Transforming Ethnohistories

Transforming Ethnohistories

Narrative, Meaning, and Community

Edited by

SEBASTIAN FELIX BRAUN

Afterword by Raymond J. DeMallie

UNIVERSITY OF OKLAHOMA PRESS : NORMAN

This book is published with the generous assistance of the Research Division and the Indian Studies Department at the University of North Dakota, Grand Forks.

Library of Congress Cataloging-in-Publication Data

Transforming ethnohistories : narrative, meaning, and community / [edited by] Sebastian Felix Braun ; [afterword by] Raymond J. DeMallie.
    pages cm
   Includes bibliographical references and index.
   ISBN 978-0-8061-4394-1 (pbk.)
1. Ethnohistory—Research.   2. Ethnohistory—Methodology.   3. DeMallie, Raymond J., 1946– I. Braun, Sebastian Felix, 1970–
   GN345.2.T73 2013
   909'.04—dc23

2013015586

The paper in this book meets the guidelines for permanence and durability of the Committee on Production Guidelines for Book Longevity of the Council on Library Resources, Inc. ∞

Contents

Illustrations

FIGURES

TABLES

Acknowledgments

Every book is a team effort; this is all the more true for an edited volume. I would like to thank all the authors for the trust they placed in this work. I would also like to thank all the people who supported our work through conversations, patience, love, education, and intellectual challenges and by giving just a little bit more space, time, and attention.

This project was helped from the start by Alessandra Jacobi Tamulevich. Alessandra gave me extremely helpful advice, and it makes a world of difference to know that one's acquisitions editor trusts one's work while trying to pull a manuscript together. I also appreciate her commitment to peer reviews, and I would like to thank the two anonymous reviewers of this manuscript. Their comments and suggestions were most helpful and have led to a better result. I would also like to thank Steven Baker, Chris Basso, and Paul Vincent, who, with great care, have made sure the manuscript was turned into a finished product.

Finally, I need to acknowledge the support this publication received from my academic institution. Phyllis Johnson, Vice President for Research and Economic Development at the University of North Dakota, supported the publication costs with a considerable amount, and the then-chair of the Department of Indian Studies agreed to contribute a slightly smaller amount. This support is highly appreciated, especially for a project in the humanities/social sciences. I would like to thank everybody involved for trusting this work and for investing in it. That contribution is the real value of this book.

Preface

A crop harvested by [him]—even if he should not choose to mill the grain himself—is always capable of providing lasting nourishment for many generations of students.

Claude Lévi-Strauss (1960:351)

Twenty years after Raymond J. DeMallie's " 'They Have No Ears' " address to the American Society of Ethnohistory (DeMallie 1993), this volume brings together a diverse group of DeMallie's students, broadly conceived, since, as we know, classificatory relations are just as real as others. The narratives these texts weave show the structure of DeMallie's approach to ethnohistory, and they show to what kinds of different places that approach has taken others. The texts hopefully also create a new or renewed dialogue about ethnohistory and about the ethnohistorical interpretation of narratives. Most people talk about *method* when they talk about ethnohistory, in part because the field performs a balancing act between disciplines that use different theories (and methodologies) in their work. I hope this volume will start a new discussion about ethnohistorical *theory*. In private conversations, I have been shocked to discover that many historians in the United States deny that their discipline is based on or uses any theory; many anthropologists, on the other hand, apart from "doing fieldwork," do not think too much about methodology. I hope this text will serve to make us all think about both.

The ideas, styles, and concepts represented here are diverse, as diverse as DeMallie's students, and as diverse as his own ever-expanding interests. They also, however, address a series of connected issues that originated in DeMallie's work and teaching. Claude Lévi-Strauss (1960:351) said of Paul Radin that he had "the gift of singling out those facts, observations, and documents which possess an especially rich meaning, sometimes undisclosed at first, but likely to become evident as one ponders the implications woven into the material." This is a rare gift shared by DeMallie, and in struggling with these meanings, the contributors ponder the implications of ethnohistory. The foundation of ethnohistory is the (anthropological) realization that history as an academic discipline, in order to be truly inclusive, needs to deal with a variety of different narratives, some of which lie outside the culturally constructed academic norms of what is logical or makes sense. The question is, in other words, one of the interpretation of narratives.

Most contributors address this question through their own narratives. They provide a demonstration, a description, but not a definition of ethnohistory. Instead of using an Aristotelian approach, trying to define each separate piece of every argument—although that might be the method used in ethnohistorical research—they use a Platonic one, by consciously using and creating or recreating narratives to make people understand, which is not unlike telling myths. A definition of ethnohistory runs into the same problems as definitions of culture, history, and other complex concepts that are shared yet interpreted differently. This does not need to be an obstacle to a discussion of theory. Understanding the tropes and tropiques of other cultures is always limited by real and metaphorical distances, yet paying attention to that which is close to ourselves will lead to potential understanding of cultural structures. It is through such a dialogue that we reach a measure of community and mutual agreement. The more real (and therefore complex) relations are, the less they can be explained. We can, however, demonstrate and describe them and hope that audiences understand. Concepts like justice, culture, love, beauty, truth, and time are powerful because they are vague, and they are vague, notes George Allen (2000:108), "because they are features of the most general contexts important to us, contexts logically, causally, and temporally fundamental, contexts at our outermost horizons of knowledge and action and aspiration." A narrative approach consciously tries to leave the understanding of reality to a dialogue with the audience, who has the right and responsibility to think along and come to its own conclusions. Myths do not explain their contents. They enact them. These contributions enact ethnohistory. I cannot say it better than Elsie Clews Parsons (1991:3), who in the preface to *American Indian Life* writes that her book "is a book of pictures. . . . If the pictures remain pictures for [the reader], well and good; if they lead [the reader] to the problems, good and better. [Ethnohistory] is short on students." As Lévi-Strauss (1970:7) points out, "In science there are no final truths. The scientific mind does not so much provide the right answers as ask the right questions." Dialogues are not without conflicts, of course, and I fully hope that contradictions in writing styles, contents, and agendas will be evident between and within these chapters.

. . .

The contributions to this volume are loosely based on a double panel of papers in honor of Raymond J. DeMallie presented at the American Society for Ethnohistory meetings in New Orleans in 2009. The meetings are a conference dear to his heart, small enough to allow for personal interaction, engaged and important for its own historical reasons, while carrying enough weight and influence to inspire scholarship beyond its realm, without fanfare or self-important posturing. Those who, for various reasons, were not able to contribute to this text need to be acknowledged: their voices contribute to these chapters: (in no particular order) Darlene Dietrich, David Posthumus, Kelly Branam, Brenda Farnell, Ben Kracht, Wyman Kirk, and Carolyn Anderson. Many others wanted to participate but for various reasons could not. The selection of texts here is not based on the quality of the original presentations, but on the idea that different generations of students and different interests and approaches should be represented.

It is not customary, in either my own culture nor those I have become ethnographically familiar with, for young whippersnappers, as Douglas Parks[1] would say, to take the stage and offer opinions. I therefore need to apologize to my elders. A volume like this one, or perhaps a true Festschrift, has been talked about for many years; I remember the conversations Mindy Morgan, Carolyn Anderson, and Paula Wagoner had at the Ethnohistory meetings in Tulsa in 2007, and I know there had been others before. I simply followed in the footsteps of my elder peers and organized something, perhaps because I have the (dis)ability to disregard rational obstacles and objections when I know something is worthwhile.

Aside from all of the academic and professional help Ray has extended to me, most importantly he modeled and models what a good academic, a good professor, a good human being, a good relative, and a good advisor should be like. He always tried to protect me from the *guerres academiques*, perhaps because of his own experiences in that field (DeMallie 2001b). As both Ray and I know perfectly well, I am not a "good relative" (Deloria 1998:25). Yet, as a fascinated observer of normal kinship behaviors, I know the rules. While I have tried to go my own way, I have deep respect and gratitude for my teachers and the trust they showed to me in allowing such exploration. Ray DeMallie's lessons to me are academic, for sure. They are, perhaps more so, however, also profoundly moral. I know that I, and I suspect most of the contributors to this volume, will be trying to do my best to justify Ray's trust in me for the rest of my academic and personal life.

Sebastian Felix Braun
August 2012

NOTES

1. As several contributors point out, the collaboration between Parks and DeMallie has produced critical work for the knowledge of Plains societies, for ethnohistory, and for scholarly and applied work on Native languages. Douglas Parks' and Ray DeMallie's mastery of both ethnohistory and linguistic anthropology can perhaps best be appreciated in their definitive study on the Lakota-Dakota-Nakota issue, in which they pointed out very clearly that Yankton-Yanktonai is not "Nakota" (Parks and DeMallie 1992b). Although I had the opportunity to assist Douglas Parks in teaching Lakota at Indiana University (and

have since been using the new Lakota textbooks the American Indian Studies Research Institute (AISRI) has been developing in collaboration with Red Cloud School on Pine Ridge), the most revealing insight into Douglas Park's work for me came on a fall day in Cannonball. Doug wanted to visit a collaborator on the Yanktonai dictionary he has been working on, and Ray DeMallie, two graduate students, and I went along from the Plains Anthropology conference in Bismarck. While Doug went into the house, we were sitting in the car watching the dogs outside. When we went in, it was obvious that the elderly woman was seriously ill. I have never seen Doug so heartbroken. I learned a lot about Douglas Parks and his work that day.

Transforming Ethnohistories

Introduction

An Ethnohistory of Listening

SEBASTIAN FELIX BRAUN

Leg dein Ohr auf die Schiene der Geschichte. [Put your ear to the rail of history.]

Freundeskreis 1996[1]

I hear them all, I hear them all, I hear them all.

Old Crow Medicine Show 2006[2]

Good ethnohistory, for lack of a different metaphor, might look somewhat like a reservation dog: the product of indefinite sources and directions, compromises and fights, a bricolage at its best; and for all that, interesting and beautiful, ready to be a loyal companion but independent enough to assert its survival, and fostering many children that all look different, yet again. Here might be the time, then, to remember one of the best stories-that-might-have-occurred (Pirsig 1992:465):

> He remembered it had been spring then, which is a wonderful time in Montana, and the breeze blowing down from the pine trees carried a fresh smell of melting snow and thawing earth, and they were all walking down the road, four abreast, when one of those raggedy nondescript dogs that call Indian reservations home came onto the road and walked pleasantly in front of them.
> They followed the dog silently for a while.
> Then LaVerne asked John, "What kind of a dog is that?"
> John thought about it and said, "That's a good dog."

The cultural misunderstanding evident above makes a point that rests at the heart of ethnohistory and any attempt to investigate cross-cultural meaning: common sense ceases to be common at cultural boundaries. This means that anthropology needs history to understand the events of the past that inform the present. History, however, needs anthropology to understand the meanings of events. As Joynt and Rescher (1961:153) wrote, such an "'under-standing' calls for interpretation, classification, and assessment, which can only be attained by grasping the relationship of causal and conceptual inter-relation among the chronological particulars." Knowledge emerges from the ability to relate things to each other. Only relations provide the context for meaning; facts without contexts stay meaningless. Mommsen (1978:21) stressed that the "structures and developments in which an historical fact is embedded also make up a vast mass" and that "these structures and devel-opments are not self-evident as such; we perceive their contours only if we view them from an appropriate perspective." Holding that "culture and culture change are, in effect, the same phenomenon" (DeMallie 1993:533), it is the proposition of this book, as of many scholars, that the appropriate perspective is informed by the methods of ethnohistory. This is not a new insight—the idea of static culture is reminiscent of the idea of an uninvented tradition—but it is one that bears clear articulation and emphasis.

The necessity of firmly placing culture in history and vice versa may recall Paul Radin (1987:184), according to whom the task of describing any culture "is always the same: a description of a specific period, and as much of the past and as much of the contacts with other cultures as is necessary for the elucidation of the particular period. No more." It might be this "no more" that is deceptive: combined with the emphasis on the particular, it creates a deceptive simplicity. If Radin (1987:185) is right, and it is truly "this particu-larity that is the essence of all history," then culture change, especially if viewed from particular, individual perspectives, can be overwhelming in its cultural and historical details. A true ethnohistorical study will have to be based on an encyclopedic knowledge, amassed in patient, detailed research over a lifetime. It takes an extraordinary person and an extraordinary com-mitment to achieve this. Raymond J. DeMallie is one of those scholars who have shown "[h]ow much can be attained by the intensive study of a single document, provided one is adequately acquainted with a particular" culture (Radin 1987:186). It is the meaning of "adequate" that DeMallie has provided with a new standard, one that is higher than most can hope to achieve. In the process, he has also helped to define the methods needed to accomplish the task.

The methods of ethnohistory are not self-explanatory, and they are not simply an application of historical or anthropological method and theory to common interests. At the 2011 Annual Meetings of the American Society for Ethnohistory in Pasadena, a very prominent (ethno)historian said that she was pleased that her students are among those who have shown that ethno-history belongs in the mainstream of history as a discipline, because they have demonstrated that the issues of ethnohistory can be approached with the same methods as any other historical issues. I agree that these scholars have contributed much to history; at the same time, however, I would hesitate to characterize their work as ethnohistorical. Many historians regard ethnohistory as simply the history of Others, the construction of chronologies of those who had been denied a historical past—a reaction that predates Wolf (1982) by several decades—just as many anthropologists think ethnohistory is simply the description of historical cultures. Both distrust the use of the other's methodology and, therefore, often appropriate it in such a way as to eliminate any potential threat. This leaves them comfortably grounded in disciplinary perspectives but also eliminates valuable contributions to and critiques of these perspectives. It prevents an engagement of alternative narratives on their own terms. This volume is not trying to rebuild historical or anthropological theories, or to reargue the proper approach for a critical analysis of texts. What it is attempting to do is to show how these different approaches can be bridged to create a true ethnohistorical approach. It does so by taking as a starting point DeMallie's 1992 address to the American Society for Ethnohistory, in which he laid out the ethnohistorical method by placing emphasis on having ears: listening to narratives.

HISTORY AND ANTHROPOLOGY

Bringing history and anthropology together is not as simple a task as successful ethnohistorians make us think, perhaps because while both disciplines like to use the other's terminology, many times they do so in ways that simply reinforce, instead of question, their own premises. While both disciplines need each other, they are different disciplines, and apply different theories and methods to find different truths (Augé 1982:112). Assuming that their ideological merger is simple is deceptive. In the relationship between anthropologists and historians, wrote Burke (1990:268–69), "each partner is attracted by an image of the other that the other finds difficult to accept." This was demonstrated to me firsthand in an interdisciplinary graduate seminar at the University of Basel. The seminar on the American Southwest involved professors and students from four disciplines: history, ethnology, English literature and Spanish. Participants would meet once a week for three hours to discuss a text on Southwestern history and culture, and the pattern that very quickly developed was that we discovered every time that we had apparently read four different texts, although the words had been the same. We would spend the meetings unraveling what we had read, as the meaning of the one text always became widely disputed between the four disciplines. Attending ethnohistory meetings sometimes reminds me of that experience; it seems that the dialogue about ethnohistory within history and the one within anthropology are very clearly demarcated. This can stand in the way of truly interdisciplinary work, which is extremely rewarding but needs to be approached with an open mind and the awareness that terms like "culture" or "history" do not always carry the same meanings in different disciplines.

Every description of culture and history is selective, and so is the assignment of meaning to the facts. As Eagleton (2000:10) has observed, "It is a fact of early industrial-capitalist civilization that young chimney sweeps tended to develop cancer of the scrotum, but it is hard to see it as a cultural achievement on a level with the Waverley novels or Rheims cathedral." Assigning much value to "cultural achievements" and insisting that they are innovative, progressive, and new can easily lead to ignoring historical and cultural facts that make up their context, especially if that context is not terribly progressive, innovative, or new. Brown and Vibert (2003:xxiii) have written that it "is a truism in history that documents ought to be read and placed in context, and their authors located and understood in terms of the period and society that produced them. Yet, the apparent simplicity of this recipe creates illusions." It is an ethnohistory that recognizes the illusions of simple recipes that forces us to look at chimney sweeps and cathedrals: they both contribute and define the cultural context of the Waverley novels—as does, for that matter, Indian removal, for example. The interpretation of anthropology and history as oppositional to each other creates a similar false paradox, perhaps exactly because we deny especially the classical texts in the disciplines their context, intention, setting, and relation. Ethnohistory is often simply seen as a creation of applied anthropology during the years of the Indian Claims Commission (see Tanner 2007 for an account of that work). I think the roots of ethnohistory are much older and stem from the critical, though not oppositional, engagement of history by anthropologists, as a short ethnohistory of anthropological ideas shows.

Ohnuki-Tierney (1990:2), reflecting on a widely held anthropological origin myth or tradition, wrote that, "[i]n hindsight, anthropologists' previous failure to tackle history seriously was due primarily to their colonial *mentalité.* . . . [T]hey shared the Eurocentric belief that 'nonliterate' peoples did not really have a history." From a North Americanist perspective, perhaps especially, such notions need some rethinking. After all, Franz Boas and his students were heavily involved in historical reconstruction. They were trying to find a way to define historical Native American cultures, partly because historians were not interested in the task. Kroeber (1939:1), often criticized for popularizing a static notion of culture through the culture area approach, had this to say: "The concept of a culture area is a means to an end. The end may be the understanding of culture processes as such, or of the historic events of culture." He directly connected the cultures he classified in a superficially static, ahistorical way to Euro-American approaches to history and emphasizes that he uses the concept of a culture area "much as a historian may use 'the Eighteenth Century' as a short way of referring to the culture that was characteristic of eighteenth-century Europe" (1939:2).

I agree with Jonaitis (1995:35), who has argued that Boasian historical particularism is much more liberating than British structural/functionalism, because it does not sweep inconsistencies under a theoretical carpet and thus creates space for multiple, competing voices. True, Boasians did not take oral, or any cultural history literally. The history of nonliterate peoples had to be extracted and interpreted, as Radin (1963:1) made clear in his introduction to the *Autobiography of a Winnebago Indian*. However, this was true for all informants, wherever they be native to, and for all texts. The collection and interpretation of texts and art as a method to write history in general was certainly a method that took others' voices seriously—more seriously than a variety of other approaches before and after.

Where fledgling anthropology failed to look for Native sources, written and oral, in its quest to write the history of Native societies, it did so in part because it took contemporary academic history as its model. It was "the definition of history as a text-based enterprise" (Conn 2004:21) that excluded oral sources, and it was the established sciences and humanities that ignored sources from outside the narrowly defined "civilized" world. Krech (1991:347) has noted that early ethnohistorical methodology, for both anthropologists and historians, meant to focus on documentary sources to write the history of Native societies, in part as an echo of Lowie's distrust of oral sources. Indeed, Boas turned the stories George Hunt tried to collect into archival documents, for example, "suggesting that culturally and geographically bounded Native American communities could be represented through a variety of texts published in book form" (Briggs and Bauman 1999:490). The intent, however, was fundamentally historical. History depended on documents, after all, and Boas's (1982:284) statement that "the whole problem of cultural history appears to us as a historical problem" might in fact showcase the then revolutionary approach to accept some Native sources— carefully selected and edited—as contributions to history. Taking history seriously, in the sense of conventional, academic history depending on written documents, might not be impeded by a "colonial *mentalité*," but actually be an expression of it. Tuhiwai Smith (1999:1) might be correct then not only in her position that "the term 'research' is inextricably linked to European imperialism and colonialism" but also in her assessment that the term "is probably one of the dirtiest words in the indigenous world's vocabulary." Such is the power of hegemonic discourse, however, that the *mentalité* of turning stories into documents and trying to use these documents as tools of domination is not limited to colonial practices (see, e.g., Kurkiala 2002). Anticolonial discourses replicate it.

Conn (2004:156) wrote that "by the turn of the twentieth century American intellectual life was filled with anthropological Indians and largely devoid of historical ones." He sees historical Indians, for example, in the historical romances of Cooper, whose characters, although fictionalized, "participated in a great, if ultimately tragic, historical process, one that lay at the heart not simply of their own history but of American history writ large" (165). In direct contrast, Conn quotes Adolphe Bandelier, who wrote that "the cigar-store man, and the statuesque Pocahontas . . . as they are paraded in literature and thus pervert the public conceptions about Indians—these I want to destroy" (165). It is, of course, true that ethnography aimed to destroy "American history writ large," although most ethnographic descriptions stayed, for a long time, essentially historical projects. However, this destruction came out of the understanding that the historical process writ large described so aptly by Cooper did in fact not resemble anything laying at the heart of Native peoples' own histories—and probably not of most peoples' histories. I find the ethnographic destruction of history writ large to be, on the one hand, a historical argument, and, on the other, good academic practice.

In his work, aiming to write history and yet simultaneously finding himself trapped within the conventions of history, Boas (1982:284) noted that, "[A]s soon as [the methods of ethnology] are applied, [a] society loses the appearance of absolute stability which is conveyed to the student who sees a certain people only at a certain given time. All cultural forms rather appear in a constant state of flux and subject to fundamental modifications." Robert Lowie (1983:xviii) pointed out that "aboriginal peoples have borrowed from one another for thousands of years, and the attempt to isolate one culture that shall be wholly indigenous in origin is decidedly simple-minded." Boasian North American anthropology understood well that culture is cultural change and that particular cultures exist in particular historical contexts. It was thus well placed to create the beginnings of ethnohistory because of its emphasis on cultural dynamics. This puts into question a second accepted tradition about classic anthropology, that of the bounded culture (see Jonaitis 1995:34), a perception coming out of a superficial and literal reading of the concept of culture area. Kroeber (1939:5–6), who is often most directly tied to the concept, makes very clear that he is not happy with this perceived boundedness. Both his and Wissler's maps, which gave rise to the perception of bounded cultures by drawing boundaries around areas, he considered regrettable: "It would be desirable, therefore, to construct cultural maps without boundary lines, on some system of shading or tint variation of color; but the mechanical difficulties are great. For the present, it seems necessary to use the old devices and leave it to the reader to translate what his eye sees into the dynamic aspects that are intended" (1939:6). The acknowledgment of historical and cultural dynamics is present in Boasian anthropology, as is a desire to somehow work out a collaboration between them. What it lacked, in part because that concept was unthinkable to academic history at the time, was a well-developed understanding of the importance of alternative perspectives on the finding of historical truth and a terminology to express this perspective.

REALITIES AND TRUTHS, DOCUMENTS
AND STORIES

Accepting and understanding—not simply tolerating—different theories and meanings, different epistemologies and hermeneutics, means to accept and understand that there are different perspectives. That may seem post-modern, as such work focuses on the acceptance that other cultures, just like other disciplines, constitute reality in very different ways. These realities must be taken into account in order to write history, if we do not simply want to impose our own reality on others and thereby create a history that bears no resemblance to the historical experience of reality of the people whose history we are trying to tell. Ethnohistory, then, because history is always the history of a culture, is how history in general should be conducted. It is also how anthropology should be approached, since anthropology is always the description of a historical culture. If perspectives of reality differ from culture to culture, historical cultures had a different experience of reality from present ones, and that context needs to be explored; otherwise, the events cannot be interpreted in their context, and the analysis is stuck in presentist interpretations.

Just as many anthropologists have refused to engage a historical focus on events, however, many historians refuse a focus on perspective. Different perspectives on reality—and history—seem to deny the existence of a historical truth. A history written in search of one historical truth needs to prefer one version of an event over another. If an event carries such different interpretations and meanings that it is no longer the same event for different people, then in reality two different events might have taken place at the same time, in the same location. Declaring one event to be untrue easily becomes an exercise of ethnocentrism. Holocaust deniers and Chariots of the Gods followers can be denied historical truth because they argue within the same epistemological framework as academic history. Realities that include events or meanings of events outside that framework, however, like traditional oral histories embedded in very different cultural values of knowledge, for example, are much more difficult, if not impossible, to argue with.

Ethnohistory reminds us of the necessity to listen to all realities. This "postmodernity" is very different, and much more transformational than simply an acknowledgment of historical positionality, as it takes into account much more than the perception of history as found true by Native scholars. The "emergent new Lakota historiography," as Kurkiala (2002:446) noted, "reproduces the very logic and structure of a Western 'grand narrative' although it challenges its contents." An "alternative narrative structure and logic" which "represents a truly alternative way of representing history" is found "in Indian oral tradition." It is then exactly those stories that positivist history and anthropology have conventionally labeled as myth—as simply cultural truths that can have little bearing on academic, "morally and culturally detached" (Kurkiala 2002:452) truth—that ethnohistory demands we listen to. This is not simply the suggestion that "for better or for worse, all history can be mythical" (Augé 1999:7), or that perhaps all history is Tedlockian "mythistory" (Restall 2003a:xvi–xvii). What the ethnohistorical method demands seemingly eradicates a fundamental categorical division and bridges truths that are "of a different order" (Kurkiala 2002:456).

DeMallie's proposition in " 'These Have No Ears' " (1993) is revolutionary in its simplicity: it does nothing less than challenge the dominance of the academic discourse, yet also, at the same time, restores credibility and inclusiveness to it. After all, if we compare different narratives and the different truths they present and represent, there is still a truth to be learned. As Restall (2003a:xvii) has stated, "There are always multiple narratives of any historical moment, but that does not mean that as interpretations they cannot tell us something true." What we learn might be a meta-truth, but then all history is that: Lévi-Strauss has shown (1966:256–58) that "history corresponds to no kind of reality" because historical events "as commonly conceived never took place" (see also Passmore 1987). A deeper investigation of DeMallie's ethnohistorical method shows that it is not postmodern in the popular sense (or non-sense) that everything is simply another perspective and must therefore be accepted as true. DeMallie is going beyond one historical truth; he is still, however, looking for historical truths. The existence of one, cross-cultural truth must be deconstructed, to be sure. However, that does not mean that each culture does or did not have its own truth.

Taylor (1986:32, italics in original) has written that for deconstructionism, "questions of origin, influence, and parentage are, *in a certain sense,* irrelevant." For the ethnohistorical method, this is true in the sense that the origin of source materials, for example, is irrelevant; oral history is an equally truthful and important source of history as written documentation. Ethnohistory combines historical and anthropological perspectives, written and oral sources, the voices of dominant and oppressed people and peoples, as well as those of intermediaries. If it is the comparison of different truths that leads us to something that is true, all truths need to be heard, not just those that are documented by whoever is in control of the discourse. The differentiation between primary, secondary, and tertiary sources in terms of their credibility makes no more sense, then, than to question Dvořák about whether the influences from classical music, spirituals, Scottish folk music, or what he understood as Native music were more important in writing his Symphony No. 9, or to question the authenticity of any of these influences or indeed the authenticity of the final work. The ethnohistorical method is about as postmodern as the telling of myth or the writing of a symphony. Ethnohistory is not the telling of myth, however: it comes from and follows a very different epistemology. Origin, influence, and parentage are still important in the analysis of the cultural and historical contexts that are the focus of the investigation. Ethnohistory must take mythical reality into account, accept it, and understand it as a reality. But as a reality, it has to be analyzed, contextualized, and investigated in terms of presenting an academic truth. If the postmodern is the critique of the modern, then ethnohistory is postmodern because it critiques the random hegemonic classification of one particular historical truth as *the* historical truth. However, this insight is not *post*modern. Modernity in that sense has always been critiqued, before, during, and after the historical era of modernity. Alternative cultural narratives are always a stumbling block to hegemonic ideas. These narratives, at the intersection of anthropology, ethnography, and history, were and are the building blocks and inspiration of ethnohistory.

The distinction between history and theory, and the consequential distinction between a theory-free, methodological discipline of history and an ahistorical, theory-based anthropology, is a curious idea with a long history. Historians who openly employ theory to form thoughts (the emphasis is on "openly," as it is impossible to form coherent thought without recourse to some theoretical model), are still often seen as "doctrinaires," as Isaiah Berlin (1960:9) made clear over fifty years ago: "Such historians are accused of being prisoners of their theories; they are accused of being fanatical or cranky or doctrinaire, of misrepresenting or misreading reality to fit in with their obsessions, and the like." Anthropologists, on the other hand, often see historians as limited by an emphasis on written documentation, by emphasizing the supposedly concrete proof. Stokes (1965:234) noted that "Many anthropologists go so far as to assume that their discipline gives them a special intuitive insight into the historical processes of African societies, particularly since the central body of evidence is contained in oral tradition." Indeed, oral tradition, or rather the use of it as a reliable source of "truthful" information is often seen as the main dividing line between history and anthropology (see Abler 1982). I think the discussion about written versus oral sources and the meanings of their respective contributions to historical information is largely a consequence of a fundamental misunderstanding. Many times, it involves a political component, a competition about who may, who should, and who is able to tell the truth; this competitive "discourse on truth" does not take into account the different purpose of academic and oral histories (see, e.g., Kurkiala 1997:195–207). A more useful approach than to try and divvy out the differences between history and anthropology and oral and written history, I think, is to look at the interpretation and use of narratives, not at their form.

By convention, academia has distinguished different forms of narratives. "Every human being," Passmore (1987:69) observed, "is born into a world of stories. Unlike most societies, however, the West gradually came to draw distinctions between different kinds of story and to make correspondingly different demands upon different kinds of storytellers." At least since Ella Deloria (2006:xxv–xxvi), we have known, of course, that other societies also differentiate between categories of narratives, even though academically all of these narratives were treated as stories or myths, the content of which was only believable once verified (DeMallie 2006a:xiv). Jahner (1983:25) writes that "the Lakota names for genres include no single category that encompasses all of those narratives that scholars label 'mythic'." Obviously they would not, as they represented different categories. Conventional academia, however, made a crucial distinction that obliterates such cultural notions. It simply differentiated between document and story, science and fiction, logos and mythos, and assigned to these categorizations different levels of academic truth. While it has been trying to disentangle itself from these assumptions, it has been a slow process, and one that has met with resistance. My point here is not to repeat the critique of science nor the critique of postmodern reactions. It is simply to question whether a classification of what narratives constitute and present truth can be made according to narrator, origin, or form of the narrative, or whether it depends on the context of the narrative and the relation it assumes to its audiences.

Story and document, science and fiction, are not that far from each other when we look at texts like Ella Deloria's *Waterlily* (2009) or Elsie Clews Parsons' *American Indian Life* (1991). The methods used in both books can be summed up by Deloria's explanation of her work (in Gardner 2009:vi): "Only my characters are imaginary." For her, the "things that happen" are true in that they are based on real events. They are only fictitious in that these real events happen to imaginary characters. Kroeber (1991:13), in the introduction to Parsons's volume, emphasized that the stories "are reliable." He explains that "[t]he customs depicted are never invented. Each author has adhered strictly to the social facts as he knew them." While Parsons (1991:2) herself critiqued the notion of ethnographic truth in her preface, Kroeber's statement is reminiscent of Boas's attempt to include Native sources into his historical-anthropological reconstructions. Each author has to hold on to conventional wisdom even while trying to push the boundaries. Boas held on to history as derived from written documents but tried to include Native sources. Kroeber held on to the concept of reliable, historical and ethnographic truth even as he admitted that fiction "has definite merit" (1991:13). Parsons, who went the furthest, simply held on to the value of anthropology as a discipline, but questioned whether truth could exclusively be found in logos, or whether it could at all be found through logos, exclusively. It might be an expression of the fundamental difficulty of this question, or the difficulty (for science) of facing this question, as well as an expression of what power traditional dogma exerts over a community, that debates on this very question still abound in departments and disciplines. I find it somewhat refreshing that Kroeber pointed to Bandelier's 1890 *The Delight Makers*, and Parsons added Grinnell's 1920 *When Buffalo Ran* as examples of what an infusion of story into document or vice versa can deliver. Of Bandelier's work, Kroeber (1991:13, italics in original) wrote: "this *novel* still renders a more comprehensive and coherent view of native Pueblo life than any scientific volume on the Southwest."

A story can become a document and a document can be told as a story. The difference lies not so much in the text itself, and perhaps not even in the relation of the author to the audience, as in the relation of the audience to the text. The audience's relation to a text and their use of it determines its nature. A text might be told or written as a document, or might be a document because its audience uses it as one. The same text can be turned into a story, however. The same text becomes a document or a story depending on whether it is read or heard as one. Everything is what it is perceived to be, depending on how we relate to it, of course; and yet, this fact is often ignored or forgotten with historical texts, perhaps because we are used to seeing our reality as an archive of documents instead of the collection of stories it is. Schneider (1987:682) connected the obsession with documentation to the secularization of a society that followed the Protestant obsession with self-observation and control. If Protestantism gave us capitalism, and capitalism is simplification, as Dussel (1998:13) argued, then archives of documents—not stories—are the capitalism of history. The abstraction and simplification of culture, history, community, and the self that Dussel argued capitalism brings with it also meant the simplification of history, memory, and the past, which led to the loss of the capacity to listen to stories. It is that act of listening that makes a text a story; simplification and abstraction create archival documents. The fact that there does not exist two similarly distinguished terms for the act of reading as there does for hearing and listening might reflect the relatively recent expansion of literacy to the general public, but we can still "read between the lines" of a text and "read in" a text. Of course, all of our senses can be used in the same different ways. Lévi-Strauss (1997) showed how to use three of them as acts of attention in *Look, Listen, Read*.

Whether written or oral, it is not the truth content but the codification and selection of a source that makes a document different from a story. A document is used to document something; it places an event as the truth and is used as proof of that truth. A story is much more complex than that, and it does different things, too. "It is storytelling," wrote Jackson (1998:177) "that effects this transformation [the embedding of the human being in the world] and creates this embeddedness, connecting people to country, connecting particular experience to shared parameters of meaning." While the importance of a document lies in its content—what it documents—a story can play. It can imply. It can be incomplete. The value of a story does not only lie in its content: it lies in its meaning and in the transformation that this meaning creates. Jackson (1998:181, italics in original) further noted Biddle's observation that "the truth of stories emerges from a *relationship* between teller and listener." In contrast, the relationship between author and reader has (supposedly) nothing to do with the meaning of a document, not even with oral history as a document. Documents cannot transform because they are alienated stories.

In its telling, a story transforms not only the past but also the present, because through telling a story the past is brought into the present (Jackson 1998:123). In the overture to *The Raw and the Cooked,* Lévi-Strauss (1970:15, 16; italics mine) points out that both myth and music are "languages which, in their different ways, transcend articulate expression, while at the same time—like articulate speech, but unlike painting—requiring a temporal dimension in which to unfold. . . . Because of the internal organization of the musical work, *the act of listening to it* immobilizes passing time. . . . [B]y listening to music, and while we are listening to music, we enter into a kind of immortality." Just like music, a good story allows the audience to enter into "a kind of immortality." The purpose of telling a story, then, is not simply historical. This, again, is a transformation of relationships, and in order to understand this transformation, we need, as Ingold (2000:24) has put it, not to hear but to listen: our perception needs to be "grounded in an act of attention." It is that act of attention that leads us to put clues in relation to each other, that lets Janáček's sketches resonate with music, that lets Ingold's Cree hunter "tell." DeMallie's ethnohistorical method resonates within this act of attention, where it gives rise, as Ingold (2000:24–26) put it, to sensitivity and responsiveness, to a sentient ecology, a poetics of dwelling. Listening as an act of attention leads us to transformation. Paraphrasing Ingold's (2000:24–25) text on the hunter's understanding of the caribou, we can express how it transforms ethnohistory: "When the [ethnohistorian] speaks of how the [specific culture] presented itself to him, he does not mean to portray the [culture] as a self-contained, rational agent whose action in giving itself up served to give outward expression to some inner resolution. Like music, the [ethnohistorian's] story is a performance; and again like music, its aim is to give form to human feeling—in this case the feeling of the [other's] vivid proximity as another living, sentient being." This is the transformation DeMallie has brought to ethnohistory. His appeal for ethnohistorians to "have ears" is an appeal to base historical knowledge on more than documents. It presents the challenge to listen, in addition, to context and relationships: to community and kinship.

TRANSFORMING ETHNOHISTORIES

Sahlins (2000:471) defined historical ethnography as works "whose aim is to synthesize the field experience of a community with an investigation of its archival past." Keeping in mind what Lévi-Strauss (1966:242) had to say about archives, namely that their virtue "is to put us into contact with pure historicity," it becomes obvious that such historical ethnography is still reconstructing history and is not an ethnohistory that listens to stories. The employment of pure historicity cannot lead to ethnohistory because the method limits the ways in which we can listen. Augé (1999:4) pointed out that "Anthropologists can see and talk to their informants, historians cannot; historians know how the story unfolds, anthropologists do not." That might be true, but both anthropologists and historians, as ethnohistorians, in order to know the story, must listen to their informants. Both must listen to documents, whether oral or written, and thus transform them into stories. From such listening one develops the ability to understand, to "tell," to use Ingold's term, and to create ethnohistory, which is not so much a practice "to establish the history of the peoples [we] study as to understand *their* conception of history or, more precisely, their conception of their own history" (Augé 1999:8, italics in original). This, I would insist, is something worth holding on to, even in the face of Lévi-Strauss's (1992:412) critique of the search for greater meaning: "Between the Marxist critique, which frees man from his initial bondage—by teaching him that the apparent meaning of his condition evaporates as soon as he agrees to see things in a wider context—and the Buddhist critique which completes his liberation, there is neither opposition nor contradiction." Myth and academic truth, story and document, can lead to an understanding of reality and therefore the liberation from it. This realization not only allows the acknowledgment that academic truth is an artificial category without relevance for many sources, but also provides a better tool with which to understand ethnohistory as a field in which history, anthropology, and all other disciplines who interpret narratives have a stake.

DeMallie's cultural truth in historical context cannot be found in datasets, primary and secondary conclusions, or the measurement of quantities, and it cannot be found in documents alone. Measurement of objects constitutes truth in natural sciences; social sciences find their truth in the relations *between* objects. Documents, in their simplified and generalized nature, are different from stories, which, embedded in cultural contexts and therefore difference, provide conflicting, paradoxical, ironic, and, as such, cultural information. To understand the difference between document and story, and the necessity of going beyond documents, consider the example DeMallie (1977a:113, italics mine) gave in his testimony before the Sioux Treaty Hearing in 1974: "The treaty concepts are based upon European tradition and though you might be able to translate these words into Lakota and have them mean something, *unless they have some basis in reality* (as perceived by the Sioux), the Indians would be totally unprepared to understand what was meant." The whole hearing (Ortiz 1977) was exactly an attempt to base documents in some basis of reality. It is also an example of going beyond the archive and comparing different histories to find, in this comparison of multiple narratives of different orders, something true. "As Bateson pointed out on many occasions," wrote Harries-Jones (1995:9, italics in original), "the scientific approach to difference is not of the same order as the scientific approach to similarity. Emphasis on difference leads to *patterns,* while emphasis on sameness leads to quantification." The systems of thought DeMallie is trying to understand are patterns of meaning, and patterns are discerned from stories. An ethnohistory that has ears, that is based on the act of listening—based on stories in addition to documents—will be a transformed and transformative field.

A society *(Gesellschaft)* is created, imagined, and constructed, both in practice and as a category of thinking in research, through documents, but it is stories that create a community *(Gemeinschaft).* A society transforms into a community through stories; if the stories are replaced by documents, the community becomes a society. What is true for the places in which (or perhaps at which) we live goes for the places where we work: academia, industry, think tanks, construction companies. No amount of street signs, branding, or brochures will create a community if the people do not build and share stories. Those interdisciplinary synergies that universities are trying to create by putting departments into the same buildings or faculty in adjoining offices, for example, cannot be artificially created by administrative measures and have to be built by allowing faculty to share stories.

Of course, there are different kinds of stories, and not all of them create the same meanings. I remember the first Committee on Institutional Cooperation Graduate Student Conference in Iowa City; two students interpreted Pueblo stories according to culturally significant symbolic meanings. At the very end of the question-and-answer session, DeMallie suggested that perhaps some of these stories might simply have meanings as stories—a bedtime story is simply that, for example. Looking through my old class notes recently, I found I had written "Sometimes 'symbols' have no meaning whatsoever! Sometimes people just do things." Overinterpretation of culture—seeking great meaning in every detail of daily lives—is just as dangerous as simply taking everything literally. "The inhabitant of an anthropological place," Augé (1995:55) noted, "does not make history; he lives in it." The ability to tell stories apart, to distinguish those with different meanings, is one of the most difficult, and yet most important, tasks of cultural competency. It is often the proof of true cultural understanding, manifested for example in understanding humor, prayer, or sacredness. However, sharing stories always creates community as it brings about and cements the realization that others are, in the end, not terribly different from ourselves and transforms them into "living, sentient beings," in contrast to an analysis that hears, but does not listen.

In terms of historical influences on DeMallie and on the method of ethnohistory he proposes, it is impossible to overlook Morgan, Eggan, Lévi-Strauss, and others. Unquestionably, it was DeMallie's determination, drive, and commitment to master the grand documents of anthropology and history from a very early age that has led to his encyclopedic knowledge of the fields in which he works. However, I cannot help but wonder in what ways the stories in the stack of *Indian Chief* comic books that he collected have been responsible for his formulation of the ethnohistorical method. After all, it has been the capacity to listen to texts as stories that has engendered a capacity to weave relations of friendship with many people anchored in communities; grassroots people, as some may call them, and tricksters, if we take the transformational aspects of storytelling seriously. Ivan Drift was a trickster, as Paula Wagoner argues in her contribution to this volume. His text might not be one that is taken too seriously by conventional (ethno)historians, but perhaps we should remember what Jahner (1992:148) said about texts that emerge "from the immediate and consciously negotiated experience of radical cultural change": that "the act of writing [might be] simultaneously a development of an imaginative tradition and an attempted entry into a new cultural order." Being a trickster is not a bad qualification for such an undertaking. In this context, one might wonder anew about the reception of Lakota (or academic) texts that are today regarded as seminal, but perhaps did not receive that acclaim from everybody when they were constructed.

Transforming both anthropology and history into ethnohistory requires us to break the shackles of conventional knowledge, of common-sense facts. Ethnohistorians might have to be tricksters. At the very least, however, they need to be able to understand tricksters and to accept that what tricksters do is also fact. A transformed and transforming ethnohistory needs to accept that Cheyennes transforming into buffalo is perfectly acceptable as fact in a Cheyenne history, and must have the ears to listen to such facts (DeMallie 1993). Myths, in fact, establish communities, uphold them, give them rules to live by, and explain realities. It should not come as a surprise that DeMallie's students have tried to understand stories to understand relations. Most of us, I think, define the world we look at using three main relations that constitute reality through stories: language, kinship, and community. The three form, fittingly, a Lévi-Straussian triad, with community transcending both language and kinship—story and relationship—which both express, reinforce, and continuously reenact community itself. The chapters of this volume address all three of these relations.

David Miller ethnohistorically contextualizes DeMallie's work, a large part of ethnohistory itself, and this volume in his contribution. This context both reveals the complexity and diversity of DeMallie's approach and provides a background to the following chapters. It is revealing to see glimpses of Eggan, Fogelson, Lévi-Strauss, Schneider, Geertz, and Tax in the following chapters, whether they are clearly and consciously identified or not. Then Kellie Hogue, Sarah Quick, and Jason Jackson discuss ethnohistorical performances, ethnohistory as performance, and the role that performance plays in ethnohistory. As Jackson discussed with me, performance studies is not something that might be automatically associated with DeMallie, but I do think these contributions show how ethnohistory can profit from and contribute to other fields in which an interpretation of meaning and context is extremely important. I am also thinking here, of Brenda Farnell's paper, "Precision in Meaning," at the 2009 Ethnohistory meetings, which bridged the interpretation of movement and the interpretation of narrative. David Dinwoodie and Patrick Moore steer the discussion more directly toward narrative, although both chapters also continue some themes from the previous ones, now applied to storytelling. Both contributions enter into a fascinating, direct dialogue, and both demonstrate masterfully how texts— whether English or Native—should be analyzed, contextualized, and used to gain larger insights into history and community. Both also show the dialogues of ethnohistory with linguistics and sociolinguistics. Raymond Bucko and Paula Wagoner then approach ethnohistory from a more biographical perspective, discussing narrative as a product of a more personal history. Where Arthur John's story seems to be more concerned with and used for community, William Bordeaux clearly presents his own historical interpretation, for example. Bucko's and Wagoner's contextualizations of texts reemphasize the potential of the ethnohistorical method, while at the same time pointing to the long neglect of authors and sources writing against the large historical process held as historical standards by those who control the discourse. Mindy Morgan continues this discussion of historical text with her contribution on James Larpenteur Long. She also reiterates an important point already stressed by Dinwoodie, namely that studies of indigenous narratives, societies, and cultures extend to English texts: here because the underlying language ideologies contribute to the context of narratives; with Dinwoodie because the context of narratives contributes to underlying ideologies. Morgan's and Braun's chapters both also question which narratives are told, and, as a consequence, what histories are remembered. The selective presentation of Native peoples as "Indians" that Morgan describes can easily be interpreted as Braun's expansion of the procedural landscape.

AN ETHNOHISTORY OF LISTENING

The reader might notice that firm lines between the issues the chapters in this volume address are difficult to draw; a Kroeberian coloring scheme might be in order. Addressing language without kinship is impossible; we need to know the relationship of the speakers (or listeners) to be able to interpret the form, content, and purpose of what is said, implied, and left out. Addressing kinship without language is equally impossible; relationships manifest themselves by relating, and relating messages—communicating—is the primary way of doing this. In both cases, we need the context of community; both language and kinship build community, and community depends on language and kinship, so that each of the chapters might emphasize one of the three, but nevertheless speak to all three together. The authors approach these issues from a diversity of perspectives, and their conclusions are equally diverse. This, I would argue, does not prevent the reader from seeing a broader pattern emerge, however. Stories are always diverse, and we do not have to engage in formal structural analysis to make sense of this diversity—or perhaps we do so naturally, just like children are able to order their bedtime stories into a moral universe that makes sense: a cultural pattern. Diversity in content, form, and perspective is an obstacle for interpretation only for fundamentalists who do not understand stories because they take them literally. It is, after all, in actively listening to the different kinds and versions of Lakota creation stories, for example, that a glimpse of Lakota cultural patterns can be caught.

It is thus the emphasis on story that forces us to "have ears." Story always implies. At the same time that this presupposes familiarity with culture, locality, kinship, language, and community, it also teaches these things as the careful listener is reminded to explore further. Teaching by not explaining, without immediate lucidity, so to speak, might be a weird concept from the standpoint of document, but it makes sense when we teach and learn by story, where we are forced to make connections: to create relations (see Sharp 2001:32). Gregory Bateson (Bateson and Bateson 1987:80, italics in original) has said that "*noncommunication* of certain sorts is needed if we are to maintain the 'sacred.' Communication is undesirable, not because of fear, but because communication would somehow alter the nature of the ideas." This might be why, in fact, that "Christianity is just writhing with contradictions" (Bateson and Bateson 1987:146) and yet obviously creates a religion that makes sense of the world. As Sharp (2001:123) explains, any communication depends on the illusion of understanding of meaning. This is successful as long as the participants to a communication share close enough general meanings of reality. Intercultural communication is difficult not because the disconnect between meanings is newly introduced, but because it becomes obvious: no shared general reading of reality allows to uphold the illusion that we share an understanding of meaning.

Keeping in mind Geertz's essay "On the Nature of Anthropological Understanding" (1983:55–70), I am far from suggesting that we need to have spiritual communion with culture in order to understand it. However, intercultural understanding, including ethnohistory, requires active listening, sharing, and knowledge of a shared context to understand (and misunderstand) implied references in a difficult, long-term process. As David Dinwoodie points out in his contribution, it is, as White put it, a "process of creative, and often expedient, misunderstandings." Without the investment in such a process, which might take a lifetime to accomplish, the illusion of understanding results in what Plumwood (2001:66–67) called "oppressive projects of unity." As Todorov (1992:165) observed, "If it is incontestable that the prejudice of superiority is an obstacle in the road to knowledge, we must also admit that the prejudice of equality is a still greater one, for it consists in identifying the other purely and simply with one's own 'ego ideal' (or with oneself)." DeMallie reminds us that the past is not such a foreign country that it cannot be understood. If culture is culture change, however, we can also not simply identify the historic other with our contemporary self, as knowing our past depends on an intercultural dialogue, too. Foregoing the hard work required to understand another culture in its own right can have as dire consequences as using knowledge to destroy a culture. Cortez knew more of the Aztecs than Las Casas, Todorov (1992) has shown, and it is important to understand that empathy without knowledge can create as much oppression as enmity with knowledge. We are not able, otherwise, to truly understand the Dawes Act, for example, or Carlisle boarding school.

To get acquainted with a foreign country, whether in the past or the present, and whether for reasons of conquest or acceptance, means an act of translation. So far, I have talked about translation as a metaphor, but DeMallie, in his teachings and his work, also reminds us that linguistic translation—the knowledge of and sympathy for other languages—is a necessity for ethnohistorical work. The importance of Native languages is evident throughout DeMallie's teachings, and his intricate understanding of Lakota, especially, is evident to all of his students to whom he tried to teach it. I just recently reread the acknowledgments in Vine Deloria, Jr.'s *Singing for a Spirit* (1999)—reading those contextual materials is one lesson I have learned from DeMallie—and saw that he thanked DeMallie, "who made corrections in the Dakota words and grammatical structures." DeMallie's connections to French history and ethnography, too, go as far back as translations of French sources such as Nicollet's journal (DeMallie 1976b).

Beyond the importance of knowing a language for purposes of translation and direct reading of sources, however, DeMallie's interest in language makes a moral point. I suspect that he sees his engagement with language as a necessity to understand culture not because culture equals language but because it enables one to really understand stories, and stories enable us to understand culture. The acknowledgment that other people's perspectives are as valid as ours and contribute just as much to knowledge—and therefore deserve to be, indeed must be, read and heard—should lead to more than a generic endorsement of "diversity." In practice, it has to be translated into cultural and linguistic understanding.

Thus, as becomes very clear in perhaps the most important aspect of De-Mallie's teaching, the study and practice of community acquires a moral obligation, that is, a kinship obligation. The search for an understanding of community can only come to fruition by participating in the community. This does not mean posing as a member of a community; it means listening with humility and integrity and trying to bear witness to ideas and events instead of using communities for scholarly, political, or personal boasting. As Todorov (1992:132, italics in original) stated, "it is only by speaking to the other (not giving orders but engaging in a dialogue) that *I* can acknowledge *him* [or *her*] as a subject, comparable to what I am myself. . . . [U]nless grasping is accompanied by a full acknowledgment of the other as subject, it risks being used for purposes of exploitation, of 'taking'; knowledge will be subordinated to power." Participating in a community means engaging in this dialogue through the humility of real listening. We are thus able to participate in historic communities, too, by applying ethnohistorical methods. We must acknowledge the others as subjects, as living and sentient beings. We have to allow them to share and allow ourselves to listen. This is not as easy as it sounds: we are all, whatever our nationality, community, university, and discipline, much less inclined to listen than hear. It is, however, the complex implication of what it ultimately means to truly "have ears," to engage in listening as an act of attention. "The idea of truth appears only when one takes the other person into account," wrote Veyne (1988:128), and that might be why it "is the thin layer of gregarious self-satisfaction that separates us from the will to power." Listening in that sense, then, is in itself a transformational act, an act of which we have to continuously and consciously remind ourselves. Raymond J. DeMallie has always acted with that humility and has reminded his students of it many times: not directly, but by gently prodding us through stories and above all by setting the example to follow.

NOTES

1. Freundeskreis, "Leg dein Ohr auf die Schiene der Geschichte," from the album *Quadratur des Kreises*. Four Music, 1999.

2. Dave Rawlings, "I Hear Them All," first recorded by Old Crow Medicine Show on the album *Big Iron World*. Nettwerk Records, 2006; also on Dave Rawlings Machine, *A Friend of a Friend*, Acony Records, 2009.

1

Borders and Layers, Symbols and Meanings

Raymond J. DeMallie's Commitment to Ethnohistory, with Nods to Thick Description and Symbolic Anthropology

DAVID REED MILLER

Historian of anthropology Regna Darnell declares that Americanist anthropology is best characterized by "invisible genealogies" that must be intentionally articulated to be revealed, charted, and analyzed (Darnell 2001:1–11). Much of the begetting is found in intellectual family trees consisting of the generations of great minds and these individuals' ideas, trees where teachers and their students found places among the branches to seek out and develop their theoretical thinking in the course of subsequent careers. This journey, undertaken out of loyalty or in defiance, rebelliously, synchronistically, or independently, is always relative to academics' teachers and their intellectual progenitors. The prodigious scholarship of Raymond J. DeMallie inspires students and engenders the respect of colleagues, especially among Americanists and Northern Plains specialists. Portions of his intellectual genealogy contribute to his larger program of research. A series of issues and influences converge in the anthropology practiced by DeMallie and were embodied in his early career. The particular focus of this chapter examines how ethnohistory epitomizes his specific anthropology.

I remember first reading the essay "On Ethnographic Authority," in which the author, James Clifford (1983), suggests that DeMallie's editing of James R. Walker's collected texts, originally written by literate tribal members in the Lakota language or dictated and taken down by Walker in the English translation of his interpreters, represented the dialogic dimension so central to a new postmodern/reflexive anthropology.[1] When I read Clifford's assessment, I was a graduate student of DeMallie's. I was struck that while Clifford's might be a reasonable perception based upon his reading of these indigenous texts, he was suffering from at least a partial misunderstanding, if he was not making a misrepresentation, based upon what I had come to learn were DeMallie's intention and purpose (Clifford 1983:141, n.146; re-printed in Clifford 1988). Having often heard from DeMallie himself how he grasped his own disposition and autobiographical debts as a neo-Boasian and historical anthropologist, I disagreed with Clifford's take all the more, especially given DeMallie's devotion to ethnohistory as his unified method of choice.[2]

BEGINNINGS OF ETHNOHISTORICAL INTERESTS

DeMallie's education and early career appears to have been a straight arrow, with every step or stage taken in logical order, all moving toward an identified goal. DeMallie was born and raised the only child of working-class parents in Rochester, New York. At age seven he was out of school for a time after an appendectomy, and this was when his mother gave him Enid La Monte Meadowcroft's children's biography of Crazy Horse (1954). Simply enamored with the book, he was soon "haunt[ing] the public library looking for books on Indians" (DeMallie personal communication, June 30, 2010). On the shelves of libraries in Rochester and in exhibits at the Rochester Public Museum, the Iroquois were well represented, and he was captivated. His parents complained that the exhibits at the museum never changed, but this did not bother him. He remembers a number of times attending the annual border-crossing celebration at Niagara Falls, New York, walking across "the bridge to Canada where Iroquois from Six Nations [Reserve] set up booths and concessions in a park" and where "there was also an Indian village tourist attraction." He also remembers family vacations in the 1950s to Lake George, New York, where a "multi-tribal Indian village tourist attraction" at various occasions had in residence a Comanche chief, a young Navajo jeweler, a Hopi man, and a young man from Tesuque Pueblo, among others. "Those experiences helped to solidify my interest in Indians," he recalls. He remembers that his interests in the Iroquois were enhanced by attending the Mary Jemison pageant at Letchworth State Park in Castile, New York, and recollects what had been a simple reenactment of the kidnapping becoming eventually "a night time drama with a stage and sound effects and a large cast." He remembers that a large contingent of Mohawks were in the audience one year, speaking to one another in Mohawk with the distinctive "r" dialect. He also recalls the Indian village and dance demonstrations at the New York State Fair, where he once observed an Iroquois man in traditional dress being ignored for the most part by the passersby—until the man donned a full Plains warbonnet, whereupon parents stopped and wanted their kids to be photographed with him (DeMallie personal communication, June 30, 2010).

During high school DeMallie began to learn about anthropology, which coincided with his wanting to spend time talking with Indian people. He recalled one summer day when his parents dropped him off at the Indian village in Niagara Falls, Ontario, and how he spent the afternoon talking with an older Mohawk man, a retired high steel worker, who taught him a simple dance step and was delighted to answer questions. He also remembers that his parents several times had taken him to Chief Parker's museum on the Tonawanda Reservation to spend time talking with him and his wife. Over picnic lunch brought by his mother, conversation occurred. Parker carved false faces and his wife made corn husk masks and dolls for sale in their museum. Encounters such as these were a beginning (DeMallie personal communication, June 30, 2010).

In his first year of high school, DeMallie started frequenting rare and used bookstores in Rochester, and with advice from the proprietors he began his collecting on a limited budget. He first heard of Lewis Henry Morgan from them, but the controversy of the loss of many historic structures, including the Morgan mansion, in the building of the Inner Loop freeway in Rochester meant several detailed articles about Morgan appeared in the papers, and about this same time he acquired and read a copy of Morgan's *League of the Iroquois.* During his first year in high school, he read what he characterizes as his "first serious book" about Plains Indians, Mari Sandoz's *Crazy Horse,* which he purchased from knowledgeable Mr. Wiess of the Genesee Book Store. This led him to John G. Neihardt's *Black Elk Speaks,* which he first read using a library copy, but he knew he had to have his own. Finding a copy available from a dealer in California, he persuaded his mother for the $20 to buy it for him; this was just prior to the publication of the 1961 paperback edition by the University of Nebraska Press. Next he found Joseph Epes Brown's edition of *The Sacred Pipe* in a new bookstore in downtown Rochester. Then he read George Bird Grinnell's *Fighting Cheyennes,* and soon he was searching for anything he could find about Plains Indians.

In this sense DeMallie began as an antiquarian before he tangibly decided to become an anthropologist. He started a correspondence with Sandoz, who told him about the extent of records in the National Archives in Washington, D.C. (see Stauffer 1992: 400–402, 426). His parents decided to vacation in D.C. the summer of 1961, and went by way of Gettysburg where they visited and were in attendance on the first day of the battle's centennial. Once in D.C., his parents took him to the National Archives so he could physically see records of the Indian Office; and once there, his father fibbed about his son's age—sixteen being the minimum age for obtaining a research card, when he was still fifteen. Of course, the records were voluminous, but this was when he got his first glimpse of the importance of these historical and cultural resources.

The summer of 1964, after his graduation from high school, DeMallie worked the first of two seasons at the Cornish early historic Seneca archaeological site south of Rochester. Later that summer he convinced his parents to allow him to empty his childhood savings account for a research trip to Washington, D.C. At the beginning of their summer vacation, his parents drove him to D.C. and left him for a month. He stayed at the Hotel Plaza, near Union Station, and he made his way every day to the National Archives on Pennsylvania Avenue. He read microfilm in Record Group (RG) 75 (Indian Records) before anything could be photocopied, and was able to use original records in RG 98 (War Department Records), which had not yet been microfilmed. Carmelita Ryan, one of the archivists in RG 75, noticed his interests in Indian culture, and arranged for him to meet Margaret Blaker, the archivist of the Bureau of American Ethnology (BAE) archives at the Smithsonian. At that time the BAE offices occupied a portion of the Smithsonian Castle Building, and Blaker's office was behind the rose window, overlooking the Mall. He was immediately smitten by the setting and the Smithsonian's legacy of research about Indian cultures and their history. When not in the archives on that trip he spent time viewing the Indian exhibits in the National Museum of Natural History. One day he was scrutinizing a manikin in one of the exhibits, purported to be the Lakota Kicking Bear, but dressed in a Blackfeet shirt. A guard noting his focused attention, asked him what he was observing, and DeMallie said that he was wondering about the authenticity of the clothing. The guard told him he should ask the curator, with the comment that that is what they are paid for, and called upstairs. Consequently, DeMallie had his first introduction and meeting with John C. Ewers, the curator of Plains Ethnology in the Department of Anthropology. On the weekends he divided time between the Library of Congress and exploring D.C. by foot. Twice he explored Arlington Cemetery looking for graves of Indian war officers. Five weeks later he took the bus home to Rochester, and prepared for relocation to Chicago for university. Instrumentally, that Washington visit marked the beginning of his in-depth tutorial about the role of anthropology in the study of Indians.

UNIVERSITY INFLUENCES

In his essay for a volume about the legacy of David M. Schneider, DeMallie (2001b) autobiographically reveals many of his intellectual influences. In his account he discusses his undergraduate and graduate education at the University of Chicago, spanning the years 1964 to 1971, describing the ideological tightrope-like maze strung among his various professors, the faculty almost an edifice which students were left to scale. An easy way out was to become the student of a particular professor, and leave any integration of conflicting or challenging ideas for another time, if ever. However, this was a contentious period at Chicago, immediately following the changes in the requirements of the department, eliminating much of the General Anthropology Requirements in favor of individualized programs of study beyond the required core courses (Stocking n.d.). In contrast, DeMallie sought to merge the ideas of his professors into an integrated approach, the product of his education trajectory in this period.

DeMallie explained how this began in the spring of 1964 during his senior year of high school when he had attended and listened to Fred Eggan deliver the first Lewis Henry Morgan Lectures at the University of Rochester (Eggan 1966), and the formative effect that these lectures had upon him. Already planning to attend the University of Chicago, knowing its reputation for having the foremost anthropology department in North America, he listened as Eggan contextualized the study of kinship and comparative social relations in the study of American Indian societies and cultures. He described the lectures as having a mesmerizing effect upon him:

"When he [Eggan] mentioned in one lecture the need for someone to do comparative work on the kinship systems of the various Sioux, I knew I had found my calling. After that evening's lecture, mustering all my courage, I volunteered for duty and told Professor Eggan—it didn't occur to me to ask—that I was coming to Chicago in the fall to be his student and work on those Sioux kinship systems" (DeMallie 2001b:46–47).

Arriving at the University of Chicago, with his purpose and goal in mind, DeMallie had to be reminded that he had to get an undergraduate degree before he could proceed to advanced studies. Eager to understand Eggan's orientation, he made a studious foray into the work of A. R. Radcliffe-Brown, especially the era when the British social anthropologist was teaching at the University of Chicago, and consequently, DeMallie explored the connections to others concerned with kinship studies among British social anthropologists. He wrote a series of kinship papers for Eggan during his undergraduate years. During this same time DeMallie was informed by Raymond Fogelson who regularly admonished his students to read with care the Boasians as well as the culture and personality literatures. In course work with Sol Tax, the Redfieldian reading list was covered. DeMallie noted that he first read Clifford Geertz "under the careful tutelage of Hildred Geertz, whose undergraduate seminar on functionalism" he characterized as "one of the highlights of my college years." This was also part of his drive to understand Radcliffe-Brown and British social anthropology, as a context for his ongoing work for Eggan. Claude Lévi-Strauss visited Chicago in 1965, further inspiring DeMallie to learn about structuralism, especially its implications for kinship studies, and further expanding his horizons (DeMallie 2001b:47). Also influential was Schneider, the chair of the department during the mid-1960s and promoter of a critical culture theory situated primarily in how symbol systems such as kinship terms and relations are malleable and are, in a sense, a semantic domain. One stream of the crisis in representation was rising in these very years, as epitomized when Schneider began his theoretical rejection of kinship as a universal in social relations; DeMallie was working his way through his own forest of symbols, clarifying further his own grasp of Sioux kinship and culture.

Taking full advantage of the opportunity, DeMallie had taken four years of French in high school, and another quarter in his first year at Chicago. While in high school he had tried to learn Dakota/Lakota by study of the Riggs (1893) and Buechel (1939) grammars, but with limited success. Once in college he found the Boas and Deloria *Dakota Grammar* (1941). However, DeMallie recognized that without formal training it would be "an uphill battle." On his first trip to South Dakota in 1966, drawing upon the many words he had learned, he realized that he had not paid attention to stress (part of his influence from his learning French), and consequently people were not understanding what he was trying to say. It was not until DeMallie went to do fieldwork at Cheyenne River in 1970 that he felt he made headway in learning Lakota. In his senior year at Chicago, he took an introduction to descriptive linguistics course from the Linguistics Department with minimal success, as he described it, and a graduate-level introduction that concentrated on transformational grammar, the fad topic of that era, but neither experience quite took. This did not diminish the importance intellectually to his larger project. DeMallie then also took a language and culture class from Norman McQwon, who emphasized the value of close reading of texts and linguistic nuances, a skill in and of itself. However, DeMallie was acutely aware from his own assessment that he was not ready for field research. While working at the Smithsonian the summer of 1969, he approached Paul Voorhis, the linguist in the Department of Anthropology there who agreed to give him some practical instruction. He arranged to visit Father Vine Deloria, Sr., at his home near Baltimore, and in that afternoon he had his first lesson in spoken Lakota, taping words, sentences, and a couple of brief texts. Unable to find a Lakota or Dakota speaker in the Washington, D.C., area, Voorhis and DeMallie were able to ask Mary Natani, a Winnebago speaker, for assistance, and they met with her once or twice a week during the summer, which DeMallie describes as "incredibly valuable to me" (DeMallie personal communication, June 30, 2010).

Into this configuration of influences at the University of Chicago and the Smithsonian, DeMallie brought his increasing encyclopedic knowledge of Sioux history and culture based mostly upon extensively surveying the published literature. His roommate through his undergraduate years was Tom Tax, nephew of Sol Tax. DeMallie also worked part time for *Current Anthropology,* during the academic year in his second and third undergraduate years when Sol Tax was editor. Both venues allowed him to know Sol Tax outside the classroom. Meeting Blaker on his first research trip to Washington, D.C., was also particularly fortuitous. With her encouragement, DeMallie had applied for a National Science Foundation Research Participation Grant for the summer of his sophomore year and was accepted by Ewers for an archival research project in which he needed DeMallie's historical research skills, seeking out information about Captain Ezra P. Ewers, an officer during the Indian wars, for an article Ewers was writing. This research foray did not yield much and was completed fairly quickly, but this was at a time when DeMallie was increasingly interested in objects. Once he had searched out the last of the retrievable documents for Ewers, Blaker encouraged him to examine Sioux manuscripts and photographs in the collections of the BAE archives. DeMallie returned the following two summers with grants from the same program to work, with Blaker basically helping in a series of small projects that prepared for the move of the archive collections across the Mall to the National Museum of Natural History, soon after to be renamed the National Anthropological Archives (see Glenn 1996:xiii–xiv). This work allowed him to identify the extent of unpublished archival materials in Washington, D.C., and elsewhere, epitomized in his still helpful inventory contributed to the volume edited by Ethel Nurge, *The Modern Sioux* (DeMallie 1970b). The 1965 working conference that led to this volume provided the venue for him to meet Ella Deloria, already known to him for her knowledge as a Dakota speaker trained in linguistics and fieldworker for Franz Boas, and subsequently the volume of so much of her unpublished manuscript material about Dakota language and culture. During this period DeMallie also became fascinated with the career and writings of James Owen Dorsey, George Bushotter's collaborator who authored texts in Lakota with Dorsey's guidance in 1887 (see DeMallie 1978, also a collection upon which Ella Deloria had worked).

DeMallie found that historical data became increasingly interesting for its possible source of information for historical reconstructions of events and interactions in Sioux culture history, but also for the promise of expanded ethnohistorical interpretation through the cultural perspectives of individual expression in the form of elicited texts. Blaker planned to attend the 1967 meeting of the American Society for Ethnohistory, and urged DeMallie to come as well. While he recollects having heard the term "ethnohistory" probably from Fogelson's conversations and lectures, DeMallie caught a ride with anthropologists James Van Stone and William Sturtevant (who was visiting in Chicago at the time) to the meeting in Lexington, Kentucky. DeMallie described his experience at this meeting, which "made me understand the potential of ethnohistory" (DeMallie personal communication, June 30, 2010).

During his first year of graduate school at the University of Chicago, DeMallie was awarded a National Endowment for the Humanities (NEH) Museum Internship at the Field Museum. Under the direction of Van Stone, the North American curator, DeMallie studied the Plains collections and organized the archival material assembled in the first decade of the twentieth century by Dorsey. This experience extended his ethnological scope of interest, and directly contributed to his developing his long-standing appreciation for material and expressive culture; his long interest in winter counts is the foremost example.

FORMATIVE EXPERIENCES

DeMallie's fieldwork on Lakota reservations, characterized most importantly by his stint at Cheyenne River in 1970–71 added to his insights, but often left him with more questions than answers. His first visit to Sioux country was in 1966, when he traveled with John L. Smith to Rosebud Reservation. He remembers they drove old man Thin Elk and Delbert Thunder Hawk up to Green Grass on the Cheyenne River Reservation, and then the return trip back to Rosebud where they attended a sing *(lowanpi)* in St. Francis, at the home of Laura Black Tomahawk; Smith was a serious student of Lakota religious traditions with whom DeMallie had been in correspondence (DeMallie personal communication, June 30, 2010). In 1967, DeMallie was involved in arranging for an urgent anthropology grant to enable bringing a microfilm camera to Kyle, South Dakota, to film the word slip file for the Buechel Lakota-English dictionary, which he did with assistance from Tom Tax. The file of 30,000 slips was located in the residence of Father Paul Manhart, S.J., who was editing what would become the published edition in 1970, but the trailer where Manhart lived was physically vulnerable and the linguistic resource so valuable: Father Eugene Buechel had spent his long career, from his arrival in 1902 till his death in 1954, collecting words (Buechel 1970:v–vi, 1–2; DeMallie personal communication, June 30, 2010). During his work on this busy but brief trip, DeMallie was also able to meet and talk with Frank Kills Enemy, a respected elder.

In 1970, having finished his MA thesis and defense (DeMallie 1970a), DeMallie returned to Washington, D.C., to spend time at the Smithsonian. He went to see Franklin Ducheneaux, then a young Bureau of Indian Affairs lawyer, whose father was the tribal chairman at Cheyenne River Reservation. Ducheneaux advised him to visit his father when he arrived on the reservation. DeMallie had driven by way of Denver to see the Walker papers that were first being made available to researchers at the Colorado Historical Society, and then drove to Cheyenne River. On his way to the reservation, he stopped in Vermillion, South Dakota, to visit with Ella Deloria. She asked him about his facility in Lakota, which is when she meticulously corrected his pronunciation and provided him with contacts at Cheyenne River. In late May he arrived in Eagle Butte, South Dakota, and found the chairman's office. His secretary, Delphine Red Fox, reported the chairman was in Washington, D.C., but offered to help. DeMallie indicated that he wanted to learn to speak Lakota and that the chairman's son had sent him for a conversation with his father. She reported that Moses Bad Male, one of the older councilmen, had a white son-in-law whom he had taught to talk Indian, and suggested that maybe he could be of help. When he was not in meetings, he was often sitting on a bench by the front door. Finding Moses there, DeMallie expressed his desire to work on learning the language. DeMallie stressed his flexibility, but was surprised when Moses declared "How about now?" Moses led DeMallie to a nearby church building, where the pastor showed them a room to use and this allowed DeMallie to set up his tape recorder. After an hour of working on eliciting sentences, Moses announced that he had to get back to the council meeting. Appreciating how serious DeMallie was about learning Lakota, Moses said that he would not be able to give DeMallie the time he needed because of his council duties, but suggested a friend who he was sure would be able to help him. Not immediately aware how conspicuous a car with New York license plates would be in Eagle Butte, DeMallie said he could be found at the motel:

> I checked into the motel and drove across the street to the drive-in restaurant and sat in my car while I waited for my food. I was engrossed in a Dakota Hymnal that the pastor had sold me when suddenly there was a knock on the passenger side window. There stood a man about 45, wearing a cowboy hat, gesturing for me to unlock the door. I did so, and he slid into the front seat. "I hear you're looking for me," he said. "Are you Moses Bad Male's friend?" "Yes, I'm Silas High Elk," and he shook hands with me. I explained what I wanted to do and he said he would like to help. "Can we start now?" he asked. I was beat, having driven from Chamberlain and [also] worked with Moses. "Could we wait until tomorrow?" "Well," he said, "see that car there?" He pointed to a red Impala in which sat a woman (his wife); the rest of the car seemed to be boiling over with kids. "I have to feed them tonight so I was hoping to start work now." I figured if we were going to develop a relationship, trust would have to be part of it. I told him that I was supposed to pay a dollar an hour and suggested that I just give him $10 up front and he could earn it later. He was impressed and took the money. He told me to come to his house in Green Grass the next day so we could start. "When should I come?" "About sundown," he said. The next day I found his house (having driven to the Looking Horses' place first by mistake) and arrived just as the sun was going down. We worked until 11:00 [P.M.]. I slept there in my station wagon and ended up staying for about three months.
>
> [DeMallie personal communication, June 30, 2010]

For a couple of weeks in September, DeMallie made a trip back to Chicago and Rochester, accompanied by Lauren Curley, a young Lakota, and during the trip they worked on transcribing Lakota texts.

After his stay in Green Grass, DeMallie moved to Iron Lightning and stayed with Whitley Marrowbone who recorded his repertoire of stories for him. Elders in the community, Tom and Marie Elk Eagle, got word that a relative of Marie's had died at the Standing Rock Reservation, and she wanted to go there. DeMallie drove them, along with their grandson David West, a boy about fifteen who was a good translator. While the Elk Eagles stayed with relatives in Fort Yates, West and DeMallie were sent on to Cannon Ball to stay with the Martinez family. This was the historic Yanktonai community of Chief Two Bears's people. This was DeMallie's first meeting with Lillian Martinez, whom he would interview repeatedly in later years. About a decade later, Lillian would telephone to report that she had a dream in which Tom Elk Eagle, who by that time was deceased, wanted DeMallie and Lillian to become brother and sister. And it was a number of years afterward that DeMallie learned that Mr. Martinez, Lillian's husband, was a biological son of Black Elk, the Oglala holy man whose life DeMallie had studied. At the time, DeMallie stayed in Iron Lightning until November 1970 before heading back to Chicago and Rochester.

Arriving in Chicago, DeMallie parked his car at O'Hare and flew to San Diego to attend the American Anthropological Association meetings and this was where he first met Vine Deloria, Jr. His book, *Custer Died for Your Sins,* had been published in 1969 and included his satirical chapter about anthropologists, especially those who had studied the Sioux, and so Ray felt like their meeting could go in any direction. In his conversation with Ella Deloria earlier, she had reassured him that her nephew was simply trying to get attention for what he was saying. There was a session at the meetings about Vine's critique of anthropologists; Margaret Mead chaired the session and Nancy Lurie was among the presenters. The sparring turned out milder than expected. At a party later hosted by Sturtevant and the *Handbook of North American Indians* staff, Vine appeared, as did other well-known Americanists, including Bill Fenton, Louis Kemintzer, and Bea Medicine. He was not really interested in talking with Ray, however; at least this was the latter's reaction. Running into Vine the next afternoon, Ray tried to tell him about his time at Cheyenne River and his planned dissertation on Sioux kinship, but Vine did not seem impressed and they parted. Shortly later they ran into each other again, and Vine, said something about Ray reminding him of his aunt, meaning Ella, whom he characterized as "always being interested in old things that were irrelevant today." Vine asked him, "Why don't you do something useful?" Ray was incensed and made a passionate defense of Ella's work and career accomplishments, and Vine responded: "You're a surly son of a bitch; let me buy you a drink." The bar was crowded near where they stood, but they conversed at some length about the potential of historical research that could be relevant to the tribes—the beginning of their friendship and future collaborations (DeMallie personal communication, January 3, 2001).

DeMallie returned from the meetings to be informed by Eggan that his fellowship had been reassigned so that another student could pursue fieldwork, but arrangements had been made for him to be supported at the Smithsonian; however this meant getting to the dissertation. Writing between January and July, Ray returned to South Dakota for the Sun Dance at Pine Ridge. He missed the blow-up over the Sun Dance at Wounded Knee by a day, but he followed it over to Crow Dog's Paradise at Rosebud. He returned briefly to Cheyenne River at the summer's end and defended his dissertation (DeMallie 1971), receiving his PhD in December 1971. Early in the new year he had the opportunity to participate in a study of American Indian economic development organized by Sam Stanley of the Smithsonian's Center for the Study of Man. During the late spring and summer of 1972 Ray did fieldwork at Pine Ridge, collecting information for the economic development survey article (DeMallie 1978b). As part of the American Indian economic development project, a series of meetings were being held among the participating scholars. The meeting for late summer was held in Seattle. Ray drove for a number of participants at the event. Vine Deloria, Jr., was in attendance, and when the meeting was over, he wanted to visit Hank Adams at Frank's Landing and the protest there. Vine was treated like royalty, and Ray shared in the hospitality: "When we were about the leave, a man showed up with a huge box containing two salmon (one a King) and dry ice." Vine insisted that Ray had to come home with him to help with all of this fish, and so, after ticket changes, Ray was on his way to Golden, Colorado. He stayed for the big salmon feast which turned out to be inserted into a block party for the McGovern presidential campaign, and the next day left-over salmon was eaten with Vine and his family watching the Democratic Convention in Miami on television. This series of adventures forged the beginning of their close relationship (DeMallie personal communication, January 3, 2011).

CONSTRUCTING ETHNOHISTORY

In the fall of 1972 Ray began his NEH fellowship at the Smithsonian (DeMallie personal communication, 2011). His first academic appointment was in the Anthropology Department at the University of Wyoming (1972–73) before he secured an appointment at Indiana University beginning in fall 1973, where he has taught to the present. Ray invited Vine to Laramie to talk in 1973 and at Bloomington in 1974. During both of these visits they talked about the kinds of research Ray was doing on his own with historical records. During the Bloomington visit, Vine's appreciation for the kinds of knowledge Ray was developing about historical detail and bibliographic accuracy came into clearer focus. Vine soon arranged a small subsidy for this kind of research through the Institute for the Development of Indian Law, and this was also when Ray began his collaborative work with Vine on the unratified treaties. Irrespective of these professional activities, a personal friendship further flourished.

In 1974 Mrs. Looking Horse sent him a flyer announcing the Green Grass Sun Dance, and he returned that summer and spent some time at Cheyenne River. He also did archival research elsewhere in South Dakota, funded once again by the Urgent Anthropology program at the Smithsonian (DeMallie personal communication, June 30, 2010). Also in 1974, Ray was involved as an expert witness in the second of the Wounded Knee Trials, this one in Lincoln, Nebraska, and this was again because he had been asked by Vine to testify about the Sioux perceptions of treaties and treaty making. Consequently, the relevance of his work on Sioux kinship and ideas of nationalism were also discussed in his testimony (DeMallie personal communication, January 3, 2011; DeMallie 1977a).

DeMallie's attention as a professor to his students cannot be emphasized enough. In my own case, I had arrived at Indiana University with a relatively uninformed sense of what I wanted to make the focus of my research, beyond wanting to engage with a Northern Plains topic and to draw upon my own concentrated interest in Sioux culture and history. His acceptance of me as his student coincided with his own recognition that he needed a better conceptual handle about contemporary Sioux country and specifically what was happening within the Dakota and Lakota reservations communities in relation to his own research agenda. He proposed a trip to tour extensively during the summer of 1976 all of the reservations in North and South Dakota and several in Montana. Jointly, we assessed what might be possibilities for fieldwork and research as we traveled and talked to select individuals that we encountered in the various communities. I was seeking a place where I wanted to work, and found that in Montana among Assiniboines whom I met at Fort Peck and Fort Belknap Reservations. DeMallie informally ended the summer with a partial inventory of places, issues, and questions that might be pursued, and began a sorting out of what might be his own priorities, developing opportunities for students at Indiana, and what might be larger initiatives in language, culture, and history, which naturally meant ethnohistory as well.

The import of ethnohistory in DeMallie's scholarship is multifaceted, and has part of its beginnings in the preparation represented by linguistic research, coupled with his interests in primary sources of Native perspectives, that began to cohere into his methodological commitment to ethnohistorical interpretation. He began to merge his evolving notions of reconciling the basic historical method with ethnological detail, built upon positivist and historiographically critical notions of the verifiable "fact," with the interpretative frameworks of his expansive anthropology. His work on Sioux ethnoontology and ethno-epistemology arising from translation issues reinforced his commitment to ethnohistory as a method, exemplified by the early article he co-authored with Robert H. Lavenda, entitled "*Wakan*: Plains Siouan Concepts of Power" (DeMallie and Lavenda 1977). Utilizing data from several primary sources, the authors provide a constructed framework of Lakota ideas that allows readers to ascertain the complex yet elegant dynamics of this principle within Lakota religious thought.

In DeMallie's first course on ethnohistory that he taught at Indiana the spring semester of 1976, he assigned Robert Berkhofer's *A Behavioral Approach to Historical Analysis* (1969), insightful in its reinforcement of the rationale of positivism through the incorporation of the findings of ethnoscientific orientations in the social sciences.[3] DeMallie has always had a fascination for the information arising from texts elicited in one language and then for the daunting tasks of translation during which the levels of meaning emerge, revealing the given text contributor's/speaker's contributions of information and perspective. Only then does a text illuminate the indigenous cultural lessons. Precisely, DeMallie has the conviction that it is this information that must be incorporated as data for ethnohistorical interpretation to occur, which makes ethnohistory more than supplying the mere context, but rather demonstrating the central factors to a culturally, even cross-culturally informed historical interpretation. In the chronology of the larger discipline, by the early 1970s the shine was coming off ethnoscience, and DeMallie was sorting out his influences, as were his students. Symbolic approaches in anthropology exemplified by Geertz's writings as a model of descriptive power was on one end of the continuum, and Schneider's wrestling match with the redefinition of culture on the other.

Fogelson has explained in his essay about the Schneider legacy that historical anthropology was being forged in the research endeavors of various faculty and students in the department at Chicago in the late 1960s and 1970s (Fogelson 2001:34). Notably, it was Fogelson, one of DeMallie's professors, who in 1974 and again in 1989 cautioned ethnohistorians to remember they are often really doing ethno-ethnohistory, or even ethno-ethno-ethnohistory, which means "taking seriously native theories of history as embedded in cosmology, in narratives, in rituals and ceremonies, and more generally in native philosophies and worldviews" (Fogelson 1974, 1989:134–35). DeMallie was moving in the same direction, and supportive of these refinements.[4]

The 34th Plains Anthropology meetings in 1976, held in Minneapolis, hosted sessions organized to assess the state of anthropology on the Great Plains. Papers were topically assigned, and the assessment of ethnohistory as a method was presented in a joint paper by Mildred Wedel, research associate in the Anthropology Department at the Smithsonian, and DeMallie. The published essay reveals a tension between Wedel's conservative literalism and DeMallie's broader vision for the potential of ethnohistory. Through critical editing, Wedel believed in using a full range of historical documentation, including early maps, to elaborate cross-cultural interpretations where possible, very much believing solely in a positivist reconstructive view of history. DeMallie, however, was particularly contrastive about the ways by which various forms of indigenous evidence might be revealed in what had been nontraditional sources previously not taken seriously or dismissed by historians. By drawing out the substances of worldviews and cultural frames so intrinsic to specific indigenous peoples and their views of their own histories in these unutilized or underused sources, DeMallie argued that this was the critical value of ethnohistory, the application of anthropological theory to interpretation of evidence, and, consequently, its contribution to an historical anthropology (Wedel and DeMallie 1980).

DeMallie refined his ideas about ethnohistory as he moved forward on a variety of research projects in the 1970s. One baseline was his articulation expressed in his 1972 paper, "Using Historical Data: A Dakota Example," delivered as part of the "Historical Documents and North American Indians" session at the 71st American Anthropological Association meetings in Toronto, when DeMallie declared, "ethnohistory consisted in the meaningful patterning of the [historical] data of past behavior by using the culture concept." He conscientiously saw that he was following in the footsteps of others who had worked in the same kinds of sources, and named those whom he saw as his immediate predecessors: "Fenton, Hickerson, Sturtevant and Vansina, among others" (DeMallie 1972:4). In his 1976 essay on "Teton Dakota Time Concepts" he wrote that the "primary goal of ethnohistory is to write Indian history in a way that incorporates Indian cultural understandings" (DeMallie 1976a:7). This was also said in light of another statement he made earlier on the same page: "True Indian history, written by and for Indians, is an intriguing and promising possibility both for the new light it sheds on the past and for the expression of Indian self-images in the present."

One of his projects at the time was the collecting of historical data about treaties and documents of proceedings, especially the treaty negotiations, in his collaboration with Vine Deloria, Jr.—volumes not published until 1999 (Deloria and DeMallie 1999). Ray's friendship with Vine also informed his ideas about applied scholarship (DeMallie 2006b). Ray became involved in presenting a series of workshops sponsored by the Institute for the Development of Indian Law, co-founded by Vine, contextualizing treaty history for a number of specific tribal groups. After writing about the interpretation of treaties (DeMallie 1977b, 1980, 1981), he turned his energy to producing his meticulously edited and annotated publications of primary texts by Sioux individuals, notably those represented in the Walker collected texts (DeMallie 1993; Walker 1980, 1982, 1983), including those of George Sword (upon whose texts he is still working) (DeMallie 1999). These efforts again found integrity with the involvements with many materials already analyzed and translated by Ella Deloria, and in 1981, once Vine Deloria, Sr., had relocated in his retirement to Pierre, South Dakota, Ray was able to work with him on the Sword materials in particular, becoming literally the anthropologist in the basement. In Ray's words:

"Sword's writings would remind him of some anecdote or custom and frequently he spoke of his personal view of Christianity and the Sioux adaptations to it. This usually led back to stories of his father, one of the first Sioux men to be ordained an Episcopal priest, and his grandfather, who converted from his traditional religion to Christianity near the end of his life" (DeMallie personal communication, January 3, 2011).

These dynamics of research and personal interactions had the effect of weaving a new fabric of kinship between DeMallie and the Deloria family.

The Neihardt-Black Elk interviews transcription effort was also begun, eventually culminating in *The Sixth Grandfather: Black Elk's Teachings Given to John G. Neihardt* (1984). DeMallie's discovery of the shorthand transcriptions of the interviews between Black Elk (translated by his son Ben Black Elk) and Neihardt, recorded by Neihardt's daughter Enid, made possible more detailed perspectives on the interactions between the two men that led to the latter's 1932 literary creation, *Black Elk Speaks* (Neihardt 1932). DeMallie's extensive introduction and elaborate annotations make both men and their relationship more accessible to future generations of readers.

Amidst his preparation of *The Sixth Grandfather*, DeMallie was invited to the University of Alberta in 1982 to give a paper at a conference on cultural interactions organized by Darnell, and papers from this conference were eventually published in 1988. His contribution, "Lakota Traditionalism: History and Symbol," clarified ways in which he contended that Lakota held concepts about their identity, and particularly how various symbols in the course of a century came to represent how traditional ways and means have secured the "basis for Indian identity [competitively] in the white man's world." He took the opportunity to elaborate upon the basis for "symbolic anthropology":

> The field of symbolic anthropology does not assign primacy to mental phenomena over behavioral ones, although it recognizes that human beings strive to find meaning in interaction. Still, the obvious fact that participants in interaction do not always share the same understanding of the situation, even though in a broad sense they share the same symbols, points to the complexity of symbolic analysis. The 'culture' constructed by the anthropologist out of people's statements about themselves and out of observations of interactions forms a model, an outsider's approximation, of consensual meaning within the group. Such a model does not differ in kind from the models that the people themselves construct, collectively or individually, as expressions of group identity directed towards themselves or others. Given the

impossibility of intersubjectivity among members of even the most homogeneous of groups, any people has the potential for many variations in the interpretation of 'culture,' of the meanings that structure and give form to their world.

[DeMallie 1988b:2]

DeMallie explains that if "culture" is the object of study, it is also the product of the research: "until we (or they, the people themselves) feel the need to draw boundaries around the group and define its uniqueness and diversity, the symbols through which the world is objectified are on the whole unconscious givens. It is only the people's own philosophers, or the outsider anthropologist, with the ceaseless question 'Why?' that forces identification and definition of cultural symbols" (1988b:3).

He suggests that it is the anthropologist who seeks an explanation for how this is done, a question not of particular or necessary interest to a given people's own philosophers. He then states a rationale for symbolic anthropology, but also a succinct declaration of his own rationale for his own body of work to this point in time:

for the anthropologist the patterns of behavior, the ways of doing, are far easier and more direct to record and provide the basic starting point for study. Yet the message of the symbolic approach is that one cannot read simplistically from how to why, from behavior to meaning. The symbol intervenes, the complex meanings, multidimensional and ever-changing, that defines the uniqueness of a way of life. To understand a people one must be able to speak their language, to behave in appropriate ways; but more importantly, one must know what it means. This is the level of understanding which far too few anthropological studies have achieved—few have even tried.

[DeMallie 1988b:3]

Coupled with the inspiration to achieve the explanatory forms of "interpretive anthropology" exemplified by Geertz's famous essays ("Ritual and Social Change: A Javenese Example," and "Thick Description," both in Geertz 1973), DeMallie proceeds with his own projects in a variety of parallel directions.

DeMallie's interpretation of the symbolic power of kinship among the Dakota/Lakota arose from the charge that he accepted from Eggan's 1964 Morgan lectures, carried through to his honors paper, master's thesis, and PhD dissertation, and then consequently extended to his refined analyses under the often distinct influences of his teachers. His long-standing interests concerning changes in kinship and social organization among the Dakota and Lakota are represented in his Sol Tax Festschrift essay (DeMallie

1979), his Eggan Festschrift essay (DeMallie 1994), his Schneider legacy contribution (DeMallie 2001b), and his contribution to the Fogelson Festschrift (DeMallie 2006c). In the last and most recent piece, DeMallie demonstrates how culture change in the social organization of the Eastern and Middle Dakota and the Lakota has been obscured by misinformed interpretation and supposition made upon supposition. He emphasizes how important knowing the full range of source materials, primary and secondary, published and unpublished (often archival), oral or written is. These sources contribute to a critical understanding of where error or misinterpretation can be separated for verifiable detail and context. By following Eggan's example, DeMallie has assembled the documentation of culture change among Dakota and Lakota as reflected in social organization, and specifically formulated their models as reflected in their systems of kinship.

Equally profound, DeMallie has demonstrated his ability to probe various collections of texts by literate Lakota and Dakota writing in their own language to reveal further cultural thought and principles. For example, his focus on the interpretation of symbol and construction of culture is epitomized in his discussion of the White Buffalo Calf Woman's gift of the pipe to the Lakota in the *Sioux Indian Religion* volume (DeMallie 1987). DeMallie demonstrates how this origin story for the pipe constitutes a social charter for Lakota both in the range of symbolic associations with this particular pipe and then all other pipes as descendent relatives, and its significance for social and moral order among the people. DeMallie explores this symbolic import of the pipe and its meanings in more detail, supported by a fuller discussion of his conclusions about Sioux kinship, in his essay, "Kinship and Biology in Sioux Culture" in the Eggan Festschrift volume (DeMallie 1994). DeMallie elucidates how the anthropological methods of the more traditional social-structural approach can be complemented by the cultural or symbolic approach with greater results as a basis for "cross-cultural comparison of native understandings of kinship" (143).

The most definitive summary made by DeMallie about the methodological and theoretical contributions of ethnohistory is found in his essay, "'These Have No Ears': Narrative and the Historical Method."[5] Using as an illustration Lakota ways of describing the act of listening, and the problems of a series of scholars interpreting Sitting Bull's prophetic vision prior to the battle of Little Big Horn, DeMallie demonstrates ways to interpret the imagery of ears in the context of Lakota culture. In an example of what he called his "brief cultural exegesis," he noted:

> Metaphorically, the act of opening ears had reference to ear piercing, the ceremony by which every Sioux infant had tiny slits cut into the ear lobes, through which earrings were later hung. Until the ears were pierced, a child was not considered fully human, a true member of

society. Semantically, it appears that the piercing, opening, or mere acknowledgment of possessing ears expressed a willingness to listen to and accept a significant message, and served, moreover, as a pledge that the parties involved were able to speak truthfully. To have open ears was to be adult, sensible, and responsible.
      [DeMallie 1993:521]

DeMallie demonstrates how through the use of documented texts taken in cooperation by a number of fieldworkers, Lakota individuals have related in their stories or accounts perspectives that embody their culture. As they reflect upon their past, the traditions and narratives inherited from their relatives and associates carry ethnohistorical insights unavailable by other means. DeMallie makes his connection to Paul Radin's admonition that it is better for the ethnologist to begin from a document, however framed and created, a fixed expression of a individual as a source, and representative of specific cultural experience (DeMallie 1999, making reference to Radin 1987:186). Darnell points to the methodological principle of standpoint and ethnographic perspective as one of the gifts of the Boasian paradigm, and DeMallie sees himself in this stream.

    DeMallie's commitment to an historical anthropology is extensive. His work with the texts of ethno-philosophers of the Lakota, especially George Bushotter (DeMallie 1978a), the various Lakota who contributed to the Walker texts, foremost of these George Sword (DeMallie 1993, 1999, and Walker 1980, 1982, 1983), and Nicholas Black Elk (DeMallie 1984), were extensive. In 1992, DeMallie joined with Douglas Parks to summarize this refocused intention and purpose, the turn toward method with a central concentration upon indigenous literatures in the languages of particular societies and cultures (Parks and DeMallie 1992:105–47). DeMallie's contributions to ethnohistory instigate a return to the framing and study of the indigenous language text and suggest various approaches to interpretation. What is especially intriguing is his blend of historical linguistic standards, coupled with the insights and interpretative power of symbolic anthropology, and the descriptive power as well as the logical dynamics of narrative devices inherent in "thick description." DeMallie's various articles in the *Plains* volume of the *Handbook of North American Indians* which he also edited attest to his personal standard about requirements for an informed culture history (DeMallie 2001a, 2001c, 2001d; DeMallie and Ewers 2001; DeMallie and Miller 2001; DeMallie and Parks 2001). This is not to say that many other ethnohistorians have not worked with texts, and based their work upon the critical reading of documents. However, DeMallie has brought to our attention the importance of such sources of substantive information in indigenous languages, and demonstrated how previously unconventional or idiosyncratic sources can be interrogated and investigated, especially through the anthropological insights applied to the interpretation in historical reconstructions and contemporary reflections upon the past.

Darnell, discussing the original Boasian agenda, stresses how much the textual tradition was methodologically central and how the production of a corpus of literature that is a substantial portion of the ethnographic record about Indians is owed to the Boasians (Darnell 1992). There is a case to be made for DeMallie to be considered as neo-Boasian (Bunzl 2004; Bashkow 2004). Foremost, he has contributed tangibly to the emergence of a historical anthropology collaboratively within his commitment to ethnohistory as a method. The borders of anthropology and history, and so many other disciplines, have been extended in recent decades, and have variously been crossed or overlapped in places, with ethnohistory being one frequent bridge. DeMallie has certainly been a frequent traveler to these borders and his selective crossings have been impressive; he has returned and given us masterful accounts descriptively and theoretically. His colleagues, students, and readers continue to be privileged that he has shared so many of his insights so reflexively, and demonstrated his ideas so persuasively.

NOTES

The author thanks Raymond J. DeMallie, Susan Elaine Gray, and David Mc-Crady for their comments on various versions of the essay.

1. The Walker texts were just published when Clifford was writing his original essay; see *Lakota Belief and Ritual*, ed. Raymond J. DeMallie and Elaine Jahner (Lincoln: University of Nebraska Press, 1980); *Lakota Society*, ed. Raymond J. DeMallie (Lincoln: University of Nebraska Press, 1982); and *Lakota Myth*, ed. Elaine Jahner (Lincoln: University of Nebraska Press, 1983). A volume of George Sword texts, collected by Walker, is in preparation (see discussion in DeMallie 1999).

2. DeMallie is neo-Boasian in the sense that he is a historical particularist in his disposition toward culture, as reflected in his scholarship on the Sioux, and is grounded in the linguistic aspects necessary to comprehending culture, focusing on the idiosyncratic expression.

3. Berkhofer's interpretive orientation as a historian has shifted with developments in narrative theory (1995).

4. During DeMallie's years in graduate school, the fascination with French structuralism and ethnoscience was viewed as an advance partly extended from the third stream of anthropology, beyond that of the Boasians and the social anthropologists. At Harvard, anthropology was instead building upon Talcott Parsons's systemic distinctions between culture and society, basically a resynthesis of ideas arising from Max Weber earlier in the century. Among DeMallie's professors at Chicago were Clifford Geertz and David Schneider, as

well as Victor Turner, all trained in this "third stream" and part of the new prac-titioners of symbolic anthropology, as were his fellow students, James Boon, Karen Blu, and Sherry Ortner. James Peacock (2005:52–62) describes this devel-opment when historical context was being rediscovered among Geertz and his contemporaries.

5. The essay is the written version of DeMallie's American Society for Ethno-history Presidential Address delivered November 13, 1992, at the annual meeting held in Salt Lake City, Utah.

2

Swing Time

Narrative, Collective Improvisation, and the Ethnohistorical Method

KELLIE J. HOGUE

On a crisp November evening in 2009, Professor Raymond J. DeMallie began our seminar on ethnohistorical methods by stating: "I don't lecture, I tell stories." A lecture, he explained, could consist of a series of unrelated facts, whereas a story requires putting together all of the evidence so that it may infuse historicity into material that is fundamentally not historical. Framed appropriately, this itinerant combination of narrative and data illuminates a formerly undetectable comprehensive pattern. Hewn from a disparate set of seemingly ahistorical materials, identified and authenticated, a competent ethnohistorian can then transform this pattern into ethnohistory. As DeMallie intimated that evening, over the past fifty years scholars in the field of ethnohistory have consistently found creative ways to negotiate the tension between history and culture, synchrony and diachrony, and anthropology and history. Musician and composer Wynton Marsalis (1995:105–17) describes a similar creative negotiation of seemingly antithetical tensions when he discusses a central concept to New Orleans–style jazz called "collective improvisation." Driven by rhythm, "the organized motion of sounds, the most basic component of music," and structured by meter, collective improvisation consists of personality traits manifested in the form of "signature things." Consequently, individual music styles are fused into a recognizably distinct, complex, collective sound. This sound is the combinative result of "spontaneous musical invention," that is, the process through which musicians create and structure a cooperative group conversation in the moment using a knowledge-based set of techniques— groove, polyphony, registers, call and response, riffs, breaks, virtuosity, and syncopation.

To begin, I propose to consider DeMallie's discussion of narrative and data as patterns and to take a look at it in the context of collective improvisation, using a jazz-inspired theoretical approach. Then, I "collectively improvise" an ethnohistorically derived theory of origin for the Mardi Gras Indians of New Orleans to demonstrate how such an approach might be applied to a complex historical situation.

As he sought to introduce the ethnohistorical method, it could be said DeMallie was in a "groove"; a groove occurs when differing rhythms are brought together. His claim that a lecture is a series of unrelated facts reminds one of the necessity of "in the moment" spontaneity and "on the spot" invention to the creative process. Statements gain context when illustrated with an example through the sharing of details concerning the personalities of early ethnohistorians: James Mooney was so concerned about making sure he used historical source materials in his study of the Ghost Dance to complement his experiences in the field that he went beyond mere description and searched for the historical antecedents of the phenomenon; and John Swanton pioneered a method of integrating history and anthropology using a typewriter, scissors, and paste. Virtuosic details like these take formerly ahistorical ethnographic facts and infuse them with a personalized sense of historicity in the ear of the listener.

Polyphony is the combination of more than one melody. As DeMallie explained, the ethnohistorical method brings a diverse set of noncompatible sources into a range of analysis. These sources could be likened to Marsalis's idea of a polyphony; that is, differing melodies equal different types of data. Consideration of these sources, and their potential use value, is similar to his idea of registers. Registers can be understood as having any number of metaphorical planes in the air, all at different altitudes—some occupying higher ranges, some lower. Some ethnohistorical sources may have cultural details that are present at higher meta-narrative levels of understanding. Some may be more easily understood. Some may be more appealing than others in terms of veracity. During analysis, an ethnohistorian must pay close attention to any call-and-response activity between the sources; such activity in the musical context is the repetition of one instrument's musical phrase by another. Any riffs or breaks, observable as repeated phrases or solos among the evidence, should be investigated. Riffs are composed by repeating a phrase, and a break is when one of the musicians in the group treats the audience to a solo. Notable musicians use none, some, or all of the above techniques, have a strong personality, and express it eloquently. As with jazz, the goal of ethnohistory is to ultimately seek a combination of narrative and data that makes possible the illumination of a formerly undetectable comprehensive pattern. Masters who have the rare capacity to create, sustain, and etch particular musical phrases into the minds of listeners are said to be virtuosos. The most expressive virtuosos are known for their ability to inject something "rhythmically unexpected" into the sound. This quality is known as "syncopation." Those who can syncopate with grand flourish and personal style distinguish themselves from their peers and stand the test of time (Marsalis 1995:105–17).

According to DeMallie, with the proper combination of formerly incomparable sources and a crucible, fusion moment (what Marsalis calls "swing time"), it is possible to make the collected documents actually "speak" for themselves and to tell their own story. Once identified, these patterns are then artfully transformed into stories by a competent ethnohistorian. I argue that this process, so central to the genesis of good ethnohistory, constitutes an academic form of collective improvisation. Following Marsalis, I suggest that what distinguishes an ethnohistorian from other more disciplinary-bound colleagues is the addition of "something unexpected" into the narrative. For an ethnohistorical virtuoso this ability stems from a deep knowledge of the relevant literature and the opportunity to express that knowledge. Such virtuosity can appear verbally or in writing. Whether this act occurs in the middle of an article, the recitation of a story in class, or at an event where the individual may have the occasion to speak, it exemplifies the ethnohistorian's ability to "syncopate."

In a course entitled "Intensive Study of a Culture: Lakota," DeMallie taught us his method of close reading and the subsequent sociocultural categorization of text evidence to yield Native and non-Native perspectives. He discussed the importance of social organization and the centrality of kin relationships to Lakota society and culture. His approach of bringing culture, history, and language together (the "next step" for the analysis of descriptive cultural data for Boas [1936] and reminiscent of Washburn's "history in the round" [1961] or Simmons's "holistic, diachronic approach" [1988]) was strikingly interdisciplinary. During this course I became enchanted by the intellectual confrontation between the diachronic and the synchronic and have spent the years since then exploring ways of placing these concepts into dialogue with one another in meaningful, understandable forms. As DeMallie has emphasized in his own work, it is important to be as careful as possible not to jump to conclusions that may not be accurate. Whether in the field or in the archive, it is necessary to stay as close to the sources as possible. When a particular set of incompatible sources seem to form a believable pattern that then could be fashioned into a narrative, it is important to seek out additional sources across registers and in other frameworks to cross-check this emerging story. However, one must also be open to that potentially illuminative moment where data and narrative merge to form a comprehensible pattern. DeMallie's approach consistently challenges ethnohistorians to consider the multiplicity of interpretations that can be applied to a single statement or act. A researcher should be able to acknowledge the unexpected, or perhaps contribute the unexpected, in order to produce that striking syncopation which signals the opportunity for virtuosity of the improvisational kind. A detailed knowledge of ethnohistorical literature, commitment to the publication of sources that demonstrate a Native perspective, and willingness to entertain alternative explanations encourages fresh answers to old

questions, new inquiries into matters believed laid to rest, and cognitive innovation from potential intellectual decay.

A particularly memorable instance of DeMalliean syncopation occurred
when a scholar came to campus to give a talk about how torture in the *Jesuit
Relations* could be read as a moment of religious conversion for the individual undergoing the torture. As the question-and-answer session was coming
to a close, DeMallie began to carefully parse the details of a particular scene
the scholar had identified as the "conversion moment." After a brief verbal
exchange, the scholar suggested that the person being tortured had completely left his culture behind as he neared a violent death. DeMallie then
carefully posed a simple question drawn from an intimate knowledge of the
account, asking: "But wasn't he singing?" He inferred that the act of singing,
a detail that had not yet been noted by the scholar, indicated the continuing
resonance of culturally appropriate behavior.

DeMallie's mastery of the sources and his ability to add an unexpected
detail to constitute a conversation between the data, the narrative, interpretation of the narrative, and the contemporary discussion of both are well
documented. In the hands of an intellectual virtuoso, the ethnohistorical
approach reveals the reflective capacity of ethnohistory and demonstrates
evidence for collective improvisation as a promising theoretical tool. De-
Mallie's observation concerning the man's singing as historical evidence of
the continuance of culture in the face of crisis was for me that little something unexpected that makes ethnohistory such an engaging endeavor. This
moment consistently lingered with me as I endeavored to complete pre-
dissertation research on a culturally creative group of African Americans
who have been performing their history and culture for more than a century, the Mardi Gras Indians of New Orleans.

MARDI GRAS INDIANS

The term "Mardi Gras Indian" is broadly applied to groups of African
Americans who parade throughout the streets primarily in the black neighborhoods of New Orleans during the carnival period attired in costumes
reminiscent of Great Plains American Indian regalia from the 1800s. The
history of New Orleans is tightly bound to the color line; while whites faced
no limitations to their participation in Mardi Gras, Africans and African
Americans were generally not allowed to participate in the yearly parades
that have become synonymous with the city. Denied the opportunity to
participate in the traditional Mardi Gras festivities, African Americans began their own parades in their own neighborhoods. Separate parades assured
them the right to participate in the larger cultural tradition of their city and
at the same time allowed them to reaffirm their resistance to white hege-
mony and demonstrate their affiliation with American Indian groups.

Cumulatively, the tribes of the Mardi Gras Indians make up what is called the Mardi Gras Indian Nation. As Draper (1973:42) explains, members of the various tribes were considered to be African Americans who were associated residentially with low-income areas and housing units that were historically part of the City of New Orleans urban renewal projects. These were primarily working-class residents who spent their lives contributing their labor and love to their communities. Men and women who worked as laborers or maids in the American and French Quarters would return to their neighborhoods at the end of the day and occupy roles of increased communal importance because they were Mardi Gras Indians. One of the best known Big Chiefs, Tootie Montana, was a lather who spent his life building and installing the support structures which must be in place before plaster can be applied to a building. One former chief of the White Eagles, Clarence "Bo" Davis, Jr., was a postal worker, waiter, and truck driver prior to his death. And Chief of Chiefs Lawrence "Big Chief" Fletcher was an employee of the Sewerage and Water Board before he passed on.

Prior to Hurricane Katrina, differentiation of tribal identity within the Mardi Gras Indian "nation" had three levels: neighborhood, ward, and region. At the level of the neighborhood, participation in Indian life brings people of the same race and socioeconomic status together in self-affirming benevolent social associations. Within the larger New Orleans social landscape, each tribe is associated with a specific neighborhood and ward. However, wards can have any number of tribes and there were six of them in the Ninth Ward alone. For example, Big Chief Larry Bannock and his "tribe," the Golden Star Hunters, are from Gert Town, an area located within the Sixteenth and Seventeenth Wards. Big Chief Tootie Montana (now deceased) and his "tribe," the Yellow Pocahontas, is associated with the Seventh Ward. Big Chief Charles Taylor's White Cloud Hunters are from the sixth ward, and the Wild Magnolias, led by Theodore Emile "Bo" Dollis, are from the third ward. Indians from one ward may also participate, or "mask," in tribes from different wards.

Since 1852, the established wards have remained relatively unchanged, and new wards added to accommodate city expansion. In addition to ward boundaries, the city is also divided into two distinct regions commonly known as Uptown and Downtown. Wards located downriver from the American Quarter, the area north and west of the Mississippi River beginning with the northern boundary of the French Quarter at Canal Street are considered as part of Uptown. Areas of town south of the American Quarter, or downriver from the Central Business District, are considered to be Downtown. In terms of demographics, as the city grew larger, whites tended to settle and conduct business in the American and French Quarters, in areas known today as the Garden District, the University District, and Magazine Street. Systematic social and residential segregation resulted in the areas outside of the French and American Quarters, both Uptown and Downtown, being settled by people of African descent and other nonwhites. Some of the more commonly known areas associated with these groups are the Ninth Ward (upper and lower), Algiers, Carrollton, and Gert Town.

While their tie to the land has historically been explicit, often indicated in the names of the tribes themselves, for many groups their identification with a specific neighborhood or district has consistently been significant. Consequently, there are four basic kinds of Indians—Uptown, Downtown, Back of Town, and Across the River. According to Draper (1973:30), the most important level of differentiation between groups was the rivalry between Uptown Indians and Downtown Indians. Differences between them were not simply residential, they were also visibly reflected in costuming and language. Uptown Indian costumes featured aprons upon which story panels were displayed, crafted from rhinestones and feathers; Downtown Indian costumes did not display stories on their aprons, instead they utilized geometric designs made from sequins and feathers.

Confrontations ("showdowns") or meetings between chiefs on parade days are ritualistic yet open to spontaneity. Showdowns between tribes only take place if it is mutually agreed by both big chiefs that their costumes are of comparable merit, value, and workmanship. Showdowns involve both rivalry as well as prestige, often playing in important role in determining the reputation of the chief as well as his tribe. Prior to the 1960s, these confrontations were often violent. After that period, the showdowns took the form of miniature musical battles (Draper 1973:117–18). The winner of a particular battle is the chief who demonstrates his singing and dancing prowess in excess of the other chief in public and wins the approval of the community members who have gathered to watch the showdown. Big chiefs "compare feathers," that is, they evaluate the other chief's costume and musical talent against their own and a winner emerges from this confrontation. The chief that wins the most competitions on parade days and over the course of his lifetime renders invaluable service to the community is given the honor of being "the Prettiest" and bestowed with the title of "Chief of Chiefs." These titles elevate the individual to a higher status within the Mardi Gras Indian nation. Individuals who bear these titles are treated with both deference and reverence. The ceremony to designate a chief of chiefs includes a walk along a red carpet, the pouring of libations, and the shaking of the tambourines. This chief of chiefs is then translated into a culture hero of sorts, one that will be remembered in both song and tradition.

ORIGIN NARRATIVES

There are two dominant narratives of historical origin associated with the phenomenon of Africans, and later African Americans, adopting costumes and cultural practices reminiscent of American Indians. The most popular idea, or riff (repeated phrase), is that these groups began primarily as a response to the visit of Buffalo Bill to New Orleans in the late 1800s, or what I call the Cody Thesis. A less discernible notion, which I call the Polyphonic Proposition, lies in the deeply intertwined, not too easily unraveled, historical experiences of Europeans (British, Spanish, French), Africans, and Indians in pre-historical and colonial Louisiana. It is good to remind oneself that Mardi Gras as we currently know it did not originate in New Orleans, but in Mobile, in 1703. From Mobile, it is thought that this tradition moved westward and arrived in New Orleans in 1723. The Mardi Gras parades which have become the hallmark of this tradition did not begin until 1835.

Historical debate about the origins of the Mardi Gras Indians has garnered a measure of public interest that often focuses upon the arrival of Buffalo Bill's Wild West show in New Orleans in 1884. Hoping to profit from the crowds expected to attend the World Industrial and Cotton Centennial Exposition, William Cody's appearance in the Crescent City was, for him, a disappointing one. Having lost his livestock and stage props in the Mississippi River shortly before arriving, it looked like the show might not go on. But in a city at the height of preparations for Mardi Gras that was also hosting an exposition which featured agriculture and education, Cody was easily able to outfit his show in time to open along with the exposition on December 19, 1884. Four months later (a stint which featured forty-four straight days of rain), Cody departed the Big Easy over $50,000 in debt. Despite his extreme financial loss, the "Wild West" of Cody's show remained embedded within the carnival culture of New Orleans well beyond his 1884–85 visit.[1] This traveling show is credited with being the founding historical moment for the Mardi Gras Indians of New Orleans largely because one of the original groups within contemporary Indian lore is known as the "Creole Wild West." Riffing off of one another, a number of scholars (Smith 1994; Lipsitz 1988; Kinser 1990; Berry 1995; Lohman 1999) (as well as many Mardi Gras Indians themselves) have suggested that a short time after Buffalo Bill's departure, African Americans in the city began masking as American Indians under the name of the Creole Wild West, modeling themselves after the Indians they had seen when they attended the show at the racetrack located toward the back of town in Metairie.

Most scholars who have written about the Mardi Gras Indians have inserted their own individual breaks into the narrative, performing their particular solos but still falling back onto this familiar riff. Berry (1988) places their origins firmly in transplanted African ritualizations and cites the year the tradition began as 1883, with the Creole Wild West. Acknowledging that "the tap root of this Carnival hybrid lay in a shared sense of rebellion," he suggests that "Africans and Indians were oppressed peoples, each steeped in a spiritual past" (Berry 1988:8). Lipsitz (1988:102) building upon Berry, comments that they represent "visual and narrative references to Native American Indians" yet they are not enough of a "resemblance to genuine Indian celebrations and ceremonies." Suggesting a bricolage-like mechanism at work, he believes the practice of masking Indian "projects a cultural indeterminacy, picking and choosing from many traditions in order to fashion performances and narratives suitable for arbitrating an extraordinarily complex identity" (Lipsitz 1988:102). For Lipsitz, the "real impetus for the creation of these mock Indian tribes" was Buffalo Bill's Wild West show and the origination of the Creole Wild West, quite in tune with an African aesthetic that is manifested through musical sensibilities reminiscent of the Africanisms documented by anthropologist Melville Herskovitz. Smith (1994) provides evidence that blacks were parading dressed as American Indians as early as 1836 through an 1845 narrative that cites "a well dressed company of 'Native American' militia . . . [who] marched hurriedly along to the old familiar tune" (Durell 1845 in Smith 1994:35–36). Smith links the practice to Afro-Caribbean tradition as well as the founding of the Creole Wild West in 1885.

I do not wish to dispute the impact of Buffalo Bill's Wild West upon the African American population prior to the turn of the century in New Orleans. Nor do I dispute the creation of the Creole Wild West as a visible manifestation of culture contact between performers (Indians, in this case, Pawnee and Sioux) and their audience (descendants of Creoles and Freedmen) within the context of a deepening European-enforced segregation. Given the complexity of sifting through large quantities of material that comprise the archive of colonial Louisiana: the multiplicity of languages required (French, Louisiana Creole, Spanish, and English); the variety of locations where these documents are stored (France, Spain, England; and the United States), issues of time and funding, the Cody Thesis makes for convenient historical and cultural sense.

The complexities of unraveling Mardi Gras Indian origin narratives are made even more difficult by attempts in the contemporary period (Draper 1973; Smith 1994) to get inside Mardi Gras Indian culture that led to the characterization of these groups as "gangs," a label which left an uneasy and bitter legacy. This generalization, when combined with the belief held by some Mardi Gras Indians that they should be financially compensated by researchers for interviews and information, as well as the complexities of the post-Katrina landscape, makes the possibility of further study even more precarious. Regardless of the potential work environment, the narrative dominance of the Cody Thesis groove in the academy, I believe, leaves little room for other stories. This riff draws on too many similar repetitive registers and has over time become its own comfortable groove concerning this extraordinarily complex identity. At the same time, however, the Cody Thesis also obfuscates some issues, in particular the stories the Mardi Gras

Indians tell about themselves, narratives located primarily in the lyrics of their songs.

One of the most important aspects of Indian life beyond parade-day participation is the performance of distinctive songs and music that actively creates a sense of shared community within each tribe and within the greater Indian "nation." While costumes and behaviors visibly document this unique tradition, the less tangible philosophical, intellectual, and cognitive aspects of Mardi Gras Indian history and culture reside within their lyrics and music. Mardi Gras Indian culture has retained a cohesive sense of community through the performance of ritual chants and music. Each leader is charged with creating his own lyrics for songs and chants. Lyrics are usually derived from personal experiences of "masking Indian" or from events from past parade days and confrontations with other leaders and other tribes. One of the frequent topics within Indian music lyrics are the big chiefs who have passed on, the "fallen chiefs." Prior to the 1970s, Indian music was largely unrecorded and performed only in two settings: private evening practice sessions and public parade days. Over the past thirty-five years, a few big chiefs have taken Mardi Gras Indian music to a wider audience, recording and releasing compact discs as well as performing their music in national and international venues. As articulated collectively through their music, Mardi Gras Indian lore and legend is saturated with imagery that proclaims a close connection between American Indian and African. Remembering that the combination of more than one melody is polyphony, it is perhaps reasonable to consider that Mardi Gras Indian identity is simply not a melody all of its own; rather it may be better understood as a polyphony comprised of cultural and historical melodies—African, Indian, British, Spanish, French, and American.

A POLYPHONIC PROPOSITION

As the less popular origin narrative of Mardi Gras Indians goes, after the arrival of Africans into the New World, and specifically in Louisiana, those who fled the brutality of plantation life often sought the refuge of neighboring American Indian groups. Over time, Africans and American Indians intermarried and formed alliances in opposition to the movement of Europeans, and later, Americans, into their territories. The formerly captive Africans found much to be admired about American Indian life. Subsequently, the Africans chose to adopt the costumes, language, and imagery of American Indian resistance as a way of honoring them as well as keeping the spirit of group solidarity alive.

A few scholars have inserted their own break into the Cody Thesis groove and investigated this premise. Trying to make sense of it using different approaches, these approaches-as-registers seriously take into consideration the contention that the African and Indian could capably find common ground. Roach (1992) represents the first attempt to place the Mardi Gras Indians into an American/American Indian context, through the lens of the narrative of the vanishing Indian as an intercultural performance. Like others Roach accepts the influence of Buffalo Bill as a factor in Mardi Gras Indian history and culture, but he is careful to leave enough wiggle room in the story to consider a tale about the famous jazz musician Jelly Roll Morton: "Mr. Jelly Roll, who was a Spy Boy around the turn of the century, recalls that the tribes 'wanted to act exactly as the Indians in days long bye ... to dance and sing and go like regular Indians.' They would 'form a ring, in a circle, dancer in the center, sending his head way back' while the tribe members made a 'kind of rhythm with their heels'" (Roach 1992:471). He suggested that there might actually be some continuity between historic descriptions of the Choctaw Eagle Dance and the activities of the Mardi Gras Indians (Roach 1992:478).

Drawing from a different register, Bellour and Kinser (1998) compare and contrast the Mardi Gras Indians with a carnival group in Trinidad called the House of Black Elk. They feel that the historical reliance upon the Buffalo Bill theory of origins of this phenomenon "is too simple an explanation." Citing the consistent development of a Plains aesthetic imprecated with African patterns over the dress and rituals of the local Choctaw groups, they argue that oral historical information which suggests mixed Indian-African ancestry is also too simple. However, they follow a similar trajectory as others, suggesting the practice is "outright resistance and defiance" during a "time of carnivalesque inversion" (Bellour and Kinser 1998:152, 154).

Seeking to locate the ethnohistorical origins of this tradition beyond the parade season, my own research into the Mardi Gras Indians sought to take seriously the contention by the participants themselves that their history and culture was the product of both African and Indian. Taking my cue from DeMallie, I endeavored to pay close attention to the sources and to listen to them carefully, hoping that at some point they would "speak" a pattern that might make syncopative sense. To better understand this unique polyphonic identity, it is important to consider not only the African and the Indian, but also the British, Spanish, French and American aspects of culture and history. What follows is my alternative, polyphonic origin narrative. It is partially speculative, yet the pieces in this story "swing" together.

Although both Indians and Africans were subject to, and classified by, differing notions of race and ethnicity depending upon which colonial power controlled a specific territory or region, there is documentary evidence to suggest there had been a strong historical Choctaw presence in the city by the time of Buffalo Bill's arrival in New Orleans in 1884. This presence was particularly established in the part of town known as the French Market, by a group of Choctaw from St. Tammany Parish, one of a group of parishes known as the Florida Parishes (which included the north shore of Lake Pontchartrain). The St. Tammany Choctaw were a cultural fixture in early New Orleans, and women from this group "gathered canes, split and dyed them, and made baskets that they sold along the waterfront and on the streets of New Orleans" (Galloway and Kidwell 2004:516). The St. Tammany Choctaw had a special relationship with a Roman Catholic priest, the first Native Creole priest in New Orleans, named Adrien Emmanuel Rouquette. After spending his childhood years on the Northshore, he was educated in Kentucky and France, and ultimately given the name of "Chahta Ima" or "Choctaw-like" by the Choctaw. "Père" Rouquette became a missionary to the St. Tammany Choctaw and, inspired by the writings of François-René de Chateaubriand and excited by the idea of a new American nation, lived with them on Bayou Lacombe until the end of his life in 1887. Rouquette has been characterized as a culture hero and over time he "entered into Northshore tradition" (Gregory 1999). A complicated historical figure that requires further research, his funeral in 1887 brought large numbers of Choctaw into New Orleans a short time after the Wild West show. To African Americans in New Orleans, neither the sight of Choctaw Indians from St. Tammany Parish in town nor the sight of a Creole priest "masking Indian" would have been out of the ordinary, as apparently Rouquette frequently dressed as an Indian during his visits to the city in the years prior to his death.

The Florida Parishes across Lake Pontchartrain which form the Northshore were not originally part of the Louisiana Purchase. St. Tammany Parish was one of a group of parishes that were at one time a short-lived independent republic before forced annexation into the United States in 1810. It is located directly to the north of New Orleans and directly across the lake from the Tchoupitoulas Coast (present-day Metairie) and Bayou St. John, areas toward the back of town historically known for the perpetual presence of Africans and Indians. As early as the 1700s, the Northshore had garnered a reputation as a haven for runaway slaves from the numerous plantations in Louisiana. In 1847, the St. Tammany Parish jail, located in Covington, was identified by the legislature of Louisiana as a depot for runaway slaves from the nearby parishes of Livingston and Washington, as well as St. Tammany. The continuous existence in the area of groups known as "Freejacks," descendants of blacks, whites, and Indians who lived in separate, inclusive communities that were "ethnically distinct," confirms that there was a great deal of interaction among the various populations (Posey 1979:179). The free blacks and runaway slaves, Indians, French, British, and Creoles in the area have a long intertwined history that has yet to be satisfactorily unraveled. The object of intense colonial attention, the area changed hands from France to England prior to the American Revolution, then came under Spanish control and became a refuge for British loyalists.

Unlike other parishes in Louisiana, St. Tammany Parish was not named for a Catholic saint, but for a seventeenth-century Delaware leader, Tamanend. A leader of the Delaware who garnered a reputation for actively favoring peaceable relations between Europeans and Indians in the early colonies during the eighteenth century, Tamanend became a powerful symbol of disappearance and rebirth among colonists along the Eastern Seaboard which spawned a number of social groups, commonly known as St. Tammany societies. These groups "gathered on May Day for dinners that featured songs, tobacco, a huge dinner, and prolific toasting with bowls of potent alcoholic punch. May 1 was proclaimed King Tammany's day, and, to celebrate the return of spring, revelers sponsored maypoles, dances, vigorous speeches called longtalks, and Indian-costumed parades" (Deloria 1998:3). "Tamanend" over time became "Tammany" and the observance of "King Tammany's Day" along with its rituals and celebrations led to the "sanctification" of Tamanend as an "Indian saint." St. Tammany societies "allowed colonists to imagine themselves as both British citizens and legitimate Americans protecting aboriginal custom" (Deloria 1998:34). As Deloria (1988:26) explains, "carnival and misrule thus spring from European roots and became infused with revolutionary messages through the figure of the Indian." St. Tammany societies existed from Maine to South Carolina, and it is quite possible that this tradition was carried westward as the emerging nation acquired more territory.

The colony of British loyalists that found themselves annexed into the United States against their will in 1810 of course interacted with their African and Indian neighbors. While the loyalists might or might not have sponsored a St. Tammany society, the naming of the parish reveals the symbolic importance of the "indianization of misrule" (Deloria 1988:26) at the time. The African and Indian groups would have come into contact with a "masking Indian" tradition which could be incorporated into already existing cultural practices. This suggestion is somewhat consistent with the contentions of an earlier scholar, Rayna Green, who studied the Mardi Gras Indians. She rejected any idea that they had any commonalities with American Indians and situated them firmly in an Afro-Caribbean tradition, likening them to hippies, hobbyists, and Marxist critics who all at one time or another sought to resist the status quo, placing them in the "Boston Tea Party mainstream of masquerade" (Green 1988:43). Thus, while it is possible that Cody's visit may have resulted in a new "tribe" of Mardi Gras Indians—the Creole Wild West—it is also possible that these "tribes" had already been participating in New Orleans Mardi Gras (and other celebrations in other cities and parishes) perhaps as many as one hundred years earlier. It is not unlikely that a tradition perhaps initiated by a St. Tammany society could have migrated from the Northshore to New Orleans through the interchange between African Americans and Choctaw along the edges of the lake, with

Mardi Gras being a suitable cover for all kinds of parade traditions and activities.

Originally, the St. Tammany Choctaw lived in Mississippi. Due to the increasing desire for land, the state of Mississippi and the federal government initiated the removal of the Choctaw with the 1830 Treaty of Dancing Rabbit Creek. This decree paved the way for European-settler appropriation of Indian lands and began the slow erosion of Choctaw property rights that would continue throughout the rest of the nineteenth century. In exchange for their lands in Mississippi, the Choctaw were given lands in Louisiana, Alabama, and Texas. Like the British loyalists, the group to be historically known as the St. Tammany Choctaw had moved to Louisiana in hopes of escaping the advancing American nation. Additionally, "in 1830, the State of Mississippi extended its jurisdiction over the Choctaw Nation within its boundaries, declaring that it was illegal for any person to declare himself a chief of an Indian nation" (Galloway and Kidwell 2004:516). This decree made calling oneself a "chief" an act of outlaw resistance. This legislative act by the state of Mississippi as applied to the Choctaw Nation perhaps found resonance among the African and Indians who found common ground within this historically based parade tradition.

Mardi Gras Indian culture might indirectly celebrate a Delaware leader. It definitely celebrates the Sauk leader Black Hawk, who is identified as the quintessential Mardi Gras Indian hero. To this day, Black Hawk is also venerated in a number of spiritualist churches within the African American communities of New Orleans. It has been noted that the costumes utilized as new suits serve other purposes beyond parade days; they are also used sometimes during church services throughout the year as living embodiments of Black Hawk. The Black Hawk War in the upper Illinois country during the 1820s and 1830s was a pivotal event in the history of the Old Northwest. After his surrender, Black Hawk visited the East and was received by the president as well as the rest of society as a celebrity of sorts. The notoriety of Black Hawk after his capture was embedded in an emerging national culture that interpreted the disappearance of American Indians as the rebirth of a uniquely American identity, not unlike St. Tammany decades earlier. Even after his death in the late 1830s, Black Hawk was a continuing part of American culture for many years.

The implied connection between sacred and secular in Mardi Gras Indian culture is maintained through the belief that Black Hawk is, as one song performed by the Wild Magnolias states, "an Indian saint." It lends credibility to the notion that within Indian music and culture the big chiefs themselves are affirmed and reaffirmed as living "saints." Lyrics by the Wild Magnolias include a section during which the lead singer, in essence, begins to "call the saints" of Mardi Gras Indian history much as Catholic services feature the Litany of the Saints. Although it is widely believed that Mother

Leafy Anderson introduced the worship of Black Hawk into New Orleans society during the 1920s, I suggest that the veneration of "Indian saints" by African Americans may have existed long before her arrival and may have taken place along the Northshore and in the rural areas surrounding Lake Pontchartrain as part of the vestiges of the enmeshed practices of the British-derived St. Tammany societies, French-originated Mardi Gras, and religious practices in which Africans and Indians were participating. This clear connection to a historical figure from the early 1800s represents further evidence for the viability of a polyphonic proposition that effectively predates the Cody Thesis groove.

When Buffalo Bill arrived in 1884, the mixed African American, Indian, white, and Creole populations in the city were a fusion of different religious and spiritual practices. Religions like Roman Catholicism, Southern Baptist, and Episcopalian came into contact with folk religions such as Voodoo, Hoodoo, and Obeah. Prior to Cody's arrival, however, there also was another type of religion that had flooded New Orleans Creole society: Spiritualist. One aspect of Spiritualist practice is the belief in Indian guides. "The Indian Spirit holds a prominent role in the practices of American Spiritualism," writes Wehmeyer (2002:10), "as well as in belief systems that it has influenced or been influenced by—American Shakerism; Pennsylvania-German Braucherei." The Indian Spirit called Black Hawk, considered an "Indian saint" by the Mardi Gras Indians, may have been one of many. "A spirit called Black Hawk," was "making regular appearances as a spirit guide and messenger at séances and Spiritualist demonstrations throughout the North" as early as the mid-1850s. In one account from 1858, Black Hawk as an Indian Spirit carried a message from New York to Washington to save a child who was ill (Wehmeyer 2002:133). The combination of Spiritualist veneration of Black Hawk along with the presence of reverence for Tamanend by the St. Tammany societies could have introduced this practice of making "Indian saints" into local cultures, thus making any mythic Indian hero suitable for adaptation as a saint. Black Hawk, a figure who the Mardi Gras Indians suggest was such a saint, was a suitable personage that could be adopted and honored just as Tamanend had been.

In this exposition I have tried to carefully weave a narrative that incorporates history and culture, synchrony and diachrony, and anthropology and history such that our understanding of the ethnohistorical origins of the Mardi Gras Indians moves beyond the repeated explanation of Buffalo Bill's 1884–85 visit. Where possible I have collectively improvised using available documents and sources where I could find them. Mostly though, I just tried my best to listen to the sources and take them seriously, wherever they may have been. Regardless of which theory one chooses to believe about the ethnohistorical origins of the Mardi Gras Indians, their ambiguous status as both black and Indian places them on the margins of society in a town where political and social power are often tied to lineages that can be traced back to first-generation French and Spanish ancestry.[2] In this combination of cultural and historical melodies, a polyphonic approach makes better sense, and hopefully a more interesting story, than just sticking with the same riff and adjusting the groove to add one's own unique twist.

COLLECTIVE IMPROVISATION AS A THEORETICAL TOOL

As I have tried to demonstrate above, DeMallie's ethnohistorical method constitutes a sustained intellectual engagement between diachrony (history as a cultural concept) and synchrony (culture as a historical concept). Embedded within this distinctive methodology are a set of key conceptual considerations: the importance of historical and cultural patterns (Fenton 1952; Kroeber 1935; Boas 1936); an awareness of micro- and macroprocesses (Washburn 1961; Kroeber 1935; Boas 1936); ideas of culture as indeterminate sets of mutually reciprocal, co-constituent historicities that influence interpretations of the historical record and the ethnographic present (Berkhofer 1973; Simmons 1988; Whitely 2004); and a consistent emphasis upon the importance of multiple cultural contexts at every level of understanding— act or event, individual or society, anthropologist or historian (Washburn 1961; Simmons 1988; Fogelson 1989).

Patterns. Processes. Historicities. Contexts. These points of convergence constitute the core aspects of the ethnohistorical method as it has been practiced to date. Invariably, ethnohistorians have sought to make cohesive sense out of patterns that emerge from their preferred types of sources (often a scant cache of discrete documentary and nondocumentary materials), some focusing on individuals within larger webs of significance, others working from the societal level toward complicated lives of individuals. Of the utmost importance to every ethnohistorian is an undaunted care for, and emphasis on, getting interpretations of context as accurate as possible with the sources at hand. Each scholar engaged in the act of creating an ethnohistorical product must attempt to balance the examination of primary documents with not only contemporary concerns, goals, and trends, but also with a secondary literature that has, in some instances, misrepresented social and cultural contexts due to the historicities of previous researchers. The (ethno) history of the Mardi Gras Indians of New Orleans reveals the complexities of this balancing act.

If we were, however, to view this set of points as a pattern on its own, we could tentatively conclude that not much has changed about the method of ethnohistory since its formal inception in the 1950s. For instance, one could claim that Fenton's (1952) "upstreaming" is really not much different from Whiteley's (2004) exhortation that to understand the anthropological present we must reexamine the epistemologically familiar to rediscover a formerly credible historic past. In this same vein, Kroeber's (1935) "phenomena" that lie in between smaller and larger less visible processes sound like the macroscopical correlate to Fogelson's (1989) microscopical demonstration of the cultural multivocality of events. This extended commitment to methodological consensus, I believe, is a strong foundation upon which we can now begin a larger discussion of what constitutes ethnohistorical theory.

When Fogelson's (1989) impassioned call for philosophical consideration of a theoretical approach that expands understanding of the complexities of context and moves ethnohistory beyond its primary existence as a method is combined with the notion of a reciprocal relationship between past and present (Berkhofer 1973), ideas of how to reconstruct pastness (Fenton 1952) and presentness (Washburn 1961), and the historicity of patterns and processes (Kroeber 1935; Boas 1936), it becomes clear that cultural conceptions of time should be integral components of an ethnohistorical approach. Building on such an acknowledgment, we are then forced to discern the critical relevance of culture change to our understanding of history as a cultural concept in the context of ethnohistory. Further, what we believe should happen after the identification of patterns or processes, in their abstracted meta-narrative form, is of the utmost importance in our task. For, once these are found, the ethnohistorian must then recontextualize the patterns within the narrative structure of whatever story they are attempting to tell. In the telling of these stories, one is forced to balance multiple cultural logics and philosophies of the temporal. How then can we approach the creation of ethnohistory, using the ethnohistorical method, in a way that takes these concerns into consideration? The answer to this question, I argue, is for ethnohistorians to acknowledge they have moved beyond the limits of method to theorize narrative development as an act of collective improvisation. "Time," suggests Marsalis (2008:16), "is the lifeblood of jazz." And theorization of the concept of time—in this case, ethnohistorical time—I believe, is the first step toward the development of a theory of context.

Fogelson (1989:145) characterizes ethnohistory as an "important field of study [that] has for too long been stymied by the avoidance of theoretical issues and been impeded by naïve epistemology." While careful to remind ethnohistorians of their reliance upon Western forms of historical consciousness, he urged them to embrace the universality of human ability to perceive the past, whether it may or may not conform to a Western, literacy-based definition (Fogelson 1989:143). To shift their historical consciousness toward a comprehension of non-Western histories, Fogelson (1989:134) suggests ethnohistorians might cultivate not only "an expanded conception of what constitutes documentation but also a determined effort to try to comprehend alien forms of historical consciousness and discourse."

Building on Fogelson's call for theoretical vigor, DeMallie illustrated the promise of theoretically informed collective improvisation for the development of ethnohistorical narrative in his 1992 presidential address to the American Society for Ethnohistory. In "'These Have No Ears': Narrative and the Ethnohistorical Method" (1993) DeMallie presents three case studies, and in each case he constructs a narrative that combined Native and non-Native sources in such a way that both understandings are effectively represented. The resultant "story" is a powerfully nuanced, balanced narrative of the ethnohistorical method as a "common commitment" that unites historians and anthropologists. While he insists on characterizing the activity ethnohistorians engage in as a "method," his narrative is, I believe, at its heart, a work of collective improvisation. Early in his career DeMallie (1993:523) realized that "any serious attempt to synthesize the historical record" when writing ethnohistory must include not only familiarity with written and nonwritten source materials, language study, fieldwork, and archival research, but also source material that needed translation, editing, and publication. Although he suggested there is no "singular" ethnohistorical method (DeMallie 1993:533), it is apparent that the complex set of skills and activities required to write ethnohistory is more than just a process one must go through to write a believable story. To tell us the "story" of the story of a method, he had to "listen" to the sources carefully and pay close attention to breaks and riffs. He had to identify patterns and rhythms in the polyphony of seemingly disparate materials. In a similar fashion, my polyphonic proposition, crafted from a wide variety of source materials, has attempted to tell the "story" of the story of the Mardi Gras Indians.

"Swing time," writes Marsalis (2008:17), "is a collective action." This particular kind of time is the result of a collective attempt to negotiate actual time and perceived time such that one's "actions are perceptive and flexible enough to flow inside that ultimate constant—swing" (Marsalis 2008:17). Much like swing time in jazz, how well anthropology and history are combined in a narrative affects the quality of ethnohistorical time. This negotiation takes place within and among a variety of registers in the creation of ethnohistory: abstractly between history and anthropology, individually between committed colleagues, and concretely among the variety of source materials ethnohistorians draw upon to construct narratives. As a meaningful groove in the ears (and minds) of ethnohistorians, DeMallie's narrative invention concerning the importance of the ethnohistorical method not only describes how to write ethnohistory, but also presents a suitable framework for understanding why we must continue to negotiate "the tension that occurs between analytical and narrative modes of reconstructing the past" (DeMallie 1993:533).

Ethnohistorical time, as an expression of swing time, depends upon how well a scholar manipulates actual time and perceived time. At its core, swing time is about the quality of communication among the registers, such that it results in a mutuality of understanding, acceptance, and reciprocal responsiveness founded upon active listening (Marsalis 2008:41). An important aspect of swing is that it requires a communal effort on the part of the audience as well as the musicians. Just as DeMallie (1993:534) reminds us that "we need to listen to one another and keep our ears open," to reach swing time, "the purest possible expression of community," all must listen and be listened to equally, remain steadfast in the face of challenges, and engage in the reciprocal exchange of ideas (Marsalis 2008:80).

DeMallie makes the rhythm section of ethnohistory—anthropology and history—swing. Suggests Marsalis (2008:16) of the rhythm section: "If they get along, things go smoothly. If they don't, you have a lot of interesting stories to tell." Seen from this context, we could infer from DeMallie's opening statement, "I don't lecture, I tell stories," that the historical relationship between narrative and the ethnohistorical method has not been a smooth one. And yet, as we all know, good stories always swing.

NOTES

1. I am greatly indebted to Steve Friesen, Denver Parks and Recreation, Buffalo Bill Museum, for his assistance and depth of knowledge as it relates to the experience of Buffalo Bill in New Orleans. During an extended set of email conversations in February 2007, he made me see that my idea that the African Americans were involved in the sewing and recostuming of the show was not a very plausible one, given the complexities of Indian bead- and quillwork and the amount of time Cody had to get the show up and running.

2. Editor's note: It is important to mention the contemporary Native presence in Louisiana and New Orleans in this context. Especially in Louisiana, the controversy over the Houma's federal recognition drive, for example, shows how arguments about origins, ethnogenesis, and traditions have political, social, and economic implications beyond academic discussions (Davis 2001; Campisi and Starna 2004). In addition to the American Indian presence, Jolivétte (2007) also presents an introduction to the subject of American Indian identities and cultures within Louisiana Creole communities.

3
Invaluable Intangibles

Raymond J. DeMallie, "Fictive Kin," and
Contemporary Heritage Performance

SARAH QUICK

What I remember perhaps most from Professor Raymond J. DeMallie's classes is that he taught through telling stories about real people. Every professor uses this technique, but not with the same adept narrative form. DeMallie's stories included scholars he knew personally, from hearsay, and from historical texts. In the first course I took from him, History of Anthropology, I remember Alice Cunningham Fletcher coming alive in his descriptions of her first field experiences on the Plains: her Victorian, northeastern demeanor contrasting sharply with those of the bureaucrats and Natives she met. DeMallie provided the context for understanding her voice in describing the Lakota dancers she observed in her account (titled "Life among the Indians" and never published). Although I happened to know about Fletcher before because of my interest in Native expressive culture in North America, I had not really contextualized her field experiences, nor had I any empathy toward her circumstances. DeMallie's narratives provided such cues. His lecture-stories were often humorous and formally rich; he took the listener on several seemingly off-track paths but always circled back to the key themes he wanted to evoke. The professional and the personal were woven together, and through these lectures and eventually in one-on-one meetings, I began to feel closer to many historical scholarly figures like Lewis Henry Morgan, J. O. Dorsey, George Dorsey, Franz Boas and the many Boasians, A. R. Radcliffe-Brown, Fred Eggan, James Howard, Claude Lévi-Strauss, and David Schneider (to name a few). He showed students how to think of scholars and other historical figures through their relationships to each other, be they institutional or personal: he taught us to think in terms of scholarly genealogies.

On reflection, I realize his manner of relating the work and practice of anthropological figures in such contextual detail is what one strives to do in ethnohistorical accounts. DeMallie (1993:523) characterizes the ethnohistorical method for his own research in his well-known speech later published as an article: "knowledge of the literature, study of the Lakota language, fieldwork with contemporary Sioux people, archival study of historical documents (including the fieldnotes and unpublished writings of previous anthropologists who worked with the Sioux), and the study of museum collections." Nevertheless, within the same paragraph, he conveys his ambivalence toward an ethnohistorical project providing *the* narrative for a cultural history of a people, even while his own understanding of Sioux culture and the necessary documents for such a project had strengthened. As he wrote, "the firmer the anthropological foundation, the farther off my writing of narrative history seems to be" (1993:524).

In " 'These Have No Ears,' " DeMallie ultimately constructs an argument in support of the scholarly enterprise that ethnohistory provides by bridging anthropology and history. However, he also reflexively highlights how attuned anthropologists (and by implication historians as well) must be to their own and to those they study's cultural premises: how such frameworks, or what might be called assumptions, direct ideas about history, events, and how they are then fashioned in particular kinds of narratives. My appreciation of DeMallie's reflexivity over such matters stems even more from my student years as an attentive listener; these narratives often included his own thoughts on his personal inadequacies and biases when he included his past self as a participant. While " 'These Have No Ears' " forges the necessity for continuing the bridge between history and anthropology "through the tangible products of our work" (DeMallie 1993:534), I view DeMallie's influence on my own research as also deriving from such intangibles in the reflexive narratives that he creates for his students.

My own doctoral research took up the ethnohistorical mandate to consider archived sources and other historical documents against the ethnographic present. In my case, I did not originally set out to understand "the past" or a particular period through such methods, but sought to unravel the various contexts contributing to what contemporary performers (fiddlers and jiggers mainly) represent as Métis culture and history, or what is often described as heritage. I saw ethnohistory as a means to an end, as a way to inform my study of the present. However, what resulted in parts of my dissertation were chronological sequences of earlier periods of (mainly) Alberta Métis political history and performative practice. In these sections, I became a historian, only occasionally breaking these narratives of past periods with some anthropologically minded analysis. I also began to see other sections describing the "ethnographic present" as outdated, since I was aware of changing participants and organizations in the contemporary heritage scene. Nevertheless, I heeded DeMallie's emphasis on studying the symbols from the point of view of the culture at hand, in this case the culture of those involved with performing heritage often (but not always) labeled as Métis. I analyzed heritage as a set of meaningful symbols that contemporary Métis (and others) invoke in personal narratives as well as in public and more intimate performances.

Here, in order to more directly honor DeMallie's insight when considering a culture's symbols and not the analyst's own assumptions, I use his 1994 essay "Kinship and Biology in Sioux Culture" to set up the following analogy: are heritage performances the "fictive kin" of *real* cultural practice? In "Kinship and Biology in Sioux Culture," besides providing an account of how the Sioux view family relationships and an explanation of the relationships rendered through Lakota kin terminology, DeMallie puts Schneider's critique (1984) of the common approach to studying kinship in anthropology to use. DeMallie pointedly takes on anthropology's "fictive kin" or those known by common kin terms but whose relationships are not rendered in the "normal" fashion through genealogical or biologically based relationships. He sees the term "fictive kin" as an obvious reflection of the conceptions of family relations from a Western standpoint, but one that only obscured other cultural understandings of kinship:

> [U]nderstanding kinship as the Sioux themselves understand it is more impeded than aided by the social-structural approach. By ignoring the religious dimensions of Sioux culture, a social-structural approach misses what is to the Sioux the heart of the kinship system—its basis in a contract with *wak'an t'anka*, which thereby unites all forms of being into an unbroken network of relationship. It also misses the understanding of kinship as the foundation of morality. The social-structural approach excludes consideration of all nonhuman relations. Moreover, it artificially limits even the domain of human kinship by excluding nongenealocially specifiable relationships—"friends"—that from the Sioux perspective are a very important component of kinship. By restricting kinship to genealogy, the social-structural approach fails to note that the Sioux define relationship in terms of a set of conceptual categories and the logical relationships among them based on proper "feeling" and behavior, rather than on concrete links of marriage and birth. Although those biological factors are at the basis of Sioux kinship, they are in fact deemphasized by the system, both in terms of classification and behavior. Biological relatedness is frequently overridden by a plethora of adoptive mechanisms; although anthropologists generally relegate adoption to the category of fictive kin, for the Sioux, adoption constitutes genuine kinship.
> [DeMallie 1994:142]

This essay explores the "fictive kin" position that heritage performance has played in academic scholarship—including the disciplines of anthropology, history, and folklore. By "heritage performance," I refer to those staged performances that are undertaken in order to showcase a particular group's cultural heritage, performances that in my field research were usually oriented toward representing iconic music/dance forms, sometimes even in combination with narratives or other performative representations of past lifestyles and events. These performances come under the scholarly umbrella of music and dance revivals (Livingston 1999; Nahachewsky 2001; Roginsky 2007), invented traditions (Briggs 1996; Handler and Linnekin 1984; Hobsbawm and Ranger 1983; Linnekin 1983), and heritage production (Kirshenblatt-Gimblett 1998; Lowenthal 1996; Olwig 1999).

To many scholars, such performances reveal invented or partial truths. Some go as far as to portray heritage as necessarily fabricated, a faulty ersatz for the accounts put forth through methodical analysis in an historian's study of cultural pasts (Lowenthal 1998). They are the "fictive kin" of the seemingly more natural forms of cultural performance, often read as failing cultural ideals since they create national myths and pander to commercial and state interests.

HERITAGE CREATES FICTIONAL CONTINUITIES FROM THE PAST TO THE PRESENT—OR DOES IT?

Historian Eric Hobsbawm (1983:1) defined invented traditions as "a set of practices, normally governed by overtly or tacitly accepted rules and of a ritual or symbolic nature, which seek to inculcate certain values and norms of behaviour by repetition, which automatically implies continuity with the past. In fact, where possible, they normally attempt to establish continuity with a suitable historic past." Popular accounts and live public narratives that represent Métis heritage *do* often present it as a continuation from the golden days of Métis origins as a culture, creating a fictional continuity of a thriving Métis culture from the fur trade days up until today. It is easy to come to the conclusion that "as heritage" these performance traditions become icons of an imagined nation while also skirting over specific periods of practice and local differences. For example, Back to Batoche—an annual festival that commemorates Métis's 1885 stand against the Canadian government at Batoche, Saskatchewan—has featured a musical that dramatizes Métis history. *The Batoche Musical* in 2004 featured a jigging buffalo and a traditional fiddler in conjunction with a story depicting the nineteenth-century lives of Métis in the Batoche region. Also, that year's "Back to Batoche" festival, as well as others since its modern beginnings in 1970, featured the widely entered jigging contests, fiddling contests, and many exhibitions of fiddle and dance performers, and emcees often point to the these performances as evidence of Métis's sustained cultural traditions. An attendee might reach the conclusion that Métis have been fiddling and jigging in the same way since the birth of Métis culture, an uncontested set of shared practices remaining as vital today as in the past; or they may conclude that this is the story that contemporary Métis want to tell.

However, attendees at Back to Batoche may also note stylistic differences in the sounds, movements, and dress between performers—and not only superficial differences. They may even realize variant narratives in some of the discourse present around such performances, both in the public discourse as well as in private discussions of what is being observed; uniformity of representation does not necessarily prevail in these settings. The repeated formalization in Hobsbawm's (1983:2) characterizations for such "invented traditions" is not always in evidence.

Another case in point comes through a CD produced by a Montana family. During the preliminary phase of my doctoral field research, I entertained the notion that I would compare U.S. Métis to Canadian Métis experiences, and in Montana I visited the Fort Belknap reservation as well as Lewistown to the south, places where Métis historically and more recently have had a presence (Fowler 1987:14–16; Foster 2006; McCrady 2006).[1] Fort Belknap's official tribes are Gros Ventre and Assiniboine; but Métis have historically lived near the borders of the reservation and had intermarried into reservation families (Foster 2006:204; McCrady 2006:82, 90). In 2002, I met two young sibling fiddlers from Harlem, Montana (a town on the northern border of Fort Belknap) at the annual Lewistown Métis Celebration. They had been exploring their Métis identity through fiddling; their guitar-playing father was Gros Ventre but their mother identified in part as Métis. And even though U.S. Métis are not recognized in the same way as they are in Canada, these siblings became involved with several heritage projects under the direction of Montana folklorist Nicolas Vrooman (Quick 2009:266, 306), whom I also met in 2002. In 2008, they recorded a CD titled *Fox Family Fiddle: Métis Tunes from Montana*. Below is the CD's web description and liner notes written by Vrooman, who was also the executive producer:

> Fiddle players Vince and Jamie are the children of Jim and Krystal Fox. Jim is Gros Ventre and Krystal is Métis/Gros Ventre. When Jamie was five she used to go around and make like she was a fiddle player. A fiddle came to her that Christmas. When she was seven, she left it out one day. Vince eyed it, picked it up, and without hesitation began to play. . . . Jim learned to play guitar so he could chord for his kids.
>
> The Michif tradition of fiddle playing on the Fort Belknap Reservation was on its last legs just as Vince and Jamie fell in love with the tunes. Old Fatty Morin was still around, and the Doney Brothers were still playing, but that was about it. The kids' playing affirmed their mother's cultural background and brought great pride. Vince and Jamie, through their love of the Michif tunes, brought a new healing

to an old discord between cultural sectors of the tribal society. As word got out, others on the reservation and along the Montana Hi-Line were incredibly enthused to see youngsters taking on a music that was in jeopardy of vanishing.

Vince and Jamie have been fortunate to play with master traditional Métis fiddlers Jimmie LaRocque and Mike Page of the Turtle Mountain reservation, Johnny Arcand of Saskatoon, and Fatty Morin in Montana. Additionally, they have been mentored by Métis elder Al Wiseman of Choteau, an archivist of Michif fiddle tunes. Vince and Jamie were brought into the fold of contemporary fiddle performance through family friendships with nationally renowned pianist Philip Aaberg and fiddler Darol Anger, both of whom have nurtured the talent you find herein. Although having expanded musical interests, and learning numerous tunes and styles from many traditions, their experience with elder Métis fiddlers is exceptional and singular. Those old-style, customary example, traditional-lineage players firmly root Vince and Jamie in the Métis tradition deep into the 19th century. Coming from within the tradition themselves, they represent the continuance of this generation maintaining a style and repertoire that dates back to the fur trade era of the 17th century and the first generation of European and Aboriginal mixing in the upper reaches of the North American continent.

[Fox Family 2008]

Vrooman's account of the heritage these fiddlers continue with their fiddle practice obviously creates a narrative reaching back to Métis's origins in the early fur trade days. The most obvious phrases supporting such a narrative come in the last couple sentences: "Those old-style, customary example, traditional-lineage players" and "they represent the continuance of this generation maintaining a style and repertoire that dates back to the fur trade era." I can easily point out discrepancies for the notion that these fiddlers are continuing this fiddling tradition unabated. For example, many of the recorded tunes stem from Canadian Métis fiddler-composers John Arcand and Andy DeJarlis, who composed and recorded these tunes commercially; they are not categorically "the old Michif tunes" Vrooman portrays. In addition, all the Métis mentors except Fatty Morin and Al Wiseman come from outside Montana, and in terms of a fiddling lineage, they could be viewed as suspicious as well: Wiseman is not a fiddler but an interested historian and collector from another region of Montana; Morin's fiddling was a mix of many tunes and styles, some more "mainstream" than would be considered to be part of the Métis tradition. Morin's history as a performer, however, is not unique since most recent fiddlers billed as Métis fiddlers have dabbled in other styles in their lifetime.

In many ways Vrooman's account lives up to scholars' claims that "as heritage" personal and cultural accounts must negate certain experiences and put others to the forefront, that is, customary practice and ties to elders. Nevertheless, Vrooman's account does not hide what might be considered questionable links in this story of cultural continuity. He references external influences and does not completely skirt over historical tensions and the marginal position that Métis hold in this region of Montana. Although he paints a perhaps euphemistic picture of a fiddle tradition's continuity from the past through its rebirth in the Fox family, he does not hide all the interruptions, which are the rationale for such a rebirth. In addition, while Vrooman's account does not shed light on his own influence as a "heritage producer" (Kirshenblatt-Gimblett 1995) in these siblings' lives, he does not conceal others obviously tied to the Fox family in their roles as professional performance-mentors. Kirshenblatt-Gimblett (1995:373–74) depicts such production values as necessary in the settings that frame heritage in the heritage industry but ones that are ideally hidden. Yet Vrooman does not eliminate the production-end or professionalization of these fiddlers' growth as performers even though such statements obviously detract from a story of a more "customary" apprenticeship.

One final example provides an even more obvious counter to the assumption that heritage is presented as a straight-line continuation from a culture's heyday or origins. What follows is a description of a small portion of the events I witnessed during the Métis National Council's Annual Assembly in 2003:

> The Edmonton downtown Westin Hotel is bustling. In one section an Alberta Massage Therapists' association meets, and in another the Métis National Council holds its Annual Assembly. The Métis National Council Talent Show is a welcome change for the provincial and national representatives and other delegates, having spent two days discussing agendas and finalizing policy. After the evening supper serving to honor the legacy of Métis Veterans, the hall begins to fill with performers and supporting audience and guests for the evening Talent Show. Tables are cleared and moved off the dance floor, while chairs are vacated and refilled as the audience and judges prepare to watch the contestants perform their abilities in Red River jigging, fiddling, or vocal performance. The microphone is passed on to the Talent Show emcee; many locals know him as a wry and humorous speaker. He grew up on a northern Métis Settlement and has been active in Métis Settlement affairs in many capacities. He introduces the judges and explains the contest sequence. He then comments on the backdrop banner's infinity symbol, the flag symbol for the Métis Nation said to represent "Métis forever" as well as the coming together of

European and Native cultures in Métis's ancestry. He suggests that later in the evening the banner will be turned so that the symbol will be standing upright—as in the number eight, although he does not go so far as to even mention the number eight. He leaves his statement at that.

I used the above description as a lead in to a dissertation chapter explaining historical and contemporary institutions that have affected and continue to affect Alberta Métis identity. The emcee's status as a settlement Métis at this Métis National Council event is itself interesting. Membership in the Métis National Council through the provincial organization (the Métis Nation of Alberta) and membership in the Alberta Métis Settlements, the two organizations representing Métis in Alberta, are not mutually exclusive, but they are separate organizations. I interpreted the emcee's verbal modification of the flag as a reference to the number eight, an index to Treaty 8. Treaty 8 enacted a treaty process starting in 1899 and continuing with additional policies until 1942 that irrevocably separated some families into those who identified as Indians and those who identified as "half-breeds"—First Nations and Métis in contemporary terms. I believe the emcee was calling into question the distinct Nation discourse the Métis National Council had been promoting for Métis (especially at this assembly), since Métis identity had also been arbitrarily defined by Canadian institutions during the treaty period. While I do not know if I correctly interpreted the emcee's reference to an upright infinity sign (the eight could also index the eight provincially designated Métis Settlements), this particular introduction to an evening celebrating Métis musical and dance heritage did not evoke a seamless set of national symbols nor a timeless Métis cultural heritage. The emcee's reference obviously pointed to the arbitrariness of the flag symbol, a no-no for representing a seamless national identity—yet I regularly witnessed such untidy references occurring in public events.

PERFORMANCE DISPLAYED AS HERITAGE IS EVIDENCE OF DISJUNCTURE—OR IS IT?

While recognizing that heritage performances may indicate a shift in orientation, an objectification of culture that other performances or "everyday life" may not emphasize, I do not see them as totally divorced from the (past and current) cultural ideals their practitioners believe are meaningful and are trying to encapsulate, celebrate, and even revive through such acts. Yet, similar to the dichotomy emphasized between history and heritage (Lowenthal 1995, 1996), scholars often emphasize the dichotomy between heritage performance and other kinds of cultural performances. Because heritage consciousness can freeze performances to a certain idealized period as well as add to such performances (as in the production values mentioned above), scholars emphasize that they should not be seen as direct continuations of cultural performance in their "second life" as heritage. While I agree that "heritage is a new mode of cultural production in the present that has recourse to the past" (Kirshenblatt-Gimblett 1995:369), scholars tend to emphasize that in their new phase marked as "heritage," these forms have turned the irreversible corner, creating a complete disjuncture with their links to past forms of cultural performances.

Scholars have long distinguished between "first" and "second" existence music or dance forms once they enter into a revival phase or once they become staged events representing a particular culture (Livingston 1999; Nahachewsky 2001; Royce 2002). Standing far enough back and comparing the more distant past contexts to more recent contexts for the music/dance forms now considered significant to Métis heritage, I do see a trend toward exhibition, toward heritage display. I even titled the dissertation chapter where I detailed the historical contexts for such performances over time "Emerging as Heritage." However, along with other scholars, I have begun to see this process as much more complex. It would be arbitrary for me to pinpoint the exact moment when performers turn that irreversible corner.

By chronicling the varying contexts for the music and dance forms now often marked as "traditional Métis" through archival research and oral recollections, I was able to index the associations such forms have had in various time periods: as taken-for-granted fiddle and dance forms enacted on festive occasions; as sites for showing off individual and collective prowess; as signs of a stigmatized background; as ways to create Native solidarity in dealing with city life; as signs for celebrating multiculturalism; and as signs celebrating Métis identity more specifically. The previous list could represent a sort of chronology from the nineteenth century to the most recent performance contexts, yet it would oversimplify each of these associations as distinct phases.

Many nineteenth-century sources note the appreciation of fiddle dance music by Natives, "half-breeds," and fur traders alike. Unfortunately for the scholar interested in understanding the details of these earlier performances, many early sources provide only generalized and often judgmental descriptions. Many accounts were written much later, after the fact, and likely suffer from the nostalgic overgeneralizations of which historians are wary. Overall, their usefulness as accurate portraits of music and dance is rather limited. Nonetheless, these early sources provide a glimpse into the social dynamics and performance practices in these earlier settings.

Across references to fiddle-accompanied dancing are some similarities.[2] First, these accounts describe festive gatherings within which dancing is a centerpiece, and the revelry sometimes causes alarm to those recording the events. Over and over again, references are made to dances lasting all night, or even several nights. During the winter months especially, not traveling home in the dark of night was practical. Besides dancing, these festivities were interspersed with feasting and sometimes also with the singing of French, voyageur, or even Métis nationalist songs.[3] In the case of what was sometimes referenced as the "half-breed dance," dancing was the main reason for gathering, while during Christmas, New Year's, or wedding celebrations, dancing was an expected part of the overall celebration. New Year's festivities, in particular, took place in many Native communities well into the twentieth century. Sometimes lasting several days, these festivities involved families visiting one another and socializing, feasting, and dancing into the night. Known as "Kissing Day" or *Ocehtokîsikâw* in Cree, relatives and friends would reward each other with good cheer through the kissed greetings that would accompany the visits from home to home.[4]

In Alberta, later post-fur trade references to these performance forms indicate they were also being embraced as heritage to be celebrated, and not necessarily Métis heritage specifically. In 1896, the Edmonton Old Timers sponsored a ball that included several dance forms now considered a part of the traditional Métis dance repertoire—the Reel of Eight, the Reel of Quatre (known today as the Reel of Four), the Duck Dance, and the Red River Jig (Gardner 1992:25–26). The Edmonton Old Timers, organized officially in 1894, met as a social club in order to celebrate their members' past exploits during the fur trading and frontier days earlier in the century (Northern Alberta Pioneers and Descendants Association, n.d.). In Calgary, a similar association was formed in 1901, much later becoming the Southern Alberta Pioneers and Their Descendants (Mackie 2010). The Edmonton and Calgary Old Timers gatherings as well as others indicate the likelihood that both Native and non-Native peoples participated in at least some the dance forms currently marked as traditional Métis near the end of the century and into the twentieth century (Carpenter 1977; Kemp 1909; Lafond Historical Society 1981; Mackie 1993).

Both of these Old Timers associations continued to sponsor gatherings that nostalgically featured such music/dance forms into the twentieth century, eventually featuring Native performers for these forms. While these associations framed the heritage they were celebrating as based on an idealized and imagined yesteryear—not necessarily a particular culture—the performers in such settings did not necessarily share this view. For example, Joseph F. Dion, an activist pivotal in establishing Métis recognition in Alberta, emceed for a Métis dance troupe with members from regions near St. Paul, Alberta, in the early 1930s. Before touring with this troupe, Dion had already set about documenting Métis elders' recollections of nineteenth-century music-making and dancing, and it is more than likely he incorporated this research into his on-stage introductions to the troupe (Quick

2009:140–43). The troupe performed at the pioneers cabin the Northern Alberta Pioneers and Old Timers established for social and exhibition events in Edmonton (Florence Mitchell interview with author August 5, 2004) and at a Calgary folk festival sponsored by Canadian Pacific Railroad in 1930 (Holmes 1930); they reportedly toured throughout Alberta and even in eastern Canada (Dempsey 1979:vi). This group toured as a Métis dance troupe, not as a group performing historical nineteenth-century dances.

These early public settings displayed such music/dance forms as heritage, albeit with competing narratives for what this heritage was meant to signify, but they simultaneously remained in the social dance and musical repertoire for many Native peoples. For much of the twentieth century, exhibition, social dance situations, and music-making existed simultaneously for the music and dance now marked as traditional Métis, most especially for the Red River Jig—although concert, exhibition, or contest formats are the primary formats for most of these dance forms most recently (Quick 2009:140–70). While obviously these forms were used as heritage beginning in the early twentieth century, these staged displays did not indicate or cause their disappearance as socially relevant forms in other, more localized settings.

Nahachewsky (2001) urges scholars to realize that some dance forms experience revivals at the level of institutionalization or exhibition while also continuing to or even reviving their function as informal social dances in other settings; he uses chronologies of different dances to show how forms go through several phases that may or may not be marked with the same historical consciousness that "second existence" or "second life" usually indicates. Overall, pre- and postrevival phases may not be as simple a transformation as scholars have envisioned, and Nahachewsky (2001:23) argues that "'first' and 'second' existences are relative terms, conventions used when speaking of dances that are actually embedded within larger timelines and more complex chronological pictures" (23). Roginsky (2007:46) has also emphasized this kind of complexity in folkloric dance displays in her close attention to the history of the Israeli Folk-Dance movement, suggesting "a *thirdhand* process" whereby the second life of "Israeli folk dances" created through governmental sponsorship is now competing with younger performers with more commercialized interests.

Heritage performances may also elide another common division between performance settings and their assumed functions. In describing the functions that dance serves in cross-cultural settings, Royce (2002:164–65) distinguished between informal and recreational versus formal and symbolic dance forms: "dances that fall into the category of formal are those used explicitly as a symbol of identity on occasions when more than one cultural group interacts or when there is a desire to create a feeling of group solidarity even in the absence of outsiders." This is a description that could easily apply to contemporary Métis's use of "traditional Métis dances" in public heritage performances. Yet, closely following through time one of the most famous of these dances, the Red River Jig, poses a difficulty in positioning it as either informal/recreational or as formal/symbolic. For one, it appears early on as a dance used to show off individual skills and endurance, making it unique within the gamut of other social dances practiced in the nineteenth century and into the twentieth (Quick 2009:135–40, 173–72). It should perhaps not be a surprise, then, that the Red River Jig has a relatively long history as an exhibition and competitive dance, since its function in social dance settings was similar to more contemporary contest or staged dances emphasizing display and skill. Surely spectacle is available for cultures not yet marked by the institutions of modernity, meaning those nineteenth-century communities connected to the fur trade industry that included First Nations and Métis members.

In many contemporary festival settings it is also difficult to draw a line between whether these forms function as purely as heritage display or as music/dance forms promoting sociality, or what ethnomusicologist Thomas Turino (2008) has called participatory, in contrast to presentational, performances. I see both at work. The continued appreciation of the Red River Jig and more generally "jigging" as a form of step-dancing that appears in the Red River Jig and in many of the traditional dance forms has in turn helped to maintain, or, in some cases, has renewed jigging's presence in social dancing. I observed many people jigging beyond the stage in more informal settings during Old Time dances—during a rendition of the Red River Jig or other tunes or even during other dance forms such as the Sideways Polka or the Heel and Toe Polka, dances that usually do not appear on stage. Emcees will also encourage Red River jigging outside of competition. During an afternoon break in competition at Edmonton Métis Festival 2002, noncompeting jiggers of all ages were called upon the stage, and eventually young and old joined together to show off their moves.

During another afternoon at this same festival, a rather spontaneous square dance troupe formed and performed on stage, its members once having performed in separate competing groups when Edmonton's Canadian Native Friendship Centre had sponsored the All Native Festivals in the 1960s, 1970s, and 1980s; and as I learned in interviewing and meeting several past competitors, they came from a variety of backgrounds—from First Nations reserve families, from Alberta Métis Settlement families, and from mixed First Nations and Métis families who had moved to the city (Quick 2009:155–59). Over a decade later at the Edmonton Métis Festival, these performers were dancing not as competitors or demonstrators of "Métis culture," but in memory of their previous dancing days and the now "old fashioned" square dancing style that still utilized callers and dance forms less oriented to the stage. As Royce suggests, performers not only "perform heritage" to audiences of outsiders, in this case to not only legitimize Métis's place in North America but also to create solidarity with and legitimize their skills for other knowledgeable performers. In addition, these performers were also performing not only to live up to an ideal of Métis solidarity (or more broadly "Native" solidarity since some identify as First Nations); they performed with an understanding of their own local history and for personal reasons that may have had little to do with representing the collective heritage of the Métis Nation.

EXCLUSIONARY, YES, BUT SOMETIMES ONLY ON THE FACE OF IT

Scholars have also highlighted how heritage creates a unified vision of the past for some while excluding others (Lowenthal 1996; Olwig 1999). Lowenthal (1996:128) writes that heritage brings "exclusive myths of origin and continuance, endowing a select group with prestige and common purpose," while Olwig confirms such exclusionary discourse in the recent emphasis on a particular historical event in contemporary heritage discourse at the exclusion of other periods (and peoples) on St. John island in the Caribbean. Furthermore, Olwig as well as Briggs (1996) correctly assert that anthropologists should consider the conditions whereby certain heritage meta-narratives become popularized and acceptable while others do not, taking anthropologists to task for not recognizing how they may also contribute to such heritage discourse.

In considering the meta-narratives that Canadian Métis have used in public discourse and heritage performances, I (and many others) have noted the prominence of the Red River Métis narrative of origins and dispersal. While this narrative has remained prominent in signifying a certain nineteenth-century lifestyle, it has waned recently in asserting that the Red River region is *the* place of origins for the Métis Nation. A court case stemming from Sault Ste. Marie, Ontario—not the place where Métis were seen to have dispersed in the previous narrative—opened the door to a nationalized meta-narrative beyond the Red River origin story. Named after its main defendants, the Powley case began in 1993 when the Ontario Ministry of Natural Resources charged Steve Powley and his son for shooting a moose without licenses. Steve Powley contested the charge on the basis that as a Métis from Sault Ste. Marie, Ontario, he had the Aboriginal right to hunt. Shortly after, the Métis Nation of Ontario formed as a provincial affiliate to the Métis National Council in order to support Powley's claim. After several years in provincial and federal courts, in September 2003 the Supreme Court of Canada sided in favor of Powley, ultimately reaffirming Métis's status in the 1982 Constitutional Act and guaranteeing the harvesting (hunting and fishing) rights to some Métis in Western Ontario.

With the Métis National Council's support of the Ontario case, a dialogue over identity and origins was catapulted into a more public and political sphere; it also has refashioned the Red River origins narrative to one where multiple historical Métis communities can be designated. Now multiple communities historically connected to a specific Métis lifestyle, instead of the Red River region alone, may be considered legitimate for establishing Métis rights. Nevertheless, not all are in agreement about what the new narrative should be; Métis's historical origins and how they affect contemporary Métis identities are still debated.[5] Furthermore, in considering this shift from a meta-narrative of Red River exclusivity in origins to one of multiple historical communities, it could be argued that the political impetus for establishing Métis rights was perhaps the greater push to refashioning the long-standing Red River origins narrative, especially since specific scholars and communities have long been asserting a more inclusive historical understanding of Métis origins.

The Powley case and its spin-off agreements and court cases in other provinces have created wide-ranging implications for how Métis membership is established by provincial Métis organizations. The national rhetoric is seemingly more inclusive for allowing origins beyond the Red River. Nevertheless, provincial organizations did not necessarily require establishing Red River origins for membership previous to this narrative shift; and with the potential for harvesting rights becoming available to their members, Métis organizations have generally enacted *more* stringent requirements for establishing membership, in part because of the pressure from the governmental agencies that allow them to exist. Furthermore, federal and provincial governments are now more attuned to shoring up the boundaries between different Aboriginal organizations and the assumed divisions between Aboriginal identities. Individuals who may have had both First Nations and Métis statuses through their unique personal and family histories are not legally allowed to assert all these identities; they must claim one or the other.

When it comes to heritage performance, however, the cultural boundaries that the government promotes also belie the actual lived experiences for those participating in these forms, creating a discursive dividing line between First Nations and Métis (and others) who participate in these forms of music and dance. Government support creates a niche for Métis fiddling and jigging in such occasions as Canada's Aboriginal Day festivities every year. Aboriginal Day posters, for example, signify each of the groups the Canadian government recognizes (First Nations, Métis, and Inuit) in different ways; Métis are more often than not marked by their sashes, fiddling, and jigging. During the opening ceremonies of the 2010 Olympics in Vancouver, each Aboriginal group danced as they entered the stadium center although all were accompanied by the same orchestra-accompanied singing: Métis jigged into the stadium center, Inuit danced in a different manner (although one female appeared to jig), some of the males carrying the Inuit-style hand drums, while most of the First Nations performers danced into the stadium performing various powwow dance styles.

Nevertheless, in practice, First Nations and Inuit also fiddle and jig; and these non-Métis performers also appear in public settings fiddling and jigging. Although the frameworks of support and the meta-narratives for who performs what may be exclusionary, individual performers cross these lines all the time. A recent example comes from *Canada's Got Talent 2012*: three First Nations teenage jiggers calling themselves "Sagkeeng's Finest" (after their reserve) auditioned in Winnipeg, Manitoba, and won spots to the next round. "Frontstage" appearances may align with the common narratives of heritage discourse; however, "backstage" identity alliances are more complex and more localized and performers, at times, playfully or humorously invoke the arbitrariness or blurriness of these national heritage distinctions "frontstage" (Quick 2012).

Furthermore, official settings may actually support some interlopers. Again, I recount a scene from my doctoral fieldwork:

> At Canada Place in 2002, where federal government offices are housed in downtown Edmonton, people have begun to gather for the lunchtime celebration of Aboriginal Day. Dignitaries and performers assemble near the small yet colorful stage with a prairie scene backdrop in the middle of the walkway that runs between the various glassed-in, governmental departments. Around a hundred chairs eventually fill, while the rest of the audience mills at the edges. The celebration begins with opening prayers (one in English, one in Cree), a color guard of Aboriginal war veterans accompanied by the beating drum of an honor song, and official introductions that precede the mix of honorees and performers. Amongst the performers are Métis singer-songwriter Laura Vinson and Inuit fiddler Colin Adjun, who both point to their latest CD recordings. A guest in Edmonton, Colin Adjun performs with a Métis guitarist originally from northern Alberta; the guitarist publicly remarks that they just met today and "it's an honor to be able to play with him." Adjun plays a version Fisher's Hornpipe, a couple of his own tunes, and ends with the Red River Jig. At the sounds of the Red River Jig, some in the audience get on their feet to jig; and when Adjun finishes, many request the Red River Jig again while urging a young male jigger to get up to show off his steps.

The above event was part of the official commemoration of Aboriginal Day sponsored by Edmonton's department of Indian and Northern Affairs Canada, and across Canada scores of such celebrations were happening; this was just one of the many events occurring in Edmonton during that day and later weekend. The participants involved in this particular event were not solely locals from Edmonton or even Alberta and included an Inuit fiddler who came from Nunavut and me, an ethnographer-observer from the United States. In addition, not all the performers were living up to the heritage slots for their cultural identities: the Inuit performer was not singing with a hand drum, he was fiddling. He also played the unofficial Métis National Anthem, the Red River Jig, to an appreciative audience, who did not see him as infringing on their cultural identities.

CONCLUSIONS

For each section above, I took a position against what scholars have either pointedly asserted or blindly assumed when it comes to analyzing and depicting heritage performance. Nevertheless, I hope it is clear that I also agree (in part) with the previous scholarly assertions about heritage. What I see as problematic is when these positions limit an understanding of the meanings performers and producers themselves create, evoke, and experience through their engagements. DeMallie makes a similar point in "Sioux Kinship and Biology" when he critiques what he calls the social-structural approach to kinship. He writes that "understanding kinship as the Sioux themselves understand it is more impeded than aided by the social-structural approach" (DeMallie 1994:142). He offers an analysis of cultural symbols in order to consider a Sioux understanding of kin relations, whereby "fictive kin" and even nonhuman relationships could come under the analytical fold not as anomalies but as significant features of what kinship means to this particular culture.

Considering the music/dance forms now marked as heritage for contemporary Métis in North America, I also looked at the symbolic intent that these performances evoked. In many cases, these performances presented seamless continuities with a glorified Métis past and were also intended to enhance the distinctiveness of Métis as a culture; and such representations were done in a conscientious manner unlike the communal functions of their distant past. Therefore, they fulfilled what scholars have pointed out: such constructed performances tend to fulfill once marked as heritage; they created false continuities and exclusionary discourse that then mark them as fulfilling different functions than they had before.

Nevertheless, as I pointed out, these were not the only meanings evoked in such performances. Performers *and* producers are willing to create storylines that do not fit the stereotypical and expected meta-narratives representing who Métis (and others) are. Many other scholars have recently noted this complexity for performers, producers, and consumers in what may be constituted as heritage (Brumann 2009; Bruner 2005; Bunten 2008; Clifford 2004; De Groot 2009).[6] Some have even suggested that although objectified or produced as heritage such performances are not necessarily completely constrained: they do allow a certain amount of dynamic flexibility in allowing participants to influence the discourse beyond commonly constructed meta-narratives (Bruner 2005; Bunten 2008). Furthermore, while the performances and the discourse that coincides with them can be seen as more contrived and conscientious than earlier periods, they do offer some continuity with these earlier settings. While some formal features have probably irrevocably changed because of performers' attention to audiences and judges for the fiddling and dances I studied, there are formal musical and movement qualities that have remained continuous with earlier periods: the continued use of the fiddle played in a particular style, especially for those dances now deemed "traditional," and the continued practice of jigging, which is then coordinated to change with certain melodic shifts in certain fiddle tunes/dances.

While contemporary settings could easily be classified as markedly different from earlier settings, continuity exists between some settings and the social functions that these music and dance forms enhance for specific families as well. These performances continue to mark certain occasions: "In the nineteenth century and into the twentieth century, these occasions were weddings, holidays, and house party dances. Of late, these occasions are more likely organized festivals, contests, heritage celebrations, and educational settings" (Quick 2009:172). However, family events—weddings, anniversaries, reunions, and funerals—still feature such fiddle dances. Also, perhaps more importantly, how performers experience what they are doing, which is not so easily analyzed through verbal discourse, is as significant to continuation of these form as what they are purported to represent in terms of heritage discourse. The *affect,* the emotional and physical qualities that performers create and evoke for themselves and others, was evident in numerous fiddle observations as well as in what performers (fiddlers and dancers) and listeners (dancers and other participants) would occasionally convey in their comments about music, dance, or particular performers.

While DeMallie critiques the social-structural approach as limited for understanding cultural beliefs in "Kinship and Sioux Biology," he still positions the approach as useful for cross-cultural comparisons between societies. In an earlier writing, he more pointedly notes the necessity "for understanding contemporary life by analytical separation of cultural symbol and social pattern, understanding the independence and separate histories of each" (DeMallie 1988b:19), in part in order to highlight the dynamic social interactions that American Indians have and to not see these as pollutants to culture. While I did not initially seek in my study of Métis heritage performance to pull apart these analytical spheres, I began to see how performers' identities often did not live up to the recent ascriptions for who actually participates in these cultural forms. Nevertheless, in knowing these social distinctions (albeit many arbitrarily based on government policy) for the performers, I became more attuned to additional symbols and alternative interpretations in the meta-narratives framing these performance forms.

In some ways, I think DeMallie's storytelling style of lecture was just as insightful and invaluable for pushing me to analyze the symbols put on display during heritage performances as dynamic and more subject to nuance than has been suggested by past scholars. Furthermore, taking a longer view of those who historically participated in these forms provided another sense of the continuity of these traditions in some families (be they First Nations, Métis, or both); and this view was greatly enhanced with the ethnohistorical approach. I came to see the social interactions enhanced by and reproduced through heritage performance as significant, in part because of the meanings attributed to them; whether they were living up to common cultural interpretations for Métis identity, whether they were playfully undercutting such interpretations, or whether they created another narrative altogether. Nevertheless, the intangible, often unvoiced, experiential quality of these performances is also a part of their significance to contemporary performers, this intangible quality is also what I (albeit nostalgically) attribute to my memories of DeMallie's story-lectures. And it is, then, this intangible that is invaluable in ethnohistory.

NOTES

1. I eventually realized I did not have the resources or time to undertake such a comparative study for my doctoral dissertation, and I ended up primarily focusing on Canadian Métis.

2. See Quick (2009:135–44, 330–32) for a more complete account of these sources. They include artist Paul Kane's account of his travels in the West (1846–48); travel writings in *Harper's New Monthly Magazine* (1859 and Marble 1860); recollections from Kemp (1909) and Robinson (1879); and accounts of life in the Red River Settlement (Begg 1871; Healy 1923; Macbeth 1897).

3. Cowie's description at Fort Qu'appelle (1913) in the 1860s and Vrooman's field recordings at Turtle Mountain Chippewa Reservation in the 1980s attest to these singing traditions (see also Prodruchy 2006). I also observed "an old Métis love song" regularly sung in French by a Métis woman at Jamborees around Edmonton, Alberta.

4. In *My Tribe the Cree*, Dion (1979:64–65) attributes the adoption/practice of Kissing Day by Plains Cree to their observation and participation in the New Year's festivities at a Hudson's Bay post. Other sources also indicate Kissing Day's widespread practice (e.g., Jackknife 1979; Howard 1977; LeClaire et al. 1998).

5. Chris Andersen's recent article "Moya 'Tipimsook ('The People Who Aren't Their Own Bosses'): Racialization and the Misrecognition of 'Métis' in Upper

Great Lakes Ethnohistory" (2011) reviewed these debates while also pointedly arguing that the recent court cases (and ethnohistorical research) supporting Métis national identity in more eastern Canadian contexts is through a lens of racialization.

6. Brumann (2009), in particular, makes a very similar critique to mine in designating the common scholarly assumptions placed on projects designated as heritage. I found his article after I had written the majority of this chapter.

4

What Can We Make of James Adair's "feast of love"?

Contextualizing a Native American Ceremonial from the Lower Mississippi Valley, ca. 1765

JASON BAIRD JACKSON

A long-standing concern in folklore studies, in linguistic anthropology, and in cultural anthropology, the investigation of cultural performances has proven to be a particularly productive vantage point from which to view a range of issues in the life of diverse social formations, from the most intimate of informal groups to the most sprawling of nation-states. There is not a single unified performance theory operative within these fields but instead a series of overlapping and complementary research orientations that span the territory from the close study of communicative activity—spoken, but also gestural, material, and so forth—in microscale social interactions, to the investigation of elaborated and highly marked cultural enactments that organize the activity and orient the attention of vast numbers of people. At the former end of the continuum would stand such phenomena as the telling of a joke among friends, the setting of a table for a dinner party, and the assembly of a set of garments into an outfit worn during a night on the town. At the latter end of the spectrum, we encounter such human creations as a nationally televised parade, a popular music concert staged in a sports arena, or the Olympic closing ceremonies.[1] At all scales, performance is reflectively shaped by, and in turn reflexively shapes, important social and cultural dynamics, including questions of aesthetics, responsibility, value, knowledge, and power. When they escape the most intimate realms, such performances are, in the classic formulation offered by Marcel Mauss (1990:78–79), "total social facts" that integrate and contribute to all aspects of social life.

Between the intimate and the spectacular lies a vast territory of performance activity that has been of particular salience for the study of social and cultural life in smaller-scale societies approached as analytic wholes. Scholars

working in such classic ethnographic situations as villages, urban neighborhoods, towns, rural districts, and smaller indigenous communities characterized by unique languages and distinctive cultural practices have found
such middle-scale performances to be of special interest and relevance. They
have also proved valuable for the understanding of particular subcultural
networks operating within larger social contexts, such as in wider regions or
the major cities of the contemporary world. Expressive practices typical of
this intermediate range are those that are widely participated in (rather than
simply viewed) but that possess a range of formal features and that organize
a diversity of participants while incorporating a rich mix of expressive activity (oratory, music, food, gesture, adornment, architecture, and so forth)
into a coherent and larger whole that is bounded in space and time and
thereby marked as a special event. Viewed cross-culturally, rituals, festivals,
dances, feasts, games, and masquerades are all instances occurring within
this broader domain.[2] These modes of performance are also those central to
the particular ethnohistorical analysis offered in this chapter.

The study of such expressive practices are at the heart of many multigen-
erational theoretical projects in anthropology and folklore studies, as is evidenced by enduring ethnological interest in such phenomena as the Northwest Coast potlatch ceremony, the kula ring found in parts of Papua New
Guinea, and European and European-derived calendar festivals (Graeber
2001; Noyes 2003b). Such studies have been of wide interest in these fields,
but they also have particular histories and significances in Native American-
focused research, including in the region in which my own projects unfold.
As will be evident below, ethnographers working in Southeastern North
America have made significant contributions to the field of performance
ethnography. Frank Speck's work on masking and, especially, Raymond D.
Fogelson's studies of the region's ballgame complex are especially founda-
tional and noteworthy in this regard (Speck 1950; Speck and Broom 1951;
Fogelson 1962, 1971). The analysis of a Southeastern Indian ritual/festival
event that I offer here is intended as a contribution to these ongoing conversations. In this chapter I aim to bring ethnographic sensibilities and experiences, born out of fieldwork undertaken within a performance-oriented
framework, to bear on the task of making sense of the historical record for
this region.

"[A] GREAT SOLEMN FEAST OF LOVE"

Among the Southeastern Indian rituals described by the trader and proto-
ethnographer James Adair in his great work, *History of the American Indians,*
published first in 1775, is a springtime celebration that he refers to in English
as "a great solemn feast of love." Embedded within an extended discourse
promoting his discredited theory of North American Indian kinship to the

ancient Israelites, Adair's account of this ceremonial among those peoples he refers to as "Mississippi Floridians" correlates remarkably well with other springtime religious celebrations found among the Native peoples of eastern North America. Using historical and present-day ethnographic data, this chapter offers an ethnohistorical assessment of Adair's account and places it into a comparative context, thereby seeking to enrich scholarly knowledge of the region's cultural history, particularly of the ceremonial life of its Native peoples.

Well-known to students of Southern Indian history and ethnology, Adair was a prominent Indian trader, diplomat, and student of Native American affairs. Born in Ireland about 1709, he lived and worked in the backcountry among the Native peoples of Southeastern North America between about 1735 and 1768. Knowledgeable concerning most of the region's Native peoples, he is most closely associated with the Chickasaw, with whom he lived at greatest length and among whom he found a wife. While there is much more that students of Adair and of the cultural history of the American Southeast would like to know about his life and career, the period culminating in the publication of his book is now reasonably well understood. For this history, as well as rich insight into Adair's study and its enduring significance, readers are urged to consult Kathryn E. Holland Braund's critical edition of the *History* (Adair 2005), along with Charles Hudson's (1977) perceptive essay "James Adair as Anthropologist."

The specific focus of my discussion is a passage from Adair's work that is presented below. John Swanton (1928b), William Sturtevant (1955), Fogelson (1962), and Fogelson and Walker (1980) had already cited it as ethnological evidence, but Braund first directed my attention to this passage in 2003 when she queried me about its potential significance. In collecting my thoughts on this ethnographic fragment for her, I recognized its potential usefulness to a larger study of Woodland Indian ceremonial life that several colleagues and I have been pursuing (Jackson 2000, 2002a, 2002b, 2003a, 2003b, 2004, 2007; Jackson and Levine 2002; Jackson and Linn 2000; Levine 2004b; Urban and Jackson 2004; Waselkov 2004:694–96). Begun as raw comments intended for one of Braund's endnotes, this chapter is a further step down the path toward this larger purpose—a regional understanding of ritual, festival, and ceremony, inclusive of their constituent expressive genres, in social and cultural context.

ADAIR'S DESCRIPTION OF THE "FEAST OF LOVE"

Adair's description of the "feast of love" is given as follows:

> Every spring season, one town or more of the Mississippi Floridians, keep a great solemn feast of love, to renew their old friendship. They

call this annual feast, *Hottuk Aimpa, Heettla, Tanáa,* "the people eat, dance, and walk as twined together"—The short name of their yearly feast of love, is *Hottuk Impanáa,* "eating by a strong religious, or social principle;" *Impanáa* signifies several threads or strands twisted, or warped together. *Hissoobistarákshe,* and *Yelphòha Panáa,* is "a twisted horse-rope," and "warped garter."

They assemble three nights previous to their annual feast of love; on the fourth night they eat together. During the intermediate space, the young men and women dance in circles from the evening till morning. The men masque their faces with large pieces of gourds of different shapes and hieroglyphic paintings. Some of them fix a pair of young buffalo horns to their head; others the tail, behind. When the dance and their time is expired, the men turn out a hunting, and bring in a sufficient quantity of venison, for the feast of renewing their love, and confirming their friendship with each other. The women dress it, and bring the best they have along with it; which a few springs past, was only a variety of Esau's small red acorn pottage, as their crops had failed. When they have eaten together, they fix in the ground a large pole with a bush tied at the top, over which they throw a ball. Till the corn is in, they meet there almost every day, and play for venison and cakes, the men against the women; which the old people say they have observed for time out of mind.

[Adair 1775:113–14; 1930:119–20; 2005:155–56]

This passage provides the basis for the interpretations offered below. Before pursuing an explication of the ceremonial that it describes, however, I must assess the troubled question of whom Adair is referring to in this passage when he refers to "Mississippi Floridians." Various scholars have addressed this issue.

"MISSISSIPPI FLORIDIANS"

The oldest proposal is that made, without detailed elaboration, in Swanton's (1928b:262–63) study of Chickasaw ethnography. There, he quotes Adair and offers the relevant passage, providing it as evidence that the Chickasaw shared a similar ceremonial dance culture to the Creek. Later, Sturtevant (1955:418) adopted this same interpretation.

Because Adair lived among the Chickasaw and knew them best, this linkage has some contextual common sense going for it. In further support of this view, Swanton and later Muskogeanists can identify the Native language names that Adair offers, while improving upon their translation. Marcia Haag, a scholar working in the field of Choctaw and Chickasaw linguistics, has examined Adair's data and notes that, while most of the words are clear cognates in both Chickasaw and Choctaw, *Impanáa* 'twisted together' is found in Chickasaw but not in Choctaw (see Table 4.1; personal communication, October 30, 2003). Like Swanton (1928b:262, n.21) before her, Haag notes that the "strong religious, or social principle" element in Adair's rendering is absent in a formal literal translation of the words given, although contextually we can perhaps understand why Adair would have added this sentiment to his glosses. In either language, the full name for the event, as recorded by Adair and translated and polished by Haag, can be given as "people feast there, dancing intertwined" (cf. Swanton 1928b:262). Its short name would be "people twisted together." The linguistic data encourages a Chickasaw interpretation, but the strong possibility remains that Adair simply rendered interethnic data in the Native language that he himself knew best.

A second contemporary reading of the problem has been provided by Patrica Galloway (personal communication, September 16, 2003). In correspondence with me, she wrote:

> I've had a look at Adair and can't be positive who he is talking about —note that there's no good evidence for where he might have been, west or south of the Chickasaws (he was among the Choctaws in the 50s I think, but it's not clear where, and he may have only been up in Neshoba County). Still given his orientation in the world I assume he must be referring to the Choctaws or the Choctawans on the lower reaches of the Pearl, Leaf, or Chickasawhay [Rivers]; I would think NOT the small tribes of the lower Mississippi ([as] elsewhere in the book he refers to the Mississippi country as east of the Mississippi).

Working independently at an earlier period Fogelson made the same Choctaw or Choctawan identification as Galloway in his valuable essay on the Cherokee Booger Dance (Fogelson and Walker 1980:98).

Taking Adair's ethnic identification pretty literally, Braund (personal communication, March 18, 2003; Adair 2005:134, 496, n.117) has postulated that he was speaking of "West Florida" Indians living near the Mississippi River, by which she means those peoples often grouped as the "Petite Nations" or the "Small Tribes of the Mississippi" as the British of Adair's time termed them. If this is accurate, then Adair is referring to "Louisiana" tribes such as the Houma, Biloxi, and Tunica.[3] This solution was also that adopted by Braund's predecessor, Samuel Williams, the editor of the 1930 edition of the *History* (Adair 1930:119, n.40). In contrast to Galloway's interpretation, Braund (in Adair 2005:496, n.117) notes that some of these tribes lived "on the eastern side of the Mississippi River in territory that became part of British West Florida after the Seven Years' War."[4] She continues:

TABLE 4.1.   Linguistic Notes on Adair's Text

Long Name

ADAIR	Hottuk	Aimpa	Heettla	Tanáa
MODERN CHOCTAW	hattak	aiimpa	hilha	tvnna
TRANSLATION	man	feasting place	dance	woven together
MODERN CHICKASAW	hattak	aaimpa'	hilha'	tanna'
TRANSLATION	man	feasting place	dance	something knitted
ADAIR'S GLOSS	'the people eat, dance, and walk as twined together'			
MODERN GLOSS	'people feast there, dancing intertwined'			

Short Name

ADAIR	Hottuk	Impanáa
MODERN CHOCTAW	hattak	*
MODERN CHICKASAW	hattak	impanna
TRANSLATION	man	twisted together
ADAIR'S GLOSS[a]	'eating by a strong religious or social principle'	
MODERN GLOSS	'people intertwined'	

Note: Transcriptions and translations provided by Marcia Haag (personal communication, October 30, 2003) and supplemented by Pamela Munro and Catherine Willmond, *Chickasaw: An Analytical Dictionary* (Norman, University of Oklahoma Press, 1994).

[a]Swanton (1928b:262) previously noted the absence of these concepts from an accurate literal translation. Adair redeems himself when he more closely translates the Chickasaw *impanáa* (impanna) as "several threads or strands twisted or warped together."

Adair's use of the name "Mississippi Floridians" is a puzzle. Usually when Adair is referring to common cultural traits of the major southeastern Indian tribes, he simply uses the term "Indians." In some cases, when he specifically points out events relating to or characteristics of specific tribes, he uses their proper names, such as Chickasaws, Choctaws or Creeks. So I think it is significant that he specifically uses the term "Mississippi Floridians." This is an odd name, and to my knowledge, it is not in widespread use. Indeed, it seems to be unique. Of course, Adair's *History* is full of odd, literary constructions that would have been easily recognized by his contemporaries but which confound modern readers.

Braund also points out that in another passage in his work, Adair mentions "a friendly feast, or feast of love, in West-Florida" (Adair 2005:134). In this passage, he clearly indicates he was in attendance and relates a long conversation with an "old rainmaker." In this instance, Adair clearly seems to be among the Chickasaw, whose territory by that time was part of the British colony of West Florida (Adair 2005:134; Braund, personal communication, August 18, 2007).

As an ethnologist, I cannot take the matter of ethnic identification much further, but my analysis of the ceremonial that Adair describes may alleviate some of the burden posed by his lack of specificity. Despite my ethnological emphasis, I do hope that scholars with more familiarity with the full range of available evidence will return to the problem.[5]

UNPACKING THE "FEAST OF LOVE"

I suggest that what Adair called the "feast of love" be understood first in a general way as a community-oriented, as opposed to martial, ceremony. More specifically, Adair's description is of a springtime event, which resonates with other Woodland Indian ceremonials held during this season, as well as with their autumnal counterparts in which the same basic set of ritual acts are inverted to emphasize an opposing or complementary set of concerns.

Having named the event, Adair begins his description, reporting that "They assemble three nights previous to their annual feast of love; on the fourth night they eat together. During the intermediate space, the young men and women dance in circles from the evening till morning" (Adair 1930:119; 2005:155). Four days is the basic temporal unit around which Southeastern Indian ceremonies are organized. This ritual structure is a manifestation of the region's basic "pattern number" (Jackson 2003:76). In the Southeast, segmentation by fours permeates every aspect of traditional culture, from grand cosmology to practical herbalism. In the case in question, I would note that while almost universal, the event structure described here most closely matches that of the Shawnee Bread Dance (Howard 1981) and the Horned-Owl or Hunting Dance, an event that has been documented for the Alabama in Texas, the Choctaw in Mississippi (Swanton 1931:223), the Creek, the Seminole in Oklahoma and Florida (Capron 1956; Sturtevant 1955; Swanton 1928a:525), and for the mixed Coushatta-Alabama-Choctaw-Tunica

Fig. 4.1. A Snake Dance performance among the Choctaw of Bayou Lacomb, St. Tammany Parish, Louisiana, photographed in April 1909 by David I. Bushnell, National Anthropological Archives, Smithsonian Institution, BAE GN 01102B30 06227600.

settlements of Kinder and Marksville, Louisiana (Levine 1991:195). As I suggest below, these are the ceremonies to which the "feast of love" appears to be most closely related.[6]

Structuring communal events around an all-night dance is similarly ubiquitous among the peoples of the region (see Figure 4.1). Almost every communal ceremony in the Southeast combines formal rituals and other daytime activities (such as feasts, games, and speeches) with a nighttime dance that complements the daytime events with which it is linked. Fundamental to the larger ritual of which it is a part, these nighttime dances are often less solemn and more social in character than other phases of the ceremonies within which they are held. This social character is evident in the fact that visitors from beyond a local community often participate in such dances but not in the ritual feasts and other ceremonies that accompany them. Despite this social dimension, such dances are not ancillary to the events within which they are held. They are almost always a core component and the success of the event as a whole is often measured in the enthusiasm and enjoyment registered by dance participants. Such dances remain important in many Southeastern communities today. Their nature in areal context is explored in my book *Yuchi Ceremonial Life* (2003) and various other ethno-graphic sources. Among the less frequently used of these is Victoria Levine's fine dissertation documenting the ceremonial life of the Choctaw enclave established among the Chickasaw near Ardmore, Oklahoma, during the so-called late removals that co-occurred with allotment (Levine 1990, see also Levine 2004a). I call attention to it here because it documents the persistence of town/ceremonial ground ritualism in a context that brought Choctaw and Chickasaw together to perform rituals akin to that described by Adair.

Continuing with Adair, he notes that in the ceremony "The men masque their faces with large pieces of gourds of different shapes and hieroglyphic paintings" (1930:119; 2005:155–56). This is an especially interesting observation because it provides, as Fogelson and Walker (1980:98) have already demonstrated, useful comparative data on masking in the Southeast. As both they and Sturtevant (1955:418) have recognized, it suggests that the community discussed by Adair performed a dance akin to the Old Man Dance of the Creek and Seminole and to the better-known Booger Dance of the Eastern Cherokee (Figure 4.2). While the Cherokee Booger Dance, in an

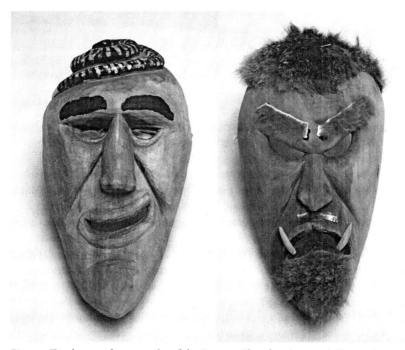

Fig. 4.2. Two booger dance masks of the Eastern Cherokee (ca. 1969) illustrating a twentieth-century manifestation of the Southeastern Indian mask dance tradition. Mathers Museum of World Cultures, Indiana University, (left) 1969-01-0003 and (right) 1969-01-0002. Photographs by Matthew Sieber.

analysis first developed by Speck and Leonard Broom (1951), has been interpreted primarily as a masked parody lampooning the behavior of foreigners and thereby reinforcing Cherokee community solidarity, it also shares themes with the Creek-Seminole Old Man Dance, in which young men wear gourd or watermelon rind masks and dance as buffoons, pretending to be old men and exploring social tensions along the axis of age cohorts (Fogelson and Walker 1980; Howard 1984:177–79; Jackson 1997; Speck and Broom 1951:25–39; Sturtevant 1955:418; Swanton 1928a:534, 556; for mask ceremonies across the entire Eastern Woodlands, see Fenton 1987 and Speck 1950).[7]

Adair next points to the inclusion of a Buffalo Dance within the "feast of love." In it, some of the men "fix a pair of young buffalo horns to their head; others the tail, behind" (1930:119; 2005:156). Like the region's masked dances, the Buffalo Dances of the Southeast are also typically episodes incorporated into larger ceremonies rather than stand-alone events.[8] Although the music and choreography of the Shawnee and Yuchi Buffalo Dances set them apart as distinctive manifestations of a wider tradition, all of the extant Muskogean groups, except the two main bodies of Choctaw (in modern Mississippi and Oklahoma), are known to have, or to have had, a Buffalo Dance that shared the same specific songs and basic choreography. My own archival work on dance music has shown that these same Muskogean Buffalo Dance songs were also used in the Eastern Cherokee version of the dance, as documented in unpublished work undertaken by Speck in the 1930s. The lesson that we can derive from the distributional evidence is that the Buffalo Dance, like all of the traits recorded by Adair, is a widely shared custom that appears to have deep historical roots in the region.

Continuing with his account, Adair (2005:156) writes: "When the dance and their time is expired, the men turn out a hunting, and bring in a sufficient quantity of venison, for the feast of renewing their love, and confirming their friendship with each other. The women dress it, and bring the best they have along with it; which a few springs past, was only a variety of Esau's small red acorn pottage, as their crops had failed." What Adair is describing here is a paradigmatic instance of gendered food exchange. Permeating Woodland Indian ceremonialism, it is found in exactly this form in the fall Horned Owl or Hunting Dance of the Creek and their congeners, and in the fall and spring Bread Dances of the Shawnee.[9] In my own experience, I have participated in this pattern of food exchange during the Yuchi Soup Dance, a ceremonial feast sharing many themes with these other ceremonies (Jackson 2003:241–71).

In the last phase of his report, Adair describes a final ceremonial activity ubiquitous in the Southeast. He notes: "When they have eaten together, they fix in the ground a large pole with a bush tied at the top, over which they throw a ball. Till the corn is in, they meet there almost every day, and play for venison and cakes, the men against the women; which the old people say they have observed for time out of mind" (Adair 2005:156). This is the ball game in which men compete against women in a contest of hitting a target atop a pole. Played today by the Western Cherokee, Creek, Seminole, Chickasaw, Caddo, and Yuchi, it is reasonably well documented, although no one has yet written a modern overview for the region.[10] In Oklahoma today, the target atop the pole is usually either a carved wooden animal effigy or an actual animal skull, usually from a cow. In Florida, the ball pole among the Seminole is even more like that described by Adair. There, a pine tree is used, from which the side branches have been removed. The green top of the tree is left in place and used as the target (Capron 1953:182–83). In this game, men typically use a pair of stickball racquets, while the women catch and throw with their bare hands. As in Adair's account, the game in post-removal Oklahoma is played first in the spring and then continues as a part of community gatherings throughout the summer. Although a fun, social game, it is closely associated with community ceremonial activity and is an expression of the gender duality fundamental to the religious and social life of the region (Jackson 2003:123–24).

Contextualizing Adair's comment that they "play for venison and cakes," I can note that gendered betting, in which women provided corn bread to men following a loss or, alternatively, the men provided wild game to the women after a defeat, was a common aspect of ceremonial games throughout the Woodlands. Swanton (1928a:555) documented it for the Creek and Speck and Broom (1951:81–82) described it for the Eastern Cherokee, as have present-day Yuchi elders with whom I have worked. This is another modality of gendered food exchange, a mechanism generating minor community feasts modeled on major ones such as those already discussed (Jackson 2003b:124).

CONCLUSION

If, with due caution, we read Adair's description against later ethnographic sources, a description that would otherwise be a somewhat enigmatic footnote makes wider sense and is a useful contribution to our comparative knowledge of traditional religious life in the Native Southeast. I conclude by offering some synthetic comments, particularly regarding the place of this event within the significances attached to the calendrical round across the region (see Figure 4.3).

For present purposes, the fall Horned Owl or Hunting Dance has been adequately documented for all the historic Muskogean tribes except the Choctaw and Chickasaw. The data is also reasonably clear for the ethnically more complex Choctaw-Alabama-Coushatta-Tunica communities of Louisiana. For the Mississippi Choctaw, Swanton (1931:223) gathered a

Summer

Green Corn (and other Harvest/Thanksgiving) Ceremonies

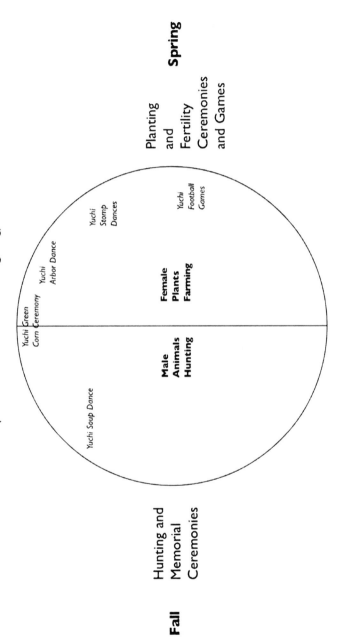

Spring

Planting
and
Fertility
Ceremonies
and Games

Yuchi Stomp Dances

Yuchi Arbor Dance

Yuchi Green Corn Ceremony

Yuchi Football Games

Female Plants Farming

Male Animals Hunting

Yuchi Soup Dance

Midwinter (Petitioning) Ceremonies
and/or Nonceremonial Social Events

Winter

Fall

Hunting and
Memorial
Ceremonies

Fig. 4.3. The seasonal and economic round characteristic of community ceremonial life in the Eastern Woodlands illustrated through reference to contemporary Yuchi ceremonial events.

compelling fragment suggesting that they too once shared the ceremonial. This leaves only the Chickasaw, for which we have no data. In the Horned Owl Dance, local communities gather for dancing, games, and a feast that is preceded by a male hunt and the segregated preparation, by women, of corn bread and other vegetable foods. In the feast itself, the genders formally exchange their respective contributions with each other, thereby enacting the fundamental principles of the region's gender ideology (cf. Bell 1990; Braund 1990; Buckley 1989; Jackson 2002). Among the other purposes of this ceremonial are marking the transition from the horticultural to the hunting season and, in some contexts, placating the venomous snakes that threaten hunters in their travels.

While twentieth-century ethnographers did not document fall ceremonialism as fully as the Green Corn Ceremonials of midsummer we, none-the-less, have a coherent sketch of autumnal ritual. What is missing is a clear exposition of its articulation with spring ceremonialism, about which little has been written. For this purpose, the Shawnee Bread Dance offers some clues. The modern Shawnee towns hold their Bread Dances twice each year. Its form is approximately the same in each season, but its rituals are inflected differently depending on its position within the annual round. In the fall, it strongly echoes the Muskogean Hunting Dance and the Yuchi Soup Dance and is performed under the leadership of men, while in the spring it emphasizes horticulture and is under the direction of female leaders. What I am describing as inversions in the ritual can be witnessed in such gendered patterns as who—men or women—leads specific dance episodes or, as among the Loyal Shawnee, whether the fire is kindled on the women's or men's side of the town square. Here Shawnee ritual partakes of areal patterns in which the seasons of the year, each with its characteristic economic emphasis, are linked to a rich constellation of gendered beliefs and practices.

Adair offers us a picture of such a spring ceremonial, one timed with (and, I think, thematically concerned with) planting rather than harvesting. Like those that I have had the fortune to participate in, in modern Oklahoma, it embraced feasts, dances, games, and ritual gestures that all affirm community solidarity while highlighting the distinctive but interlocking contributions men and women each make to the social fabric and to economic life. In this light, the Chickasaw names that Adair recorded—twisted, knitted, woven, and twined—with their rich textile imagery, reveal again the sophistication of Woodland Indian social philosophy.

If the later ethnography can be relied on as a basis for interpretation, I suspect that the "feast of love" also helped insure the success of the upcoming crops and celebrated the end of the social "downtime" of the winter season. If I have overstepped Adair's data in this last proposal, I can at least retreat to my own experience among Woodland peoples in Oklahoma today and note that these are the significances that they attach to their own very similar spring celebrations.

We cannot make any claims with certainty, but the comparative ethnography suggests that being unable to fix the ethnic identity of the "Mississippi Floridians" does not undermine the usefulness of Adair's description. Through a comparative lens, his data provide an eighteenth-century account of ceremonial patterns that would otherwise be known almost completely from twentieth-century sources. Reading Adair's description against the ethnography strengthens my own sense that not even Swanton, with his rich knowledge of most Southeastern groups, fully appreciated the convergent, sprachbund-like quality of the region's cultural patterning (cf. Jackson and Levine 2002; Speck 1945). Reviewing a bit of this ethnological data here, I have emphasized form over meaning. In moving on to a more elaborate treatment of these issues, I hope to use my firsthand experiences among Woodland peoples to foreground the profound significance and beauty of the traditions that most non-Native peoples first glimpsed in sources such as Adair's *History*.

In connection to the larger themes explored by the contributors of this volume, I hope to have offered a modest empirical contribution illustrative of the continuing fruitfulness of ethnohistorical research in the ethnological or culture history tradition. While often understood in historical terms as the theoretical and substantive core of North Americanist and North American anthropology in the pre–World War II period, such work is neither strictly Americanist nor solely a product of that era (see Boas 1940; Goldenweiser 1937:443–526; Herskovits 1948; Kroeber 1963; Lowie 1940:356–90; Sapir 1916; Wallis 1930 for theoretical treatments and Hallowell 1926; Lesser 1933; Radin 1911; Bennedict 1922 for empirical studies). Contemporary American anthropologists have revisited the continuing vitality and productivity of work undertaken in this paradigm in this period (Fox 1991; Darnell 2001) and, with its hallmarks of regional comparisons aimed at the construction of regional culture history, such work has remained consistently central to a number of research traditions in scholarship. Americanist ethnohistory (Eggan 1954; Fenton 1952; Fogelson 1962; Sturtevant 1966; Trigger 1986), European ethnology/folklife studies (Fenske 2007; Noyes 2003a; Noyes and Bendix 1998), American cultural geography (Kniffen 1965; Zelinsky1958), and North American folklore and folklife studies (Glassie 1968; Yoder 1976) all represent domains in which such work has proved durable and vital. My own introduction to these traditions of scholarly inquiry traces back to my socialization and enculturation in the workshop of Raymond J. DeMallie and I remain deeply grateful for his generous tutelage and his inspiring example (DeMallie 1993, 1998, 2009).

ACKNOWLEDGMENTS

My debts to countless Native people in Oklahoma are immeasurable and it is a pleasure to record again my appreciation for all of the individuals and communities that have welcomed and instructed me over the past twenty years. Support for the field and archival research upon which this chapter is based has been generously provided by the Wenner-Gren Foundation for Anthropological Research, the American Philosophical Society, the Oklahoma Humanities Council, the Whatcom Museum Society, and Indiana University. Appreciation is extended to Kathryn E. Holland Braund for prompting this project, as well as contributing very substantively to it. The author is also grateful for assistance generously provided by Leroy Sealy, Patricia Galloway, and Marcia Haag. None of these individuals or agencies are responsible for the interpretations offered here. A version of this chapter was initially presented at the 2003 Annual Meeting of the American Society for Ethnohistory. A generous audience in the Department of Anthropology at Southern Illinois University provided feedback and well-informed questions about this project during a March 2008 visit. In particular, I want to acknowledge Anthony Webster, Paul Welch, and Jonathan Hill for their hospitality on that occasion.

NOTES

1. A recent assessment of performance approaches in folklore studies, including the theoretical questions at stake, is offered in Bauman (2012). For an introduction to the face-to-face end of the continuum that I am describing, see Duncan (1992). For the case of spectacle at its other end, see Manning (1992).

2. For conceptual orientations to the study of these performance events, see Rappaport (1992) for ritual, Stoeltje (1992) for festival, Kaeppler (1992) for dance, Goode (1992) for feasts, Georges (1972) for games, and Tonkin (1992) for masks and masking. For the social formations at issue in the study of expressive life, see Noyes (2003b, 2012).

3. For ethnographic and historical background on all of the peoples discussed in this chapter, see the various chapters gathered in the "Southeast" volume of the *Handbook of North American Indians* (Fogelson 2004).

4. To deal with this question, we might also survey the range of meanings given in the period to "Mississippi" and "Floridians." Finally, we might systematically document the accuracy and inaccuracy of Adair's own cultural geography. I have not attempted such a rigorous analysis.

5. In a very helpful review of the account provided in this section, Braund made the following additional observation regarding her identification of Adair's "Mississippi Floridians" as the "Small Tribes of the Mississippi" in her edition of his work: "I suppose I should have said Adair likely meant the Small Tribes and he might very well have meant the Chickasaw. That was my trouble

in trying to pin it down for my edition – I was hoping the ceremony would reveal identity" (Kathryn Braund, personal communication, August 18, 2007).

6. The number four articulates with Southeastern Indian ceremonial event structures in a number of ways. One of these is the number of days over which a ceremonial is staged. While minor ceremonies may occupy a single day (often conceptualized as sunrise to sunrise), major ones are understood and organized as four-day affairs. This is typically the case, for instance, in the basic form of the Green Corn Ceremonial. This four-day structure is sometimes doubled, as in the more elaborate eight-day Green Corn Ceremonial described by Swanton for the Creek (Swanton 1928a:577). The four-day unit can also be tripled into a twelve-day event. Such is the case with the ancestral form of the Yuchi Green Corn Ceremony, as it is still practiced by the people of Polecat town. In this ceremony, an eight-day Green Corn Ceremony is concluded with the four-day Soup Dance Ceremony. The Delaware Big House Ceremony was similarly built out of constituent rituals into a twelve-day ceremonial (Grumet 2001; Miller 1997).

7. I would note here that Braund (2005:496–97, n.120) differentiates more strongly ("very different") the Cherokee Booger Dance from the Muskogean Old People's Dance (Old Man's Dance) than I do. In seeing commonalities between the two, I follow Fogelson and Bell (1980) in recognizing "Old Man" themes in the better documented Booger Dance. This perspective does not invalidate the "resistance to non-Cherokee outsiders" interpretation of the Booger Dance offered by Speck and Broom (1951); it only suggests that, like all known Southeastern Indian rituals, these dances conveyed and explored multiple, complex messages, meanings, and concerns.

8. The Buffalo Dance is performed among Native Southeastern peoples today, both in Oklahoma and Florida. (The Yuchi have their own version of it, but the Creek version seems widespread in the Southeast.) As described in James Howard's *Oklahoma Seminoles* (1984) and elsewhere, it is most often a phase of the Creek and Oklahoma Seminole Green Corn Ceremony. This same version is performed today among the "North Ground" Absentee Shawnee in their annual War Dance (where it is led by Creek or Seminole singers), but the Loyal Shawnee have their own distinct version of the Buffalo Dance that does stand alone as an event. This, and the cognate Delaware ceremonial, is described in Howard's (1981:288–96) Shawnee study. There is a Creek Buffalo Dance performance available on a commercial recording published by Indian House Records (1970), and a Florida Seminole recording of Buffalo Dance music is available online in the "Florida Folklife from the WPA Collections" of the American Folklife Center, Library of Congress. This recording has been assigned the following designations: Call Number AFS 3893B:2, Digital ID Number afcflwpa 3893b2. A relatively easy path for those wishing to hear this recording is to search for the Seminole recordings within this collection (http://memory.loc.gov/ammem /flwpahtml/ffgroups.html, consulted May 25, 2005).

9. As noted later in this chapter, this same kind of food exchange was found in the betting that once accompanied men-versus-women ball games among the Yuchi in Oklahoma and the Cherokee in North Carolina (Speck and Broom 1951:82–83; Jackson 2003:124, 133).

10. In discussing the game comparatively, Fogelson (1962:243) has cited the Adair passage as an early description of Chickasaw practice, but the reoccurring question of the ethnic identity of Adair's subjects is again relevant here. See Howard and Lena (1984:181–83) and Swanton (1928:467–68) for the game among the Oklahoma Seminole and Creek. For the Oklahoma Cherokee, see Heth (1975:69–70) and Fogelson (1962:242–47). Play among the Natchez is discussed in Galloway and Jackson (2004:612–13). The Yuchi game is touched on throughout Jackson (2003). I have played the "social" game many times among the Yuchi and on occasion among the Hasinai Caddo and the Western Cherokee. I have witnessed many games among the Oklahoma Cherokee and Creek and know indirectly of its revival among the contemporary Chickasaw. The best source for the Florida Seminole is Capron (1953:182–83).

5

"He said he would show [the tobacco] to M. Ogden"

Voice and Historical Role in the Tsilhqut'in Fur Trade

DAVID W. DINWOODIE

The matters of "voice" and "historical role," important to ethnohistory in general, are at the heart of a debate in Tsilhqut'in studies. The Tsilhqut'in are a First Nations group living in west central British Columbia, in the area between Williams Lake on Highway 97 and Bella Coola on the coast. They number roughly thirty-five hundred and live on five reserves as well as in Williams Lake, Kamloops, Vancouver, and elsewhere.

The Tsilhqut'in appear to descend from a population of loosely organized subarctic hunter-gatherers who entered the Chilcotin River corridor as late as 1650 (Dinwoodie 2010:653; Matson and Magne 2007:7). They evidently consolidated sociopolitically in the context of the coastal fur trade as the interior fur traders perceived them to be an ethnic community at the time of the onset of the interior trade in the area (Dinwoodie 2010:662–68). Though initiated by the Russians and the British, the Pacific Northwest maritime or coastal trade was dominated by Americans from the last decade of the eighteenth century to the end of the first decade of the nineteenth (Gibson 1992:58). During this time the primary focus of the trade was the sea otter. In that phase Tsilhqut'in played a peripheral but not insignificant role, trading with coastal middlemen such as the Bella Coola such pelts of lower value as beaver, goat, and marmot. With the decline of the sea otter and the shift of the trade to the interior and to the beaver, and in the context of the reorganization of the trade in Oregon Country by the Hudson's Bay Company (HBC) following the merger in 1821, Fort Chilcotin was established in the heart of Tsilhqut'in territory in 1829 (operated consistently after 1834) (Turkel 2007:153), and the Tsilhqut'in came to be viewed as primary suppliers of beaver (Turkel 2007:155).

The Tsilhqut'in language is increasingly featured as a cultural and political symbol today so that while the practice of some registers (for example, deference to family heads) is maintained continuously from previous times, the practice of others (for example, styles of political discourse tailored to Canadian public spheres) is being newly cultivated today. Historically, the situation regarding language and communication remains uncertain. It appears that varieties identified as Tsilhqut'in were prevalent among those who identified as Tsilhqut'in. Nevertheless, as Tsilhqut'in ethnicity likely took shape in the context of the coastal fur trade, a time when economic and kinship networking necessitated communication with speakers of regional coastal languages, regional interior languages, European languages, and others. It seems likely that individuals effectively involved in trade and exchange were at least partially bilingual or multilingual in the varieties integral to their activities in their preferred region of activity. Though certainly some Tsilhqut'in individuals were proficient in Chinook Jargon, evidence suggests that most were not.

In *Contact and Conflict: Indian-European Relations in British Columbia 1774–1890*, Robin Fisher (1977:xviii) argues that a full appreciation of the role of Indians in the history of British Columbia required a careful consideration of Indians "acting in terms of the priorities of their own culture," even as they were responding to "the European economic system" (xi). The Tsilhqut'in case, Fisher (1977:35) argues, represented one in which Indians "preferred not to be involved in the fur trade and found it possible to exercise that choice." In his recent book, *The Archive of Place: Unearthing the Pasts of the Chilcotin Plateau*, William J. Turkel (2007:146) respectfully challenges Fisher's (1977:35) claim that, essentially, "the Chilcotin had opted out of the fur trade." Based on broad use of HBC records, Turkel marshals considerable evidence that the Tsilhqut'in sought to augment their role. He explains:

> Far from opting out of the fur trade, the Tsilhqot'in did everything in their power to be a part of it. They were willing to fight with the Carrier for direct access to the HBC traders. They repeatedly expressed an interest in having a post of their own. When the company failed to establish a post year after year, brought goods that the Tsilhqot'in thought were inferior, charged high tariffs, and depreciated the furs that Aboriginal people brought in to trade . . . even then some of the Tsilhqot'in persisted in dealing with the company men at the post. When the company men did something outside the bounds of propriety—treating important Tsilhqot'in with a complete lack of respect, for example, or trying to capture their most valuable and unpredictable food source—the Tsilhqot'in were forced to take their business elsewhere.
>
> [Turkel 2007:160]

More specifically, Turkel argues on the same page that even when confronting the HBC on one matter or another the Tsilhqut'in were trading furs with aboriginal middlemen along indigenous trade routes to the sea. Based on my ethnographic experience and on the study of fur trade and missionary records, I believe the evidence supports Turkel's view that "the Tsilhqot'in did everything in their power to be a part of it." Nevertheless, a key point remains unclear, namely whether in their participation in the fur trade the Tsilhqut'in as a collective were "acting in terms of the priorities of their own culture," as Fisher put it, reactivating indigenous trade routes as Turkel suggests, or whether specific actors sought to innovate by persuading their Tsilhqut'in colleagues and their HBC interlocutors to accept new priorities based on their reading of the opportunities presented by the rapidly shifting terms of trade (Fisher 1977:xi).[1] What I hope to do in this chapter, in addition to addressing this question of Tsilhqut'in cultural history, is to highlight a kind of evidence that opens to view the matter of historical innovation in regard to political economic opportunities.

A key emphasis in Native American studies today is the documentation and analysis of voice (Dinwoodie 1998; Hymes 1981; Moore 1983; Parks and DeMallie 1992a; Sherzer and Woodbury 1987; Tedlock 1983; Webster 2009). A key stimulus to this research has been the recognition that the record of Native American speech in the mainstream media and in history written for the majority has been either biased and highly selective, or fraudulent. One logical avenue of inquiry, as a result, has been the pursuit of texts composed by Native Americans in Native American languages, or, more recently, digital audiovisual "self-representations" of communicative practice by self-identified Natives, that is, the pursuit of sources relatively free of Western influence (Hymes 1981; Parks and DeMallie 1992a; Sherzer and Woodbury 1987; Tedlock 1983; Singer 2001; Webster 2009). Although I am fully supportive of the goal of actively cultivating a richer record of Native American communication in history, including attention to Native language documents, I nevertheless argue here that there remains a place for the study of Native communication on the basis of historical records generated by historical actors who are not co-ethnic, records that do not overtly depict the code of what is believed to have been the Native language, but which nonetheless were composed by people with firsthand knowledge of those they depict, and which do depict crucial aspects of setting and circumstance, and even depict—albeit selectively—aspects of the communicative repertoire of the contact community.

Conceptualizing communication holistically requires that the Native language emphasis be carefully considered. First, there is a Western ideal of a primordial "aboriginal vocal origin," an active modern political construct that has been used to shape a distinctly American political consciousness from revolutionary times to the present (Dinwoodie 1998; Looby 1996). The continuing presence of this ideal complicates historical interpretation. The fact that presently we have no self-standing method or theory for differentiating between our perception of aboriginal vocal origin as an active Western political ideal and our perception of it as an historical expression of aboriginal voice raises questions about calls for decolonization that have not addressed the challenge of differentiating between the two in a systematic and principled way (Mignolo and Escobar 2009; Noble 1971; Thiong'o 1986).

Second, given the extensive history of interaction among Native American and European populations, there is the question of whether we can effectively understand any particular voice or voicing without a consideration of the historically specific mediation of "social relationships among particular populations" (Wolf 1982:19).

Third, a key impulse in the ethnohistory of communication today questions received ways of thinking about what have been termed, *communities* and their assumed isomorphisms with what have been termed, *languages*, particularly isomorphisms projected back from the present. As Michael Silverstein puts it, we "must avoid equations of contemporary sociopolitical groups, communicative economies, and languages (well defined denotational codes) and project these back indefinitely as a timeless and unchanging cultural configuration" (Silverstein 1997:130). In addition Silverstein cautions, we should not assume the existence of "stable, language-bounded, one-language cultural units" rather, we should shift our attention to the study of "speech communities," organizations of communicating peoples "by regularities of language-in-use" (Silverstein 1997:126,7; on speech community, see also Gumperz 1972). To address the challenges facing the study of voice in terms of aboriginal vocal origin, I propose to build upon Douglas R. Parks and Raymond J. DeMallie's goal of exploring Native voice in the "fullest possible historical and cultural context" by including along with representations of speech "the careful evaluation" of historical role, a consideration that requires an analysis of participation in political-economic history (Parks and DeMallie 1992a; White 1983, 2011).

As it happens, while fur trade records are short on Native language documents per se, they are rich in descriptions of communicative practice made in varieties that were integral to the contact speech communities, descriptions of verbal acts in which fur trade roles were being delegated or contested. While not utilizing the semantico-referential codes of aboriginal languages, such descriptions are composed in varieties that were at least partially reflective of the speech communities they purport to describe. They can be indexically rich in the sense that the linguistic descriptions are contiguous with descriptions of what was at issue politically and economically, and so can be triangulated with other descriptions and indexes of the time.

VOICE AND HISTORICAL ROLE

Before exploring a documentary representation of a verbal negotiation of political-economic role, I first proffer a relationship between "voice" and "historical role," concepts not often linked due to the distance between the fields in which they reside. "Voice" can be used to address two different aspects of a unitary phenomenon. In regard to music or speech it can be used to represent the sound quality, sound patterns, or acoustics of a particular performance. On the other hand, it can also be used to foreground the signaling of relations among participants, as in, say, the way a singer indexes in their vocal tone and manner their solidarity to audience and nation in the performance of a national anthem. Due perhaps to the extensive written record, Native American text analysis has emphasized the poetics of sound-patterning over the signaling of relations among participants (Hymes 1981; Tedlock 1983; Webster 2009; on this point see Parks and DeMallie 1992a:131).

More or less at the same time that "voice" arose as a subject in Native American studies, it was drawing interest among social scientists more generally. Social scientific research on voice, writes Webb Keane, "directs attention to the diverse processes through which social identities are represented, performed, transformed, evaluated, and contested" (Keane 1999:271). For the literary critic Gerard Genette (1979), the concept of voice is used to explore the mutual fashioning of persons (authors, characters, and so forth) internal and external to the text. The *social* approach to "voice" centers on the intricacies of the semiotic management of "who is speaking," the dynamics of participants' alignments, sets, stances, postures, or projected selves (Genette 1979; Goffman 1981:128; Keane 1999).

Key to clarifying the structural underpinnings of the dynamics of social alignment is Erving Goffman's study, "Footing" (1981:124–59). In it Goffman challenges the dyadic speaker-hearer model of communication. Observing that the presence of unratified "adventitious" participants "should be considered the rule, not the exception" (Goffman 1981:132), and that three or more ratified participants are common (133), he suggests the study of participation within communicative process should attend to the relations among speaker, addressed recipients, and unaddressed recipients.

Goffman also shows that interlocutors regularly attend to at least three communicative roles associated with speaking. For any message we can differentiate between the animator, the party who activates the message in space and time; the author, the party who composes the message; and the principal, the party on whose behalf the message is delivered (Goffman 1981:144). This represents the minimal set of social factors we must take account of when analyzing speech production (145). Paraphrasing Keane in a way that highlights his grounding in the emerging field of metapragmatics, we can generalize the insights of Goffman and Genette by saying that the social scientific study of "voice" is the study of the metacommunicative representation of the co-articulation of social personae via discourse (Keane 1999:271; Silverstein 1993).

While I am not aware of a mature analytic literature on historical role parallel to that on voice, the insights of political-economic anthropology and history are seminal. Such works as Eric Wolf's *Europe and the Peoples without History* (1982), Arthur J. Ray's *Indians in the Fur Trade* (2005[1974]), and Richard White's *Roots of Dependency* (1983) showed that changes in economic role were primary factors in the reconfiguration of aboriginal and European societies, resulting in the emergence of new peoples in many cases. Such political-economic studies were rightly criticized for failing to adequately show "how local peoples attempt to organize" their experiences "in their own cultural terms" (Sahlins 2000:416), thereby reducing their historical role to their economic role, but they nevertheless foreshadowed the emergence of a new range of inquiries. While relying primarily on a modes of production approach, as Marshall Sahlins charges, and secondarily on such overarching economic categories as the fur trade, slave trade, and the Industrial Revolution, Wolf, for example, nevertheless broke new ground by emphasizing the economic not for its own sake but for the purpose of trying to "understand more precisely how cultural forms work to mediate social relationships among particular populations" (Wolf 1982:19). And, White innovated by shifting his attention from radical discontinuities determined by European ascendency to the ambivalencies of the history of intercultural accommodation and realignment (White 1983, 2011). As White (2011:xxvi) observes, such accommodation, if not the rule in Native American history, nevertheless took place "for long periods of time in large parts of the colonial world."[2] While White emphasized the idea that a special environment, a "middle ground," "a place in between: in between cultures, peoples, and in between empires and the non-state world of villages," arose and eventually declined in the Great Lakes region the French called the Pays d'en Haut (2011:xxvi), the book has broader implications. This is especially apparent in White's reframing of the way peoples adjust their differences in history from political-economic determinism to the communicative negotiation of historical role:

"On the middle ground diverse peoples adjust their differences through what amounts to a process of creative, and often expedient, misunderstandings. People try to persuade others who are different from themselves by appealing to what they perceive to be the values and practices of those others. They often misinterpret and distort both the values and the practices of those they deal with, but from these misunderstandings arise new meanings and through them new practices—the shared meanings and practices of the middle ground" (xxvi).

In this wonderful passage, White links historical participation to "a process of creative, and often expedient understandings."

Just as White is reconceptualizing his long-standing interest in political-economic participation in more symbolic or more communicative terms, contemporary linguistic anthropology is attempting to reintegrate a concern with the material asymmetries underpinning social life with the study of linguistic varieties. Once we consider the similarities of purpose, it is perhaps not too surprising to sense resonances between political-economic history and the social science of communication. Compare, for example, the passage from White above with Asif Agha's (2007:165) recent reconceptualization of communicative practice in terms of material differences:

"differential register use is indexically linked during interaction to ongoing activity frames and identities maintained through that use. Since individuals differ in their register range, they differ in their ability to inhabit distinct register-mediated **social personae** in encounters with others, or to perform different **voices** (Bakhtin 1984) or characterological **figures** . . . as features of self through acts of performance. Interlocutors respond to such personae, voices or figures in ways that depend on their own register range." Both emphasize the reciprocal, reflexive character of action and reaction set within historical parameters. Interlocutors respond to such personae, voices, or figures in ways that depend on their own political-economic circumstances, their own register range, and their perceptions of the political-economic circumstances and register ranges of their interlocutors. The work of Wolf and White points to the need to address communicative dynamics in political-economic transformation, and recent work in linguistic anthropology points to the need to better contextualize communication within political-economic circumstances. Conceptualized as a dynamic interface of material and social asymmetries, "voice" might provide an especially productive window upon the processes through which historical role is configured.

NEGOTIATING HISTORICAL ROLE(S) IN THE FUR TRADE

The Fort Chilcotin post journal of the winter of 1838–39 (the fourth season since the post was fully activated) contains a description of an interesting dispute centering on the respective roles of the Tsilhqut'in and the HBC. The post journal indicates that numerous Tsilhqut'in men were trapping beaver and other fur-bearers and trading regularly. As described by the postmaster and journal keeper William McBean, a situation arose on December 23, 1838, when Chief Allaw came to the post not to offer furs for trade but to visit with McBean in his office. McBean refused to see Allaw and offered no tobacco or any other gift and the chief departed angrily.

The next day Allaw sent word that he "had forbidden all the Indians to hunt" and that he looked forward to them departing from his lands so he and his fellows "might have the pleasure of burning the fort." The chief elaborated that his people were not free to smoke when they wished, that the fort was destitute of goods, and that pricing was unfair. McBean sent word back that while they were free to hunt or not, he was master of his goods and would not vacate until instructed to do so by his superior, a man so eminent that Allaw was not worthy to carry his shoes.

Two days later, on Christmas Day 1838, McBean observed that a Tsilhqut'in passerby named John warned the HBC men to be on their guard due to the possibility that Indians from Long Lake might exact retribution for an unexplained death. The fort became unnaturally quiet and McBean began to suspect that Allaw and his band, and perhaps also the party from Long Lake, were planning an attack. The following day, on December 26, McBean wrote that Chief Allaw returned to the fort asking whether he was welcome. Temporarily relieved, McBean explained that he was. He reported that Chief Allaw concluded the interaction by warning them to stay on guard against the bereaved Long Lake Indians, who were expected imminently.

Several days passed uneventfully. Then Allaw returned. At this point I quote directly from the January 2, 1839, entry:

Wednesday 2nd Snowing all day. Men employed cutting firewood and hauling it home &c.

Four Indians came to the Fort at the time Grant & Liar[d] were in the wood and that I was alone with Bte. These were Allaw (Chief), his first Cousin Sâpâh, and two Brothers of the deceased, these two's Looks and Motions forbade nothing good. I will remark first that last fall when I gave the Chief his present he delivered a large Beaver Skin (which is all I have received from him Since) telling me at the time that he would ask for his payment at a more convenient opportunity. I pressed him to take it at once and I intended to send my Beaver Skin with the rest of my Furs to Alexandria very soon_ and that he would not get more than one Made Beaver by leaving it longer. He answered that I might send it and did not expect more than the usual price_ to day he came along with the 3 others above mentioned and demanded his payment saying he wanted Balls and tobacco. I ordered Bte. to give him 5 balls as a/c [?] for Skin & 9 In: Tobo. for the other, and 3 In: gratis to smoke his pipe_ this he sent me back & said it was too little_. I went to him in the Interpreter's House and measured the Tobo. before him and counted the 5 Balls which I told him was his due and he would not take it_ You sell your Goods dear, well I shall make my own price for my Beavers_ If you had not sent it I would have taken it out of the Store for which the Atnah [?] would have given me a Lg. Blkt. but since you

have not got it here_ you will give me 5 Cats in the place of it_ I burst
out laughing and told him he must be joking; but I soon perceived
he was in earnest_ and insisted upon having them seconded by the
3 others_ Seeing this, I positively told him that I would not_, that I was
no Child to give 5 Beaver for one neither his slave to force me to give
my property away_ immediately they showed signs of a premeditated
attack and I put myself on defence [*sic*] and laid hold of my pistols_ Bte
did the same_ At this critical moment I heard Grant & Liar[d] come
into the Fort_ I immediately called out to them to Bar the Ft. Doors
and to come in with their arms_ here they became as mild as they had
been bold and the Chief requested to give him what I had previously
offered him_ 5 balls & 12 In: Tobacco_ took the balls with him but
left the Tobacco to the charge of Bte which he said he would show to
M. Ogden and that if he gave him no more he should tell him they did
not want his Trade and with this they scampered off_ glad no doubt to
get out of our arms reach.

 It is very evident these fellows wish for our blood and it may be seen
what a Scamp is that Allaw.

What was at issue for Allaw was clearly the role of the Tsilhqut'in within
the Columbia District of the fur trade. From the HBC's standpoint, the
Tsilhqut'in were not middlemen but rather primary suppliers of furs, as
Turkel (2007:155) observes. In the wake of the 1821 merger with the Northwest Company, Governor George Simpson reorganized the HBC's practices
to more effectively manage the trade west of the Rockies. With the merger
the HBC achieved a monopoly in the interior and the hope was that by
maximizing efficiency there it could maintain the core zone of the profitable
trade against the Russians to the north, and the Americans to the south and
along the coast. Along with building new posts, opening new routes, cutting
employees, tightening discipline, and reducing wages, Simpson also attempted to "standardize" fur prices (Gibson 1985:15). What John S. Galbraith
(1957:156) observed of the coastal trade after 1839, applied well to the interior
after 1821, namely, that the HBC proceeded "to alter the price structure of the
fur trade . . . to accustom the Indians to more modest returns for their furs."
What concerned Allaw was that HBC postmaster McBean seemed to believe
in 1828 that he (McBean) had the authority to exact Tsilhqut'in furs essentially as tribute, requiring that trappers take whatever value the HBC set.
Chief Allaw, conversely, sought to make the point that the Tsilhqut'in should
be recognized as free traders, or capitalists, to paraphrase Allaw, and should
be allowed to set their own price for their beavers, just as the HBC set its own
price for its goods (on tribute versus capitalistic modes of production, see
Wolf 1982:72–100).[3] Allaw perceived accurately that the HBC was attempting
to turn back the economic clock, and he registered his disapproval.

In terms of evidence, the episode represents not an analyst's inferences from cumulative economic data, nor a simple confrontation, nor or a single reported utterance, but an unfolding interactional text of actions and counteractions taken in regard to economic roles. The interactional text of actions and counteractions can be analyzed in terms of twelve action-responses:

1a. Chief Allaw sought to visit with Postmaster McBean in his room.
1b. McBean refused to meet Allaw and offered no tobacco or any other gift.

2a. The chief departed angrily and sent word the next day that he "had forbidden all the Indians to hunt," thereby showing that the hunters felt no obligation to the HBC to hunt without fair compensation. So as to underscore his disinterest in tribute-based fur harvest, Allaw further stated that he looked forward to McBean and his men departing from his (Allaw's) lands so he and his fellows "might have the pleasure of burning the fort." The chief elaborated that his people were not free to smoke when they wished, that the fort was destitute of goods, and that pricing was unfair.
2b. McBean replied that while they were free to hunt or not, he was master of his goods and would not vacate until instructed to do so by his superior, a man so eminent that Allaw is not worthy to carry his shoes!

3a. Tsilhqut'in trappers avoided the fort, sending the message that they were displeased with the HBC.
3b. McBean began to suspect that Allaw and company were planning an attack on the fort, perhaps in conjunction, in some way, with a party from Long Lake. On Christmas Day 1838, McBean wrote that a Tsilhqut'in passerby warned the HBC men to be on their guard due to the possibility that Indians from Long Lake might exact retribution for an unexplained death.

4a. Chief Allaw returned to the fort asking whether he was welcome.
4b. McBean welcomed him back.

5a. Chief Allaw concluded the interaction, to that point a civil one, by warning the HBC men to stay on guard against the bereaved Long Lake Indians, who were expected imminently.
5b. McBean indicated in his journal that he was aware that Allaw was raising a new threat in his description of Allaw's message.

6a. On January 2, 1839, Chief Allaw returned and demanded his payment for a large beaver skin deposited the previous fall, saying he wanted balls and tobacco (though McBean had insisted that he would receive no more in value by leaving it longer, Allaw had refused his payment in the fall).

6b. McBean responded by ordering his interpreter Baptiste Boucher to give Allaw a little more than he had promised in the fall.

7a. Allaw sent word from the Interpreter's House that McBean offered too little.

7b. McBean met Allaw in the Interpreter's House and measured the tobacco before him and counted the five balls which were his due.

8a. Allaw again refused McBean's payment, indicating that he would set his own price.

8b. —

9a. Allaw requested that McBean return the value by providing him with "5 Cats" in its place (since McBean was no longer in possession of the original large beaver, and since he could have traded the large beaver with an Atnah for a large blanket).

9b. McBean refused this proposition.

10a. Chief Allaw and company threatened to attack.

10b. McBean and Boucher prepared to defend themselves by laying hold of their pistols. McBean called out to others for assistance.

11a. The chief changed strategy and requested the payment he had previously refused.

11b. McBean complied.

12a. Chief Allaw accepted the balls but left the tobacco to the charge of Boucher. He threatened to show them to the district head to seek his opinion on whether McBean was acting in HBC interests.

12b. McBean writes in the journal that Allaw is a "scamp."

The Oblate scholar of early British Columbia, Father Adrian-Gabriel Morice, well described the formal institution whereby the HBC appointed or recognized chiefs. The company recognized chiefs to serve as "the spokesmen of the traders to the village folk, and help the Company in securing the departure of the hunters for their usual expeditions, and smooth over any difficulty that might arise between whites and reds." In return, as Morice (1978[1906]:199) puts it, "they received certain gratuities, mostly in the line of wearing apparel."

Allaw initially tries to visit McBean in his office. When McBean refuses to see him, and even refuses "certain gratuities," Allaw reads this as an indication that McBean fails to appreciate the HBC's dependence on the entrepreneurial initiative of the Tsilhqut'in trappers. Allaw therefore forbids all the Indians to hunt to underscore the point. Continuing, Allaw states that he looks forward to the HBC departing from Fort Chilcotin, since they do not permit Tsilhqut'in to smoke when they want, they are often destitute of goods, and they pay low prices for beaver and then sell their goods at a premium. In other words, Allaw is observing that the HBC fails to treat Tsilhqut'in people like individuals, they inhibit commerce when they fail to offer goods, and they persist in framing the trade in terms of tribute rather than supply and demand.

McBean senses that the terms of commerce are at issue, replying that there was no compulsion in the trade, that the chief is at "liberty" to do as he pleases. He attempts to turn the tables on Allaw and to suggest that it is the Tsilhqut'in who through their "menaces" compromise the terms of free and open commerce, mentioning the "Instructions" of the "Chief" of an enterprise different—and qualitatively more modern—than the one Allaw serves.[4] When Allaw requests of the Tsilhqut'in trappers that they cease trading at Fort Chilcotin, which they do, he shows that McBean is incompetent in failing to understand the supply and demand basis of HBC business.

In action-response pairs 6–12, Allaw enters into a tricky negotiation of payment for furs intended to show McBean that he will not acquiesce to the tribute model of exchange. He *will* set his own price. When McBean negotiates him into near compliance, Allaw name-drops, threatening to appeal McBean's rigidity to M. Ogden, the head of the New Caledonia district, a man Morice (1978[1906]:206) characterized as "the great magnate and first representative of authority within New Caledonia."

The twelve communicative actions can be looked at as a series of linguistic invocations of role-dyads, or as a six part unfolding interactional structure of voicings, culminating in Chief Allaw establishing himself as a little-capitalist, or relatively free trader compared to the postmaster (Goffman 1961; Linton 1936; Silverstein 2003):

1a. Chief : Postmaster
1b. Postmaster : Peon
_____   **I. Chief status rejected**
2a. Not Peons : Illegitimate Traders
2b. Trader : Peon
3a. Not Peons : Illegitimate Traders
3b. Postmaster : Savage
_____   **II. Trader status questioned**
4a. Peon/Chief : Postmaster

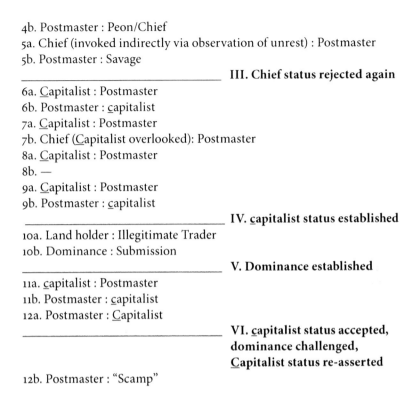

4b. Postmaster : Peon/Chief
5a. Chief (invoked indirectly via observation of unrest) : Postmaster
5b. Postmaster : Savage
_____   **III. Chief status rejected again**
6a. Capitalist : Postmaster
6b. Postmaster : capitalist
7a. Capitalist : Postmaster
7b. Chief (Capitalist overlooked): Postmaster
8a. Capitalist : Postmaster
8b. —
9a. Capitalist : Postmaster
9b. Postmaster : capitalist
_____   **IV. capitalist status established**
10a. Land holder : Illegitimate Trader
10b. Dominance : Submission
_____   **V. Dominance established**
11a. capitalist : Postmaster
11b. Postmaster : capitalist
12a. Postmaster : Capitalist
_____   **VI. capitalist status accepted,**
                                     dominance challenged,
                                     Capitalist status re-asserted
12b. Postmaster : "Scamp"

This extended interactional structure allows us to enter into the experience of the negotiation of the political-economic transformation of the moment. What we see from the interactional sequence as a whole, however, is not a "middle ground" between European and Native American traditions, not a syncretic "composite of traits defined by their supposed origins," but rather an unfolding negotiation of respective roles and standings (Hanks 2010:xvii, 8). The negotiation runs counter to expectations in that Allaw, the aboriginal chief, is determined to enable the Tsilhqut'in hunters the perquisite of being treated as free traders, or capitalists. The European corporate man, Postmaster McBean, on the other hand, is determined to maintain—even upon the threat of death—the incremental trading advantage of quasi-feudal peonage. In the end, McBean survives, but Allaw gets the last word, in this interchange at least.

Given that the coastal trade long involved competition between traders and nationalities, and that prior to 1821 the interior fur trade involved competition, Allaw's sensitivity to the difference between peonage and free trade is perhaps not surprising, but it is still interesting. He was unquestionably attuned to the modern political-economic environment of the day and he well understood its constraints and opportunities. By using the role descriptor "capitalist" I do not mean to suggest, however, that by his actions that he intended to forfeit his role as an aboriginal chief. I mean only to highlight the clarity of his insight into the economic role options.

The Allaw-McBean communicative interchange provides a window upon a situation that defies expectations. It allows us to map out "the voicing structure of a social universe," the universe of negotiating fur-harvesting in the Columbia District. And it "reveals how identities and interests come together at different institutional sites of social interaction around various issues, in plot-like conditions of potential transformation" (Silverstein 1999:3–4).

CONCLUSION

In *The Middle Ground,* White (2011:xxvi) points to the relationship between historical role and voice when he reframes political-economic history as a study of how "diverse peoples adjust their differences through what amounts to a process of creative, and often expedient, misunderstandings," peoples trying "to persuade others who are different from themselves by appealing to what they perceive to be the values and practices of those others" and in the process fashioning new meanings and new fields of interaction. While if we look carefully, we can see an openness to such an approach even in Wolf (1982:19), too, the fact remains that White and Wolf fail to sustain attention on the communicative practices that we would have to examine in order to begin to approach "a process of creative and often expedient, misunderstandings." Parks and DeMallie observe that although:

"American Indian native language texts have received increasing scholarly attention in recent years, most studies have been of mythology and folklore and have focused on the structure and style of oral literature. Following the lead of Dell Hymes and Dennis Tedlock, many scholars have sought to discover the narrative structure of native language texts. Important as their work is, it does not exhaust the possibilities" (Parks and DeMallie 1992a:131).

In this text I attempt to follow their lead and use ethnohistorical methods to enrich our understanding of aboriginal-fur trader communication. While, obviously, HBC records and other such documents lack systematic depiction of Native languages, and are limited in that respect, they are nevertheless indicative of aspects of the contact speech community and are rich in the kinds of contextual information that help us appreciate the fashioning of historical role via communication. And thus while limited in certain respects, these historical records present opportunities in others. Parks and DeMallie draw attention to the ethnohistorical potential of a heretofore underutilized source, Native language texts, and they certainly do not oppose the use of others. I differ from Parks and DeMallie only in suggesting we include alongside Native language documents primary historical documents depicting the communicative interchanges that bear on the configuration of historical role.

An impulse in Latin American historiography parallel to DeMallie and Parks' emphasis on Native language documents goes by the name of The New Philology (for an overview of this developing approach see Restall 2003b). Indubitably valuable for directing attention to the rich record of Native language documents, this approach prioritizes Native language documents relative to all others somewhat more emphatically than DeMallie and Parks. Given the growing interest in Native perspectives at the heart of these two approaches, it is especially important to recognize that Native language documents are not the only primary documents that bear on matters of voice. Moreover, an overreliance on linguistic code identity might well lead to the exclusion of materials essential to an appreciation of the material bases of voice.

At issue in a great deal of Native American history is the verbal negotiation of historical role. This includes but is not limited to economic role. Though it can be accompanied by force, or threat of force, a verbal component is typically integral to such negotiation, and in the verbal component a good deal of the action centers on, as Keane (1999:271) presents the problem, who is speaking, and on whose authority he or she is speaking. And as Michael Silverstein (1999:4) has long demonstrated, political economic roles, no less than communicative ones, are worked out in "plot-like conditions of potential transformation." In the particular case of interest here, the interchange between Chief Allaw and Mr. William McBean, developing this perspective enables us to move beyond the question of whether the Tsilhqut'in were opting in or out of the fur trade. I believe the evidence from the Fort Chilcotin Post Journal shows that the Tsilhqut'in participated in the fur trade, as Turkel argued, and were acting in terms of their priorities as Fisher argued. However, I do not think it is adequate to say that they were "acting in terms of the priorities of their own culture," as Fisher put it, because this characterization fails to describe their insightful analysis of the political-economic moment (Fisher 1977:xi). Allaw innovated in the way he analyzed the situation and in the way he encouraged his fellow Tsilhqut'in and the HBC to consider a new set of priorities, a new understanding of the situation.

ACKNOWLEDGMENTS

I hereby register my deep appreciation for the intellectual generosity of Raymond J. DeMallie. I also must acknowledge my gratitude to Douglas R. Parks and Sebastian Braun. Financial support for the research upon which this study was done came from the Research Allocations Committee of the University of New Mexico, the Melville and Elizabeth Jacobs Fund of the University of Washington and the Whatcom Museum, and the American Philosophical Society. I am grateful for access to the Hudson's Bay Company Archives, a division of the Archives of Manitoba, which house the documents of central concern in this chapter, and grateful for permission to reproduce passages from the Fort Chilcotin post journal.

NOTES

1. In passing in his superb study, Turkel (2007:146) claims that the "story of the Tsilhqut'in during the fur trade should be seen as a failed bid on the part of the HBC to change the **spatial ecology** of the region." While this connects his eminently historical and cultural work to the traditional concerns of environmental history, one frame of the study, it underplays, I believe, the contemporaneous character of Tsilhqut'in actions in this episode.

2. As key figures in political-economic history, I cite the works of Wolf, White, and Ray in order to bridge political-economic and linguistic anthropological approaches. A more recent study especially notable for centering analysis on what I am calling "historical role" is Gerhard J. Ens, *Homeland to Hinterland: The Changing Worlds of the Red River Metis in the Nineteenth Century* (1996). For example, Ens (1996:4) marshals evidence to show that nineteenth-century Metis identity "was not defined by biology, blood, or religion, but rather by the economic and social niche they carved out for themselves within the fur trade."

3. On the basis of rich evidence regarding Native trading acumen, James R. Gibson (1992:119) offers a pithy encapsulation:
"As traders the Natives proved not only as keen as the Euroamericans but also just as shrewd and just as sensitive to supply and demand, as well as equally vulnerable to fashion. A picture of artless and gullible indigenes being duped by white carpetbaggers could scarcely be farther from the truth. And this fact was recognized early by the whites themselves."

4. In different ways, John The Baptist's evaluation of Jesus as being spiritually so much higher that he is not worthy of handling his shoes is depicted in each of the four Gospels (Matthew 3:11, Mark 1:7, Luke 3:16, John 1:27).

6

The Contemporary Significance of Native Language Texts

Arthur John, Sr.'s Account of John Martin and the Kaska Stick Gamblers

PATRICK MOORE

Among scholars working with American Indians, Raymond J. DeMallie is well known for emphasizing the unique value of indigenous materials for cultural and ethnohistorical studies and for encouraging his students to gain a degree of fluency in American Indian languages to facilitate their linguistic, cultural, and ethnohistorical research. He has argued that materials written by Lakota Sioux and other North American Indians constitute a different understanding of their past than that provided by the records of Euro-Americans, saying, "in a fundamental sense they represent conflicting realities, rooted in radically different epistemologies. The challenge of ethnohistory is to bring these two types of historical data together to construct a fuller picture of the past" (DeMallie 1982:5). DeMallie's work has built on earlier Boasian descriptions of American Indian languages and cultures, in which texts served to exemplify indigenous genres of oral performance as well as cultural beliefs and practices (see, for example, Goddard 1904; Boas 1912; Lowie 1912; Sapir and Hoijer 1942), as well as more recent studies that have explored the poetic structure of performances and their significance as ethnohistorical evidence (e.g., Jacobs 1959; Hymes 1981; Harkin 1997; Tedlock 1999). This chapter complements these approaches to the analysis of American Indian narrative texts by examining the significance of a Kaska narrative told by Ross River elder Arthur John, Sr., for local audiences. His story about Gwich'in Anglican minister John Martin is particularly appealing to Kaska audiences because of the symbolic importance of stick gambling for contemporary indigenous identity in the Yukon and because of their appreciation of John's sophisticated use of Kaska. Just as indigenous histories are often rooted in different epistemologies, so too are the indigenous responses to ethnohistorical accounts based on a different set of experiences, values, beliefs, and linguistic aesthetics.

One indication of the contemporary importance of narratives is the extent to which they are known by members of the local communities where they are told. It is appropriate, then, that I first heard about one of the key events in John's account of Martin in 1987, more than seven years before hearing the story itself. One evening, while attending a community stick gambling competition in Ross River, Testloa Smith, one of the younger community leaders, mentioned that a missionary had once tried to discourage people from drumming by burning their drums. Later, in 1993, while listening to John at a Kaska language workshop held in Ross River, I realized that the missionary who had burned people's drums was the Gwich'in Anglican minister John Martin, who was stationed in Ross River from 1929 to 1935, and that the story was widely known among the Native adults in this small community of four hundred people. John's complete two-part narrative about Martin is presented at the end of this chapter.

Arthur John, Sr., is of Northern Tutchone and white ancestry and is a member of the *Mésgá* (Raven) moiety, which is locally referred to in English as the Crow Clan.[1] He was born around 1910 and he is the senior member of the *Mésgá* moiety in Ross River, Yukon. His father, Bob Hobin, joined the Canadian Army in World War I and never returned to the Yukon. When John was a still a young boy, his mother died, and he was subsequently raised by his stepfather, Long Haired John, and by his mother's mother, Chuɤtsayme ('Loon Woman' in Northern Tutchone). He worked as a hunter, trapper, woodcutter, highway worker, prospector, band councilor, and during World War II as a guide for the U.S. Army surveying the route of the Canol Highway and Pipeline. John is fluent in Northern Tutchone and Kaska as well as English and is respected as an authority on Kaska and Northern Tutchone history and cultural practices.

John Martin, whose activities are the subject of John's account, was renowned for his skills as a hunter and guide. As a young man he led a record number of the arduous mid-winter patrols between his home in Peel River Fort (later called Fort McPherson), Northwest Territories, and Dawson City, Yukon. Like many Gwich'ins, Martin's family had been recruited to the Anglican faith by Archdeacon Robert McDonald (Moore 2007:27–53). In his youth Martin became literate in Gwich'in and gained a fundamental understanding of Christian doctrine while attending church services and classes offered by Archdeacon McDonald and Gwich'in ministers and teachers at Peel River Fort. In 1929, he was recruited by Bishop Stringer to be the first resident minister in Ross River. John's story describes aspects of Yukon First Nations relations in the early 1900s and of Martin that are not found in either the written records of the Anglican Church or the written historical accounts of the period. John alleges that Gwich'in continued to raid the Kaska and Northern Tutchone areas well into the early 1900s, and that when Martin came to Ross River, he was on a revenge mission for the death of his grandfather that occurred on one of these raids.

Although I do not attempt to evaluate John's claims about Martin in this chapter, as these will be treated in a future article, I focus on two main aspects of the story with wider significance: the symbolic importance of stick gambling for indigenous identity among members of Yukon First Nations and the emblematic narrative use of terminology relating to lived experience and place, including deictic expressions. Martin appears below as he was photographed in the Ross River area in the 1930s by amateur photographer and Royal North West Mounted Police corporal Claude Tidd. In the first photograph, Martin is dressed for Sunday church services in Ross River and in the second he is eating moose meat beside a campfire (Figure 6.1).

THE IMMEDIATE CONTEXT OF THE PERFORMANCE

The audience for John's story was a small group of Kaska-speaking elders and language teachers who were gathered at the Ross River School for a language workshop that I organized in 1993. I lived in Ross River from 1985 to 1992, and the workshop, the first held after I left the community, was one in a series of gatherings over several years held to promote the Kaska language and to develop teaching materials. The audience was clearly familiar with John's story about Martin because several people asked him to "tell the story about John Martin." The narrative was recorded in two parts because John ended the first part of the story when a group of grade one students arrived for their scheduled class, prompting him to change to topics more appropriate for their interests and fluency. When the students left, Kaska elder Charlie Dick said, "He still never tell the story yet," at which point John completed his story with an account of how one evening Martin heard a group of Kaska men stick gambling on the hill beside the old Ross River townsite, snuck up to the gamblers, grabbed their drums, and threw them into the fire.

The audience clearly enjoyed hearing the story even though they had all heard it before, in part because of the dramatic conflict between Martin and the Kaskas, in part because John's descriptions resonated with their shared life experiences, and in part because they appreciated his masterful use of the language. In important ways, John's performance was a coproduction with his well-informed audience (Jacoby and Ochs 1995) because their common experiences and knowledge of the story, as well as their fluency in Kaska, were essential for his telling. In telling the story, he addressed Kaska elders Amos Dick and Charlie Dick, who were especially knowledgeable about the story and the area north of Ross River where the story takes place. While Amos Dick and Charlie Dick were both recognized elders, they were sufficiently younger than John that he took on the role of elder teacher in recounting events that occurred before their time.

Fig. 6.1. (Top) John Martin, Ross River, Yukon, ca. 1930. Yukon Archives, Claude and Mary Tidd Fonds, #7387. (Bottom) John Martin (right), near Ross River, Yukon, ca. 1930. Yukon Archives, Anglican Church, Diocese of Yukon (86/61, no. 42).

YUKON LAND CLAIMS AND CULTURAL REVITALIZATION

The symbolic importance of stick gambling, and its depiction in John's story, stems from cultural revitalization processes that were set in motion by indigenous activism concurrent with the Yukon Indian land claim. The Yukon land claim arose from a period of indigenous–government contention in the late 1960s that followed developments such as the Civil Rights movement in the United States and the Quebec Sovereignty movement in Canada. In 1968, in an effort to achieve broader recognition of their rights and reverse decades of social and economic marginalization in Yukon society, Yukon Native leaders founded the Yukon Native Brotherhood, and soon after indigenous organizations, including the Union of British Columbia Indian Chiefs (1969) and the Indian Brotherhood of the Northwest Territories (1970) were formed in neighboring regions. One key event that sparked indigenous political activism in Canada was the "White Paper" policy statement of the federal government in 1969 that proposed terminating indigenous rights. Native political leaders responded with their own document, *Citizens Plus,* which became known as the "Red Paper" (Indian Chiefs of Alberta 1970) and, in 1972, Native leaders in the Yukon and the Northwest Territories threatened to impose a moratorium on mining and oil and gas development. In 1973, a month after the Supreme Court of Canada recognized indigenous land rights in a split decision in the Calder case, the federal government agreed to negotiate with Yukon Native leaders. Elijah Smith, president of the Yukon Native Brotherhood, traveled to Ottawa with a group of Yukon Native political leaders to present Jean Chrétien, the minister of Indian Affairs, with a historic document titled *Together Today for Our Children Tomorrow* (Yukon Native Brotherhood 1973). John was a signatory to this document along with other band councilors, chiefs, and community delegates who met to establish the basic elements of the Yukon claim. John was also a close personal friend of Smith and they visited each other frequently. Although the Yukon land claim was formally initiated in 1973, the umbrella final agreement was not ratified by the Canadian government until 1993, and negotiations to finalize agreements with individual Yukon First Nations continued until 2004. By 2004, ten of fourteen Yukon First Nations had ratified land claims agreements; however, the two Kaska First Nations in the Yukon, the Ross River Dena Council and the Liard First Nation, ultimately rejected the land claims process, preferring to retain their lands and other indigenous rights.

The success of Yukon political leaders in asserting their political rights was paralleled by a sweeping cultural revitalization movement. Cultural practices such as storytelling, traditional subsistence activities, Native artwork, potlatches, and the use of Native languages blossomed during this period. Along with the development of Native political organizations, the land claims period saw the development of many still-prominent cultural institutions, including the Yukon Native Languages Project (later the Yukon Native Language Centre) (1977), CHON FM radio (1984), Northern Native Broadcasting Yukon (1985), the Yukon International Storytelling Festival (1988), and the Yukon Arts Centre (1992).

THE REVIVAL OF STICK GAMBLING

Stick gambling, also known as hand games, was one indigenous cultural practice that resurged during the period of political activism after the Yukon land claim was initiated. Stick gambling is a guessing game in which opposing teams of players attempt to win counter sticks by hiding an object in one hand in such a way that the captain of the opposing team (who uses hand signals to indicate the hand of the opposing players in which their token is hidden) is unable to guess its location. The Kaska version of this game is essentially the same as versions played in the Northwest Territories as described in June Helm and Nancy Lurie's 1966 study *The Dogrib Hand Game*. It is likely that the versions of the game in which two objects are hidden in the hands, one marked and one unmarked, were at one time played in much of the Yukon since they were documented for the Han in the Yukon, for Sekani and Carrier in northern British Columbia, and for Tlingit in southeast Alaska (Culin 1907:272–74, 287–88; Swanton 1908:444–45). In contemporary play, however, the version using a single hidden object is universal at Yukon stick gambling events.

Historically, the major stick gambling competitions occurred when people were gathered at trading posts in early summer or when groups of men visited other communities. In the land claims period, impromptu stick gambling competitions were held at events such as the Annual General Assembly of the Council for Yukon Indians (previously the Yukon Native Brotherhood and more recently the Council for Yukon First Nations) and the Ross River Cultural Exchanges. Since 1987, an annual Yukon Stick Gambling Championship with both youth and adult categories has been held each summer, rotating between host Yukon First Nations communities. First prize in the adult category has averaged $10,000 in recent years. Although all-male teams were the norm in the past, women now compete as well, and female teams have won several Yukon championships. The three-day Yukon Stick Gambling Championship attracts an average of thirty-two adult six-person teams and sixteen six-person youth teams as well as numerous family and community members. Recent competitions in the Northwest Territories have been even larger with even more substantial prizes. Stick gambling is one of the recognized indigenous sports of the Arctic Winter Games and tournaments are also held at the annual Sourdough Rendezvous in

Whitehorse and at other community events in the Yukon. The sport is the subject of blogs and YouTube videos that evoke the spirited competition (yukonfawn 2008; Nerdball3 2008; Meandering Michael 2009) and involvement of youth (yukonfawn 2009). In the Yukon, stick gambling has become a symbol of Native identity that continues to evolve and attract young participants who have introduced new songs, movements, outfits, and other innovative practices such as face painting.

As one of a group of Ross River elders who competed in widely attended stick gambling tournaments at the Council for Yukon Indians (CYI) general assemblies and the Ross River-Fort Norman (now called Tulita, NWT) cultural exchanges, Arthur John played a central role in the revival of stick gambling in the Yukon. He is pictured below in Ross River at the 1985 cultural exchange with Fort Norman (see Figure 6.2). Along with the Northern Tutchone community of Pelly Crossing, Ross River was one of the communities where many elders were still familiar with the game, and Kaskas played a leading role in reestablishing stick gambling in the Yukon.

Many younger Ross River stick gamblers learned how to play from John, Amos Dick, and other elders after weekly stick gambling evenings were organized in Ross River in 1986. John is pictured below teaching children how to drum at one such session in the Ross River Band Hall (see Figure 6.3). Two of the students who are watching him at this event, Dempsey Sterriah

Fig. 6.2. Arthur John, Sr., drumming at Fort Norman cultural exchange, Ross River, Yukon, 1985.

Fig. 6.3. Arthur John, Sr., drumming at Ross River, 1986.

(smiling broadly immediately to John's left) and Greg McLeod (whose face is visible in the bottom middle), went on to become members of the Ross River drummers and winners of the Yukon Stick Gambling Championship. Within Yukon stick gambling circles, Kaskas are well known for their skill and competitive spirit. Teams from the Kaska First Nations have won more of the Yukon championships than any other group and they often comprise as many as half of the teams. Stick gambling is such a ubiquitous part of contemporary Kaska culture that during any spare moment many Ross River students spontaneously drum their pencils to the double beat of stick gambling drumming.

Within the context of resurgent Native identity, and the symbolic importance of stick gambling for Native identity in the Yukon, Martin's attempt to eliminate the practice in the 1930s has become an epitomizing event. John was in his late teens or early twenties when he witnessed this event, one of the young stick gamblers whose drums were seized by Martin. He began the second part of his narrative with the dramatic confrontation between Martin, the Kaska stick gamblers, and Kaska elder Jack McKay:

John Martin tedze nā́ts'e'ā́,

"Hwe!

   Hwe!
      Hwe!"
John Martin sedetān ahdą̄sī gūyéh
gédā́detān.

Dâhch'ah dene tah łâyālī.
Drum,
all about five drum,
all nedílaī.
"Megā́nahtān," dī'.
Tses degedelaī́.
Tsíyedīlā t'é.
Old Jack come too,
Old Jack McKay.
I don't know yē kah dahyā sā́.

Megāts'enehtān *he burn 'em up.*

"Don't gamble no more.
Don't make drummin no more," dī.

Īt'é',
Old Jack łā́ denīzā́'.

"Why you do that? Kid they play

with that all the time.
All the time that's all the fun they
have.
Yē doge ent'īna?" yéhdī.

Īyéh,
kḗgedī t'éh łets'ī́' degenezā́'.

Jā̧ nedį̄

"Dédū nénen'ā́ t'é,
nénenā́ t'é',

John Martin [came to us while]
we were stick gambling at night.
"Hwe! [stick gambling singing to
drumming]
   Hwe!
      Hwe!"
John Martin woke up [from the
noise of the drums] and sneaked
towards us from up above.
Suddenly he came among us.
Drums,
all five drums,
he gathered all of them up.
"Look at them," he said.
He put more firewood on the fire.
Then he put them all in the fire.
Old Jack came there too,
Old Jack McKay.
I don't know why he happened to
come there.
We watched John Martin burn
the drums up.
"Don't gamble no more,
Don't make drummin no more,"
he [John Martin] said.

Then,
Old Jack McKay was really
angry.
"Why did you do that? The kids
play
with that all the time.
That's all the fun they have all
the time.
Why did you do that?" he said to
him.
Then,
they were mad at each other
about what they had said.
What could they do?

"Now, if you stick gamble
if you gamble,

nete'e dādāl lā" yéhdī.

Old Jack ts'į́',
John Martin.

Kolā ī *Jack,*
"Nenī k'ī ah'áné nekēyeh ts'į́'

nedinjá̃ t'é',
dūłą́ łéndendāl lā." yéhdī.
Kű́hyegé neden'íł lā." yéhdī.

you're a dead man." he [John
Martin] said to him,
to Old Jack [McKay].

Finally Jack [said],
"You too, if you go back toward
your
country,
then you won't come back.
You'll die there," he [Jack
McKay] said to him.

At the conclusion of their dispute, Martin and McKay exchanged death threats in the iconic manner of a "medicine fight" between two spiritually powerful men (Ridington 1968; Blondin 1990:131–34, 137–38, 172–76). John describes Martin's threat and McKay's subsequent death from a heart attack while stick gambling to support his contention that Martin was a dangerous medicine man. The medicine fight incident follows from John's description in the first part of the story of how Martin came to Ross River seeking revenge for the death of his grandfather at the hands of Ross River people. John seems to theorize that since Martin was unable to kill his grandfather's murderer by ambushing him in the bush, he resorted to using his medicine powers to get revenge.

When I discussed this narrative with John in 2002, his comments about how Martin had burned their drums led to more general reflections on the mistreatment of Native children, including his own, at the Indian residential schools in the period after World War II. He connected Martin's threats and his opposition to cultural practices such as stick gambling to the beatings and forced acculturation of the later residential mission schools. After World War II, John's children attended the newly built Catholic residential school at Lower Post, British Columbia, although later he was deeply troubled by the way they were treated there. As Lila Abu-Lughod (1990) has suggested, acts of resistance point to wider power relations in society. The pride Kaska take in their resistance to cultural assimilation through practices like stick gambling points to the dramatic power imbalances that have long prevailed between indigenous Yukoners and Euro-Canadians. The period between World War II and the initiation of land claims was a particularly sad one when Kaskas and other Yukon First Nations people were marginalized within society and their children were taken from them to attend residential mission schools.

LIVED EXPERIENCES ON THE LAND

John's account especially resonated with his Kaska audience because they shared many experiences of life on the land that are poetically expressed in his account, experiences that became especially salient during land claims debates. Other writers have noted the prominence of Yukon land-based narratives in the land claims period. Julie Cruikshank (1997) argued, for instance, that elders at the Yukon International Storytelling Festival in 1993 and 1994 were united in relating their performances to the land. Whether they chose to evoke histories of exchange between coastal Alaska and the interior of the Yukon; clan prerogatives over lands and resources; the personal emotions of their ancestors as they traveled Yukon rivers; or the tragic history of forced removals of Native people, Cruikshank says that they were prompted to share these traditions because of ongoing debates over land claims. Daniel Tlen and I (Moore and Tlen 2007) have argued that the former president of the Yukon Native Brotherhood, Elijah Smith, a close friend of Arthur John, recorded Southern Tutchone elders' accounts of land-based history for radio broadcast in 1984 because of his concerns about land claims negotiations, which were then at an impasse. In the land claims period of cultural revitalization indigenous practices, including the telling of traditional narratives, the use of Native languages, and stick gambling assumed tremendous symbolic importance.

Although it has often gone unrecognized, many indigenous Yukoners, including Arthur John and his entire Kaska audience, experienced long periods of removal from their homeland. The younger members of the audience at the Kaska language workshop, including Kaska language teachers Grady Sterriah and Josephine Acklack, left the community for many years to attend residential mission schools in Whitehorse and in Lower Post. The elders present at the workshop never attended residential schools, but after fur prices collapsed in the mid-1950s, out of economic necessity many of them relocated to other communities. Until the late 1960s, Arthur John, Amos Dick, Charlie Dick, and others lived in Upper Liard, Yukon, near the Alaska Highway, where they found periodic employment as woodcutters, guides, laborers, and prospectors to supplement their subsistence activities. Because these elders spent years away from their home community, John's accounts of travels and subsistence activities were doubly precious to them, triggering memories of the happy times spent on the land with their families.

By mentioning key locations, individuals, and modes of travel, John was able to evoke the social networks and subsistence activities of Kaskas in the Ross River area before the construction of the Canol Highway. He identifies the main families and their excited return to alpine hunting ranges by naming the owners of the fully loaded boats that they roped up the fast-flowing Ross River once the water levels fell in late summer. The members of his audience had undoubtedly camped beside the sloughs he mentions on the Ross River fifty and sixty miles upstream from its confluence with the Pelly River, where fish and moose were dependably plentiful.

John code-switches between English and Kaska which was a prestigious mode of speaking for successful men of his generation who worked with English speakers. Although he code-switches to English, John is completely fluent in Kaska and he makes effective use of the highly developed resources of the language in his narrative. As Michael Silverstein (1998) has pointed out, performances in times of social flux become sites where identities are negotiated in relation to intersecting cultural allegiances. In the wake of language shift to English and contentious political debates over land claims, uses of indigenous language become emblems of identity and also evidence of what is happening in the wider social matrix (Silverstein 1998:411). Linguistic anthropologists have drawn attention to a variety of similar contexts in which indigenous languages, grammatical structures, and modes of discourse have been used to project particular identities (Hill 1985; Basso 1996; Collins 1998; Silverstein 1998; Dinwoodie 1999, 2002; Ahlers 2006; Moore and Tlen 2007). John projected a prestigious bilingual identity by code-switching between English and Kaska, but his use of the Kaska language to orient his audience to narrative events and to evoke traditional life in the Kaska homeland was still particularly sophisticated.

KASKA DEICTIC DIRECTIONALS

While many well-known anthropological studies have examined the cultural significance of place names (e.g., Rosaldo 1988; Basso 1988, 1996; Cruikshank 1990a, 1990b, 2005), fewer have explored the uses of other terms relating to place and narrative accounts of place. In his account of John Martin, John makes particularly productive use of directionals, a specialized word class that is used in northern Athabaskan languages to indicate location and direction of movement (Moore and Tlen 2007; Leer 1989). Kaska directionals are deictic expressions that depend for their meaning on the relationship between a speaker and their audience. Deictic terms are of particular social importance because their use and interpretation depends on what William Hanks (2005:196) has summarized as "Background knowledge, memory and anticipation, and all that is part of the social setting."

Kaska directionals are based on different grammatical categories than English spatial terms, and John makes extensive use of these linguistic resources for social ends in his narrative. While, in the context of language shift, all uses of Kaska language signal indigenous identity, John's grammatical and narrative sophistication is particularly emblematic. In Kaska there are four primary sets of directional terms (see Table 6.1) differentiated by historical suffixes that indicate movement to a location (allative),

TABLE 6.1.   Kaska Directional Stems

	Allative	Ablative	Areal	Punctual
Gloss	going toward	coming from	circling	fixed location
'to the side'	'áné	'ą́dzīh	'ǫ́gí	'ą́dī, 'ą́t
'across'	náné	nádzīh	nógí	nádī, nát
'down'	tsá	tsį́dzīh	tsų́gí	tsį́dī
'ahead'	degé	dąsī	dōhhí	—
'upstream'		dasī	dōgí	
'uphill'				
'down'	yegé	yīdzīh	yōgí	—
'there'				
'back'	dá	dádzīh	dų́gí	dą́dī, dą́t
'downstream'				
'beside'	ná	nídzīh	—	—

TABLE 6.2.   Kaska Directional Prefixes

jah-, dah-, júh-	'nearby'	e.g., jahdegé	'a short distance ahead'
kúh-, gúh-	'distant'	e.g., kúhdegé	'far ahead'
	(exact location known by both speaker and addressee)		
de-	'distant'	e.g., dedegé	'far ahead'
	(exact location known by the speaker, but not the addressee)		
ah-	'distant'	e.g., ahdegé	'far ahead'
	(only general distant location is specified)		

movement from a location (ablative), circling, or indirect movement toward a location (the so-called areal directionals), and location at a fixed point (punctual directionals). The directional stems can be used as free forms or used with one of the prefixes listed below which indicate relative distance and the speaker's and audience's knowledge of locations.

Kaska directionals indicate more than simple location or direction of movement; the choice between classes of directional stems also serves to identify members of an in-group as opposed to outsiders, and to imply that the outsiders may have malicious intent. In the John Martin story, John tracks the group of characters that includes his younger self through his use of the allative directionals (in bold below).

In the passage below, events are pictured as viewed from Ross River, where John is telling the story. Key reference points marked by the directional prefix *kúh-* 'distant location known by both speaker and audience' include the white man's cabin (*kúhyegé* 'there') and the trail to Blue Hill (*kúhdegé* 'up ahead'). Having established these locations, he uses unprefixed forms when people propose crossing (*nắné* 'across') the river. The three uses of *degé* 'up ahead' imply three days of travel to Blue Hill (camping one night at the lake along the way). At the end of this passage, to indicate that their campsite on Blue Hill was chosen on the spot and was not at an established location that would be familiar to everyone, he uses *ah-* in *ahdegé* ('up ahead, uphill').

Kűhyegé ts'įh, "**Nắné,** **nắné** hés ts'į̀ ' téts'edūdélí," gedī'.	**From there,** "**Across,** let's go **across** to the mountain," they said.
Kűhyegé *cabin* t'ắt.	They put everything inside the cabin **there.**
Nắné bōt yéh déts'es'ēdlī', **kűhdegé** dene désdētl.	We landed the boats **across,** and people walked **up there** [to the mountains].
Etene tūgūts'edéhhétl **degé.**	They had marked the trail going **up there,**
dene datsé̀,	the people who had traveled there before,
Blue Hill.	to Blue Hill.
Ī men mekā etene tūgūgājān.	There is a lake that the trail passes beside.
Ī memā **dắ** etene tūgūts'edéhhédlī **degé.**	We even marked the trail **down** along its shore **on the way up.**
Łą̀ *straight* **degé** hés ts'į̀' téts'esdētl.	We went straight **up to** the mountain.
Ahdegé hés ts'es'įh shets'enéhtēts.	We went to sleep **up there** just before we got to the mountain.

The story has a filmic quality as John zooms in on the action as viewed from the camp of the Ross River hunters on Blue Hill by shifting to directionals with the prefixes *jah-* and *jűh-*, which indicate nearby locations. The shift of the deictic ground in the passage below enables the audience to visualize subsequent events from the point of view of the members of John's group camped on Blue Hill and to identify with their perspective on events. Keith Basso (1996:89) finds that Apache are similarly concerned with precisely visualizing events in their stories, saying, "Nothing is more basic to the telling of a Western Apache story than identifying the geographic locations at which events in the story unfold. For unless Apache listeners are able to picture a physical setting for narrated events—unless as one of my consultants said, 'your mind can travel to that place and really see it'—the events themselves will be difficult to imagine."

Tā́chą̄ *in the morning* Denechō̌,

hés **dą̄sī** yā kah ts'édāne nénah'aha?

"Jah'áné ejenūsyáí," dī'.

Oh yes, two nights shets'enehtēts
lî lā kų́hyegé.
Jahdegé ejegesdētl; *all nothing.*

The next morning why was
Jack Sterriah,
sending his children **down
from** his camp?

"I'm going hunting off this
way," he said.
We slept there two nights.

They all went hunting a short
ways up that way without
success.

In marked contrast to the way that the members of the Ross River group are depicted through the use of allative terms, Martin and his grandfather are cast as hostile outsiders through the repeated use of punctual and ablative directionals to describe their movements and locations. Through the use of these terms to the exclusion of the more common allative terms, John connects Martin's revenge mission to the earlier raid on which his grandfather was alleged to have been killed. Giving Martin and his grandfather an spatial positioning allows John to imply their dangerous intent without stating it directly. This pattern is established early in the story when Jack Sterriah quotes Martin's comments: *"Jahdádzīh gūts'į́' estsíe dede 'į́h lēgūht'ē"* ("It seems like my grandfather disappeared **coming from a short distance downstream**"). The quote evokes memories of the earlier Gwich'in raid by depicting events from the immediate spatial perspective of the Ross River group camped at Tenas Lake. The members of this group, which included John and Sterriah, would have viewed the raiders as coming from a short distance downstream. Sterriah's quote of what Martin said is repeated in a slightly different form when Sterriah advises people not to travel alone, *"De'ą́dzīh ts'į́' estsíe dede 'į́h lā, lēgūht'ē.' dī lā"* ("'It seems like my grandfather disappeared **coming from way off to the side**,' he [John Martin] said"). These events are viewed from John's perspective in Ross River, from which Tenas Lake is relatively distant and from which the Gwich'ins would be viewed as coming from the side (relative to the Yukon and Pelly River Valleys) in traveling from their country to intersect the trail from Ross River to Tenas Lake.

John draws a parallel between the way Martin stalks the members of the Ross River group as they hunted on Blue Mountain and the way Martin's grandfather and the other Gwich'in raiders came after the people camped at Tenas Lake nearly two decades earlier. Just as his grandfather is twice depicted through the use of the ablative directionals as coming toward the Ross River group, Martin is twice characterized as a silent stalker through the use of punctual directionals to pinpoint his fire. In this region, members of distant groups traditionally shot in the air to announce their approach and they responded to visitors by firing a welcome shot in the air or by shouting a greeting. Martin, like the Gwich'in raiders before him, did not observe these conventions, and quickly extinguished his fire when hailed. From his vantage point at a moose kill on the mountain, Sterriah, referring to Martin's fire says, *"Kón désk'án. Kónchō' désch'ele **nā́dī**"* ("There is a fire burning. There is a big fire burning brightly **across** [the valley]"). The second quote, which is attributed to the group as a whole, is also from their perspective on the mountain as they looked down and pondered who could have lit (and extinguished) the fire below. The members of John's group say, *"Mā et'ā **etsį́dī** kón dáhk'ána et'ā?"* ("Who could it be **down there** starting a fire?"). By identifying Martin only through the location of his fire, and never through the use of the allative directionals, John casts him as a loner waiting to ambush the hunters in revenge for his grandfather's death.

CONCLUSION

The context of the language workshop at which Arthur John told his story called for a performance that would be emblematic of indigenous identity and make sophisticated use of the Kaska language. Because of the symbolic importance of stick gambling for the revitalization of Native culture in the Yukon and because of their appreciation of his skills as a storyteller, John's audience urged him to tell the story about John Martin. Even though he was likely still exploring what sorts of stories were appropriate to tell at such a workshop, and even though he was interrupted in telling his story by a class of first graders, John made effective use of the linguistic resources of Kaska to rekindle his audience's memories of life on the land and to engage them as eye witnesses to the events he experienced. Identifying reasons why the Kaska workshop audience may have found John's story about Martin particularly satisfying highlights the importance of contemporary indigenous revitalization processes and the emblematic uses of Native languages, such as Kaska, for building indigenous identity.

Important questions remain unanswered about whether Gwich'in raided the Ross River area in the early 1900s and whether Martin sought to revenge the murder of his grandfather by Ross River men. Although these questions are not conclusively settled, John makes a strong case for his argument through his use of parallelism to link the Gwich'in raid at Tenas Lake with Martin's later statements and actions and by providing copious details of the events he witnessed. He raises the possibility, if not certainty, in his audience's minds that "He didn't seem like a medicine man, but it looks like John Martin was really a medicine man."

APPENDIX: JOHN MARTIN'S STORY AS TOLD BY ARTHUR JOHN, SR., AT ROSS RIVER, YUKON 1993

Part One

Summertime,[2]	Summertime,
summertime.	summertime.
August gū́jáí. Dene tédedéł	August came and people were
dege.	ready to go.
Ī t'é' dene tédedéł, *get ready*	People were getting ready to leave
negūts'edī.	[hunting].
John Martin dene ts'į́' kenedah.	John Martin came to visit people.
Ī ssą́,	It must have been,
"Jahdádzīh gūts'į́'	"Just off to the side up there,
estsíe dede'į́h lēguht'ē,"	it seems like my grandfather
	disappeared coming from a short
	distance downstream,"
dī lā, Denechō',	he [Martin] said to Jack Sterriah.
Denechō' ts'į́'.	
"Estsíe lā dá gūts'į́' edede'į́h į	"My grandfather disappeared down
lēgūht'ē sa'ǎ ts'į́' et'ā."	this way a long time ago."
Kūlā dene tédedélí	Finally people were ready to leave
ī t'é' téts'édésdētl.	and then we started to go.
Boat tắts'edéslūs degé,	We started to pull the boats
	upstream,
two boat,	two boats,
three boat.	three boats.
John McKay yéh.	John McKay's as well.
Jimmy Keen bōdé' téts'ālū́s;	We pulled Jimmy Keen's boat
	upstream;
Selkirk Billy k'ī bōt tégālū́zí.	they also pulled Selkirk Billy's boat
	upstream.
Denechō k'ī bōt tégālū́s.	They pulled Jack Sterriah's boat
	upstream as well.
Old Jule k'ajī dene yāda' lî lā	Old Jules was looking after people
kū́h.	at that time.
Ī k'e bōt tégālūs kū́hdegé.	They all pulled their boats up there.
"Dułą́ degé dene chenetḗdzī,"	"People shouldn't sleep while they
	are up there,"

Denechō' kédī.   Jack Sterriah said.
"Ī késtān dédī lî edīa?   "That stranger, what did he say?
'De'ą́dzīh ts'į́' estsíe dede'į́h lā,   'It seems like my grandfather
                                        disappeared coming from way off
                                        to the side over there,'

lēgūht'ē,' dī lā."   he [John Martin] said."
Ekų́h dene dejī lēdī.   That's what people were saying at
                                        that time.

Ī dene esą̨hdī gódah gūsen.   People can't go around alone.

"*Two apiece all the time* dene   "People should travel in pairs from
                                        now on,"
gūdedélī, jāni gūts'į̄h degé," dī.   they said.

Iyéh *there we camp.*   Then we camped there.

Iyéh, ī en*trapline*é' sa'ă   Then across from where your
kéndéhdah   [Amos Dick's]
nã́sdį̄'   trapline comes out

kų́hyegé łégādéł.   they arrived there.
Boat degé tédzālúzí.   We pulled boats upstream to
                                        there.

Jimmy Keen dahtlah ah'áné   Jimmy Keen went off hunting up
degé.   there.
Fifty Mile kų́htsą́ kedīya'.   He walked out to the river down at
                                        Fifty Mile
kedā se'ų́n lā.   Slough where he shot a moose.

No,   No,
Sixty Mile yegé lą̆.   it was at Sixty Mile Slough.
Fifty Mile kedīya', dī.   He said that he walked out to the
                                        river at Fifty Mile Slough.

River gagáh teseyāí.   He walked up along the river,
Sixty Mile łâdālí.   and he came to Sixty Mile.
Raft zų́ze nelái dedeskīn lā.   He made a small raft and started
                                        rafting
Nã́sdį̄', kedā se'ų́n lā.   across. On the other side he shot a
                                        moose.

Mā *boat* tắts'ālús.   We pulled the boats upstream the
                                        whole way along the shore.

Just gūdātsé kedā déhhīn lā.
Īyéh łéts'adélí tāchą
eyéts'esdētl.
All łégeyētēlí;
everybody eat.
Degé *boat* tágālús.
Otter Creek ts'és'į́ ,
ten mile this side są́ gūt'ē nā

cabin, ī atsą́ netene kūgūdejān.

Kų́hyegé dé ną́sdį̄' *cabin* se'ān
lā,
skūkānī *cabin*é.

Kų́hyegé ts'į̄h, "Ną́né,
ną́né hés ts'į̄' téts'edūdélí,"
gedī'.
Kų́hyegé *cabin* t'át.
everything kūgeyela'í.
Ną́né bōt yéh déts'es'ēdlī',
kų́hdegé dene désdētl.

Etene tūgūts'edéhhétl degé,

dene datsé,

Blue Hill.
Ī men mekā etene tūgūgājān;

ī memā dá́ etene
tūgūts'edéhhédlī
degé.

Łą́ *straight* degé hés ts'į̄'
téts'esdētl.
Ahdegé hés ts'es'į̄h
shets'enéhtēts.

Gūyéh tedze gūjá'.

| | Just ahead of us he killed a moose. |

Just ahead of us he killed a moose.
Then the next day after we arrived
we went to get meat.
They brought it all back, and
everyone ate.
They pulled boats upstream.
Just before Otter Creek,
ten miles on this side there is a
cabin,
down where the trail to your
[Amos Dick's] cabin comes out.

Across from there, there was a
cabin, a
white man's cabin.

From there, "Across,
let's go across to the mountain,"
they said.
They put everything
inside the cabin there.
We landed the boats across,
and people walked up there [to the
mountains].

They had marked the trail going up
there,
the people who had traveled there
before,
to Blue Hill.
There is a lake that the trail passes
beside, and
We even marked the trail down
along its shore
on the way up.

We went straight up to the
mountain.
We went to sleep up there just
before we got to the mountain.

Night came upon us.

Tāchą̄ *in the morning,*
Denechǒ'
hés dą̄sī yā kah ts'édāne
nénah'aha?
"Jah'áné ejenūsyáí," dī'.

The next day, in the morning, why
was Jack Sterriah
sending his children down from
his camp?
"I'm going hunting off this way," he
said.

Oh yes, two nights
shets'enehtēts
lî lā kų́hyegé.
Jahdegé ejegesdētl; *all nothing.*

We slept there two nights.

They all went hunting a short way
up that way without success.

Łénts'adélí neshets'enéhtēdzī

ts'edesdētl.
Etene gwēgílí *near* degé

dene néstlōn ādéł dene k'éh.

We all came back and went back to
sleep;
then we went again.
There was a really good trail up
there
where lots of people followed each
other.

Ī̧yéh,
"Jah'áné hés kā ejets'edū'ą́zī,"
dī'.
Joe meyéh k'édah lā.

Ejegedés'āts.

Then,
"Let's both go hunting on the
mountain," he [Jack Sterriah] said.
Joe Sterriah walked around with
him.
They both went hunting.

Ī̧yéh hés ts'į́' ts'edésdētl.
Hés łą́ dedīe nétlōn.

Boy, tłį' yḗdé łą́ nédébét.

Dedīe *fat* tłį' tah négeyet'ás.

Gūdzį̄h k'e endúé,
hés kāge, he.
Ī̧yéh kų́hdegé łéts'ādélí.
Denechǒ' kedā se'ún lā, ah'áné.
Ī̧yéh tedze negedest'āts.

Then we went to the mountain.
There were lots of marmots on the
mountain.
Boy, the dogs were really hungry,
so
they cut up marmot fat for the
dogs.
There were no caribou
on the mountain.
Then we came up there, and
Jack Sterriah shot a moose there.
Then at night two of the men went
walking.

Tedze jahdegé ts'edesdētl;
meyḗsdíh lā.
Jū́hdegé négāt'ásí.

We went up ahead a little;
I remember.
They both walked up ahead a
little.

"Kón desk'án," dī.

"Kónchö' désch'ele nắdī.

Gee, mā lî et'ā?

Mets'į̃' eden'ữn, déja kā," dī.

Mets'į̃' edes'ữn.
Īdéh kón tsedits'et;
fire out.
Īdéh tsį́dzīh déh negedést'āts
degé.

Tedze degé t'ę́s gę́gūht'ē łégā'ás.

"Mā et'ā etsį́dī kón dáhk'ána
et'ā?"
gedī.

Nobody,
nobody been there.
Here John Martin dene gę́ne'į́'.

Denechö', *he want to kill*
Denechö'.
Detsíe łą́, "Ī lā estsíe déhhīnī,"
dī.

Ī sa'ă ts'édāne eslīn,
dene gedéhhīn lą́
Tenās *Lake.*
Dene tsá' gedésdēdlī,
all the man gedésdēdlī.
Tenās *Lake* dāsgúh tahtlah
ts'į̃' dene tsá' kedésdētl.
Tenās *Lake, this side,*
dedeslīnī łą́ *lots of jackfish* lā,
slough gagáh.

"There is a fire burning," he [Jack
Sterriah] said.

"There is a big fire burning brightly
across.
Gee, who is it?

Shoot towards it to see what
happens," he said.
I shot toward it.
Then the fire was put out;
the fire was out.
Then from below, they both [Jack
and Joe Sterriah] climbed up.

It was as dark as pitch when they
arrived up there.

"Who was that down there starting
a fire?"
they said.

No one,
no one had been there.
That was John Martin sneaking
around.
He wanted to kill Jack Sterriah.

"That's the one that killed my
grandfather," he [John Martin]
said.

Long ago when I was a child,
they killed a person
at Tenas Lake.
People went there for beavers,
all the men went there for beavers.
Way down to the end of Tenas Lake
people went for beavers.
On this [south] side of Tenas Lake,
where it flows out, there were lots of
jackfish in the slough beside [the
river].

Ī ts'į́' *move* ejá' dąsī,

light load yéh łégādélí.
Gūhłīnī *tent* degeslaī. Tehmíl

tāgestlū́n lą́ tāchą̄.
Cache kah gedésdēdlī.
Dene degą́dedeh gedī, degé.

Tlį̄', *grandma*tlī̧́é' łą́ deyedīht'ē
lā.
Dene géndegojī są́, gedesgot lą́,
bēs yéh.
Łą́ mechené' *big cut*
tlī̧' łénāgōł.
"Ī dūłą́ gūhłīnī lēgūsenī," gedī.

"Bēs k'éh lēgūht'ē," gedī

łą́gādélí.

Ī są́, kūlā tedze gū́já'
Dą́gū́ht'ē tedze, *all night*

kūgūdāt'īn hę.
Kūlā sā gūnī́'ąnī́.
supper łą́gādélí;
supper gūjá'.
Ts'édāne eslīnī kēsdíhí lā.

Dedé̄ *tent* t'ą́t gūdenest'ę̄dze

I don't want to eat.
Rice sehbēts, *Mom.*
Rice esyénekān
tent t'ą́t.
Gee, gūdenest'ę̄dze kón nídzīh.
I go down;
kón nídzīh kenāsja',
sesda'.
Ahnǫ́gī tl'ūtsen kę́t'ē dlą́se'ą́ tah
łą́ *nothing.*

They moved down to there, coming with
light loads.
They put up some kind of tent. Then they
set a fishnet the next day.
We went to the cache there.
They say that people chased each other up there.

The dog, my grandmother's dog, was really ferocious
It must have attacked someone who slashed it with a knife.
There was a big cut on its back
when the dog came back.
"That wasn't done by just anything," they said.

"That must have been from a knife,"
they said when they came back.

Then finally night came.
It was like now when it is light all night.

Finally the sun set and
they returned for supper;
it was suppertime.
I was a child, but I remember about it.
Sitting in the back of the tent it was dark
and I didn't want to eat.
Mom boiled rice.
She gave me a bowl of rice
inside the tent.
Gee, it was dark beside the fire.
I went down,
came back by the fire,
and sat down.
Across in the sage and all around there was nothing.

Ī sedāgī dá̄ gūts'į̄h,
"Ū́k!
 Ū́k!
  Ū́k!
   Ū́k!"
gūdlī' kāgūdehchōde.
Gee, Uncle Ollie Grandma ts'į̄'

kénātlah.
"Mekā edzedū'ū́nī," gedī'.
"Łōgī'! Łōgī'! Dédahdīa?

"Don't do that," dī'.
Ī entsíe, *Pelly Smith* yéh,
Jim Smith yéh,
Uncle Ollie yéh,
three geneht'ē.
Ją endî?
"Lōgī," gedī ghólí *he start*

to shoot kū́hnā́né.
Gūdē,
"Tał!
 Tał!
  Tał!
   Tał!
    Tał!
     Tał!"
Nagū́dī́gá̄' kūgudest'į̄,

nā́né négesdētl.
Tses kāge edelé' gū́līn, gedī'.

Ī lā *John Martin* metsíe lā genlā
lî.
Yē kā dene gḗne'į̄a?
Késtāne elīnī denelá' et'ón nā,

sure.
They want to steal some kids I
guess;

Then from down the hill,
"Whistle!
 Whistle!
  Whistle!
   Whistle!"
came the sound from all over.
Gee, Uncle Ollie came to visit
Grandma.

"Let's shoot at them," they said.
"Don't! Don't! What are you
saying?
"Don't do that," she said.
Your grandfather, Pelly Smith,
and Jim Smith,
and Uncle Ollie,
there were three of them.
What were they to do?
"Don't," they said, but even so they
started
to shoot across.
Like that,
"Bang!
 Bang!
  Bang!
   Bang!
    Bang!
     Bang!"
In the morning, when it was light
enough to see,
they went across.
There was blood on the dry wood,
they said.
That was John Martin's grandfa-
ther they did that to.
Why did he hide from people?
He was a stranger, he should have
shook people's hands,
sure.
They wanted to steal some kids, I
guess;

sá get'īn nā.

that must have been what they were doing.

Charlie Dick: *Maybe.*
Arthur John: Īdéh tāchą̄ gūjáí
dene tēdésdētl.
Pelly Smith k'ī łą́ dzī'īya',
Ī lā *Uncle Ollie* k'ī.
Jim Smith yéh lā *three* geneht'ē

nēgede'ún lā ną́né.
Ī lā dene gedéhhīn lā.

Maybe.
Then the next day
people started to go.
Pelly Smith left,
Uncle Ollie too.
With Jim Smith there were three of them
who shot across.
Those were the ones who killed that person.

Ī tl'ą́ sa'ǎ gūjáí,
Uncle Ollie, "Kų́hdá
Tenās *Lake* kų́hdá ejenesyā,"
dī.
"*Graveyard* ts'ī́ kī́sya'," dī t'é'.
"Dene gedéhhīn lî," dī'.

A long time later,
Uncle Ollie said, "Back there,
back there by Tenas Lake I was hunting.
"I came upon a grave," he said.
"It was that person they killed before," he said.

Dene gedéhhīn.
Kedā edégīhhātl lą́.

They killed a person.
The strangers left a moose [that they had killed].

Ī k'īde,
ī k'īde
"Dene dūs-hē," doge dene
gūne'į́'
ī *John Martin* kų́hdegé hés kā

dene tedesdētl lą́.

Because of that,
because of that,
"I'll kill someone," [he was thinking]
and because of that John Martin hid
from people when they went up there on the mountain.

Īyéh dene *two the piece* dene
nḗndḗlī
yéh, *they can't do nothing*, eh.

Then people went in pairs while they were
living there and they couldn't do anything.

Īyéh *Jimmy Keen* zedlé' esą̄hdī
k'édah.
He see trap.
He trap groundhogs,
killed two hundred groundhogs
trap yéh.

Then only Jimmy Keen [John McKay] was walking around.
He was checking his traps.
He trapped marmots,
killed two hundred marmots with traps.

Ī sá̧,
"Yā kā sá̧ dāsgűh
dūgūnūstēl dege ūdá̧ *tea*
deseszīl," dī
Tsį́dzīsgűh nédésja'.

Gūdehtűhlī kedā kísya'. Kón,

kón désk'á̧. *Tea* desbēts," dī.

"Estlīé' edíts'ek," dī', "ahtsȩ́,
gűle tah ts'į́'.

Kết'ē ghōlí dūłá̧ mekah
kesest'ah," dī'.
"Īdéh tlį' neshenéstīn ūtsȩ́.

Tsį́de'ōde déh neshenétīn.

Łá̧ eyegé gūts'į́' déh yedéts'ek,"
dī'.
"Tses dege tsȩ́ déh medētes sa'ǎ
t'é'
kāsda'," dī'.
"Łá̧ da'įh esjá' sá̧. *Everything*
estlīé'
yédé dánesdȩ́stl'ūn, hį́.
Packsack yédé
nāsjaí.
Nasedenāsja mekah űnē
dádenāsla',"
dī'.
"Bōh!
   Bōh!
     Bōh!
       Bōh!
Five time mekah dās'űn," dī'.

"sǎ gűle tah gűhtsá̧."

Łá̧ sá̧ egede'űn ī sá̧.
Can't see 'em.
Īyéh tadáhtlah kűhyegé.

It must have been,
"Why was it
I was warming tea for myself down
in
the valley," he said. "I went back up
and
I came out on top of a little hill.
Fire,
I started a fire and boiled tea for
myself," he said.
"My dog was listening down below
to something in the willows," he
said.
"I turned to see what it was," he
said.
"Then the dog went back to sleep
down below.
It was paying attention and then it
went back to sleep.
It was really listening intently
down there," he said.
"I went down below to look for
firewood," he
said.
"Then I put on a pack and put
everything else
in my dog's pack.
With my packsack and all
I went back down.
I turned around and loaded my
gun," he said.

"Bōh!
   Bōh!
     Bōh!
       Bōh!
I shot five times at something
among the
willows far down below," he said.

They must have really shot.
Couldn't see him.
Then he ran off down there.

Óǵí ts'edesdētl senī k'e,
John McKay yéh dene yéh
dzedes'āts
kúh'áné.

We circled ahead;
I went there with John McKay.

Tedze,
tedze gūjáí,
"Mā et'ā kón dáhk'ána tsídī?"
gūdī'
gudlī' ahdegé hés kā gūts'īh,

Night,
night came,
"Who started that fire down
there?"
it sounded like someone said up
above,

Jack McKay, eh.

Jack McKay, eh.

John McKay,
"Gūhhīnī lēts'īht'ē.
Jānī debē gedāsghān
shechenehtēts
lā," yéhdī.

John McKay said,
"It's us.
They killed some sheep here and
we're going to
sleep," he told him.

"Enzí', enzí' lā, enzí' dúgúyā?"
dī'.

"Your name, what's your name?"
[Jack McKay] said.

"Enchūé' *John McKay* lēst'ē,"
yéhdī.

"I'm your son John McKay," he said
to him.

"Ham, nahts'í' gūtódūsyá sí,"
dī'.
Tedze lá t'és gégūht'e.
Tedze gōghąh łådāl.
Dene de'āsgą sí.

"Yes, I'll come to you," he said.

It was dark as pitch.
He [John McKay] came in the dark.
Maybe they killed someone.

"Nahgāne desdene segedéhhīn.
Gēdedésk'edze yéh lēgūht'e,"
dī'.
Gūghąh łådālí.
Twenty-two shell one box John

"A bushman just about killed me.
I shot to protect myself," he [John
McKay] said.
He came down beside us.
John McKay gave him one box of
twenty-two
shells.

McKay yéne'ān.
Twenty-two yéh ede'ún dege.
Gūdzīh yēge'ún dé'.
Īyéh
three dzenéht'ē nedzedesdētl.

He used twenty-two shells.
They shot caribou then.
Then
the three of us went back.

Dene ahlāde *they don't believe it.*
They want to go hunt some more
gedī.
Ejegedél.
Gūhīnī kǫ́ą nedzedesdētl.

"Dene dāsgą sį́.
I know dene lēt'īn," dī.
Ejegedesdētl.
Kǫ́ą *nothing, everything good.*

All everybody good.

Ī lā *John Martin* gēne'į́ lā lēt'īn lî lā.
Ī detsíe tl'ą́ dene dūhhē dege.

Kūlā dene ts'į́' sedāī dene gedéhhīn
są́, *okay.*
Dene gēne'į́h yéh ejá, *everybody get scared.*
Kę́sgų́h lā gīyedzéhhīn lā, metsíe.
Dedī metsíe lajáí dene se'ų́nī.

"Ī lā yádze'ų́nī," *three.*

Amos Dick: Estsíe *Pelly Smith, tough man.*

Arthur John: Ī łénādāl
Denechō' dǎdī'a' yéh
mets'édāné
two nédela'

The other people didn't believe it.

They said that they wanted to go hunt some
more.
They went hunting.
We went back to camp.

"Maybe he will try to kill someone.
I know it was a person," he said.
They went hunting.
At camp everything was good,
nothing had happened.

Everyone was good.

That was John Martin sneaking around.
Because of his grandfather he wanted to kill someone.
He must have thought the person sitting there
killed [his grandfather].
Because someone was sneaking around,
everyone was afraid.
They had killed his grandfather.

His grandfather was the person who was shot.
"That must have been who we were shooting at, those three [who were there, Pelly Smith, Jim Smith, and Uncle Ollie, said later].

My grandfather Pelly Smith was a tough man.

When he [Martin] returned
he bullied Jack Sterriah and took two
of his children

nedésjaí:
Joe,
Chiney.

when he went back:
Joe Sterriah
and Chiney Sterriah.

Lucky thing Joe Ladue k'ī
gűhdá
néde' yéh,
senī k'ī gűhdá nésde' yéh ekűh.

It was a lucky thing that Joe Ladue

and I were living down there [at
Fort Selkirk] at that time.

Īyéh nedzedela'; *Joe Ladue*
negedela'

Then we took them, Joe Ladue took
them.

<u>Amos Dick</u>: *John Martin.*
<u>Arthur John</u>: *Ya, Selkirk* yegé

edígeyela',
Selkirk yegé edégīyela' lá,
He left them there.

John Martin.
Yes, he left them down at Fort
Selkirk,

he left them down at Fort Selkirk,
he left them there.

He go Mayo, eh.
Mayo kűhyegé *pneumonia* ejá'.

He went to Mayo, eh.
Down at Mayo he came down with
pneumonia.

Doctor ghąh łégeyētel gólí,

They brought him to the doctor,
but

he get double pneumonia.
He just die quick.
God sąt'īąn nā;

he got double pneumonia.
He just died quickly.
It must have been God that did
that;

he do wrong, eh.

he did wrong, eh.

Dá dechedle, degūdīe ghąh
nǎseja'.
Dawson gūdīe

He visited his brother down there.

His older brother in Dawson
City

missionary man elīn lā.
Ī dégūdech.

was a missionary.
He [John Martin] told his brother a
story.

"Estsíe tl'ą dene dūs-heī.

"Because of what happened to
Grandfather, I wanted to kill
someone.

Kǎsja ǫ endűé éhdī lą."

Because of what I did, I'm going to
die,"

Ī degūdīe dāł.

he told his brother about it.

Īyéh, ekū́h,
summertime déh kū́hdā́.

Then, at that time,
in the summertime, we were down
there then.

Dawson łédzesdētl; *Dawson*
tédzes'ēdlī.
Tses yēdzeskēt lā, *Little Sam*
yéh.
Little Sam, "*I got friend*,

Megā́dzū'ā́zī," séhdī.
K'ā *Moosehide* gedī kū́hdā́
łédzā'ás.
Kū́hyegé gūdégūdech.

We came to Dawson; we landed at
Dawson City.
We sold firewood, Little Sam and
me.
"I've got a friend" Little Sam said to
me,
"Let's go visit him," he said to me.
They call that place Moosehide,
and we both went down there.
Down there, he [Richard Martin]
told the story.

"Yā kah nechétsétlah lî et'ā?
God punish yénla' nédé'īn"
yéhdī.

"Why did he do that?
God took him to punish him," he
[Richard Martin] told him [Little
Sam].

Dene gēne'į́' lî k'ede

degé. Ī lā *all* dene kēgīyéhdī
lāt'ā
łénādālī
Dawson.

He was sneaking around [after
people] up there.
That's what people told Richard
Martin
when he came back
to Dawson City.

Ah'áné *long way* kūdené' lēt'ē
endīa,
Fort McPherson.
Kū́h'áné ts'į̄h łégādélī́.
Dene gēgene'į́'.
*They wanted to take somebody
from
Ross River.*
Tenās *Lake* są̄ nahgā́nī gets'į́'

łā́ngededéł.
*They should just come there,
shake hands.*
Yā kah dene ghą̄ nejetgendētl
yéh

He was from distant people

at Fort McPherson.
They came from way over there.
They wanted to take people.
They wanted to take someone from

Ross River.
Those people must have been the
bushmen
that came to them at Tenas Lake.
They should have just come there
and shook hands.
Why did they persist in bothering
people?

Dene gedéhhīn lā.

They can't report it;
They can't make war.
That's their own fault, that's all.

Because of that they killed
someone.
They couldn't report it;
they couldn't make war.
That's their own fault, that's all.

Part Two

Gu*drum*é segīdīyelaī.
John Martin tedze nâts'e'â̗',

"Hwe!
   Hwe!
      Hwe!"

John Martin sedetān ahdą̗sī
gūyéh
drums gédādetān.

They put our drums in the fire.
John Martin [came to us while] we
were stick gambling at night.
"Hwe!
   Hwe!
      Hwe!" [stick gambling singing
to drumming]
John Martin woke up [from the
noise of the
drums] and sneaked towards us
from up above.

Dâhch'ah, dene tah łâyālī.
Drum,
all about five drum,
all nedílaī.
"Megánahtān," dī'.
Tses degedelaí.
Tsíyedīlā t'é.
Old Jack come too,
Old Jack McKay.
I don't know yē kah dahyā są̗.

Megāts'enehtān *he burn 'em up.*

Suddenly, he came among us.
Drums,
all five drums,
he gathered all of them up.
"Look at them," he said.
He put more firewood on the fire.
Then he put them all in the fire.
Old Jack came there too,
Old Jack McKay.
I don't know why he happened to
come there.
We watched John Martin burn the
drums up.

"Don't gamble no more.
Don't make drummin' no
more," dī.
Īt'é'
Old Jack łą̗ denīzą́.
"Why you do that? Kid they
play

"Don't gamble no more,
Don't make drummin' no more,"
he [John Martin] said.
Then
Old Jack was really angry.
"Why did you do that? The young
people

with that all the time.
All the time that's all the fun
they have.
Yē doge ent'īna?" yéhdī.

Īyéh,
kégedī t'éh łets'į' degenezá'.

Ją̄ nendį̂?
"Dédū nénen'á t'é',
nénen'á t'é',
nete'e dādāl lā," yéhdī,

Old Jack ts'į̂ ',
John Martin.

Kūlā, ī *Jack,*
"Nenī k'ī ah'áné nekēyeh ts'į̂ '

dułá̧ łéndendāl lā," yéhdī.
Kúhyegé neden'į̄ł lā," yéhdī.

Next year gūjáí,
Old Jack McKay ahdegé nédésjā
lá̧.
Otter Creek kúhdegé *trap* et'īn
wédé.
Ejeneyā, dâhch'ah
drum ehheł gūdlī'.
"We!
  We!
    We!
      We!
        We!"
dī gudlī'.
Mekah kāda', kāda'.
Dech'ūe *three* dedenéhts'ī.

Two ná̧'á̧', *one he hit drum.*

play with those all the time.
That's all the fun they have.

Why are you doing that?" he said
to him.
Then,
they were mad at each other about
what they had said.

What could they do?
"Now, if you stick gamble,
if you gamble,
you're a dead man," he [John
Martin] said to him,
to Old Jack McKay.

Finally, Jack [said],
"You too, if you go back toward
your country,
nedīnjá t'é',
then you won't make it back.
You will die there," he [Jack
McKay] said to him.
The next year,
Jack McKay went back up [the Ross
River].
He usually trapped up by Otter
Creek.
He went hunting and suddenly
there was a sound of drumming.
"We!
  We!
    We!
      We!
        We!"
came the sound.
He looked for it and looked for it.
Three porcupines were sitting up in
a tree.
Two were stick gambling, one was
hitting a drum.

John Martin dāghā́dé sā̧ gūt'īn
nâ.
Ī sā̧ *Old Jack McKay* łâdāl t'é',

dech'ūe
drum yéh edídel tēdeyés.

Īyéh
kū́hyegé *all winter* trap ejá' lā̧.

Pelly Bank ts'į́ ' nedesjá';
Pelly Bank ts'į́ ' négedésdēdlí;
Pelly Bank kḗngededélí.
Summertime gūjáí,
"Nā́ts'ū'áī," gedejá lā̧.

Amos Dick: Ekū́h sā̧ gedī nā
Springtime gōl łá'ā̧ ł, gíhdī nā.

Arthur John: *Ya'* ekū́h.
Amos Dick: Ī *Fox Lake*
kū́hdegé,
kū́hyegé *cabin* se'ān, gíhdī lā.
Big lump of gold.

White man, he see 'em.

Arthur John: Īyéh dene néde'á'.
Łā̧ dūłā̧ geyétset.

Nothing!
Two time twenty-one kí'ān.

Ī lá *he fall down, he dead.*
Dūłā̧ geyétsede t'é', sék'ādé,

Old John die.
Ekū́h *that summer* t'é'
John Martin k'e éndéskīn lá.

He move out,

They must have been there because
of John Martin.
When Old Jack McKay came there,
the
porcupine
threw away his drum and jumped
up.
Then
he [Jack McKay] trapped there all
winter.
He went back to Pelly Banks;
they all went back to Pelly Banks;
everyone went back to Pelly Banks.
It was summertime,
"Let's gamble," they said then.

That was the time they say
in the springtime he [Jack McKay]
brought gold

Yes, that was the time.
Up at Fox Lake,

there was a cabin there, they say.
[Jack McKay had] a big lump of
gold.
A white man saw it.

Then people started to gamble.
They couldn't catch him [Jack
McKay].
They never got him.
He twice won the last stick [to enable
his team to start hiding again].
Then he fell down dead.
They still hadn't caught him
[correctly guessed which hand he
had his token in],
when Old Jack McKay died.
At that time, that summer
John Martin also went back by
boat.
He moved out,

dūłą́ me*bossé'* ké̜yéhdī ghółí.

Denechō' ts'édāné *two* nédelaí,

he go down.
Whole family.
Selkirk kų́hyegé téseyá̜'.
Steamboat gétl'eje lā ekų́h.

Ī̜yéh *steamboat* gāgáh dá̜ dūdīé'

nāsejá' lą́.
Medégūdech lą́,
what he do up here.
Medāł gwēdéjī.

Łágādélí
Mayo ts'í̜ ' łeh,
kų́h'áné dekēyeh ts'í̜ ' nédésja'.

Mayo ts'í̜ ', *Mayo* ts'í̜' łâdālī,
he get pneumonia.
Ī̜yéh *hospital close right there,*
eh.
Doctor there too.
Ī̜yéh *hospital* kūgīyehtīn ghółí,

he die,
Old Jack ké̜yéhdī k'éh.

Ī̜ k'ī *John Martin* k'éh,
gô *die* ejá' nā.

See łą́ dūłą́ nédet'ē gét'ē ghółí,

John Martin looks like it really

medicine man.

even though his boss never told
him to.
He took two of Jack Sterriah's
children and
he went down [the Pelly River].
His whole family.
He got off down at Fort Selkirk.
The steamboat was going around at
that time.
He took the steamboat back down
to visit
his brother.
He told him stories about
what he did up here.
He told him stories about it.

They arrived
at Mayo instead and,
he started to travel back to his
country.
At Mayo, when he arrived at Mayo,
he got pneumonia.
There was a hospital right there, eh.

There was a doctor there too.
They put him in the hospital, but
even so
he died,
just the way Old Jack [McKay] said
he would.
Him too [Jack McKay],
he died the way John Martin said
he would.

He didn't seem like a medicine
man,
but it looks like John Martin was
really a medicine
man.

NOTES

1. The Kaska orthography used in this chapter is the same as that used by the Yukon Native Language Centre in its publications as described online at http://www.ynlc.ca/languages/ks/ksalphabet.pdf, except that "h" is used for the voiceless velar fricative [x] and short "i" and short "u" are not used in this orthography.

2. Arthur John's narrative is written in an ethnopoetic style in which breath groups are represented by double-spaced line breaks. Breaks between sections are represented by an extra double-spaced return. A version of this story with interlinear text and a prose translation can be found in my dissertation (Moore 2002:759–84).

7

"Conquering the Mighty Sioux"

An Ethnohistory of William Bordeaux

RAYMOND BUCKO

In the fall of 2007, I was invited to write an introduction to William Bordeaux's 1929 *Conquering the Mighty Sioux,* which was about to be formally republished. Bordeaux's story is a unique and interesting one, but his book contained some problematic material that needed to be addressed, so I agreed to annotate his book and to write an introduction that would bring together the published material on his life. My initial research revealed that biographical material on Bordeaux was based entirely on this book and his book on Crazy Horse, both of which he self-published.

Having found so little primary material on Bordeaux, I began a different approach to the research. I have known Lakota on the Rosebud Reservation since I first came to South Dakota in 1976; in 2002, I had spent a sabbatical year at the Buechel Memorial Lakota Museum, creating a digital catalog and resource for Father Buechel's material culture collection there. During that time, I met many new people and renewed old friendships. Among these relationships was a particularly warm friendship with a generous couple who fed me whenever I visited. Needless to say, they eventually assigned me my own chair at their table. In conversation with them, I mentioned my research on Bordeaux and one of them exclaimed, "Oh! Uncle Billy!" It turned out this friend's family is closely related to Bordeaux. The couple later introduced me to relatives who were even closer relations. As I got to know Bordeaux's family, however, I discovered that none of them knew of the proposal to republish their deceased relative's book. Initially, there was some confusion about my role in the project. Some relatives believed that I myself was publishing the book. I assured them that this was not the case and that if the press published without their consent, I would withdraw permission to publish my introduction. I also promised that I would work closely with them and that I would not publish anything that did not meet their approval. With those issues cleared up, I went to work on the introduction, which follows.[1] I finished the introduction with the help of many people on the reservation, Raymond J. DeMallie, and others. When the introduction to

the book was complete, I provided it to several members of his family to review what my research had uncovered. Bordeaux's family approved my introduction, but by then I understood that they did not want *Conquering the
Mighty Sioux* reissued at this time. I made that fact known to the publisher;
eventually the decision was made not to publish it after all.[2]

WILLIAM BORDEAUX'S FIRST BOOK

William James Bordeaux's *Conquering the Mighty Sioux,* self-published in
1929, is a work built on interviews with elders, personal reminiscences, and
winter counts. The book also illustrates an awareness of a larger world comprised of many people who were and continue to be interested in the Sioux
past. The complexity of this work mirrors the life of its author. Billy, as family and friends knew him, was both a chronicler of the past and a participant
in contemporary Native affairs. Through his own determination, he published a variety of books and articles on the Sioux and made his way through
life on the Rosebud Reservation and later in Sioux Falls, South Dakota.
Much of his life was regulated by a paternalistic federal government that
judged both him and his actions. He moved across a spectrum of compliance with the government and resistance against it. He chronically dealt
with questions about his reputation, and struggled with family and financial
concerns. Nevertheless he managed to create this and other historical works
and established himself as an advocate for his people.

Since *Conquering the Mighty Sioux* was privately published by Bordeaux,
he sold subscriptions to the book in order to meet production expenses. Bordeaux believed his book would eventually help support himself and his family.[3] In turn, Bordeaux enlisted his family to assist him in supporting his
book. In September of 1931, his son Wilbur wrote to Rosebud superintendent
W. O. Roberts requesting the balance of his Sioux Benefits.[4] He wanted to
use part of the money for clothing and school expenses and to invest the rest
in the publication of the second edition of his father's book "on the life of the
Sioux Indian" and to share in the eventual profits as a co-partner.[5] Bordeaux
was suffering severe financial hardship at the time, a dire circumstance he
expressed in a letter to Charles J. Rhoads, commissioner of Indian Affairs.
He stated that the depression had hit Sioux Falls particularly hard and he
was unable to work due to a hip injury. He sought financial relief at the local
Welfare Office but was told that since he was Native he would have to apply
for help through the Indian Office. The Indian Office would not help him as
his son Wilbur still had money available from his Sioux Benefits. Bordeaux
stated that Wilbur was sick with an "appendix ailment" and therefore unable to attend school. Wilbur also took odd jobs to help support the family.
Bordeaux requested the remainder of Wilbur's Sioux Benefit fund to assist
his family through their financial difficulty.[6] The Indian Office eventually

decided to issue payments of $50.00 a month to Bordeaux rather than to transfer the balance of Wilbur's account, arguing that it would not be "in the best interests for this boy to have his entire balance at one time."[7] In fact, J. Henry Scattergood, the assistant commissioner, in a letter to Senator Peter Norbeck, doubted "the wisdom of using the entire balance belonging to his son to assist him in publishing his books."[8]

NATIVE HISTORY

Bordeaux clearly had a passion for Sioux history that was already evident during his grade school days. He described how a fellow student at the Rapid City Indian School related his experience at the Wounded Knee massacre some ten years previously:[9] "I was just a child," he proceeded, "but I can distinctly recall how my mother pulled and dragged me over the snow-covered ground in her flight. I was shot through the ankle, and with a scream I fell. My mother picked me up, and resumed her flight. Finally we reached a dense thicket, and were later rescued by some of our people passing by" (Bordeaux 1929:289).

Bordeaux portrayed Sioux history with large strokes, including the arrival of the Sioux on the North American continent, their migration to the Laramie Plains and the Dakotas, warfare with other Native groups and the Americans, and present political concerns for the contemporary Sioux. The Sioux, for Bordeaux, were both conquered and unconquerable, a complexity that was mirrored in his own life. Bordeaux's wide cultural and personal experiences were also embodied in his many ideas and theories. On the one hand he spoke evolutionarily when he embedded the Sioux in the ideology of progress and civilization. On the other, he was a cultural relativist, appreciating Lakota culture as it was and is. He engaged in memory ethnography, asking tribal elders for their recollections of the past, and he also commented on people of mixed ancestry and the future of the Nation. He used a florid and colorful vocabulary with words considered distasteful today. His language was, however, successful in transmitting his enthusiasm for his subject.[10] He portrayed precontact Sioux culture as well as the role of mixed ancestry individuals as intermediaries between the United States government and the tribe. He relied on participant narrative, recollections of family members, winter counts, and at times his own conjecture in this comprehensive albeit sometimes unsystematic treatise. He set up many of his chapters to solve historical questions, such as: who killed Custer, who killed Preacher Smith, who killed Logan Fontanelle, how the Minnesota war began, and what the true circumstances were around the killing of Crazy Horse. He also focused on the culture and language of the Sioux, providing descriptions of various rituals and customs as well as providing topical word lists. Most of all, the work focused on war and battles, first between different tribes, and finally with the United States government. Into his history, he integrated a family portrait, highlighting his kinship connections with various historical actors.

Bordeaux stated early in his work that the Sioux were descended from the Romans. He held neither for the Bering Strait theory popular at the time nor for the Sioux belief that held for an autochthonic origin. Few if any would accept this proposition today. Bordeaux, however, wanted to portray the dignity of his people and relied on analogy rather than archaeology, archival research, or tribal tradition. Years later artist Gutzon Borglum referred to the Sioux as "the Romans of the Plains" (Wilson 1941:31). Not everything Bordeaux related in the book was historically accurate and the work needs to be read and utilized carefully. Like a pointillist painting, however, it is important to step back and see the entire work rather than to judge if each point corresponds to a specific reality.[11] There are larger truths in this work, and in the history Bordeaux also portrayed himself and his own understanding of history. So, too, he portrayed the historical dignity of his people, their transformation and continuity, and their hopes for the future. While Bordeaux did not have a sophisticated education, even his detractors admitted to his intellectual capacity and curiosity. He had a lifelong passion for Sioux history, a history into which he himself was born and in which he and his family participated. In interviews, family members recalled his enthusiasm for local and world politics and the gusto of his discussions. They also remembered his long conversations in Lakota with elders when he and his family returned to the Rosebud Reservation for gatherings and to visit. The richness of Bordeaux's work lies in its narratives, not only by the elders and family members to whom he listened carefully, but also his own views on such things as how history should be written, how Native people should make their way in the world, and what the role of mixed-descent people in tribal society should be.

NATIVE NARRATIVES

William Bordeaux clearly set out in his work to correct the historical record through reproducing extended first-person narratives by Native historical participants and so to preserve these valuable commentaries on historical events. As he insisted throughout his life, the Native perspective on events needed to be told and recorded. Thus Bordeaux quoted only one non-Native source, Cyrus Townsend Brady's *Indian Fights and Fighters,* and then only to refute Brady's account. In the chapter entitled "Thirty-two against Three Thousand," Brady (1971:40–58) laid out a detailed description of the 1867 Wagon Box Fight based on the testimony of military survivors, Captain and Brevet-Major James Powell, Mrs. Anne Powell, and Colonel Dodge's record of a frontiersman's testimony. Brady used no Native sources for his account.

He estimated the number of fighters at "no fewer than three thousand war-riors, the flower of the Sioux Nation" (41).[12] Brady also claimed that Red Cloud was present at the battle (41, 46).[13] Bordeaux (1929:219–21) countered this testimony with reports given directly by Sioux combatants: Little Bull, Ring Bull, and Little Hawk. All three asserted that Red Cloud was neither in the vicinity nor was he ever wounded in combat.[14] Little Bull (in Bordeaux 1948:219) did not enumerate the Lakota force but stated there was "an unusu-ally large party of hunters." According to Ring Bull's testimony (Bordeaux 1929:220), there were only eight Lakota wounded and three killed. Bordeaux concluded this section confidently: "I feel free to state that the information I obtained from the Brules and Ogalala Sioux, relative to the historical Wagon Box Fight, or thirty-two against three thousand, back in 1867 at Piney Creek, is reliable and authentic history" (221). Another example of Bordeaux's fo-cus on interviewing participants was his description of the Battle of Crow Butte (37–42). The event took place in October of 1849 (Hanson 1969), although Bordeaux (1929:37) incorrectly gave the date as 1856, which illus-trates the importance of working carefully through Bordeaux's text, yet not abandoning it.

In addition to first-person narratives of the event, he added something very characteristic of Lakota life but neglected in many other histories: hu-mor. Bordeaux recorded the testimonies of Cloud Man and Red Leaf, two participants in the battle. One narrator described how the Sioux attempted to race up to the top of the butte to engage the Crows who took refuge there (Bordeaux 1929:41–42):

> Disregarding our warning they arose and proceeded to resume their climb, but they did not get far, when they were forced to race down in an attempt to out-distance huge rocks which the enemy rolled down on them. This was no time to laugh for we were all in a serious mood, but the spectacle of a group of scared Indians in a wild flight for their lives, to escape these huge rocks thundering down after them, was enough to make us forget our troubles for the time being. I laughed until my sides ached. Big Turkey was hit back of the ear from a flying missile and knocked unconscious for some time. Landing safely in our midst they were satisfied with their experience.

As seen above, Bordeaux both corrected Native history but also inadver-tently introduced some error into the record. In another example of this, Bordeaux (1929:39, caption opposite page) misidentified a picture of his fa-ther and a group of Lakota chiefs as "The Second Delegation who visited Washington in 1869."[15] He correctly identified his father as one of the trans-lators in the delegation photograph, however the image was taken of the 1875 delegation to Washington when it stopped on the way in Omaha, Nebraska.[16]

William Garnett stands in the center while the man on the right, unidentified by Bordeaux, is Julius Meyer.[17] Charles E. Hanson, Jr. (1966:10) accepted Bordeaux's date and photograph at face value but goes on to say that James Bordeaux also translated for the 1875 delegation, another example of the necessity to use Bordeaux's work carefully. Bordeaux (1934a:11) again misidentified the date of the delegation to Washington as 1869 in one of his short articles. Plans for that delegation, motivated by Spotted Tail and Swift Bear, began in the fall of 1869 (DeMallie 1988a:xxxvii).

Bordeaux was aware of the errors in the initial printing of this work. In 1932, his son Wilbur mentioned in a letter that he wished to help his father publish a second edition of the book.[18] In January of 1937, Bordeaux advised Everett Pitt Wilson, a professor at Chadron State Normal School in Nebraska, that he had revised and supplemented this work based in part on working on all seven South Dakota reservations as a special investigator under ex-governor Thomas Berry's administration.[19] In a subsequent letter to Wilson, Bordeaux explained that he had made minor corrections to the text, added illustrations, and doubled the book's length. He also worked with a proofreader at the Sioux Falls *Argus Leader* and renamed the book *Un-Veiling the Sioux Romantic Past*.[20] It is unclear at this writing whether he republished the expanded corrected work; what became of that manuscript is unknown.

COMPARABLE LITERARY WORKS AT THE TIME

Bordeaux neither lived nor wrote in a vacuum. His life intertwined with his relatives, tribal members, Indian Office officials, residents of other reservations, Sioux Falls politicians, and ordinary people. Conquering the Mighty Sioux joined a body of works at a time when other Sioux people were raising their literary voices. One of the first Sioux authors was Flying Hawk, an Oglala Sioux born in 1852, thirty-two years before Bordeaux, near what was to become Rapid City (McCreight and Flying Hawk 1947:3–4). He was a member of the generation who were enthusiastically interviewed by Bordeaux, and his memoirs were recorded by Major Israel McCreight. McCreight's text included a wide variety of Native narratives and history beyond the material on the Sioux provided by Flying Hawk. He generally had Flying Hawk comment on these discourses. Flying Hawk's topics closely parallel some of Bordeaux's interests: warfare with other Natives and the Americans including the Battle of the Little Big Horn; origins of the Sioux people, biographies of Crazy Horse, Sitting Bull, and other notable leaders; winter counts; and a social critique of the white man. As with Bordeaux, Flying Hawk wanted to record the Indian side of history and correct inaccurate non-Indian history (McCreight and Flying Hawk 1947:3).

Charles Alexander Eastman, a Santee Sioux who married an American woman, published a series of articles and books written with his wife's assistance (Ruoff 1991:xi). He was born in 1858, about twenty-six years before Bordeaux, and worked for the government in many capacities, including as a physician (Wilson 1983:13; Ruoff 1991:xi–xii). He published his first book in 1902 (1991a).[21] His writings covered in depth many of the themes that Bordeaux touched on in his work, including religion (1980), contemporary Native issues (1915), famous Indian leaders including Crazy Horse and Spotted Tail (1991b), and folk stories (1976; Eastman and Eastman 1990). Like Bordeaux, Eastman also wrote journal articles (Eastman 1894, 1906a, 1906b). Another Sioux author, Luther Standing Bear, was a Teton born in the 1860s, two decades before Bordeaux (Ellis 1975:ix). Like Bordeaux, Standing Bear was discontented and had also been cast in a bad light by the agent. Standing Bear stated in 1931: "I was a bad Indian, and the agent and I never got on" (Ellis 1978:ix). Also like Bordeaux, he believed that Native people should write their own histories: "White men who have tried to write stories about the Indian have either foisted on the public some blood-curdling, impossible 'thriller'; or, if they have been in sympathy with the Indian, have written from knowledge which was not accurate and reliable. No one is able to understand the Indian race like an Indian" (Standing Bear 1975: preface).

A third contemporary author, Zitkala-Ša, also known as Gertrude Bonnin, was a Yankton Sioux born in 1876, eight years before Bordeaux. Many of her writings appeared in the journals *Harper's Monthly Magazine, Everybody's Magazine,* and *Atlantic Monthly.* She protested against the assimilation policy of the government and was involved in Native politics, founding the National Council of American Indians (Fisher 1985). Like Bordeaux, although on a far grander scale, she sought reform in Native–white relations. In addition to her numerous articles, she published two books. Her first (1985b), published in 1901, was an anthology of Sioux stories. The other (1985a), containing a collection of previously published stories, including her essay entitled "The Soft Hearted Sioux," was published in 1921. She also wrote a Native performance piece called *The Sun Dance Opera* (Hafen 2001). As we shall see, Bordeaux also wrote a piece for public performance.

OTHER LITERARY WORKS BY WILLIAM BORDEAUX

Before and after *Conquering the Mighty Sioux*, Bordeaux wrote articles for publication in a variety of venues.[22] Pine Ridge superintendent James H. McGregor stated in 1934 that Bordeaux published small pieces on Indian affairs.[23] In 1926, Bordeaux wrote a short piece for the *Sunshine State,* a journal published by the South Dakota Development Association intended to promote immigration and tourism in the state. Bordeaux's article (1926), entitled "The Early Day Squaw Man," discussed his grandfather, asserting the importance of French traders who acted as intermediaries between the government and the Sioux, as well as their role in advising the Sioux to sign the

Treaty of Fort Laramie in 1868. He subsequently (1927) wrote a second piece for the same journal, a biographical article on Hollow Horn Bear, in which he explained how Hollow Horn Bear vehemently opposed the sale of the Black Hills and was a key force in what became the Black Hills claim. Hollow Horn Bear favored the sale of the reservation land that was to become Gregory and Tripp counties, which he saw as worthless prairie lands in comparison to the rich Black Hills. Bordeaux also detailed Hollow Horn Bear's relationship to U.S. presidents Roosevelt and Wilson.

Bordeaux had been in an automobile accident that had tossed him from the car and injured the ball of his right femur, for which he underwent a series of painful treatments.[24] Despite his disabilities, he struggled to maintain his literary career. When Bordeaux's health prevented him from engaging in physical labor, he supplemented his income by writing stories for the Associated Press and the Newspaper Enterprise Association.[25] In 1934, he wrote a series of five articles for another local South Dakota journal, *The Dakotah Traveler,* that also promoted immigration and tourism. In a short introduction to the series, the journal editor wrote that Bordeaux was well known to readers in the state (in Bordeaux 1934a:11). The first article (1934a) was a short biographical piece on Chief Spotted Tail. The next (1935b) chronicled the shift from nomadic to settled life by the Sioux and the beginning of Western education among them. The subsequent article (1934c) described the ritual of the Sun Dance in the context of a dance held for the fiftieth anniversary commemoration of the establishment of the Rosebud Reservation. The fourth article (1935a) outlined Sioux techniques of hunting, following a trail, and eluding enemies. The final piece (1935b) explained Sioux mourning and burial customs. Eight of the nine photographs and line drawings in the article series had appeared previously in *Conquering the Mighty Sioux.* Bordeaux also used some of the topics and text from the book for some of the articles. In one article, he stated the importance of Native perspective when writing tribal history, a consistent theme in his writings: "Historians, who have portrayed the primitive Sioux as a brutish, savage demon, lack a true conception of the Red Man. No matter how near he may be, or even a peep behind their secret scenes of tribal activities and mode of living, a white man obtains only an obscure picture of the real significance behind the veil of operations; hence practically all historians rely only on vague and visionary ideas for history" (Bordeaux 1934b:20).

Bordeaux wrote other books, including one on Crazy Horse entitled *Custer's Conqueror.* He became interested in writing about Crazy Horse in 1917, the year of his father Louis's death. Louis had accumulated records on Crazy Horse's life, and Bordeaux used these documents in concert with personal interviews with Mrs. Joe Clown, who he says is Crazy Horse's sister, and other Native people to compose the manuscript. He completed it around 1945, but waited until 1948 to put it into publication, six years after

Mari Sandoz (1942) published her own work on Crazy Horse.[26] According to Yeager (1948), Eligha [*sic*] Smith of Rosebud, South Dakota, Bordeaux's brother-in-law,[27] drew the illustrations for this book. Bordeaux's interest in Crazy Horse went beyond written commemoration; he was also in support of plans to memorialize Crazy Horse with a sculpture in the Black Hills (Yeager 1948). Sculpting officially began on June 3, 1948, one month after the publication of Yeager's article (DeWall 1983:149).

Bordeaux also penned and produced another short account of the life of Crazy Horse, *A Warlord of the Mighty Sioux*, which he claimed contains the only true version of the Battle of the Little Big Horn. He based this book on his interviews with the oldest of tribal members on various Sioux reservations.[28] He wrote this piece in the literary style of a historical novel. Another of his books, *Sitting Bull, Tanka-Itotaka*, was a biography that sought to provide Native historical perspective on this important leader and the events surrounding him. The Custer Ephemera Society republished the work in 1974 (Bordeaux 1974). In addition to books and articles, Bordeaux also composed a "festival" entitled *The Seven Camp Fires* which his wife Nannie directed. The piece was performed for many years at Terrace Park in Sioux Falls, South Dakota (Nelson 1958).

In addition to his own writing, Bordeaux assisted other scholars. He carried on an active correspondence with historian Everett Pitt Wilson from 1937 to 1940. Wilson was involved in the Sioux Memorial Project, an initiative to commemorate the Lakota along with their allies, the Cheyenne and the Arapaho (Sheldon 1941:40). Despite support from many Natives and scholars, the project never came to fruition. Wilson wrote to Bordeaux about identifying the precise location of Crazy Horse's camp at Red Cloud Agency as well as the original location of Bordeaux's grandfather's trading post.[29] Wilson (1941) later published an article on Lakota history as part of this project.[30]

BORDEAUX'S SCHOLARSHIP

Bordeaux was not without his critics and supporters in the literary community. Sandoz wrote to Eleanor Hinman, an author who turned over her own Crazy Horse research to her, questioning the accuracy and originality of Bordeaux's work on Crazy Horse: "I'm saving the enclosure in it [a letter sent to Hinman that was returned to Sandoz] for you, a copy of Bill Bordeaux's admission that our version of the breed wife of Crazy Horse was correct. He even confirms your notion, which I had heard too, but with neither of us very sure—that her name was Nellie. He had not told anything of this story, or anything else much that was true in the book on Crazy Horse as ghost written for him by a Dakota Newspaper man."[31]

Sandoz also communicated with Joseph Balmer, a Swiss bibliophile particularly interested in Sioux history,[32] about her concerns about Bordeaux:

"Just a word of caution: The Bordeaux book was written by a newspaper man and is completely unreliable, as Bordeaux knows very well. I have a letter he wrote to Scotty Philip about Crazy Horse'[?] second wife. It indicate [*sic*] that he knows a lot of history well. But the book is perhaps the poorest on the Sioux, unless it is the Dodge book."[33] Balmer responded to her letter: "The Bordeaux book is a scarce book and hard to obtain, but as you say, not especially good for source-material. The pictures are interesting and nice—but the writing of the Lakota words etc. it'isn't [*sic*] well done, and many historical dates are wrong. A [*sic*] only important thing is, that this book was written by a half-blood. You say that a newspaper man has written it—well, but the thoughts came from Bordeaux."[34] It is unclear to what degree the "newspaper man" collaborated in writing Bordeaux's book. In a letter to E. P. Wilson written ten years before the Sandoz-Balmer exchange, Bordeaux explained: "The Argus Leader proof reader has aided me in editing the manuscript so it is in fair shape for the publishers."[35]

The aforementioned Charles E. Hanson, Jr., a historian who wrote extensively on Bordeaux's grandfather James, knew Bordeaux personally and consulted him on questions of family and local history.[36] He wrote of Bordeaux: "One of his [Louis Bordeaux's sons], William Bordeaux, was a life-long student and historian for his people and his family. He wrote a number of pamphlets on the Sioux Indians and an excellent book, Conquering the Mighty Sioux (Sioux Falls, SD 1929), which preserved a great deal of Lakota oral history. The book includes a good account of the Crow raid on the Bordeaux Trading Post in 1849, incorporating the first-hand recollections of several Sioux participants" (Hanson 1991:7). In another article, Hanson (1972:141) stated that William Bordeaux "probably did more careful research on his ancestors and their contemporaries than anyone else in the family." In July of 1955, Bordeaux was an honored guest at the opening of the Museum of the Fur Trade near Chadron, Nebraska.[37]

Bordeaux's work should be taken "as is" in order to understand the picture Bordeaux painted of his people and of himself. On the other hand, this portrait should also be viewed critically with regard to specific historical and familial information. *Conquering the Mighty Sioux* is an amalgamation of sources, some remembered and recorded well, some inaccurately.[38]

WILLIAM BORDEAUX

William Bordeaux came from a large extended family spanning multiple cultures, several languages, and a vast geographical territory. While Bordeaux provided no direct autobiographical information in the text of *Conquering the Mighty Sioux,* he did provide a photograph of himself wearing a chief's headdress with trailer, moccasins, a blanket, and a pipe in his right hand. The caption stated that his Indian name, given to him by the Brule

Sioux, was Pte Ka-Sote-La. Only in a later book, *Custer's Conqueror,* did he devote a short paragraph to his autobiography: "The author was born on the Rosebud Indian Reservation in 1884. He completed his education at Haskell Institute, Lawrence Kansas. In 1933, to 1937, he was employed by the State of South Dakota as a special investigator at large."

Bordeaux grew up on his father's ranch on the reservation near Kilgore, Nebraska.[39] He was thirty-three when his father died in 1917, allowing him substantial time to listen to his father's reminiscences. His grandmother, Red Cormorant Woman, died the year he was born, and his grandfather, James, died six years before he was born. Bordeaux was born at a time of radical changes in the life of the Brule and the Sioux in general. His birth marked the sixteenth anniversary of the signing of the Treaty of Fort Laramie in 1868, the fourteenth anniversary of the first Brule delegation to Washington, D.C., in 1870, the eighth anniversary of the Battle of the Little Big Horn in 1876, and the seventh anniversary of the killing of Crazy Horse in 1877. He was three years old at the passage of the Dawes Act in 1887 and six years old at the time of the Ghost Dance, the killing of Sitting Bull, and the Wounded Knee Massacre in 1890.

Bordeaux spent considerable time applying for a position with the Indian Service. His desire, consistently stated, was to serve his Indian people. However, a past that included two incarcerations and other troubles impeded his success. Bordeaux remained undaunted, as the history of his correspondence shows, and he continued to apply for positions with polite determination. For example, when he sought a job with the Indian Service in 1925, he stated that if hired he would work "to the best interest of the government and the Indians."[40] Senator and former South Dakota governor W. H. McMaster sent Charles H. Burke a letter of recommendation dated March 27, 1925, describing Bordeaux as "a very valuable man" and mentioned that he worked for the State Highway Commission under his governorship. However, a penciled note on this letter stated "Bordeaux appears to be a 'bad actor.'" The note also references the 1921 court case convicting Bordeaux of possession of alcohol.[41] This was part of Bordeaux's ongoing struggle to establish a good reputation through his own testimony and that of others while certain government officials negatively evaluated his character based on his past behavior.

The election of Herbert Hoover to the presidency brought a new appointment for commissioner of Indian Affairs, Charles J. Rhoads. Bordeaux wrote to Rhoads from Rosebud in October 1930, informing him that he had injured his right femur and requesting a position once he recovered.[42] Characteristic of many of his applications, he promised his best efforts and gave his motives for seeking a job in the Indian Service: "I realize the Indian situation is one of vital importance today and I would like to be of some service to my fellow Indians towards advancing them to a state of self-support. And if appointed I intend to put forth my earnest efforts in bettering conditions among my own race who today need first hand attention."

In July 1933, Bordeaux wrote to yet another commissioner of Indian Affairs, John Collier, who had taken office on April 21, 1933.[43] He again asked for an appointment to the service and pledged his commitment to "render my services for the best interst [sic] of my people and your department." Bordeaux wrote again to Collier the next month, stating that he understood that his civil service rating had expired and that agent W. O. Roberts had "intimated" that he might be placed in service, and ended by pledging his service to assist his people if a position became open.[44] Collier replied that "persons of one-quarter or more Indian blood who qualify through an examination are given preference for appointment in this Service."[45] He also recommended that Bordeaux send a full resume to Edward L. Compton for employment outside of the Indian Service. Seven months later, Collier sent Bordeaux another letter saying that several positions had opened in the Farm Service, and while he could not guarantee Bordeaux a position, he asked him to fill out an attached application.[46] Collier sent a carbon copy of this letter to the Salt Lake City Extension Agency, the Rosebud Agency and the Pine Ridge Agency. The carbon sent to Pine Ridge elicited a response from Superintendent James H. McGregor who strongly opposed Bordeaux's employment in the service. He said that while Bordeaux had "sufficient education and intelligence," and was "modernistic enough to make a success," his character was insufficient and his advancement would discredit the Office of Indian Service.[47] Despite saying he did not want to blacken Bordeaux's reputation, McGregor remarked scathingly that Bordeaux "poses as an Indian leader," "writes little articles for the papers on questions affecting the Indians," and was involved in political questions while his political allegiance was unclear. McGregor did suggest that Bordeaux be given "one chance" away from Sioux Country, although he could not personally recommend him.

On May 12, 1934, Bordeaux submitted his application to be a farmer in triplicate along with an attached photograph of himself to the Office of Indian Affairs, Division of Extension and Industry.[48] He included a letter to Collier stating that he was also applying for construction supervisor in addition to the Farm Aids position. He told Collier that he had asked six people to send Collier letters of recommendation on his behalf.[49] Bordeaux also wrote to W. O. Roberts, the superintendent of the Rosebud Reservation, and included copies of his Farm Aids application. Roberts sent the applications to the commissioner of Indian Affairs along with a letter delicately stating that he would not recommend Bordeaux for employment due to his age and that in his judgment Bordeaux's behavior was not in keeping with the Extension Service. He further stated that the Extension Service was set up to employ young Indians.[50] Bordeaux was fifty years old at the time of the letter.

Relentlessly, Bordeaux continued to seek employment in the Indian Service. In one letter, he stated that he expected a positive recommendation "for my conduct with my own people has been unimpaired and free from depraved policies."[51] In the same letter, he also referenced the Wheeler-Howard Act "exempting Indians from the civil service status and giving them preference where applicants are qualified." He expanded on his now four-year quest for employment with the Indian Service:

> I am not alone in this appeal for recognition, for countless educated, able and qualified Indians in our state today are jobless, for the simplest reasons, "chiefly," that we are Indians and formerly have been recognized as incompetents. This attitude held out against us has been one of the stumbling blocks, discouraging any notion for advancement.
>
> To achieve success in your program, outlined for my people, you must seek the aid of sincere and desirable persons who are in a position to impart and contrive [sic] to ideas best fitted for purposes beneficial to your program. Persons well versed in our problems should be selected. Experience in the past, tolerating with selfish deceptives [sic], whose only desires were for personal benefits, should be discontinued. This corrput [sic] policy, with its discouraging environments, is wholly responsible towards transforming the Indian from a well developed, self-conscious race to a state of dependence and inferiority.

The letter ends with Bordeaux's assurance that he would work toward advancing the policies of the service.

Despite these efforts, a memorandum in Bordeaux's personnel file dated November 13, 1934, stated he was an ex-government employee, recounted his prison record and then provided quotes from the character evaluations made by superintendents Roberts and McGregor.[52] Collier wrote a short letter to Bordeaux the same month stating that he reviewed his record and "it seems unwise to consider you for a regular appointment in the Indian Service."[53]

There is more than irony in this exchange. Indeed, Bordeaux did go through a period of breaking the law. On the other hand, in a personal discussion I had with one of Bordeaux's relatives, he remembered that "Billie" worked with Native prisoners and parolees, stating that this was no doubt due to his own experience. Unlike within Native families, there seemed to have been no forgiveness of the past from the federal government. Bordeaux could only attempt to fight negative recommendations with letters of endorsement.[54] His indictment was handed down in the 1930s, not by a court but by two reservation superintendents. Bordeaux was never given a chance to directly defend himself, or to have relatives and friends testify on his behalf. He was aware of his record and asked politicians located in his new home, Sioux Falls, to intercede on his behalf and attest to his good character.

Bordeaux no doubt wished a new start away from the reservation. He actively, and at times relentlessly, sought employment. Moreover, as is clear both from his life history and his stated intentions, he sought to work not only to his fullest capacity but also for the benefit of his own people.

COMMUNITY COMMITMENT AND POLITICAL COMMENTARY

Bordeaux and his wife Dorine participated in community activities both in Sioux Falls and on the Rosebud Reservation. Bordeaux helped organize Boy Scout troops and gave talks to college students, high school students and Boy Scouts.[55] Another sign of his commitment to work for the common good was his engagement with scholars who had pressing historical and cultural questions. Dorine was active in assisting Sioux on the reservations to the west of Sioux Falls with donations of clothing and other necessities (Bordeaux 1958a, 1958b). Under the Works Projects of America program, she supervised beadwork teachers who instructed Sioux Falls children. She also worked for the YMCA, teaching dancing and arts and crafts to the "Friendly Indian tribes." As noted earlier, both Bordeaux and his wife created and directed a festival called *The Seven Camp Fires* (Nelson 1958). Through this event and their involvement in teaching and lecturing, they served as cultural intermediaries between the Native and local non-Native communities.

Both an observer and participant in the intricate relationships between his tribe and the federal government, Bordeaux was a vocal critic, and sometimes victim, of the federal Indian bureaucracy while at the same time he used this bureaucracy to reestablish his good standing. In a letter to Collier he utilized his own book as evidence of the deteriorated conditions of his people: "In writing up a history of my people I have delved into their past and present modes of living. I find conditions of today far inferior in every respect with that of their primitive era, with the exception of educational advancements which can be improved."[56] He was not totally opposed to the government's paternalistic system and bought into the evolutionist model of the day. In the same letter, he recommended wardship only for older people and those unable to manage their own affairs, seeing government supervision of Natives and the "dole system" as taking away Native responsibility and self-reliance. He stated further that the government had been negligent in managing rental of Native lands; that the Indian service was over-bureaucratized; that some civil servants sought their own betterment rather than that of the Indians, noting that some engaged in political campaigning despite federal prohibition; and that the government engaged in wasteful spending.

Bordeaux was also involved in Native assistance programs from his home in Sioux Falls. During 1958, there was an extended debate on the conditions of Indians in South Dakota in the Sioux Falls *Argus Leader,* carried out through articles and letters to the editor.[57] Bordeaux was interviewed about the situation in a feature article which introduced him as a Native author, at that point retired, who had traveled extensively to the reservations in the state.[58] In this interview, Bordeaux highlighted critical problems:

"I say without hesitation that extreme poverty and malnutrition exists among Indian families in South Dakota," Bordeaux said. "Practically 70 per cent of our Indians in the state are in dire need."

"THEIR INCOME [sic] does not exceed $500 yearly per family and is derived from land rentals in most cases. Beyond this, the state provides old age assistance and help to dependent children.

"I have visited many one room shacks erected with crude lumber. The furniture consisted of one table, a bed and old type tin stove for cooking and heating."

Bordeaux said the Indians relied in much part on surplus commodities such as powdered milk, cheese, flour, beans, and occasionally butter. He said they have no refrigeration and butter was of no benefit in the summer time.

"Men and women cannot buy decent clothing," Bordeaux said. As a result they are shabby and present a true picture of poverty in its lowest ebb."

"THE OLD AGE [sic] pensioners have many visitors on check days to share in their meals. The old people will feed their close kin until their money runs out.

"Then they grow hungry until the monthly check arrives."

In a letter, Bordeaux (1958) further criticized the government and recommended local intervention to alleviate the desperate conditions:

Indisputable facts have proven that our Indian Bureau directing their orders and supervision from the Washington office have failed, either through ignorance or maladministration in their supervision over their Indian wards. The complex situation has brought grief, despair, and extreme poverty on many families, and their pride and self confidence shattered. To restore the will to progress in the mind of the Indian, a concrete program having qualities of producing results should be initiated from the local level. Local ranchers, farmers, and business men who live neighbors to Indian families and in daily contact with them should be brought in to the clouded picture and take part in panel discussions and aid in drafting Indian policies.

Bordeaux's wife Dorine also commented on the conditions of the Sioux and their neglect by the government. She stated her opinion in a letter (1958a) to the *Argus Leader*: "The year 1957 was an era of incredible suffering among my people. Congress appropriates huge sums yearly presumed to benefit the Indians welfare and economic progress. The truth is that out of these staggering appropriations a large share is expended for administrative purposes, while a poverty stricken race goes in want." Dorine argued in another letter (1958b) that conditions were worse than ever before: "Never before during the annals over wardship control over our Indians have they experienced such hardships as they are confronted with today. Undernourished, scantily clothed, living in tents or rudely built shacks, minus proper heating facilities. Added to the depressed conditions the Government for reasons unknown have temporarily stopped the sale of all individual and inherited lands, thus increasing further privation from the sale or rental of their trust lands for their survival. . . . My people are made victims of want, in a land of abundance."

CONCLUSION

When William Bordeaux died on May 22, 1962, at the age of seventy-eight, the *Argus Leader* described him as a "champion for a better life for Indians."[59] Despite the bureaucratic wrangling over Bordeaux's character and suitability for employment, his obituary gave testimony to his commitment to Indian people: "Mr. Bordeaux labored in behalf of Indians generally, but was primarily concerned for the welfare of the elderly. 'The old, old people is where my heart is,' he once explained, discussing his work. 'Some provisions should be made to take care of them in their declining years.'" Bordeaux was a complicated person who lived at a time of radical change. He had been both a violator and then an appointed upholder of the law. He struggled to make a living for himself and his family during difficult years on the reservation, and later through difficult times during the Depression in Sioux Falls. In later life, he became an active voice advocating for his people. He also needed others to advocate for him as he struggled to establish a good reputation and secure employment. He was one voice among many Lakota who spoke and continue to speak both orally and in writing. His position was unique and yet his struggles mirrored those of many Lakota at that time. While some Americans sought and continue to seek the "true" Indian, authentic and untouched, he spoke about the diverse reality of Lakota culture, a diversity he himself embodied, speaking English, French, and Lakota, visiting elders and enthusiastically discussing the past with them, visiting relatives and debating contemporary world politics, and being funny in a uniquely Lakota way. He did not have the privilege of a university education or an advanced degree, but he endeavored to write authoritative books and tried to correct errors as he could. He was open to discussing history and culture with both his relatives and outside scholars. Neither he nor his book was flawless, yet studying both his life and his texts is of incredible value.

Joseph M. Marshall (1992:43), himself a historian and a Lakota who writes extensively on his own people, had this to say on the importance of a multivocal history of the West that includes Native voices: "There are Native Americans with an active interest in the history of their people. Some . . . have devoted much time and energy to the recording of those events, and make the time to pass those stories to young people. Those people should be involved wherever the history of the West is told or presented. And we Native Americans really should not wait to be invited to do so. We should take the initiative and take an active and aggressive role in the development of accurate histories of our various peoples." Bordeaux was one among many other Native people interested in his people's history, one who struggled to have his voice heard through a variety of media-letters, articles, books, and speeches. That voice spoke Lakota, English, and French and traveled among many different groups and situations: Natives and non-Natives, full and mixed culture individuals, reservation and non-reservation, praise and condemnation, acceptance and dismissal. His voice is teaching us to look carefully both at his work and at his life and to learn from both. Through it all he strove to give a wider voice to his people, particularly his family—which, in Native reckoning, are one and the same.

NOTES

1. Editor's note: The full Introduction, although a great example of how ethnohistory should be done and written, was unfortunately too long for this volume. I sincerely hope that it will be published as intended. With permission from the author, it was edited so that its length would be more appropriate for this publication. This editing process affected mostly a full, detailed, extremely interesting, and important account of Bordeaux's life.

2. I give my deepest thanks to the members of William Bordeaux's family who assisted me in this work with their stories, good humor, and hospitality. This work could not have been completed without the exceptional editorial and research skills of my research assistant, Kristin Fitzgerald, University of New Mexico graduate student and instructor at Creighton University. I began this project knowing only that Bordeaux wrote *Conquering the Mighty Sioux* and then, thanks to a bibliographic database, the Online Computer Library Center, three other works. Bringing together the rest of this information was a daunting and time-consuming project that relied on the collaborative generosity of a very large group of people. Tina Irvine at the Sioux Falls Public Library assisted in finding the majority of Bordeaux articles in various journals as well as obituaries and other sources. I was also assisted by Peter Brink at the Archives and Special Collections of the University of Nebraska Lincoln; Violet Catches, Lakota language instructor, Pierre, South Dakota; Raymond J. DeMallie, American Indian Studies Research Institute, Indiana University; Ann Greenia at the

High Plains Heritage Center at Chadron State College; James Griffis, webmaster, United States Marshals Service; Rhonda Kodad, department administrator, Department of Sociology and Anthropology, Creighton University; Emily Levine of the University of Nebraska, Lincoln; Marcia Poole director of the Betty Strong Encounter Center, Sioux City, Iowa; Richard Pool, theater department of Briarcliff College, Sioux City, Iowa; James Potter, Senior Research Historian at the Nebraska State Historical Society; Gail DeBuse Potter and James A. Hanson of the Museum of the Fur Trade, Chadron, Nebraska; Jodie Risley, director of the Cimarron Heritage Center; Donovin Sprague, Crazy Horse Memorial; Lynn Schneiderman, Nathan Morgan and Mary Nash of the Reinert-Alumni Memorial Library, Creighton University; Harry Thompson of the Western Heritage Center, Augustana College; Ken Steward of the South Dakota State Archives. Raymond J. DeMallie, Kristin Fitzgerald, James Hanson, Emily Levine, James Potter and Terry Strauss read versions of the manuscript and made many useful suggestions.

3. Letter from William J. Bordeaux to W. O. Roberts dated December 11, 1931. National Archives and Records Administration (NARA), Archives I, Record Group 75 (Bureau of Indian Affairs), Entry 121 (Central Classified Files), 1907–1939, Rosebud Agency, Box 68385, File 255.

4. One form of Sioux Benefits was a cash payment of $515.27 (Riney 1999:194).

5. Letter from Wilbur Lewis Bordeaux to Superintendent W. O. Roberts dated September 22, 1931. NARA, Archives I, Record Group 75 (Bureau of Indian Affairs), Entry 121 (Central Classified Files), 1907–1939, Rosebud Agency, Box 68385, File 255.

6. Letter from William J. Bordeaux to Superintendent Commissioner of Indians Affairs dated March 31, 1932. NARA, Archives I, Record Group 75 (Bureau of Indian Affairs), Entry 121 (Central Classified Files), 1907–1939, Rosebud Agency, Box 68385, File 255.

7. Letter from C. J. Rhoads to William J. Bordeaux dated June 7, 1932. NARA, Archives I, Record Group 75 (Bureau of Indian Affairs), Entry 121 (Central Classified Files), 1907–1939, Rosebud Agency, Box 68385, File 255.

8. Letter from J. Henry Scattergood to Senator Peter Norbeck dated January 22, 1932. NARA, Archives I, Record Group 75 (Bureau of Indian Affairs), Entry 121 (Central Classified Files), 1907–1939, Rosebud Agency, Box 68385, File 255.

9. Bordeaux stated that this took place while he was in school in Rapid City in 1900. He stated in his Farm Aids application that he attended school in Rapid City from 1903 to 1905. William J. Bordeaux, May 12, 1934. NARA, National Personnel Records Center, Civilian Personnel Records, Personnel file for William J. Bordeaux.

10. One editor saw in his approach over-enthusiasm (Mercatante 1974).

11. Emily Levine (1998:xxviii–xxxvi) provides an in-depth discussion of shifts in appreciation for and understandings of Native histories.

12. There is a very large literature on this battle. Historian Jerry Keenan (1972) suggests that Brevet-Major Powell's estimate of at least 60 Indians killed and 120 severely wounded is a close approximation although Keenan admits that that is an inflated number. As for numbers of Native participants, Powell's official report says there were two groups of attackers totaling 800 warriors. Keenan does not cite William J. Bordeaux in his sources.

13. Keenan (1972) asserted that the Natives engaged in the Wagon Box Fight were Oglalas under Crazy Horse, Miniconjous under High Back-Bone, some Sans Arcs, and about sixty Cheyennes under Little Wolf. Citing a variety of sources, Keenan admitted that the record is unclear on whether Red Cloud was present or not. He credited Olson, Larson, and Vestal with implying that Red Cloud was present while Big Bat Pourier and Black Horse stated that he was not.

14. In an interview with Red Cloud toward the end of his life, Eli Ricker (2005:348) recorded that Red Cloud did not remember if he participated in the Wagon Box Fight.

15. The book index refers to the first delegation to Washington but the photograph says the second delegation. Both delegations are dated 1869.

16. This error was brought to my attention by James E. Potter, senior research historian at the Nebraska State Historical Society, personal correspondence, November 2007. He stated: "This date is erroneous, as there was no such delegation in that year. By comparison with a related photo of the same individuals (dressed exactly the same) appearing in the Handbook of North American Indians, the correct date is 1875, for this was the visit by Spotted Tail, Red Cloud, et. al in the summer of that year in advance of the September 1875 Allison Commission trek to the Red Cloud Agency to attempt to purchase the Black Hills."

17. See DeMallie (2001a:795). This is a different photograph of only some of the participants taken with the same background and with participants wearing the same clothes except for Julius Meyer. Both photographs were taken in the studio of Frank Currier, Omaha, Nebraska in May 1875. Goodyear (2003:26–29) presents both photographs in his text.

18. Letter from Wilbur Lewis Bordeaux to Superintendent W. O. Roberts dated September 22, 1931. NARA, Archives I, Record Group 75 (Bureau of Indian Affairs), Entry 121 (Central Classified Files), 1907–1939, Rosebud Agency, Box 68385, File 255.

19. Letter from William J. Bordeaux to E. P. Wilson dated January 27, 1937. E. P. Wilson Papers, Museum of the Fur Trade, Chadron, Nebraska. Personal correspondence, Gail DeBuse Potter, director of the Museum of the Fur Trade, Chadron, Nebraska, December 6, 2007.

20. Letter from William J. Bordeaux to E. P. Wilson dated October 24, 1937. E. P. Wilson Papers, Museum of the Fur Trade, Chadron, Nebraska.

21. To be more accessible for contemporary readers, I refer to the newer editions of these works whenever possible.

22. Recovering all of William's writing proved to be a daunting task. My suspicion is that there are many more works that have not yet been found at the writing of this text.

23. Letter from James H. McGregor to John Collier dated May 10, 1934. NARA, National Personnel Records Center, Civilian Personnel Records, Personnel file for William J. Bordeaux.

24. Letter from William J. Bordeaux to Commissioner of Indian Affairs dated October 15, 1930. NARA, National Personnel Records Center, Civilian Personnel Records, Personnel file for William J. Bordeaux.

25. Letter from William J. Bordeaux to the Commissioner of Indian Affairs dated March 31, 1932. NARA, Archives I, Record Group 75 (Bureau of Indian Affairs), Entry 121 (Central Classified Files), 1907–1939, Rosebud Agency, Box 68385, File 255.

26. Bordeaux did not put a copyright date in *Custer's Conqueror*. The estimated date is based on evidence in Yeager (1948). DeMallie and Parks (2001:1073) cite 1952 as the publication date for *Custer's Conqueror.*

27. Rosebud Indian Census Roll, from NARA, M595, roll 430, p. 42, as posted on www.ancestry.com.

28. The publication date of this work is unclear. Grace Nelson (1958) attributes another book to Bordeaux, entitled *History of Crazy Horse*. I was unable to find any evidence of its existence. Perhaps she was referring to *A War Lord of the Mighty Sioux*.

29. Letter from William J. Bordeaux to E. P. Wilson dated November 20th, 1938. Letter from William J. Bordeaux to E. P. Wilson dated January 27, 1937. E. P. Wilson Papers, Museum of the Fur Trade, Chadron, Nebraska.

30. William J. Bordeaux's work was not cited in this article, although works by two other Sioux authors, Charles Eastman and Luther Standing Bear, were.

31. Letter from Mari Sandoz to Eleanor Hinman dated January 3, 1945. Mari Sandoz Collection (MS 080). Archives & Special Collections, University of Nebraska–Lincoln Libraries.

32. Balmer explained his relationship with Lakota people beyond scholarship: "I'm always in connection with chief James H. Red Cloud and I'm called by him 'Wanbli ista or 'Eagle eye.' My boy got the name 'Mahpiya luta' or 'Redcloud': – The chief wrote me that he will give a name to my daughter Suzy, who was born 3 months ago. The name I do not know, but it is the name of old man Redcloud's sister." Letter from Joseph Balmer to Mari Sandoz dated February 18, 1947. Mari Sandoz Collection (MS 080). Archives & Special Collections, University of Nebraska–Lincoln Libraries.

33. Letter from Mari Sandoz to Joseph Balmer dated November 28, 1947. Mari Sandoz Collection (MS 080). Archives & Special Collections, University of Nebraska–Lincoln Libraries.

34. Letter from Joseph Balmer to Mari Sandoz dated December 23, 1947. Mari Sandoz Collection (MS 080). Archives & Special Collections, University of Nebraska–Lincoln Libraries.

35. Letter from William J. Bordeaux to E. P. Wilson dated October 24, 1937. E. P. Wilson Papers, Museum of the Fur Trade, Chadron, Nebraska.

36. Hanson (1972:164, n.10) cited information in one of his articles as being based on an interview with "William Bordeaux, Hobart Bissonette and John Bissonette."

37. William Bordeaux was also invited in October 1956 to the opening of the reconstruction of his grandfather's trading house proximate to the Museum of the Fur Trade, but he was not able to attend. Personal conversation with James Hanson of the Museum of the Fur Trade, June 18, 2008.

38. A wide range of scholars have cited elements of Bordeaux's works including Susan Bordeaux Bettelyoun (Bettelyoun, Waggoner and Levine 1998), Kingsley A. Bray (2006), Robert A. Clark (1988), Raymond J. DeMallie (1984), Charles E. Hanson, Jr. (1966:12), Richard G Hardoff (2001), Royal B. Hassrick (1964), George E. Hyde (1961), John McDermott (1965), James C. Olson (1965), and Virginia Driving Hawk Sneve (1995). All cite *Conquering the Mighty Sioux* except for Clark and Hardoff, who cite *Custer's Conqueror*. Donovin Sprague (2005:71), a member of the Cheyenne River Sioux Tribe, wrote a short pictorial biography of Bordeaux and his wife Dorine.

39. Personal conversation with family member, August 3, 2008.

40. Letter from William J. Bordeaux to Charles H. Burke dated April 3, 1925. NARA, National Personnel Records Center, Civilian Personnel Records, Personnel file for William J. Bordeaux. He provided three character references including the superintendent of the Rosebud Reservation, James H. McGregor.

41. Letter from W. H. McMaster to Charles H. Burke, March 27, 1925. NARA, National Personnel Records Center, Civilian Personnel Records, Personnel file for William J. Bordeaux. United States vs. William Bordeaux, September 24, 1921, United States District Court. Within and for the District of South Dakota.

42. Letter from William J. Bordeaux to Commissioner of Indian Affairs dated October 15, 1930. NARA, National Personnel Records Center, Civilian Personnel Records, Personnel file for William J. Bordeaux.

43. Letter from William J. Bordeaux to John Collier dated July 9, 1933. NARA, National Personnel Records Center, Civilian Personnel Records, Personnel file for William J. Bordeaux.

44. Letter from William J. Bordeaux to Commissioner of Indian Affairs dated August 23, 1933. NARA, National Personnel Records Center, Civilian Personnel Records, Personnel file for William J. Bordeaux.

45. Letter from John Collier to William J. Bordeaux dated October 5, 1933. NARA, National Personnel Records Center, Civilian Personnel Records, Personnel file for William J. Bordeaux.

46. Letter from John Collier to William J. Bordeaux dated May 3, 1934. NARA, National Personnel Records Center, Civilian Personnel Records, Personnel file for William J. Bordeaux.

47. Letter from James H. McGregor to John Collier dated May 10, 1934. NARA, National Personnel Records Center, Civilian Personnel Records, Personnel file for William J. Bordeaux.

48. William J. Bordeaux's Personnel Information Blank for Farm Aids dated May 12, 1934. NARA, National Personnel Records Center, Civilian Personnel Records, Personnel file for William J. Bordeaux.

49. Bordeaux provided the following references: "Governor Tom Berry, Pierre, South Dakota; Ellis O. Smith, Sioux Falls City Commissioner; James Murry County Commissioner; Attorney Holton Davenport; John M. Cogley, all of Sioux Falls, South Dakota." Letter from William J. Bordeaux to John Collier dated May 12, 1934. NARA, National Personnel Records Center, Civilian Personnel Records, Personnel file for William J. Bordeaux.

50. Letter from W. O. Roberts to Commissioner of Indian Affairs dated June 16, 1934. NARA, National Personnel Records Center, Civilian Personnel Records, Personnel file for William J. Bordeaux.

51. Letter from William J. Bordeaux to John Collier dated August 1, 1934. NARA, National Personnel Records Center, Civilian Personnel Records, Personnel file for William J. Bordeaux.

52. Memorandum from Burton in regard to William J. Bordeaux dated November 13, 1934. NARA, National Personnel Records Center, Civilian Personnel Records, Personnel file for William J. Bordeaux. No further identification is given. The letter is not on letterhead.

53. Letter from John Collier to William J. Bordeaux dated November 30, 1934. NARA, National Personnel Records Center, Civilian Personnel Records, Personnel file for William J. Bordeaux.

54. In an incident early in his life, Bordeaux defended his reputation against claims that he was marrying women in order to gain access to their allotted land so he could sell it and dissipate the proceeds. Bordeaux directly countered these accusations in a letter in which he both spoke for himself and referred to affidavits sent to the Indian Office attesting to his integrity. Letter from William J. Bordeaux to Cato Sills dated April 4, 1914. NARA, Archives I, Record Group 75 (Bureau of Indian Affairs), Entry 121 (Central Classified Files), 1907–1939, Rosebud Agency, Box 26376-13, File 175.

55. William J. Bordeaux's Personnel Information Blank for Farm Aids dated May 12, 1934. NARA, National Personnel Records Center, Civilian Personnel Records, Personnel file for William J. Bordeaux. United States Department of the Interior Office of Indian Affairs, Division of Extension and Industry.

56. Letter from William J. Bordeaux to John Collier dated June 30, 1933. NARA, Archives I, Record Group 75 (Bureau of Indian Affairs), Entry 121 (Central Classified Files), 1907–1939, Rosebud Agency, Box 30186, File 120.

57. "S.D. Indians Not Starving, Asserts Welfare Director, *Argus Leader,* March 6, 1958; "R.C. Woman Declares State Indians Starve to Death," *Argus Leader,* March 9, 1958; "Leader Says Crow Creek Food Ample," *Argus Leader,* March 11,

1958; "Surplus Food Is Going to State Needy," *Argus Leader,* March 13, 1958; "Food, Clothing to Aid Indians," *Argus Leader,* April 22, 1958; "Hassle over Aid to Starving Indians," *Argus Leader,* November 30, 1958; "South Dakota Indians Receive Food," *Argus Leader,* December 2, 1958; "Indian Says His People Are Hungry," *Argus Leader,* December 7, 1958.

58. "Indian Says His People Are Hungry," *Argus Leader,* December 7, 1958.

59. "Champion of Better Life for Indians Dies," *Argus Leader,* May 23, 1962, p. 2A, col. 5.

8

The Search for an Honest Man

Iktomi Ȟcala as an Ethnohistorical and
Humanistic Conundrum

PAULA L. WAGONER

In 1985, Raymond J. DeMallie, an anthropologist and ethnohistorian trained at the University of Chicago with interests in Plains Indian languages and cultures, collaborated with the Berkeley-trained anthropological linguist Douglas Parks, who had an interest in Plains Indian linguistics and language preservation, to create the American Indian Studies and Research Institute (AISRI) at Indiana University's Bloomington campus. Its mission was to support, conduct, and encourage collaborative student and professional opportunities to work on research with American Indian communities. Indiana University was a particularly good site for such an undertaking because of other related American Indian collections already being curated by the staff at the Mathers Archaeological Museum, the Voeglin collection, and music archives that include fragments of music and language captured on wax drums by early ethnographers and ethnomusicologists. Much work has already been conducted by AISRI staff and students, for example, to digitize the music, enabling future researchers and other audiences to use it in a more accessible format. The AISRI became an interdisciplinary magnet that has done its best to fund eager graduate students who continue to carry its mission forward by pursuing their respective intellectual interests. The personal and professional network formed there is often invaluable for them. The representatives of American Indian nations, elders, historians, anthropologists, linguists, and folklorists whom AISRI brings together often continue productive discussions long after their time at the institute.

As a middle-aged graduate student, I was invited to become an AISRI fellow for my first year of study in 1991. One of the perks of the fellowship is wandering around the richly paneled walls on the squeaky wooden floors and poking around in all of the crannies and cubbyholes in search of books and pamphlets on the Sioux and other American Indian tribes that are not easy to find elsewhere, especially not in one place. DeMallie has a great library, and if one ever needs to find a book, he either owns it or knows where to find it, especially when it comes to literature on the Sioux. It was in a bookcase in the vestibule at AISRI that I discovered *America Needs Indians! (Unexpurgated Version),* published in 1937 and authored by Iktomi H̆cala ('The Real Iktomi' or 'The Real Trickster'). I was immediately fascinated by the text. True to the author's pen name (Iktomi usually manifests himself in the form of a spider), the theme, writing style, and illustrations seemed analogous to one of the asymmetrical webs spun by spiders that had ingested LSD in biological and psychological research experiments.

This was a text that I knew that I had to own, and after pestering my mentor mercilessly, I learned that Vine Deloria, Jr., had enjoyed this particular book enough to purchase the remainders. I hesitated contacting the man who had so magnificently captured the essence of newly minted anthropologists on early fieldwork excursions to Indian reservations in chapter 4 of *Custer Died for Your Sins* (1988). I had met him before attending graduate school at a conference at Harvard and he had told me that if I wanted to work on Lakota topics, I should be taught by Ray DeMallie. With this in mind, I thought that I would chance it, since Ray had made the suggestion. Despite Deloria's apparent distaste for anthropologists (and historians and lawyers, as he confided to me later when I was conducting my own fieldwork in Bennett County, South Dakota, where he was raised as a preacher's kid), he and Ray had worked together on treaty and federal Indian law projects for years. I called Vine and he found me a beautiful specimen of the book that included a map that laid out the author's plans for tourism, environmental conservation, and industry based on Lakota-ness for the reservation. There was some irony, of course, in getting a copy of the text by one who calls himself "The Real Iktomi" from a contemporary Lakota trickster, Vine Deloria, Jr. The book is a treasure and, if one has the patience, it can be read from cover to cover. Wine or something stronger may be necessary for reinforcement, however, due to its distinct and outrageous style and content. True to its trickster origins, it is different each time it is read, and it always yields more questions than answers.

Facts and truths are contingent on the questions asked, which is why this topic (I have convinced myself) is indeed a text that demands interrogation by ethnohistorians. This chapter deals with the larger issue of what we receive as "historical fact," and what we pass on as such. As I was preparing this chapter, I consulted Google and Wikipedia (sources that my students would not dare cite but have all consulted) to learn that the author, Iktomi H̆cala, or as he also refers to himself, Iktomi Lila Šiča ('The Really Bad Iktomi') lives on in websites and in scholarly texts. Some have stumbled upon his book and want to know more, but, interestingly, he has now morphed again in print and digitally into "a Lakota chief who was a contemporary of Standing Bear" in Spence (1999) and a "Lakota Sioux writer" in Norris (2002) respectively. I am sure that he is having himself a laugh knowing that he has

been digitally immortalized, and I suspect that he lurks in chat rooms dedicated to him, shedding available light like water off a duck's back. It pleases
me to think that Vine Deloria, Jr., would also be having a good laugh at the
gullibility of those who don't look closely at the source or interrogate it
through appropriate methods such as ethnohistorical inquiry and analysis.
This may prove to be even a more important method in a "democratic" digital age in which everyone may present truth claims in their blog or tweet
their "twuths" sans context or attribution.

IVAN DRIFT AND HIS TEXT

Once in a while one comes upon a character that captures the imagination.
One wants to slip into his head and find out what makes him tick. Ivan Drift
is that sort of character. This chapter scratches the surface by beginning an
examination of the identities of an author who calls himself "Iktomi Ȟcala
—the REAL Iktomi," the Sioux trickster whose form is that of a spider. At
times I have wondered whether he is simply the type of person that Westerners refer to as a "real character," indicating a person who is a "little off in the
head" but entertaining nonetheless, or if he is, indeed, a persona that only
springs to life on the pages of a text. Drift wrote a quirky book of devastating
satire, imminent lunacy, and egocentrism, entitled *America Needs Indians!*
(Unexpurgated Version) that was meant to be a manifesto for Indians living
at the time of the Indian Reorganization Act (IRA) of 1934, commonly
known as the New Deal for Indians. On its face, the IRA was meant to correct the abuses of the General Allotment Act (Dawes Act of 1887) that attempted to hasten the assimilation of Indians by making them into the
"ideal" of yeoman citizen farmers, regardless of whether their land was sufficient for the task, or whether Indians had learned the duties, obligations,
and legalities of land ownership. Drift refers to the New Deal for Indians
alternately as the Nude Eel, the New Dull, and the New Dole. The book is
part detailed ethnography (sans attribution), part environmental treatise,
part irreverent satire. Drift, "the REAL Iktomi," wrote a scathing critique of
how Indians had been "administered to" in his 425-page convoluted volume.
Yet, at the same time, he was jockeying to secure a position within that
same damnable bureaucracy as the superintendent at Pine Ridge. This is a
man who, like Iktomi, personified contradictions, often in the most vulgar
terms—as a good Iktomi story must be; and much like Diogenes the Cynic,
Drift trudged on with his lantern looking for just one honest man.

When I inquired about Drift around Pine Ridge fifteen years ago, I was
informed that he was the first "white hippie wannabee." This response came
from everyone I asked who had any remembrance of him at all. Based on the
Pine Ridge responses, I initially assumed that Drift was a non-Indian from
outside the region who married into the powerful Red Cloud family. His

sister-in-law, a granddaughter of Chief Red Cloud, said that she seemed to recall family stories about how Drift, a "white guy," and his wife had had a daughter who was resting in a local cemetery. Despite the unanimous identification of Drift as a non-Indian, correspondence in the National Archives between Drift and the commissioner of Indian Affairs, John Collier, indicates that he then identified himself as a Cree-Sioux.[1] He had even managed to secure sums of money from a Seminole philanthropist who had made his fortune by way of oil in Oklahoma. Walter Wise indicated in letters to Drift and Collier[2] that he was pleased to contribute to Indian intellectuals, and that he supported his perspectives on "the Indian problem"—because Drift was an Indian intellectual. While the letter states that Wise made a $1,000 investment in Drift's ideas, Iktomi Ȟcala noted in his text that his benefactor had promised him $6,000 (1937:167).

But who was Ivan Drift really? And why did he identify with Iktomi so closely? He certainly knew a great deal about the Lakota, Dakota, and Nakota people, referring to them as "'akota" when referring to the Sioux as a whole. The ethnological portions of the volume indicate that he has a certain level of mastery over the Lakota language and casual references to complex religious and cultural practices interspersed throughout indicate that he is more than comfortable in discussing them. These references appear almost second nature and do not seem to be consciously inserted for effect.

Drift knew what he was doing when he chose Iktomi as a pseudonym, and an analysis of his writing indicates that Drift is indeed fulfilling Iktomi's mandate, especially as evidenced by his later life; it is Iktomi who always ends up getting the proverbial pie in the face. James R. Walker (1980:53) notes Iktomi's place in the Lakota creation story as condemned by Skan for shaming a Goddess. Skan ordered that "he should sit at the feasts of the Gods no more, and should exist forever on the world without a friend, and his wisdom should be only cunning that would entrap him in his own schemes. He names him *Iktomi*. So *Iktomi* is the imp of mischief whose delight is to make others ridiculous." Iktomi fully enjoys making others look ridiculous and is complicit in many plots, schemes, combats, and intrigues; in the spirit of Drift's book, today he might even feel comfortable walking the halls of Congress. Walker (1980:106) noted that "*Iktomi* was the first thing made in the west that matured. He invented language. He saw all animals when they were made, and watched them grow. So he gave them their names. He was very wise in many things. He delighted in playing jokes on everything. He would fool men and spirits to get something from them and would cheat and lie to them. He was like a man, but he was deformed." Despite his gifts, he took his powers to name and to create language to the most negative level, such as manipulating language to make others appear foolish rather than using it for resolution and understanding. Instead of providing for the peace of the community, he really enjoyed "stirring up strife among the Four Winds when he can so he can have fun watching them fight" (Walker 1980:125).

THE "REAL" IKTOMI

Iktomi Ȟcala, the author, displays the traits associated with Iktomi, the Lakota trickster, himself. His interests in further complicating the language of federal policies, the de-Indianizing of Indians, and environmental concerns, on the face of it, seem almost well reasoned, if written in a flamboyant, ironic style. A closer look into his political aspirations, however, fills in the blanks of Iktomi Ȟcala's alter ego, Ivan Drift.

At the beginning of his text, Drift includes a letter written to John Collier, the commissioner of Indian Affairs in 1937. He wants the reader to know that he has boldly announced the production of this critique of Collier's and the bureau's policies concerning the Sioux. It is a brash, bold, explanation of his writing style: "How must it be written? Smoothly? The situation is too critical to spare the time. We need action! Tactfully or boldly? All the nice, sweet words by tongue or hand have helped not. The book must have guts! Not a weak, cautious criticism varying little off the median line of least resistance, but strenuous criticism and strong praise crisscrossing vigorously from opposite extremes bids to be most fair and gainful." The letter is signed, in all sincerity, "Iktomi Lila Šiča (the really bad Iktomi), June 21, 1937."[3]

The appearance of this letter as a preface to the volume leads the reader to believe that Iktomi the author and social critic has a new answer to the problems facing the Bureau of Indian Affairs that Collier might be interested to hear. In fact, Collier has heard much of it before: not from Iktomi, but from Drift. Four years earlier, Drift wrote to Collier noting that from what he had heard, Collier's policies were very much in line with some of Drift's theories on the environment and Indians.[4] In the letter, Drift noted that he had already prepared the manuscript for his book, "put in a form that would have wide appeal." According to Drift, the text took five years to write and two years to illustrate, and was "of ethnological, historical, and economic interest around a theme of conservation." He noted that the "Oglala are especially interested and pleased with what I have written on their history, philosophy, and religion, and they are hopeful about this book as a method of informing the public and enlisting public support to my Indian program which the Indians (Lakota and some other individuals) believe is most Indian and practical." He presents himself as a facilitator for Collier's policies on Pine Ridge by using his own plan to "fill in the gaps" in Collier's program.

Another letter written by Drift to Collier four months later seems to have been an attempt to gain Collier's trust by providing a rundown on factions that were seen as enemies of Collier's policies. Drift also brought forth excuses for why the secretary's recent trip to the area was so poorly attended by some local Lakotas. The tone is ingratiating, as Drift hinted that he would not be opposed to applying for the agent's job on Pine Ridge when it came open, and that he had Charley Red Cloud's support. He noted that no faction on Pine Ridge opposed his plan and promised to help Collier and "our Indians." Drift was clear that one of the problems for Pine Ridge was the factionalism on the reservation and that it would have been impossible for all the factions to support any issue unanimously.[5] To distinguish Drift's assessment from Iktomi's, I note a lengthy portion of that letter to Collier:

> It is probably not necessary to remind you that the Sioux are probably the most factional of all. Consequently, the Council is not a representative body, as it should be, and formerly was. It does represent several of the kinds of Mixed and full-bloods, and even includes something of the Indian, but this renewed imitation of the Old Council seldom agrees internally, and rarely produces or suggests anything of practical aid or solution, and is merely a fuse for allowing the Sioux Thought and Dissatisfaction to talk itself into a climax that simply melts the fuse and breaks all contact harmlessly enough—it is usually considered by a majority of the People to be but a sad sort of Joke in the form of a social gathering of phoney White-men's-chiefs who are descendents of the real leaders. Those men are my friends and I am sorry to have to admit that it will not be through their efforts or ability that real improvement will come to the Sioux. Neither do I think it easy, if possible, to pick 3 men from either Pine Ridge or Rosebud who are Typical, Courageous, Fair, Honest, Unselfish, and Understanding enough to be true and well-posted representatives of their people to you. Each will probably lack one or more of these necessary qualities.

Drift goes on to say that despite the negative picture, the people of Pine Ridge can make a go of it—with his (the future REAL Iktomi's) help, naturally.

Collier's response is dated on the day that he received Drift's first letter.[6] He was looking forward to "getting some light" from Drift on policies and procedures, and that Drift should take the civil service exam for the position of superintendent. He said he was looking forward to reading Drift's manuscript. After all, Drift had alluded to the fact that they had independently reached many of the same conclusions. This was probably not the response Drift hoped for; one trickster knows another, and Drift might have understood well enough that Collier tried to appease him with sweet nothings. Collier's own idealism had probably been considerably affected by the resistance on his plans for the IRA from the established interests, and the resistance on other reforms by Native nations.

Drift's tone as Iktomi is no longer ingratiating. In his book, Iktomi is loud in his denouncement of individuals who work for the Indian Service and argues that they are mired down in policies: *"The government has always moved like your tongue on a frosted pumphandle."* His assessment of government officials is that they are corrupt, being mired in graft and greed and that they are usually "educated, honorable, and religious GENTLEMEN" who are really political lackeys being rewarded for loyalty to their parties (Iktomi Ȟcala 1937:80).

IKTOMI'S POWER AND ILLUSION

Since Drift purports to be an environmentalist and friend of the Indians, some light might be shed on his assessment of his own role in reforming Pine Ridge and the bureau overall by a return to the first letter sent to Collier, dated August 18, 1933. In this letter, he noted that the Oglalas were especially interested in the creation of the proposed LaCreek Wildlife Refuge. He took credit for gaining Lakota support of the refuge, and saw this as an indication that he should be appointed to superintendent of Pine Ridge. Yet to this day, the specter of the wildlife refuge hangs heavily over Bennett County, South Dakota, a county in the southeastern section that seceded from the Pine Ridge Reservation in 1910. The very mention of it causes heated debate among community members, Indians and non-Indians alike. In his Iktomi persona, Drift also takes a more complex view of the issue.

Despite Drift's role in persuading Oglalas to see the value of the project, Iktomi notes that "the U.S. Biological Survey's project on Pine Ridge Reservation is a perfect illustration of what crimes may be committed by imposters or amateurs under the name of conservation" (Iktomi Ȟcala 1937:201). He goes on to correctly assess the area that was, at the time, owned by people he calls "progressive Indians" and whites. The LaCreek district's soil is rich compared to other county land and the area was originally nesting land for many waterfowl, including trumpeter swans, pelicans, and other migratory birds. The rich land grows some of the best hay in a county that overall can best be termed as semi-arid. A person could make a decent living in LaCreek. Drift described intrigues surrounding the acquisition of land since virtually no one wanted to sell their prized land, especially at the low prices offered that would not be sufficient to relocate to something more suitable. Finally, alleging high alkali content, the government condemned the land and moved everyone off. Drift argued that non-Indian landowners got a more substantial payoff than Indian allottees, but non-Indian ranchers who currently border the refuge rue the yearly encroachment of LaCreek swampland into their hayfields and decry the thousands of ducks and geese that eat the seeds right out of the ground (see Wagoner 2001).

Iktomi was prescient in his views that the Wildlife Refuge, once created, would be used as only a place for outsiders to come on hunting trips. Former South Dakota governor Bill Janklow, for example, led expeditions of hunters there every year. While Drift might have agreed that the area should be set aside as a conservation area, this was not what he had in mind. One could argue that Iktomi had been out-Iktomi-ed by the government agents, but at the same time, highly placed officials in the United States Department of Agriculture Forest Service, the Department of the Interior Soil Erosion Service, the Department of Commerce Bureau of Fisheries, and the Director of Forestry were exchanging letters as late as 1935 with Drift and helped him peddle another book, *Maka Ihangyi*[7] to publishers. I have not been able to locate that text, but it is referred to in *America Needs Indians!* as a smaller book that outlines Drift's Indian conservation plans for Pine Ridge.

Drift's writing is quirky to the contemporary eye, but the text is written in a style that was common at the time. One can read his words and "hear" how they were meant to be read. Changing the typeface to accentuate words or phrases, the text nearly screams off the page at the reader. In other places, the typeface becomes so small it seems that the author is whispering or, more precisely, thinking to himself. Drift writes in a stream of consciousness style that seems to put us intimately in touch with the mind and thinking processes of Iktomi. Often, the smallest typeface is reserved for thoughts that seem to belong more to Drift than to Iktomi. It is in the smallest font that Drift's correspondences with the government may be found. There is sometimes little resemblance between the actual correspondence and what is purported to have been written.

It is in that smallest typeface that Drift recounts his experiences in minor government positions where he was perceived as a clown. One of the most telling glimpses of Drift in close proximity to agency officials is related in the chapter entitled, "Junk Codliver's Nude Eel" (Iktomi Ḣcala 1937:161–88), in which Iktomi takes the commissioner to task on his policies. This section outlines his dealings with Collier as well as some of the moments when Drift realized exactly who he was dealing with in terms of power. He notes that any power he may have thought he had in helping facilitate Collier's policies was illusory, unnecessary, and that, actually, the joke was on him. He admitted that, "I have sometimes received courtesy from the Government, but no real favors, very little pay, no reward or much of anything else I didn't earn, and very little of what I might have a right to expect. Yet sometimes it is felt that I am **unappreciative**. I appreciate all consideration and help extended— especially by my efforts. But the kind of flattery you want is a reflection of yourselves, and not **Indian**. I'd be suspicious of any Indian who over-did the kind of flattery you thrive on" (Iktomi Ḣcala 1937:162). He alluded to a personal style that may have done him in by stating: "I might command more respect by a more guarded manner. . . . I drive my rudimentary brain, worn-out nerves, and dried up carcass daily, so why keep up a strained **front** while forced to waste pressing time playing **dignif-idle!** When not busy I relax by clowning. People expect and suspect little of a **clown**. So I am just a clowning 'upstart.'" (Iktomi H̆cala 1937:162).

He concludes that particular stream of consciousness section, which makes him appear un-Iktomi-like and vulnerable, by noting that "many neo-Colliers, semi-Colliers, sub-Colliers, pseudo-Colliers, non-Colliers, anti-Colliers, de-Colliers, super-Colliers, and other Colliers strata of the Indian office, with whom I've played Leap Frog, have been very friendly and somewhat helpful to me. So have they generally in the Forest Service, Biological Survey, ECW, Bureau of Fisheries, Soil Erosion Service, etc." (Iktomi H̆cala 1937:162).

I conclude by returning to the letter that Iktomi Lila Šiča sent to John Collier in 1937 to introduce his book. The letter ends with the following: "As for me personally, nothing can result to justify my sacrifice. I am neither dishonest nor coward enough to pretend I like to do this, for I am anything but a martyr in makeup. I have finished a great circle that has wasted a lot of time and me. My only consolation is that I am done; my only hope is that I am crazy."

AN HONEST MAN

Crazy he may have been, but one thing we can be sure of is that, like Iktomi (the true Iktomi), Ivan Drift brought trouble to himself by being all too human; a victim of his own excesses and, perhaps, his all-too-human intellectual vanity. And he was crazy like Diogenes carrying that blasted lamp looking for that one honest man. I think he thought, in his vanity, that it was he who was that man. At the end of his life, as far as I can ascertain, he was put off Pine Ridge Reservation after his young daughter was buried. He was alone and unwelcome at Pine Ridge; his name remains unspoken among the family. He finally relocated to a cave in Hot Springs, South Dakota, hoping to glimpse his own face in a lantern. Surely, for all his knowledge of Lakota people, language, and culture, he failed to grasp that, in the end, Iktomi was doomed to always outwit himself, which is what makes him so compelling as a tragic figure alone with his hubris.

Drift, however, was not alone at the end, according to an elderly informant who volunteers at the Hot Springs Historical Society. He "took up" with Mary, the mistress of the town dump. They cared for each other a great deal. Although, according to my informant, no one really knew when they died, they remain a topic of discussion among old-timers in the area. I believe that in the final analysis Ivan Drift was both, naïve and idealistic in the extreme. He was doomed to wrestle with the contradictions between his quest to be that one honest man, the savior to the Lakotas (because they had lost their independence and credibility as *true* Indians), and his political aspirations to become the superintendent at Pine Ridge to play out yet another futile experiment in his vision for what he thought Lakotas should be, just as others before him had tried and failed to accomplish. Both unable to change the system and unable to adapt to it, yet also unwilling or unable to let go of his idealism, he was doomed to tilt at windmills.

In many ways, Drift was disappointed with the Indians. On one hand he felt akin to them, but on the other he described them as argumentative and disorganized people who must ultimately change. At the same time, he sought to identify with the same government officials whom he defamed for blundering in their lack of foresight in implementing policies. Simultaneously, however, he was trying to become a bureaucrat himself because he alone is the one to solve the problems. Despite his raving and inconsistencies, I find him to be a sympathetic, if tragic, character with a deep understanding of U.S.–Indian relations. He may have been crazy, but his take on the situation and his style put the finger on many wounds that must yet be healed. While the world has moved on from Ivan Drift, without really taking notice, one can still read the specters of conquest and colonialism Drift described, and see them acted out around the world every day. Iktomi pointed out that nation building did not work out so well in the nineteenth and twentieth centuries within the borders of the United States. It is doubtful that contemporary social critics and satirists would be as creative as Iktomi when spilling ink to expose modern political and social lunacies anytime soon.

As an afterthought, Iktomi Ȟcala/Iktomi Lila Šiča now lives anew on Google and has a place forever fixed in cyberspace as a Lakota chief. Some have stumbled upon his book through online sources and want to know more, but, interestingly, he has now transformed into a Lakota chief who was a contemporary of Standing Bear. I think that Vine Deloria, Jr., would have found this an amusing turn of events and would have argued that there is still a great puzzle to solve.

As for Ivan Drift the man, for all his knowledge of Lakotas, he failed to grasp that in the end, Iktomi was always doomed to live outside the community, a tragic figure alone in his cave with hubris. And Mary.

Find me a lantern! Or perhaps an ethnohistorian?

NOTES

1. Letter by Robert Marshall (Chief of Forestry) to Frank T. Bell, Commissioner. August 31, 1934. John Collier's Papers, National Archives, Washington, D.C.

2. Wise letter to John Collier. June 25, 1934. BIA-Seminole-Walter Wise, National Archives, Washington, D.C.

3. Editor's note: For another version of the story of Iktomi's banishing, see George Sword, "When the People Laughed at the Moon," in Walker (1983:52–57).

Here, Skan says: "Because you are the son of *Inyan*, you may keep your power as a God, but you shall no more be associated with the Gods nor use your power against [any] of them. Mankind shall be warned of your tricks and all cautioned against you. You shall go upon the world and there abide alone forever without associate or friend." One could say that by authoring the volume as "Iktomi," Drift gave fair warning.

4. Ivan Drift letter to John Collier. August 18, 1933. John Collier's Papers, National Archives, Washington, D.C.

5. Ivan Drift letter to John Collier. December 29, 1933. John Collier's Papers, National Archives, Washington, D.C.

6. John Collier letter to Ivan Drift. December 18, 1933. John Collier's Papers, National Archives, Washington, D.C.

7. Editor's note: This can be translated as "Destroying the Earth."

9

Acts of Inscription

Language and Dialogism in the Archives

MINDY MORGAN

This story begins with a detour. In the course of conducting research regarding the Fort Belknap Assiniboine community in the Montana Historical Society, I decided to look up some of the files on the neighboring reservation, Fort Peck, including records dedicated to *Land of Nakoda: The Story of the Assiniboine Indians*. I was familiar with the book in both its printed and reprinted form, and knew that many tribal members appreciated it for its style and accuracy in telling about pre-reservation beliefs and practices.[1] Published by the Montana Writers Program in 1942, the book recounts early social organization, subsistence patterns, and ceremonial life of the various Assiniboine bands that came to reside at Fort Peck. The author was James Larpenteur Long, whose mother, Annie, was the only child of Charles Larpenteur, a fur trader at Fort Union, and Makes Cloud Woman, the daughter of a prominent Assiniboine leader. Larpenteur Long, whose father died before his birth, had been raised by his mother and grandmother among the Assiniboine community at Fort Peck Indian Reservation. In 1938, at the behest of Byron Crane, the director of the Montana office, Larpenteur Long began collecting stories from members of the community for a history of the tribe that was intended for use in the state's secondary schools. Fluent in Nakoda, he interviewed over twenty tribal elders regarding tribal history and cultural practices, then compiled the interviews into a handwritten monograph that was submitted to the state office for typing and editing.[2]

I was curious to see the original manuscripts and decided to take a look. In the collection were several drafts of the book as well as correspondence between Larpenteur Long and administrators in Helena, including Michael Kennedy, who succeeded Crane as director of the Montana Writers' Program. Larpenteur Long wrote meticulous drafts of the book, including detailed sketches of cultural objects and practices that were supplemented by explanatory text including examples of the Nakoda language. Some of the handwritten chapters were written on small yellow pieces of paper, while others were written on standard notebook paper. As I lifted some of the lined pages and turned them over, I found the penmanship homework of Larpenteur Long's twelve-year-old daughter, Frances. In lovely cursive, she copied the pledge of allegiance down the entire length of the page.

This discovery of the notations was by no means exceptional. In a period and a place where scarcity was the norm and there were few additional resources, it was not surprising to think that Larpenteur Long would repurpose available materials for his project. At the same time, the discovery was compelling. Larpenteur Long's act of inscription on his youngest daughter's schoolwork provides a window into the environment that surrounded him as he wrote of the Assiniboine past; he was employed by a government office to remember and record the "old ways" while pressures on American Indians to accommodate and adapt to dominant U.S. culture continued unabated. There is an irony in the juxtapositioning of Frances's text and Larpenteur Long's writing that is easily observed, but difficult to enunciate. Her side is a lesson in civics as well as penmanship as she rotely declares her allegiance to both country and flag. His side is titled, "Medicine Men" and includes a correction to an editor's change regarding the appropriate use of the pipe in requesting aid from a healer. This pairing suggests many things; among them, that the republic was not as "indivisible" as implied, and that within this historical period that ostensibly celebrated U.S. diversity, there remained an expectation of conformity.[3] This context is both political and personal, and the discovery of the reused paper suggests that in order to properly understand the text of *Land of Nakoda* these influences need to be considered. These delicate pieces of aged paper subtly illuminate the context in which Larpenteur Long produced his manuscript and ultimately help us better appreciate his work.

This chapter begins to think about how to incorporate the "flip side" in the production of historical narratives. Scholars generally do not draw attention to the materiality of their sources in writing history, and often lack ways of conceptualizing and theorizing the dialogic process that is apparent yet understudied in the archives. But as the text above demonstrates, this process shapes our understanding and interpretation of the documents. By dialogic, I simply mean that texts exist in relationships to other texts and that as researchers we need to be much more attentive to these influences. Following Mikhail Bakhtin (1981), the dialogic process is more than merely context; rather it is the way in which a single linguistic act operates in relation to other forms and thus carries the imprint of these other forms. Acknowledging this process is to view texts not as static objects that are only useful for the information that they contain, but as dynamic artifacts that retain traces of their circulation. Ann Stoler (2009) argues for just this type of attention to documents in conducting what she terms "ethnography of the archives." By tracing marginalia, edits, and strikethroughs, investigators can see how imperial projects were both conceived and executed. Importantly, she argues that attention to the hesitations, concerns, and contradictions within archival documents demonstrate colonial insecurities as much as colonial power.

The idea of a dialogic history fits well within the concerns of the larger field of ethnohistory that brings anthropological, linguistic, and historical methods to bear on the documentary record.[4] Rather than combing documents for content, this approach sees both texts and archives as sites of cultural exchange that can be interrogated. As Michel Rolph-Trouillot (1995) observes, there are many moments included in historical production: the event, the inscription of the event, the archiving of that inscription, and the later interpretation of that event. By focusing on the moments of inscription we can capture more of the history of the everyday—not the exceptional or transformative event, but rather the later recording that takes place in more ordinary time. The time between events occurring and their recording creates a space into which the author's ideas and orientation shape the final version. The resulting documents represent the concerns, issues, and ideological positioning of the period and become, as Stoler (2009:2) observes, "active, generative substances with histories, as documents with itineraries of their own."

Because inscription generally references texts, language is critical in this discussion and is the primary unit of analysis. My attention to language is both the language used in documents as well as the larger ideologies concerning language and discourse that are evident. This is particularly critical in regard to American Indian history where the use or nonuse of Indigenous language is indicative of larger operations of power. Therefore, I am interested where there are both examples of Indigenous language text as well as the metadiscursive commentary about language, translation, and editing offered by both Larpenteur Long and those in the state office. Ultimately, I am interested in how these instances illustrate the tensions between the normative ideals of the center and the lived experiences of tribal members.

I begin with some brief theoretical considerations regarding archives and the dialogic construction of history. Central to this section is the work of Raymond J. DeMallie and Douglas R. Parks, who have drawn attention to the ways in which scholars should approach texts created by tribal members, especially those that have emerged from collaborative work.[5] I am particularly interested in how we can begin to capture the dialogic process that is evident in archival work and the importance of that process to constructing historical narratives. After that, I return to Larpenteur Long's drafts of *Land of Nakoda,* as well as selections from *Indians at Work,* a periodical also generated from the Public Works program, to begin to illustrate what dialogic history looks like. Ultimately, I argue that an analytical reading of these complicated and sometimes contradictory texts helps to shed light on underlying tensions regarding definitions of Indigeneity during the New Deal era.

SILENCES, TENSIONS, AND TRANSITIONS IN THE ARCHIVES

In her book, *Along the Archival Grain: Epistemic Anxieties and Colonial Common Sense,* Stoler provides an illuminating discussion of how the archives themselves came to be a productive site of ethnographic study over the past twenty years. Taking inspiration from Walter Benjamin, among others, scholars initially wrote histories "against the grain" in which they sought out the silences within the archives and examples of erasures of local communities. This work focused on those who were often denied voice in colonial narratives (Stoler 2009:46–49). More recent work, which includes Stoler's own, does not look for what is missing but rather reads archives "along the grain" to see what is there; albeit through a different lens. This approach opens up new possibilities for understanding how imperial projects work; however, it relies primarily on the writings of those who were in the colonial administration, and not necessarily members of the governed communities. But in the case of the United States and its practices of "intimate colonialism," tribal members were often employed by the federal agencies established to oversee Indian affairs.[6] These individuals were thus both subjects to and producers of archival documents. This is certainly the case with Larpenteur Long, who was both a member of the larger Assiniboine community and employed on behalf of the federal government. The writings produced by such individuals require a slightly different analytical frame.

While focusing on Indigenous language texts, DeMallie and Parks offer a way of approaching and analyzing archival documents created by tribal members such as Larpenteur Long during the early reservation period. In their article, "Plains Indian Native Literatures," they discuss how scholars have ignored a large corpus of Indigenous language texts that are critical in understanding how tribal members viewed themselves as historical actors during the upheavals and social transformations of the nineteenth century. The reasons for this exclusion stem from multiple sources: a lack of training in Indigenous languages; an assumption that European language sources are sufficient for writing American Indian history; and linguists' views of language texts as sources of grammatical and lexical information rather than cultural and historical (Parks and DeMallie 1992a:132).

DeMallie and Parks are careful to note, however, that this incorporation is not easy. They argue that these texts are best suited to ethnohistorical analysis that can situate them "in the fullest possible historical and cultural context to allow the American Indian voices they preserve to speak through the generations and across the barriers of language and culture to become intelligible and articulate representations of the past" (Parks and DeMallie 1992a:106). Practically, this means that the documents themselves need to be understood as products of their specific time and place as well as the conditions of their creation. In particular, they investigate the collaborative project between James R. Murie and George A. Dorsey to record the narratives of Roaming Scout, a Skiri Pawnee leader, as well as the collection of Lakota texts written by George Sword, a member of the Oglala Lakota tribe located on the Pine Ridge Reservation. Both collections date from the first decade of the twentieth century and illustrate the growing ethnological interest in Plains communities.

In the two text collections, the authors argue that the context of their production influenced the content of the texts themselves. They write, "Quite explicitly, Roaming Scout, in collaboration with Murie, as well as Sword, used the opportunities presented by the requests of anthropologists to record accounts of their respective cultures as they existed in the mid-nineteenth century. Both perceived their tribal cultures to be disappearing and wished to preserve some record of those older ways for the benefit of the future. In the process, they developed a new genre of native literature" (DeMallie and Parks 1992a:131). While they are explicitly concerned with Indigenous language texts, I would argue that the method that they employ for analysis can be extrapolated to documents such as Larpenteur Long's drafts of *Land of Nakoda*. The turbulent events of war and relocation during the late nineteenth century were not far past when Larpenteur Long began his collection of Assiniboine stories. Many of the "old timers" he interviewed were born just as the reservation was coming to be, and they told stories of their grandparents who knew the time before the Lewis and Clark expedition. That said, he was also writing in a moment of significant social, economic, and political change as a result of New Deal policies.

While Larpenteur Long was writing in English, the texts that he produced can be viewed as what Elaine Jahner has termed "transitional texts." Referring to the same Sword manuscript as DeMallie, Jahner (1992:148) defines transitional texts as those "in which the act of writing is simultaneously a development of an imaginative tradition and an attempted entry into a new cultural order without known precedent and beyond any anticipation implied by the cultural past." While Larpenteur Long certainly had models of ethnographic texts, he viewed his own work as a break from previous studies precisely because of his ability and knowledge of the Nakoda language and his own position within the tribe. Similar to Sword and Roaming Scout, his collection also reflected the concerns and anxieties of the time. He worries about the future of the stories that he inscribes and, tellingly, toward the end of his author's introduction he writes, "This book is dedicated to the descendants of the Assiniboines, many of whom, even today (1940) cannot talk the language of their people."[7] He viewed his own work as something new and critical.

But Larpenteur Long's writings were also subject to the requirements of the larger project for which he was working as well as the expectations about what was considered Native within broader U.S. society. It is within this negotiated space between Larpenteur Long's intentions and the editors revisions where we can more clearly understand the pressures and anxieties that Indigenous communities felt during this transformative time. While Larpenteur Long's experience in many ways was singular, it was also exemplary. The same tensions that he experienced during the writing of *Land of Nakoda* can also be traced in the contemporary periodical, *Indians at Work*. As will become evident, both of these cases are sights of epistemological struggles regarding authoritative knowledge and the power of representation. By situating them within a larger cultural and historical context, we can better understand the insecurities, tensions, and fissures that emerge from their creation.

JAMES LARPENTEUR LONG AND *LAND OF NAKODA*

When Larpenteur Long began composing his drafts of *Land of Nakoda* he was fifty years old. He had been married to his second wife, Regina Koch for eighteen years, and had four daughters aged twenty-four to twelve, having lost his only son, Charles, in infancy.[8] At the time, he was running the Hi-Way Grocery in Oswego, Montana, a small community located on the Fort Peck Indian reservation between the towns of Frazer and Wolf Point. The grocery was the second business he had run after having co-owned a general merchandise and hardware store with his former brother-in-law. Before that he had tried his hand at ranching, which he did after serving as a clerk at the Wolf Point Trading Company. He entered the boarding school in Poplar, Montana, at age seven and by the age of seventeen he had completed an eighth-grade education. Along the way, he apprenticed as a tailor, though he "never made use of [the] trade beyond sewing a few buttons on my clothes and adjusting and cleaning our sewing machine at home."[9] He liked running the grocery, especially since it had become a place where the "old-timers" would gather and share their stories.

The grocery earned him a respected place among both the tribe and the local business community. In his own words, his "life has been of a dual nature" and he was fully ensconced in both Native and non-Native communities in northern Montana. He served as a member of the Executive Board of the Tribal Council, representing the tribe's interests to the federal government and the 1851 Treaty of Fort Laramie committee. At the same time, he was deeply involved with organizations affiliated with the Catholic Church, serving as a Fourth Degree member of the Knights of Columbus and as the secretary of the District Council of Catholic Men for northeastern Montana.

Individuals in charge of the Writers' Program valued Larpenteur Long's position within both communities. A letter to Henry Alsberg, the director of the Federal Writers' Program, praised early versions of the book and commented that "Mr. Larpenteur Long is a 'find,' a writer who knows how to present this material interestingly and from a tribal point of view."[10] In multiple correspondences, administrators in Writers' Program offices in Helena and Washington, D.C., commented on Larpenteur Long's bilingualism and his ability to translate concepts from the original Nakoda into English. As one former state director stated,

> "Mr. Long and the editors' [*sic*], Mrs. Whitaker and Mr. Henry tried to use words and terms which were within the experience of the Indian. The construction of some sentences is rather queer in English, but these constructions according to Mr. Long convey the idea as an Indian would express it. The sequence of words follows the Indian thought patterns and ideas."[11]

However, this ability to translate between the two different idioms and the two divergent worlds is minimized in the final version of the text. Larpenteur Long's skill in navigating between Native and dominant society that the Central Office praised in private correspondences was muted in the public presentation of Larpenteur Long, suggesting that the editors of the Writers' Program were more interested in conforming to popular stereotypes of the "Indian" rather than presenting contemporary American Indian life with all of its attendant complexities.

JAMES LARPENTEUR LONG, ACCORDING TO HIMSELF

Prior to starting his work on the monograph, Larpenteur Long had been a contributor to the periodical *Indians at Work,* which chronicled Indian participation in Emergency Conservation Work as well as other New Deal programs. In a piece written for the magazine, Larpenteur Long used his position as a businessman and an insider to the Fort Peck community to disabuse non-Natives about their stereotypes and preconceived notions about the tribal community at Fort Peck. He created an exchange between a local shopkeeper and a visiting salesman who has taken an interest in a group of tribal members who are working for the Indian Emergency Conservation Work program (IECW). After expressing his surprise that the men are engaged in productive work, the salesman comments, "I have often heard that Indians as a rule don't work or will not work." To this, the merchant responds, "Indians are the same as anybody. Of course some will not work, but the number is small. Since the relief jobs have been opened on the reservation it is surprising how many of the Indians are applying for work and staying on the job even in very bad weather."[12] The conversation continues with discussions of the skill of Native women in managing family finances and ends with the salesman satisfied that surrounding white communities will be happy to hear that government money is being used wisely.

The exchange, which is clearly based on his own experience, emphasizes how much Larpenteur Long drew upon his exposure to both the Assiniboine and white communities to help reconcile misperceptions that occurred between them. The shopkeeper in the above story does not identify himself as part of that community but he clearly demonstrates tremendous sympathy and knowledge about the local tribe. Perhaps Larpenteur Long believed that outsiders trust his opinions more as a local shop owner than as a tribal member; however, it is his position within the tribe that enables him to reliably report on the impact of relief work on the community.

This explicit positioning between the Native and dominant U.S. society extended into his writing of *Land of Nakoda,* particularly in his personal statement, which served as a preface to the published book. The autobiographical statement numbers twenty-five handwritten pages. Written in tight cursive with occasional letters, it begins with the simple statement "My name is James Larpenteur Long. I was born DEC. 25, 1888." From there he provides a detailed discussion of his life from birth through adulthood and the various people and places that shaped his upbringing. While the information in the statement is important, the form in which it is written also requires analysis. His organization of the text as well as other formal elements resembles Assiniboine oratorical practices, something of which Larpenteur Long was keenly aware. The first of these formal styles is the recitation of lineages and the positioning of himself within these lines as having the authority to speak about the issues contained within the text.

He first mentions his maternal relations to Charles Larpenteur and Makes Cloud Woman. Rather than discussing his grandfather, he traces his maternal grandmother's line through First Fly and Wanhi Maza (Iron Arrow-Point) and emphasizes both of these men's roles as leaders within the Assiniboine tribe, including First Fly's participation in the 1851 treaty council. At the time of the writing, Larpenteur Long had himself served on the treaty council which was still engaged in securing treaty rights and therefore this linkage is critical. In addition to the lineages, Larpenteur Long also discusses his early deeds that are recognizable as distinctly Assiniboine, such as his first kill and his grandmother's recognition of this through a feast. He also discusses key ceremonial episodes such as his naming and his initiation into the horse society. In each of these discussions he is careful to note his own age, the person who sponsored him, and the significance of the moment. The

paragraphs have a repetitive structure and are thus reminiscent of the oratorical patterns of Assiniboine speech-making where the person who is talking must first give his own biography as a way of asserting authority to speak.

In addition to these organizing structures, Larpenteur Long has other
ways of authorizing his own cultural knowledge. First, he makes connections between his own personal experiences with those recounted in the
book itself. He mentions that his mother experienced difficulties in his birth
and was attended by a healer who used herbs and "the 'turtle method' as
explained in this book."[13] Most importantly, he discusses others' attempts to
understand Assiniboine life and how they ultimately fail largely because of
their lack of community access and inability to speak the language. After
mentioning how previous researchers had been led astray by faulty interpretations and prejudiced theories, he concludes, "I wish to impress on the reader
that only a person who is a blood member and has lived in close contact with
his people is able to thoroughly understand the true meanings of the customs
and ceremonies of the tribe. The meaning and purpose of some of the religious
organization is so deep that words translated into English to interpret them
are meaningless. A person has to be one of them to really understand."[14] The
difficulty of translation from Nakoda to English appears frequently throughout the author's statement as well as in Larpenteur Long's letters to the Montana office, and he often discusses how types of knowledge are lost as the language changes. According to Larpenteur Long it is his knowledge of the
language and the sign language that distinguishes his own work from that of
previous scholars and others; it is also this knowledge of the language that
positions him unequivocally as Assiniboine despite his mixed heritage.

Larpenteur Long's identity as a full member of the Assiniboine community is solidified in a story about his time at the N-N Ranch where his
mother worked as a housekeeper for the foreman of the ranch. While his
time spent there was relatively happy, the moment of greatest significance
was when, as a young boy, he had his braids cut by the rancher, Hank
Cusker. As a member of the Assiniboine community, it would be expected
for Larpenteur Long to wear his hair long and in braids. Cutting hair had
deep symbolic significance for the Assiniboine communities as it was only
cut as sign of deep mourning. By the late 1930s, it had acquired even greater
importance as Native communities associated cutting hair with the brutal
assimilative agenda of the boarding school that was imposed on the young
students. In his story, Larpenteur Long is careful to note that the haircut was
accomplished without the knowledge or acquiescence of his mother and tells
the reader that the event was traumatic for his grandmother. During this
discussion, he also makes a point of mentioning that he has blond rather
than black hair. This disclosure is somewhat jarring as it is a reminder of his
mixed heritage in the midst of a story that is primarily concerned with an
assault on his ties to the Assiniboine community. Without his braids, he is

visibly less Assiniboine, but not because of his hair color. He mentions that his grandmother prized "his straw-colored locks," so much so that she is pacified with the token gift of one of his braids.[15] His focus on his hair color continues, noting that after the haircut he had to wear a bright red bandana because the family feared losing him if he ran off since "the needle-grass which covered the country for miles around the ranch was the same color as my shorn head."[16] It is a complex story that works to assert Larpenteur Long's authority as an Assiniboine narrator despite the fact that he may not appear to outsiders to be one.

Throughout his writings, Larpenteur Long never expresses concern or ambivalence about his own identity, but rather pulls from his varied up-bringing and experiences with others to substantiate and verify what he believes to be true. The people who were responsible for editing and publishing his work had a decidedly different view. While private correspondences use Larpenteur Long's upbringing and education as evidence that he is a reliable author, this is downplayed in the final version of the book where there appears to be great effort placed on making him as Native as he could be as opposed to a person adept at moving between communities.

JAMES LARPENTEUR LONG, ACCORDING TO HIS EDITORS

While the published version of Larpenteur Long's autobiography is clearly his own words, it was edited in significant ways that produce a different reading than he probably intended. The editing was done primarily for reasons of length; however, the decisions of what stories to cut and the ways in which existing ones were rewritten are telling in how the editors hoped to shape the reader's image of Larpenteur Long and what was clearly acceptable as "Indian" according to the general public. Some of these changes might have appeared minor, but they were precisely the elements that would be considered critical by the tribal community in Larpenteur Long's identifying himself as Assiniboine. For example, in an editorial report from the national office July of 1941, the editor observes that the changes in many of the paragraphs were "designed to avoid the monotony of beginning too many paragraphs with age data."[17] As mentioned above, Larpenteur Long fashioned his author's statement to reflect standard Assiniboine oratorical practices that would have required the pronouncement of the ages at which Larpenteur Long accomplished certain deeds.

The sections that were most heavily edited and ultimately deleted, however, were those that clearly identified Larpenteur Long as a person of mixed heritage. There is no direct discussion of this by the editorial staff—only an observation that the statement was too long—but all mention of Larpenteur Long's mixed heritage, with the exception of identifying his father of

"English descent," is eliminated from the final version of his introduction. Curiously, there is an insertion. In the description of his first wife, Mary Knapp, the final version includes the fact that she herself was one-eighth Assiniboine. Larpenteur Long makes no mention of this in his initial version, only stating her father was a trader of German heritage (Kennedy, 1961: lxiii). The published version includes his baptism that was done at the behest of his mother and grandmother and his commitment to the Catholic faith, but Larpenteur Long's discussion of his leadership roles in the church is edited out, as is his membership in the Knights of Columbus. Additionally, Larpenteur Long's comments on his involvement with the surrounding white community and his prominence in the business community do not appear anywhere in the final version. In his original, he frequently mentions correspondence with scholars and lay people about their interest in Native cultures; however, these references are eliminated in the published version. Perhaps the editors felt that too much discussion about interaction with outsiders meant that readers would assume that the narrative itself was a composite of previous interactions and discussions rather than being a reflection of the interviews with the elders with little mediation.

Most tellingly, the editors took out Larpenteur Long's discussion of his early years at the N-N Ranch. The ranch itself is mentioned in the first few sentences, but there is no mention of his mother's employment or his time spent there. Importantly, there is no mention of the episode of having his braids cut or of his hair color. The story of this haircut may appear trivial, but Larpenteur Long's inclusion of it and the editors exclusion of it illuminate how reading events from different epistemologies leads to varied interpretations. For Larpenteur Long, the event was obviously a major one in his young life that was probably recounted often by his mother and grandmother. The story of his first haircut places Larpenteur Long within the Assiniboine community while simultaneously indexing his mixed heritage. A tribal member reading the story would understand the deep significance that the haircut had for Larpenteur Long's grandmother and would also perhaps chuckle at the image of a red-capped youngster running through the tall prairie grass. For a non-Native reader, the acknowledgment of Larpenteur Long's blond hair would have cast suspicion on his position within the community and ultimately his acceptance as an "Indian" author. The edited version of the author's statement presents Larpenteur Long as an idealized Assiniboine narrator without the complexity that clearly attended the actual man and that would have made him recognizable to his own community.

The Central Office's constructed image of the "ideal Indian" can be found in other areas of the text as well. In addition to his written drafts, there are examples of Larpenteur Long's illustrations and sketches for the monograph in the archives. These illustrations serve as key texts that can be analyzed for

the ways in Assiniboine culture was created and edited in the final manuscript. Responding to requests from the Central Office, Larpenteur Long
sent in pencil sketches of many of the cultural items and practices discussed
in the elders' stories. These sketches serve as composites of the types of
knowledge that Larpenteur Long hoped to convey through the book and as
such serve as additional means for him to demonstrate his knowledge and
experience with the information contained within the elders' stories. They
are ethnographically rich and include detailed drawings of items discussed
in the various chapters of the books such as a navel bag, arrow points, and
horse and dog travois. On all of these drawings, he had explanations of the
various items including labels for what color and material would be used
in its construction. The items often appeared with the Nakoda term for it
with English translations. These illustrations were extensions of the text—
simultaneously giving details to the readers that were often left out of the
elders stories and asserting Larpenteur Long's own command of the cultural
material.

In addition to his sketches, Larpenteur Long submitted a number of illustrations for the book from his sixteen-year-old daughter, Maxine. These
sketches, which were never published, are illustrative of the ongoing tension
between Larpenteur Long and the Montana office regarding how to represent Assiniboine culture and practices. In an effort to illustrate the mud
stick game that is described in the text, Maxine sketched a young man demonstrating the overhead stick throw. In this illustration, the man has short
hair and is dressed in clothes current for the time including lace-up Oxford
shoes. Above this image is the question, "Indian Costume?" In a later series
of sketches illustrating the various positions for the Assiniboine slide stick
game, the man is dressed only in a loin cloth with moccasins and long,
braided hair. While the first image is ambivalent—it could be a tribal member or a non-Native individual—the second image is not. It is undeniably
"Indian." While it is impossible to know who questioned the attire in the
first sketch, as it does not appear to be Larpenteur Long's handwriting nor
that of Maxine, it can only be guessed that someone in the Montana office
decided that for inclusion in the book, the illustrations needed to fit within
stereotyped understandings of Indigenous life.

Ultimately, the state office decided not to include any of the illustrations
offered by Larpenteur Long and his daughter. Instead, they hired William
Standing onto the Writers' Program to illustrate the book. Standing, or Fire
Bear, was also a member of the Fort Peck Assiniboine community. By the
time of the project, he was well known as a Montana artist who did both serious and humorous work and had exhibited in Washington, D.C.[18] Despite
his renown, Larpenteur Long was hesitant to engage Standing for the project. In a dutiful letter back to the Montana office, he writes, "I will see
Mr. Larson about the artist Standing that is referred to in the Washington

letter. He is hard to handle."[19] Standing's final illustrations are evocative and capture the spirit of the stories; however, the decision not to use Larpenteur Long's own illustrations also meant that his own expertise and demonstrable knowledge were both edited and constrained.

Interestingly, Maxine's revised sketches were used as models for William Standing's illustrations of the sliding stick game.[20] In this series, as with all of the other illustrations in the book, the person is depicted in pre-reservation dress with long hair and is phenotypically American Indian. Larpenteur Long's descriptions came from watching games being played and playing them himself; however, the final illustrations did not reflect a contemporary tribal member engaging in the sports, only an idealized version of a pre-reservation Indian. Paradoxically, the information in the text was prioritized because it was firsthand knowledge, but it was represented visually as something anachronistic and distant. This became a familiar trope not only in *Land of Nakoda,* but other writings from the era as well. The issues raised in the writing and editing of *Land of Nakoda* were exemplary of the times. Many of the same strains between non-Native and Native writers can be seen in the periodical to which Larpenteur Long himself contributed, *Indians at Work.*

DOCUMENTING AND DEBATING
THE "MODERN" INDIAN

Indians at Work, published from 1933–45, surveyed relief programs, chronicled new developments in Indian affairs, and served as an important conduit between various reservation communities. The first issue was published in late 1933 and was initially described as "a news sheet for ourselves." This overtly reflexive title soon gave way to a "news sheet for the Indian and the Indian Service." It started as a biweekly publication, but became a monthly publication in November of 1937. While an official publication of the Indian Office, contributors to *Indians at Work* ranged from local tribal members employed by conservation projects to anthropologists, to government officials. Tribal members were the primary audience for the periodical and it served as a way of informing and linking tribal communities together; however, government officials, employees of the Indian service, and non-Native readers also subscribed.

Issues began with an editorial by John Collier, the commissioner of Indian Affairs that commented on either current issues in the Indian Office or a reflective essay on the topics included in the rest of the periodical. It highlighted issues that were of critical importance to Collier including educational reform and a focus on Indian arts. There are many articles from tribal members, similar to Larpenteur Long's contribution, reflecting on the progress of the IECW as well as other works projects on the reservations, and articles commenting on contemporary society and cultural practices. But the periodical also includes reprints of previously published texts from a variety of sources including reports from previous commissioners of Indian Affairs, popular regional magazines, and ethnographic monographs and articles including ones from the Bureau of American Ethnology. In Bakhtinian terms, it is quintessentially heteroglossic and is characterized by its multiple and competing discourses about what it meant to be Indian during the New Deal era and who had the authority to define the terms.

This tension was explicit, and was introduced in the second issue of the periodical where Collier himself posed a question. In his editorial, he reflects on the role of the Indian Service in helping to facilitate the blending of what he perceives as the Indian and modern world. He considers how the two seemingly irreconcilable modes of living can be brought together by "the Indian drawing upon his own native deeps" and a "modernity drawing upon its own native deeps." He continues, "The Indian Service must bring the Indian and the modern world together. But what Indian and what modern world?"[21]

The question posed by Collier is illustrative of an ideology that not only locates Indigenous peoples outside of modernity but also in opposition to it. This is ironic given its placement in the periodical that was dedicated to documenting the experiences of contemporary Native communities.

Ultimately, the periodical reflects the same problems apparent in the editing of *Land of Nakoda*; wanting to promote Native cultures, yet perpetuating stereotypes that continued to locate tribal communities in a pre-reservation idealized past. As mentioned above, anthropological discussions and ethnographic snapshots frequently appeared in the periodical. These included previously published manuscripts from individuals such as Clark Wissler, John Harrington, and Ruth Benedict. Other contributions came from anthropologists such as Scudder Meekel and Ruth Underhill who were working for the Applied Anthropology Unit that Collier established in 1935.[22] Interestingly, there are discussions and examples of Native languages as well as ethnographic description. For example, an issue dedicated to communities in Alaska has an example of the Lord's Prayer in Tlingit.[23] Where these occur, however, they are often presented as objects of analysis rather than part of community life. The ethnographic articles vacillated in both tone and scope but most reflected the objective, distanced voice common to social science discourse at the time. Some authors such as Meekel do offer informal discussions of contemporary reservation life; however, their appearance within the periodical contributed to the overall idea that Native communities needed to be represented by others both to themselves and to outsiders.

Despite this effort to define and delimit Native experience, American Indian contributors viewed the opportunity to publish in *Indians at Work* as a way of providing alternative narratives to the dominant discourses, even within standard generic forms. Unlike the contributions from the Central Office, these writers did not shy away from uncomfortable truths. They understood that they were charged with presenting Native culture to a wide audience who, in many respects, believed that those ways of life were a thing of the past. Their work, therefore, illustrates their struggle to repudiate these representations and to locate the tribes in the American present while still fulfilling the expectations of the project.

For example, in January 1937 tribal members from Fort Belknap submitted an article on the history of fires in the Little Rocky Mountains.[24] It was common in the periodical to have tribal members write on issues of public safety, hygiene, and other practices that were of concern to the IECW. The piece appears to be simply a discussion of fires that have plagued the reservation since 1883, culminating in the severe fires of the preceding summer. What is interesting, however, is how a piece that is ostensibly about fire safety and precautions is actually largely about gold mining and its role in the ceding of valuable portions of the Little Rockies in 1886. The authors accuse the miners of deliberately setting the fire, and equate the fire's destruction with the expulsion of tribal members from the area and the transformation of the space from one used for hunting and gathering to one used for mining.

These contestations over representation of Indigenous life become more overt when the theme of "traditional" Native culture appears in the periodical. Throughout the various volumes, there are examples of "traditional" Indian stories, myths, and histories. Many of these are located in a specific community, but some are general and lack tribal attribution. Some are submitted by tribal members, while others are republished from various sources. Many lack a specific author, and most stories are set in the pre-reservation, pre-contact period. Those that do not specifically mention the pre-contact period are often without any temporal context. This leads to the flattening of the stories; devoid of important context such as the speaker, place, and time, they become typical, generalized stories that can be consumed by an interested yet disconnected public. Depictions of community histories are similar. They are written as informative reports without the framing that can be typical of these stories when told in a community context.

But again, there are exceptions. The issue from June 1, 1937, has a contribution from Martin Mitchell, an Assiniboine policeman at Fort Peck.[25] In it, he chronicles a story about a hunter and his prey. The hunter, lacking proper ammunition, uses cherry pits to shoot a deer. While failing to bring it down, he encounters the same deer the following season with cherry trees growing out of its head. This story is both humorous and fantastical, and defies easy categorization, but it serves as an oppositional text to those previously mentioned. It is contemporary, its author and location are identified and specific, and it complicates popular notions of what an "Indian" story looks like. Mitchell's disruption of dominant discourse is subtle but it does move the reader from a stereotypical understanding of Indigenous storytelling.

Other times, more explicit confrontations occurred within the pages of the periodical. In March of 1937, a reader of the periodical, Mr. White Bison de Forest, submitted a response to an early article by Matthew Stirling of the Bureau of American Anthropology. Stirling had argued against the idea of extensive medicinal knowledge among American Indian communities, and stated that most communities attributed sickness to spirits and other supernatural forces, thereby illustrating a general lack of knowledge among communities regarding the nature and cure of illness. Mr. de Forest writes back, "The readers and public must have the truth so they, the readers and public will not have the wrong impression. I make this claim bold [*sic*] to our friend Mr. Stirling, young Indian doctors and the scholars of America: that no family doctor can conduct his practices, his calling as a family doctor of medicine, without using medicine discovered by Indians. I will agree they did not know about tinctures, or fluid extracts and they did not have machines from making pills and powder, but the healing power was there just the same; the idea was there." He continues, "Mr Stirling, I cannot write or talk to answer like you—but I know I know, not by books, but, I was born of Indian mother and lived both sides of the question." De Forest concludes with a long list of herbal medicines commonly used by many tribes for healing. The striking element of the letter, in addition to its content, is that it is framed as direct response and appeals directly to the readers of *Indians at Work.* De Forest prefaces his letter with the following: "I cannot express myself right but without fear of contradiction. I thank you to put this in the paper 'Indians @ Work.'"[26] It is a direct engagement with the periodical and the types of knowledge that it both values and presents. The letter writer acknowledges that he cannot match Stirling's authoritative power, but offers his own lived experience as a repudiation of it.

Despite Collier's attempt to present a comprehensive view of Native communities through *Indians at Work,* tribal members working in the projects used *Indians at Work* as an opening and an opportunity to reshape representations of Indigenous life within the United States at the time. They seized the opportunities to contribute to this periodical, imperfect and problematic as it was, to directly appeal to the American population about the current state of affairs within these communities. This periodical while highly edited and mediated, is a critical space in which divergent voices meet. Collier's influence on the periodical cannot be understated, but the voices from the communities cannot be ignored either. Reconciling them is difficult, but this is actually beside the point. The periodical is most instructive when these conflicting voices are left unresolved as they reflect the ambiguities and tensions of the time itself.

RETHINKING HISTORICAL DIALOGUE

Both *Land of Nakoda* and *Indians at Work* are key texts of the Indian New Deal. They reflect the liberal spirit of the Roosevelt administration with their attention to and acceptance of Indigenous forms of knowledge including Native languages; however, as has been demonstrated through this analysis, that acceptance only extends so far. These descriptions of Native life become complicated when a wider frame is employed that illuminates the moments of text production. While Larpenteur Long's work is impressive in its own right, it becomes even more so when the reader views the struggles with the Central Office regarding how Assiniboine culture should and should not be portrayed. The edits do not diminish the "authenticity" of the finished product—Larpenteur Long himself was very proud of the published monograph—but attention to the tensions and fissures in the book's creation gives us a better perspective on how tribal members themselves were struggling to place themselves in the dominant U.S. landscape.

Similarly, *Indians at Work,* through its sheer breadth, provides a compelling view on Native communities engaged in important relief work during the New Deal. Community members, such as Larpenteur Long, were grateful for the projects that brought employment and attention to the reservation communities. They were often happy to discuss this in the pages of the journal. At the same time, Collier's republishing of ethnographic and other anthropological works in the periodical both illustrates his view of authoritative knowledge and his assumption that the American Indian readership would be equally interested in descriptions of themselves represented through these texts. Perhaps they were; the periodical did link communities of readers together. But at times, as the above exchange over medicinal plants demonstrates, readers were not always willing to accept these representations and would write back, marshaling their own stories as a way to counter the ones they encountered in the pages of the periodical.

Bakhtin's discussions of centripetal and centrifugal forces within language and culture are instrumental in developing a dialogic approach to history. Centripetal force, according to Bakhtin, is the standardizing, routinizing discourse of the center. Its ultimate goal is homogenization and the silencing of dissent by erasure, adoption, and diffusion. Alternatively, centrifugal forces are those of the lived experiences of people in their daily lives that are altering and changing discourse through its enactment (Bakhtin 1981:272). These are the creative and heterogeneous forces that continually disrupt the normative influence of the center and provide alternatives to the dominant discourses. Importantly, these latter forces are the more powerful of the two according to Bakhtin. As the previous discussions of *Land of Nakoda* and *Indians at Work* illustrate, these forces are not forms of resistance that respond to actions by the center, but rather the dynamic forces already at play that the center tries to contain. Understanding how these two oppos-ing forces operate allows for the view taken by Stoler that colonial adminis-trators were wracked with both anxiety and uncertainty about how to gov-ern, despite the power of colonial structures over the lives of the local communities.

Both Larpenteur Long and the contributors to *Indians at Work* illustrate how Indigenous communities within the United States continually disassem-bled the nation's unifying narrative through their portrayals of contemporary Native life. What becomes clear throughout these pages is the focus on ex-change and contestation. Texts are never fully completed—they are revised, edited, republished, and repackaged. Through these various textualizing pro-cesses, they are imbued with the aspirations and concerns of the authors and readers alike and as such are reflections of the times. These reflections—fleeting, refracted, yet compelling—are what comprise a dialogic history.

NOTES

1. While the book was published in 1942 as *Land of Nakoda* as part of the Montana Writers' Program, it was republished with a new introduction by Mi-chael Kennedy as *The Assiniboines* in 1961. Despite the book being exclusively drawn from elders at Fort Peck Reservation, many people at Fort Belknap had seen the book and eagerly sought original copies of it.

2. Nakoda, in addition to being the tribal designation of the Assiniboine peo-ple, refers to the Indigenous language of the Fort Peck and Fort Belknap Assini-boine community. I have retained the use of the term "Assiniboine" as a tribal designation as that is how Long refers to it throughout his text. I use the term "Nakoda" to refer exclusively to the Indigenous language. Long mentions that not only was he fluent in Nakoda, but he was literate in the language as well. All of the manuscripts I encountered by Larpenteur Long were written in English with some Nakoda interspersed. I do not know if he wrote the elders' stories down initially in Nakoda and then later translated them into English or if the narra-tors recited them in Nakoda with Larpenteur Long recording them initially in English. Given the ages of the informants at the time of the project (average age was seventy-seven), it is likely that they were monolingual in Nakoda. In my research, I have not found any manuscripts in Nakoda.

3. Reflecting the liberal spirit of the New Deal, many of the projects associated with the Federal Writers' Program were aimed at educating the general public about the diversity of communities that comprised the United States. The fed-eral and state offices focused on documenting the experiences of immigrant communities in urban centers, ex-slave narratives, and local ethnic studies. American Indian communities were also the focus on many of these projects, though there remained an ambivalence regarding their position within the larger U.S. society. See Morgan (2005).

4. I do not mean to imply that ethnohistory is exclusively concerned with written documents. Oral history and ethnographic interviews are especially effective methods employed by those doing ethnohistorical research. But one of the primary sites of ethnohistorical research is the archive and the documents it contains and this is the site that I am interested in for this chapter.

5. Both DeMallie and Parks have addressed this issue in many of their writings. For purposes of this chapter, I am focusing on their 1992 article, "Plains Indian Native Literatures." See also DeMallie (1999) and Parks (1999).

6. For an excellent account of this in the context of the United States, see Cathleen Cahill (2011). I do not mean to imply that the United States is the only case where local individuals were employed by the colonial government, but rather that the literature so far has emphasized the writing of colonial officials rather than the community members that were also employed.

7. James Larpenteur Long, Autobiographical Statement, October 29, 1940, MC 77, Box 17, Montana Historical Society, p. 24. This observation is critical in that he is expressing the concern that younger generations do not know the language and therefore by extension the cultural knowledge contained within it. Further, it illustrates that for Larpenteur Long, who knew Nakoda, linguistic ability is the key component of identity as Assiniboine rather than blood quantum.

8. Larpenteur Long's first wife was Mary Knapp, whom he married in 1913. He had two daughters with her: Phillippena (b. 1914) and Anna (b. 1916). Mary died in 1918. In 1920, he married Regina Koch and had two daughters, Maxine (b. 1923) and Frances (b. 1926). Their son Charles was born in 1930 but died shortly later.

9. James Larpenteur Long, Autobiographical Statement, p. 15.

10. Charles Smith to Henry Alsberg, April 7, 1939, Records of the Central Office, Project Proposal File, 1936–42, Box 1, National Archives and Records Administration.

11. Byron Crane to Henry Alsberg, June 20, 1939, Box 224, Library of Congress.

12. *Indians at Work* (IAW), vol. 3, no. 3, p. 28.

13. James Larpenteur Long, Autobiographical Statement, p. 4.

14. Ibid., p. 24.

15. Ibid., p. 5.

16. Ibid., p. 6.

17. Editorial report, July 30, 1941, MC 77, Box 17, Montana Historical Society, p. 2.

18. His artwork also appeared in the periodical *Indians at Work*. Standing died tragically in a car accident in 1951, and *Land of Nakoda* remains one of the finest collections of his work.

19. James Long to Margaret Whitaker, July 27, 1939, MC 77, Box 17, Montana Historical Society, p. 2.

20. These particular illustrations are found in the original publication of *Land of Nakoda,* but do not appear in the reprinted version of *The Assiniboines.*

21. IAW, vol. 1, no. 2, p. 2.

22. Stephen Kunitz (1971) situates Collier's thoughts regarding society within the larger intellectual movement occurring at the same time. For more discussion regarding the Applied Anthropology Unit, including internal struggles between anthropologists and administrators, see Biolsi (1997), Castile (2004), and Stocking (1992:163–64).

23. IAW, vol. 4, no. 21, p. 28.

24. IAW, vol. 4, no. 10, p. 21.

25. IAW, vol. 4, no. 20, p. 44.

26. IAW, vol. 4, no. 15, p. 2.

10

Against Procedural Landscapes

Community, Kinship, and History

SEBASTIAN FELIX BRAUN

I would like to start with a story, or, more precisely, a short extract from a longer story. Like most stories, it is told from a unique perspective, but the themes it addresses are not uncommon; I have heard stories like it in many places on the northern plains. This one concerns Fort Yates in the 1930s and 1940s. The events described in this story would soon become history because the damming of Lake Oahe would make crossing the Missouri impossible.

> Everybody used the river. When I . . . Ever since I remember when I was growing up, everybody on Saturdays and Sundays we all went down by the river and swam and people fished and in the wintertime, when the river would freeze over, the people from Strasburg, across the road, the German people would come over and they would trade, they would bring their . . . in the grocery, into the store, and trade there, and it was just like—it was unbelievable. You know, people just went back and forth. . . .
>
> We had connections with people, you know, it was so fun. And they would come over and go the church, you know, during lent, they would come over, across the river, and go to our church, and we just thought it was—wonderful, you know, to see so far away people go to our church *(laughs)*.
>
> [Ketterling in Reed 2011]

This story and its implied context, the destruction of the relationships described, shows two changing relationships, that of people (both Natives and non-Natives, although in different ways) to the river, and that of the two communities to each other. In interpreting this story, the damming of the Missouri River could be seen as the ecological event that led to the changing of the community relations. Rather than following this perhaps conventional storyline, however, I want to explore the possibility that the river was dammed at the same time that the relationships between the communities were changing, and this might have been the reason why the river could be dammed. I want to pursue a storyline of changing community relations, not specifically between Fort Yates and Strasburg, but between Native people and their non-Native neighbors on the Great Plains. The damming of the river and its consequences, then, are an expression of changes between communities, a consequence of changes in the larger landscape. I propose to use this story as a starting point for an ecological approach to this ethnohistory of landscapes.

ECOLOGY, HISTORY, RITUAL, AND KINSHIP

Both an ecological approach and a cultural approach to community look at the relations in a landscape at a given time. Just as "culture and culture change are, in effect, the same phenomenon" (DeMallie 1993:533), so are ecology and ecological change. The important question to answer for an observer is not whether anything changes, but how it does and how we describe this change. Neither a cultural nor an ecological perspective measure or compare change within a landscape directly. Its history becomes apparent when one notices how different elements of the cultural or ecological landscape change over a number of descriptions dealing with different times. A historical analysis, to the contrary, emphasizes these changes and involves a direct comparison between the differences over time. In the ethnohistorical method, the two are combined (DeMallie 1993) so that both change and continuity in a given ecological, cultural, social, political, or other landscape are described.

Because history compares differences over time, it attempts to describe two different landscapes, one before and one after a chosen point in time, or a single landscape at different stages. It thus becomes impossible to focus on all elements, and with the emphasis on change, those elements that stay the same are simply background to that change: they are non-events. Raymond Fogelson has, in his exploration of "Events and Non-Events," shown how a positivist history is contradicted by the recognition of "the possibility that most history is non-eventful" (1989:141). I would add to this that most events in history are also not successful (thus becoming nonevents), yet future events and nonevents in history are still influenced by them. Fogelson (1989:134) wrote that "Events . . . have traditionally been considered as the primary elements in the study of history," perhaps because "The components of narratives are connected series of events" (140). If history is a connected series of events, culture is a connected series of meaning; we can make the same argument about nonmeaning as about nonevents. Most meanings are background and do not register consciously, and what meanings are noticeable are those that stick out for some reason, depending on the cultural expectations of the observer.

A history without ethnology and an ethnology without history can be read as essentializations: one of culture, the other of change. Just like a superficial reading and writing of culture results in the emphasis of the exotic, a careless approach to history results in times being represented by those events that stand out. While Marc Augé (1999:10) noted that the "idea of a purely evenemential history, where the substance of historical narrative would come down to a succession of dates and events, is one we no longer find credible," the methods and theories of history still remain bound to events as markers and dividers of eras. Certain events come to symbolize whole eras because they seem to impersonate the changes between different times, just like certain values and meanings come to represent cultures. Once these markers have become hegemonic, consumers of history and anthropology—and academics are also consumers of their crafts—then come to perceive times and societies as incorporating the values of the chosen events that are taken to symbolize them.

Humans make sense of culture and history in the same way that they participate in rituals. Following Edmund Leach (1976:41), explanations of history and culture can actually be perceived as participation in rituals, since they, just like rituals, are a condensation of our experiences. For example, "attending a funeral" is not simply a series of events, but really a series of symbolic acts and communications that lead, if successful, to that overarching experience. Roy Rappaport (1999:90) has argued that "the significance of ritual significance is often trivial," but this triviality is erased once the ritual fails, because at that point the trivial becomes visible and profound: an event. Perhaps, then, historical events are events exactly because they have failed on a grand scale: they have become visible and profound because they are untypical, unexpected, and (trans)formative. The irony, then, is that too often extraordinary and untypical events come to represent historical times and are as such perceived as typical in part exactly because they were exceptional and exotic. The many other nonevents that were taking place during those times, which ironically dominated more people's lives than the events, are relegated to the obscure academic domain while a succession of markers that have the quality to stand out are remembered, interpreted, and reinterpreted in the ongoing ritual that attempts to make sense of our present situations by categorizing history.

Since ritual is "perhaps the ultimate human emplacement structure" (Thornton 2008:174), an analysis of history as ritual might provide some useful insight into how history as a series of nonevents works differently from history as a series of events, or how anthropology as a series of nonmeanings is different from an anthropology as a series of meanings. The large events of history, infused with "historical" meaning provide Rappaport's (1999:164) ritual "re-creation of the primordial order." These meanings are portrayed as the changeless moral lessons of history. "If the essence of history is the passage of the particular," Rappaport (1999:233, 234) argued, "the essence of liturgical order is the recurrence of the changeless." The fact that the meaning of such history is supposed to be changeless is of course a powerful clue that it does not describe the real (non)events, or culture of any given people. Although rituals (and traditions) need to be portrayed as changeless in their meaning, obviously no two rituals are the same if we look at the (non)events that make them up as singular events. Neither history nor culture happen in a universal, generalized way in the actual reality of life. Change does not happen simultaneously in all places nor does it change everything it affects in the same way. To gain a true understanding of cultures and history— outside the liturgical order—we need to go beyond the positivist view of history. Perhaps we should look for a negativist history, search for the abortive, unexpected, and incomplete nonevents as signs for the profound that we otherwise would overlook as trivial. I propose that the profound nonevents and nonmeanings of history and culture are enacted in the trivial practice of kinship.

Kinship as a cultural practice does not seem to go out of style, but academic interest in kinship seems to have disappeared.[1] Fogelson (2001:41) declared it "a dead topic" after Schneider (1984:vii) declared that "there is no such thing as kinship." Without getting into a discussion of kinship theory, it seems obvious that "Scholars today," as DeMallie (1998:307) has noted, "including many anthropologists, frequently dismiss kinship studies as arcane and irrelevant to such larger concerns as politics, economics, or religion." However, the study of kinship is not the single-minded obsession with genealogical charts that many people imagine it to be. In thinking about kinship, DeMallie always emphasized that it is a tool for further understanding of a larger issue: the position of individuals within the local, regional, human, and ultimately universal communities they build through kinship relations. "By restricting kinship to genealogy, the social-structural approach fails to note that [people] define relationship in terms of a set of conceptual categories and the logical relationships between them based on the proper 'feeling' and behavior, rather than on concrete links of marriage and birth" (DeMallie 1994:142). Kinship relations are all relations between human and nonhuman individuals and communities who feel they are related. These relations define rights and responsibilities, that is, behavior, language, and belonging.

The study of meaningful relations between communities, for example, to get back to the story with which I began, the ecology of dams, is thus an extension of kinship studies. By extension, I do not mean that spiritual and ecological relations are simply "'metaphorical extensions' of human kinship"; I agree with McKinley (2001:132) that "such a view seriously underestimates both the power and scope of" kinship. I mean that spiritual and ecological relations truly are kinship relations. Claude Lévi-Strauss (1969:xxx), in the preface to the second edition of *Elementary Structures,* writes of culture as "a synthetic duplication of mechanisms already in existence" in nature. The extension of kinship to nonhuman relations—how we view ecological relations—is the duplication of mechanisms of culture. If kinship is what ties us to our cultural universes, ecological relations as humans define them are kinship relations, or at the very least modeled on them. This is true for all societies, including industrial ones that might be more individualistic or alienated. The denial of relationships, the relative alienation from kin, is also a kinship pattern. To speak about community, ecology, or landscape, then, is always to speak about kinship as relations to meaningful actors in the cultural environment. Approaching community relations from a kinship perspective is fundamentally different from approaching them from a political, religious, or economic perspective because kinship ties are not limited to political, religious, or economic groups, but in effect bridge them. The liturgical order of historic and contemporary communities is thus transformed into a less essentialized reality.

LANDSCAPES: PROCEDURAL AND OTHER

If community is the expression of a distinctive relationship with a specific environment, these relational structures, which constitute landscapes, change with experience. According to Tim Ingold (2000:189), "The landscape is constituted as an enduring record of—and testimony to—the lives and works of past generations who have dwelt within it, and in so doing, have left there something of themselves." In building relationships, humans attach cultural meanings to our social, natural, and spiritual environments, wherever we are. As Thornton (2008:190) argued, "comparative evidence suggests that social, linguistic, economic, and ritual structures are vitally important vehicles for place making among indigenous peoples from the Americas to Eurasia to Africa to Oceania, and even for immigrant and diasporic peoples no longer tied to their original lands." This perspective has two advantages: it allows for communities to become native somewhere, and it allows for ecological relationships to change. A view of the landscape that emphasizes nonevents and kinship thus challenges rather than recreates the ritual primordial order—the assumption that community relations take place between socially fixed groups with fixed cultures, and the fixation of politically defined groups as cultural and historical realities.

The political group in its most defined form is the liberal state, and the meanings of the state are reflected in the identities of its voluntary, forced, incomplete, or subjected constituents. David Anderson (2000:209) has argued that identities in modern states are "pre-selected by administrative agents, although people do then use these identities in creative and often unexpected ways. In Hobsbawm's words, the territorial citizen-state provides 'an institutional or procedural landscape which . . . is the setting for [its in-habitants'] lives, which it largely determines.'" The liberal state provides an abstract framework of kinship relations, an imagined community (Anderson 1991), through its procedural landscape, which it enforces upon the existing unprocedural, unliturgical relations. As Gagnon (2004:22) has stated, "Liberal systems require the active construction of a non-existent homogeneity that constructs and binds the population of a territory into a 'community.'" This is the meaning of conquest on the North American plains and elsewhere, seen at its best, or worst, in assimilation policies such as allotment or termination, rituals of citizenship, and formal education.

However, the liberal state cannot simply cover the existing landscape with its new procedural one. The processes of an expanding and contracting procedural landscape take time. The procedural landscape only exists where procedures can be enforced. While the Supreme Court may define relations between communities as those of deadliest enemies, this does not mean that relations in reality conform to this construction (Biolsi 2001). The history of the expanding modern state on the plains is just as much the history of the absence of the state as it is the history of the presence of the state. It is the history of the deliberate, yet slow and incremental construction and enforcement of a new landscape. One can argue that one visible part of this new, procedural landscape are the Pick-Sloan dams. To take the story of disrupted community relationships seriously, however, my focus is on the landscape that was covered by this procedural one.

In order to un-cover that landscape, we can look at what happens when a state fails and its procedural landscapes melt away. As archaeologists know, structural failure can give important insights into the meanings of the structure during construction. Niobe Thompson (2008) has explored what occurs when the citizen-state disappears and its procedural landscape retreats by looking at the contraction of the Russian state, the "collapse" of the Soviet Union in Siberia. Soviet settlers had been attracted to Chukotka by privileges, as the procedural landscape afforded their frontier society a high class status. When the state contracted, Thompson (2008:138) argues, Siberian settlers in the 1990s became deeply rooted in the actual landscape in order to survive. Settlers became "more palpably tied to Chukotka's landscape," and their "networks were singularly embedded in a local community" (140). Once the state disappeared, "The old hierarchy of settler privilege in relation to natives lost its monolithic aspect, for survival and success in post-Soviet conditions of statelessness became in many ways a more meritocratic and less ethnically determined affair" (114). The procedural landscape disappears, in other words, and is replaced with one whose relations are not predetermined.

I find these observations useful not because I think the postindustrial plains resemble post-Soviet Siberia, although that is actually an idea worthwhile pursuing more deeply (see Brown 2001). It is because they inspire me to re-think the ethnohistory of plains communities not as a persistent conflict between Indians and settlers but as plains communities. If we can agree that the procedural landscapes of a contracting and an expanding state present themselves geographically in a structurally similar, although opposite fash-ion, and that it is the existence of the procedural landscape that provides for distinct relations between communities, post-Soviet Siberia contributes to an understanding of the proto-American plains. The official historiography of the plains has mostly focused on the procedural landscapes. This creates a focus on conflict, a "fixation on war" that is "at best, a mixed bag" (Fletcher and Vicaire 2012:230), not only for Indians, but for everybody on the plains. The period between "relocation" and "assimilation" is thus often seen as one of conflict, massacre, and war, an era marked by Wounded Knee and Sand Creek (but who in the public at large, or even academia, remembers and teaches the actual last battle between American Indians and the U.S. Army, the Battle of Sugar Point, won by the Chippewa?). The emphasis on such events creates the idea of the procedural landscape as inevitable and a natu-ral progression, and pretends that at that moment when the conquest was "over," the state had already blanketed the landscape and changed the cultural-ecological system to one in which two distinct communities oper-ated: one, oppressed Indian and the other dominant white (a view that also ignores the non-Indian-non-white presence). A history based on procedural landscapes might come to the conclusion that Indian and non-Indian com-munities on the plains led absolutely different lives and experienced abso-lutely different histories; that they had no commonalities, meeting grounds, or shared lives, concerns, events, and spaces.

What if Indian and non-Indian communities had shared lives? What if we take Ketterling's story, with which I opened this chapter, seriously? The nar-rative of a self-evident, primoridal and perennial racial divide that is taken to be "part of the landscape" (see Biolsi 2001:4) would have to change. With it would have to change the narrative of continuous improvement of race relations. Now, the possibility exists that personal relations between Indians and non-Indians might have been better in the 1920s than today, that com-munities might have known more about each other, might even have coop-erated better. It is a narrative that goes against the grand view of history as propagated by national myths and based on carefully selected symbolic events. Yet, it might just be true.

COMMUNITIES IN THE LANDSCAPE

At the moment of conquest, if we assume that such a moment can be de-termined, Indian communities and settlers faced—as they still do—the same natural and economic environment. Climate, economy, soils, markets, infrastructure, and many other variables in their lives were the same. It is usually assumed that what differentiated them was the presence of the state; that the procedural landscape predetermined their relationships with their environments and therefore with each other. This, however, is not necessarily true.

Procedural landscapes connected to state presence first appear in places where the state has a vested interest. After the military conquest of the plains had been completed, the state was interested in places with resources: mineral, timber, and water resources were to be exploited, annuities distributed, and conquest protected. The procedural landscape on the plains extended not too far from the spots that marked the state's presence at given times. This included reservations, where procedural landscapes were present at agencies and traveled with agency personnel, policies, and directives but did not define other landscapes. While policies, where enforceable and enforced, had huge impacts on lives, the situation left room for nonprocedural landscapes to persist. As Rebecca Bateman (1996) made clear, where procedural landscapes were enforced, they worked to the disadvantage of American Indians, in part exactly because the governments of both Canada and the United States enforced their economic, social, and political ideologies on Indians, but not on settlers. Social networks and cooperative or communal approaches to the land where thus severely limited on reservations, but their presence was ignored or tolerated outside of them—an ethnohistorical fact that was later covered by the procedural landscapes of individualized, industrialized agriculture. However, even the most destabilizing, destructive practices of the state—for example, livestock reduction programs in the 1930s or military massacres before that—only traveled over the landscape, apart from extremely localized outposts of the state. Although the consequences, namely genocide, poverty, and oppression stayed, the presence of the state in its manifest forms was transient at best. The destruction was often so large that the landscapes remained changed, but resistance to these procedures could and did carve back nonprocedural spaces.

Philip Deloria (2004:232) has stated that "Indian space was not only reservation space, and reservation space was anachronistic only in white expectation." Read from the viewpoint of procedural landscape, Indian landscapes were not only procedural, and even in places where Indians were subjected to predetermination, the subjection came only out of the agents of procedure. This leaves a lot of room for interactions between communities that do not fit the predetermined or expected landscapes. Clark Wissler, in his 1938 remembrances published as *Red Man Reservations,* noted that:

> On a reservation one could shuttle back and forth from one order of life to the other. Interesting personalities could be contacted while loitering around the agency, but there the Indian felt he was in the

white man's country and acted accordingly, whereas if one of these old personalities invited you to pitch your tent near his camp or cabin, as the case might be, the tables were turned, for then you were in the Indian country. Perhaps it was part imagination, but I felt that once settled in such surroundings, those cold staring faces, so familiar at the agency, were seldom seen, having given way to kindly benign looking countenances.

[Wissler 1971:229]

Unexpected interactions can be found where expectations—the procedural landscapes—do not exist, either because the state takes no interest, or because Indians are not supposed to be there. Deloria (2004) has shown how those Indians that worked and lived "in unexpected places" were able to build unexpected lives; unexpected because they were based not simply on actions or events, but on *relationships* that did not follow predetermined expectations. We should expect such unexpected landscapes in expected places, too, for example on reservations.

One landscape that resisted very strongly against becoming procedural was the religious landscape. While the state certainly attempted to extinguish traditional religions, the imposition of action on this was impeded by the severe limitations of the procedural landscape. Sun Dances were held almost every year on Pine Ridge, for example, sometimes in hiding, sometimes tolerated, and sometimes officially sanctioned, such as in 1917, 1918, 1919, and continuously from 1929 on (Steinmetz 1998:28). Lakota people, just like other indigenous peoples, often undermined the state and weakened the intent of the government to extend the procedural landscape. John Troutman (2007) has shown how people on Standing Rock first appropriated the procedural landscape and then turned its meaning against the state: as citizens of the United States, they claimed religious freedom and the freedom to celebrate national holidays however they wanted. Non-procedural landscapes and those in which the enforcement is not saturated enough allow the flexibility to think, classify, and act relative to each situation, even in reallocating the meanings of the procedural landscape itself.

COMMUNITY

Paula Wagoner (2002:1) shares the following story about expected landscapes in Geo's in Martin, South Dakota: "I saw Indians and non-Indians come in, nod at each other in recognition, and sometimes exchange a few words. I saw people in terms of phenotype back then. . . . Things seemed pretty clear on my first day in town, and I was confident that I had found some variety of parallel societies that interacted at certain places, such as cafes, schools, and grocery stores, and at church. It all seemed pretty cut and dried." Perhaps centering her own work in Bennett County, in some ways outside the procedural landscape of today's defined reservation space, allowed her to subsequently notice instead and explain the complex community relationships she so wonderfully describes. According to Wagoner (2002:13), her study "illustrates the ways in which United States federal policies brought Oglala Lakotas, and their neighbors, to think of themselves in racial terms, where, previously, a politically loaded classification by race had not necessarily existed." I argue that such a classification still does not necessarily exist on all levels, that procedural landscapes still do not define all relations. This is not to deny the racism within and outside of Indian communities. But in the same towns, the same people that are not served in cafes because they are Indians are members of bowling teams and ranchers' associations where ethnicity is not primary. Kinship communities are not communities that never experience conflicts. Instead, they allow the situational flexibility that is characteristic of traditional, nonessential relations (see Braun 2008).

Wagoner (2002:59–60) writes about local kinship communities based on a "tenuously negotiated social equilibrium." These equilibria and communities, in the eyes of the people, were destroyed by "urban ideas" which led to ethnic differentiation rather than the recognition of neighbors as kin. While one could see this perspective as a denial of responsibility, it reminds me of Loretta Fowler's (1987:144–46) discussion of the three divisions in the Youth Generation on Forth Belknap during the same time. Could it be that those tenuous kinship communities became the victims of an expansion of procedural landscapes—including the academic landscape—that emphasized ethnic predeterminism? While, as Fogelson (1989:140) predicted many years ago, "resistance to event-centered history . . . seems to be eroding in the face of a rising tide of interest in narrativity," the procedural classification of narratives as belonging to certain ethnic groups has continued an event-centered history. Emphasis is placed on relations between these groups in the procedural landscape; communities and actions that exist between or outside the procedural and expected space are nonevents.

When elders say that in earlier years everything was better, we can assume that they are expressing nostalgia for cultural values that have changed. However, when an elder said to Wagoner (2002:59), "In the old days we were all the same out here. We were all poor," or when another elder tells me that he feels his German-from-Russia neighbor has lost his language in the same way that he has lost Lakota, I think we have to pay attention. Harold Schunk, former superintendent at Cheyenne River, Turtle Mountain, and Rosebud, told Joseph Cash the following story about the 1930s: "One of the things I always recall was a really good old friend of mine at the Cheyenne River agency. He was a real old-timer. . . . He said to me, 'Mr. Schunk,' he said, 'we're all on the same level now. The white man is in the same shape we are,' which was literally true the drought had just wiped everything out. And the old man was a real fine gentleman. We were all on the same plane at that time" (Cash and Hoover 1971:152).

It is not simply hard times that create communities, however; it is the absence of procedural landscapes. Daniel Sharfstein (2003) has argued that kinship communities existed in rural Appalachia until the state was able to enforce strict racial segregation regimes between "whites" and "blacks." In small communities in the South, Sharfstein has shown, even at the height of the Jim Crow laws and lynchings, elders still focused on kinship relations more than on categorical constructions of race. Despite racist violence, "there remained cool spots in the crucible of race, where racial identity was personal and casually worn and where rumors of race did not compel mob action" (Sharfstein 2003:1487). Similar attitudes are evident on the plains. Local people knew better, as Keith Regular (2009:32) has shown in Alberta: "Reserve, ranch and farm, town and village were adaptations to a common environment that required and encouraged co-operation. Beneath the veneer of the frequent expressions of Natives as a race in the process of extinction, there was subtle recognition of Native persistence accompanied by the realization of the need for neighbourly accommodation. The subsequent relationship between the [Indians] and their neighbours was not without its tribulations, but it endured despite fracture and fissure because its benefits were necessary for the well-being of both."

Community exists where kinship connections are built and upheld. John Saul, an elder from Crow Creek, had the following to say: "I've known different superintendents that have been in charge of this reservation. There was one good man, Major Chamberlain—he was a superintendent, and he's the one man that didn't sit in the office. He put his overalls on, and got out among the reservations and worked. . . . I've seen him pitch hay for an Indian. I've seen him chop wood for log houses" (Cash and Hoover 1971:201). The mark of community was thus the absence of bureaucracy, not necessarily because of the paperwork, but because the procedural landscape it created was preventing kinship ties, which are built through spontaneous co-operation. This extended to other areas. Johnson Holy Rock explained other relationships stemming from kinship communities in the early twentieth century, when the tribal cattle economy prospered on Pine Ridge: "And any one of those old Indians with braids could go to the bank and borrow money. The bankers in those days, they lent them the money, regardless of what the statutes said or what the Secretary of Interior's regulations were, they lent those old Indians money, and they got paid" (Cash and Hoover 1971:207).

I do not argue that the kinship communities that had evolved by the early 1900s were entirely free of procedural influences. Stereotypes and the perception of ethnic differences exist within all communities because none are completely isolated. Rather, I think that nonprocedural landscapes existed simultaneously with, and sometimes within the same places as, procedural landscapes: that kinship communities, crossing procedural markers, existed much more frequently than we assume today, and that many continue to exist. In one of the very few studies focusing on functional interactions between Natives and non-Native people, Regular (2009:12) concluded that "In the period of supposed Indian 'irrelevance,' the Bloods, at least, forged a relevant meaningful economic association with their non-Native neighbours in the period between the establishment of the reserve and the onset of World War II."

Such relations also developed elsewhere, although they have to be excavated from texts that often deemphasize them. Gordon MacGregor (1946:83) wrote that "The attitudes of the whites of [bordertowns] toward Indians varied. Employers want Indians to harvest corn and potatoes. They are invited to participate in the summer fairs and rodeos, to which they add a great deal of color. The stores enjoy their trade . . . On the other hand, the white people in the towns look down upon the Indians." While this account leaves the reader with the impression that Indians are simply exploited, this might result from the author seeing Indians as contributing nothing to the community but economic value and "a great deal of color." The participants in the fairs and rodeos—Indians and their non-Indian kinship relations— hardly felt that way. Similarly, from Niels Winther Braroe's account of (non) interactions in his *Indian and White,* a picture of general racist exploitation emerges. However, the exploiters are white people who live according to procedural, predetermined landscapes. There are also a few who are genuinely knowledgeable about their Indian neighbors, and they are the ones who had established kinship relations: "Probably no more than a few dozen Whites have even a vague awareness of Indian names. Most of these are people who lived near the reserve as children and had regular contact with the Indians. . . . I met only four men who knew any Indian names, and two of those spoke Cree. They were adults, in their fifties, who had played with Indians as children, and they knew the names of some of their former playmates, though not those of any Indians from later generations" (Braroe 1975:130). The nonprocedural landscapes of their childhood were probably replaced by the hegemonic procedural norms in adulthood. However, I think this passage reinforces that kinship relations existed, as does this statement: "I heard one White ask an Indian the purpose of the small bits of cloth hung here and there in bushes, which the latter claimed not to know (some older Whites still remember that these are offerings to spirits)" (Braroe 1975:131). Braroe concludes that "White ignorance of Indian customs is extensive" (133). This was undoubtedly true, but it was probably also true that a few Whites and Indians had extensive knowledge of and interactions with each other.

Kristin Burnett (2010), in her study of health care on the Alberta plains,[2] details the importance of Native women's knowledge for early settlers. She describes "extensive economic and social ties," especially between Nakoda laborers and ranching families (63). However, she finds that these contributions were not acknowledged.

> Despite the importance of Aboriginal women's help, Euro-Canadians were reluctant to acknowledge it. To this day, silence persists regarding the healing and caregiving interventions of Aboriginal women. . . . Indeed, of the nearly twenty addresses to church audiences that Eliza McDougall and her sister-in-law Annie delivered, none mention the women's close and important relationships with Aboriginal women. . . . In an interview with journalist Elizabeth Bailey Price in the late 1920s, Annie McDougall revealed that Mary Cecil had been very important in ensuring the well-being of the McDougall women. Was this disclosure a result of the reporter's questions or of Annie's desire to set the record straight? The latter is most likely.
>   [Burnett 2010:63]

If setting the record straight was important, this, I would propose, also shows the strength of the relationship with the Native women that Annie McDougall felt. The fact that these relationships were not revealed to all audiences probably had a lot to do with the awareness of the procedural landscapes in which the presentations took place and the expectations that prevailed in those landscapes. As Burnett (2010:3) writes, "when Aboriginal and non-Aboriginal women encountered each other, they, for a brief time, participated together in an informal system of healing and nursing care that drew on both traditions and centred on shared domestic concerns relating to childbirth and general childhood and family illnesses. Over time, as the number of white settlers grew, the formal structures of Western medicine and nursing care increasingly dominate these more informal arrangements." In other words, as the procedural landscape expanded over southern Alberta, it replaced the kinship relationships that had brought women together in community.

In the absence of a procedural landscape in rural areas, people experienced their environment in very similar ways: they were all poor and nobody but themselves did anything to remedy that. As Michael Jackson (2007:230) has observed, "when people are obliged to coexist in the same place, on roughly the same terms, they tend to see themselves and others as variations on a single human theme, different but not demonically or dangerously other." Along the Missouri River, the reemphasis on belonging to autonomous societies accelerated as the procedural landscape expanded rapidly after World War II and increasingly created different places in which people lived. Now, those who perceived themselves as not receiving the same rights and benefits as the others—and both Indians and non-Indians found reasons for feeling this way—saw themselves victimized. The flooding of the Missouri deliberately targeted reservation lands, similar to the establishment of bombing ranges on reservations during the war. These events were an expression of changing community relationships on the procedural level. Yet, because the state now was able to influence local relations, the procedural landscape became imposed on the real landscape in a more visible and absolute way than ever before.

BORDERS AND BORDERTOWNS

Anecdotal evidence and my own experience on the northern plains over the years indicates that today, as well as in the past, some of the people with strong stereotypical and sometimes racist perspectives of American Indians are very often among those who live closest to reservation communities but have no direct personal interactions with Indians, and that sympathies for Indians—albeit ones that are often not steeped in cultural knowledge—are often found away from reservations. Bordertowns are often infamous for the treatment of Indians. Fletcher (2007–2008:73) writes of "an age-old, intergenerational enmity between the people of Indian communities and the non-Indians who live on or near Indian Country." However, I think that paying attention to kinship landscapes instead of, or in addition to procedural ones, brings a different, more complex history to light and explains this paradox. Bordertowns cannot simply be seen as generally hostile environments. That perspective is dependent on a view of history as a linear progression from the establishment of reservations to a continued neocolonialist regime.

Bordertowns are, as the name says, situated close to the borders between reservation and nonreservation land. They are also, however, situated on a different border, namely that between kinship relations and ethnic relations. Kinship relations depend on personal loyalties and expectations, while ethnic relations depend on public or political loyalties and expectations. The two are often in conflict. This can perhaps be seen best in the history of trade and warfare, not only in North America. Whether groups or individuals would engage in peaceful or violent exchange depended on whether the strength of personal loyalties overcame the social and political ambiguity associated with strangers (Braun 1997; 1998; Burch 2005). Bordertowns, like all borders, are places of ambiguity for all groups. To enlist Susan Gillespie's (1991:340) study of ballcourts, public interactions in bordertowns mark "the separation of society into its component groupings, just as [bordertowns are] the loci where this separation [is] made manifest." In bordertowns, the social danger of crossing the border is always present. Therefore, those in

whose interest it is to maintain such imagined ethnic borders need to enforce it here the most.

The separation between constructed ethnic groups needs to be made
manifest the most in places where people have created kinship communities. Bruce D'Arcus (2003) has described the importance of constructing
such boundaries for both occupiers and besiegers of the Wounded Knee
site in 1973. In that context, it is interesting that when the federal road-
blocks were removed for a while, many Oglala left and were replaced by
"men and women who had driven night and day from every corner of
America, mostly from other Indian nations, but also a few whites, Asians,
and blacks. . . . Altogether, about 200 Oglalas went home, but in their place
came about 150 other Indians" (Means and Wolf in D'Arcus 2003:425). This
is not to deny the involvement of traditional people from Pine Ridge (see
DeMallie 1978b:304–10), but it is entirely possible to see the conflict as a theater for the marking of boundaries that played out between two groups of
strangers to the reservation—the federal government and the American Indian Movement. Both needed continued conflict over such boundaries to
extend the procedural landscape that allowed them to exist and therefore
were interested in enforcing and potentially escalating boundaries, on
Pine Ridge and elsewhere. Caught between them were the local people—
"traditionalists" and "progressives"—who were increasingly victimized in
their own communities.

The constructed "ethnic group in 'hard' terms," as Gagnon (2004:27–28)
calls it, "exists only if its borders are constantly enforced or reinforced. . . .
So it was no coincidence that the worst violence in the Yugoslav wars occurred in the most ethnically mixed and tolerant regions of the country,
places where such notions [of kinship communities] had a strength and reality that came from a shared sense of community." Bordertowns are places of
real and potential border crossings, whether around Indian reservations or
along other national borders. Those interested in maintaining or constructing ethnic groups need to prevent kinship communities. People in such environments often make racist remarks in front of individuals from the group
they have just denigrated, only to say, "Of course I do not mean you" or "Of
course, you are different," or other such statements. These events can be seen
as further evidence of bigoted, cowardly racism. In the simultaneous presence of kinship communities and racist concepts of ethnicity, however, they
might also be signs that people feel comfortable making stereotypical statements about another group in the presence of individuals of that group because they conceive of specific individuals not in terms of ethnicity, but in
terms of kinship. The procedural landscape, in terms of essentialized divisions between communities, and the nonprocedural landscape, in terms of
kinship ties that bridge these stereotypes, coexist for a moment, although
always in conflict.

The abandonment of the nonprocedural landscape is not a new phenomenon. Nancy Shoemaker (2004:3) has proposed that "Indian and European similarities enabled them to see their differences in sharper relief and, over the course of the eighteenth century, construct new identities that exaggerated the contrasts between them while ignoring what they had in common." Although this process of conceptualizing procedural landscapes appears to have been largely finished by the nineteenth century, the imposition of these ideas on the actual landscape is still ongoing. In the early twentieth century, kinship communities persisted against and coexisted with systemic racist stereotyping and exclusion in many rural areas on the plains. In the 1960s and 1970s, which saw a renewed interest in American Indian communities and narratives, the procedural markers that kinship communities had bridged on a personal level often became more important. The state—still expanding in the 1960s, especially with "war on poverty" programs—and its academic and economic affiliates wanted or needed neatly classified groups. An expanding cultural nationalism was based, in part, on ethnic differences. I agree with Tim Schouls (2003:79) that the liberal, Wilsonian, and perhaps paradoxically indigenous nationalist notion of the parallels between political sovereignty and distinctive culture stems from one basic assumption, namely that it is "predicated on bounded conceptions of cultural and political systems that are difficult to maintain within a technologically advanced and socially heterogeneous society." One could even argue that it is exactly the heterogeneous culture of diversity, at least as frequently deployed in popular diversity discourse, that leads to the essentialization of specific cultures. James LaGrand (2002:232) describes how Native culture became essentialized in Chicago, arguing that "a debate about identity and who was the 'true Indian' . . . could only have taken place within an urban community. . . . A challenging and foreign environment, the prospect of being misidentified by others, new economic and political obstacles, and the sheer diversity and heterogeneity of the population made presentation of an Indian identity an issue of utmost importance in the city." Without a doubt, identity becomes the most rigidly and politically defined when a group sees itself as under attack, as it becomes necessary to define who does and does not belong.

With the continued and reinvigorated expansion of procedural landscapes, both the procedures of the state and the procedures of those who opposed it divided people into ethnic groups. Indians became convinced that they had to be distinct from their neighbors in order to attract and deserve attention. Non-Indians felt that although their situation deserved as much attention as the Indians', they were being ignored. Some non-Indians also felt that their position of power was threatened by attempts to revitalize reservation economies and sovereignty. In short, in the eyes of the "outsiders"—both Indians and non-Indians—and the logic of zero-sum-game conflict over limited resources, two absolutely distinct communities existed. Ethnic loyalties became dominant over personal loyalties, and these procedural structures not only marked the political, legal, and ethnic landscapes, they were also reflected in academia. In *The Modern Sioux,* for example, after a lengthy discussion of identity patterns and stereotypes, Daniels (1970:211) wrote, "the above discussion of stereotypes and character judgments is, I believe, a true reflection of the thought patterns of the most powerful group on the reservation, the white federal employees." Although he simply accepts the categories installed by the elites, he asserts that the categories he describes—white, mixed-blood, full-blood—need to be constantly patrolled and enforced. Once we forget, however, that it is only this constant effort to enforce procedural landscapes that enables them to exist, we confuse them with the natural landscape.

AN ETHNOHISTORY OF COMMUNITY LANDSCAPES

What Eric Hobsbawm called procedural landscape finds its expression, in Benedict Anderson's (1991:174–78) words, in the map. Maps as used by colonial, postcolonial, and other states, or when used generally in the purpose of nationalism, he argued, become means of classification, alienated logos that show the supposed cohesiveness of a territory and its otherness to everything else. Nonevents and nonpeople are nonexistent on these maps, and are thus often assigned no meaning in reality. "The map," however, as we know at least since Gregory Bateson, "is not the territory" (see Harries-Jones 1995:57–80). This becomes literally very apparent on reservations. Seemingly absolute borders between reservation and nonreservation territory—on state highway maps, for example, and other logo-maps—become fractured when land-status maps are consulted. The procedural landscape on reservations shows the different legal statuses—fee, individual trust, tribal trust—of land, implying also the different sovereignties extending over the landscape. These statuses still do not present a picture of landowners' ethnicities, as many American Indians own fee land, for example. The maps give a hint, however, that uniformity is not absolutely imposed on the physical nor social landscape. Reservations are thus carved into legal, economic, ecological, and political niches, and the more detailed the maps one consults, the more they contradict the flowing, seemingly uniform procedural landscapes. In their complexity, they affirm the existence of communities that exist and hold the landscape together despite these maps, and they reveal the imagination of uniform narratives spun in much procedural history.[3]

In off-reservation landscapes, such maps, if they exist at all, are mostly lying in the drawers of experts, except where trust lands have spilled out of their supposed confinements such as in the Trenton Indian Area or in Bennett County. The popular knowledge of the existence of land-status-maps on reservations, and the necessity to constantly consult them, thus reinforces the status of difference as an anomaly. Difference in legal land-status is not what is supposed to be "normal" in the United States. Anomalies are bearable to the procedural landscape once they are classified, contained, and integrated into the grid (Anderson 1991:184), and different policies, from assimilation to termination, to the more recent narrow interpretation of federal Indian law by the Supreme Court, can be read as continuing efforts to contain the anomaly of American Indian status—to homogenize the map and create a uniform, procedural landscape. Fredric Jameson (1998:66) blamed this integration into the grid, the extension of procedure over landscapes and peoples, on capitalism, "which translates the money form and the logic of commodity production for a market back on to space itself." I agree, but I think it would also be fruitful to explore the homogenization and proceduralization of the landscape as a consequence of the liberal state in general, continued in what the Ivorian musician Alpha Blondy called "la mondialisation de l'économie à sens unique."[4] Despite the sometimes assumed primacy of the economy, the expansion of the procedural landscape has not depended on capitalism, which can be adapted to or appropriated by kinship societies, but on the presence of agents of the state.

I took the original idea of procedural landscapes from the example of the Soviet Union, which was in a sense a more liberal state in its underlying ideology than what used to be called the capitalist West (see, e.g., Khalid 2007). If so-called communism was "Soviet power plus electrification," as Lenin is attributed to have said, the plains, and the western United States in general, show a lot of similarities in their procedural development, perhaps summarized best as "access to markets and electrification." With or without the presence of a market, however, the consequence was to proceduralize the landscape—"to seize upon a landscape and flatten it out, reorganize it into a grid of identical parcels" (Jameson 1998:66). Community-building and rebuilding under these circumstances becomes an act of resistance: against procedural landscapes, against procedural anthropology, and against procedural history. It is, thus, a total political act and has to be approached as one to be successful.

Terry Eagleton (2000:122–23) has pointed out that "culture [and therefore landscape] is not inherently political at all. . . . [It becomes] so only under specific historical conditions, usually of an unpleasant kind. [It becomes] political only when [it is] caught up in a process of domination and resistance." The goal is, he argued, to restore to culture its "innocuousness, so that one can sing, paint or make love without the bothersome distraction of political strife. It is true that there are proponents of identity politics who will then have no idea what to do with themselves, but this is their problem, not ours." Nonprocedural landscapes allow communities to see and acknowledge commonalities. In the context of an increasingly urban and alienated West, Peter Iverson (1994:219) asks "can rural people, white and Indian, see commonality as well as difference? . . . Can they achieve an understanding greater than if one group had suddenly been dropped from the moon? Can they talk to each other about continuity and change—and survival?" The stories of kinship relations and nonprocedural landscapes might allow rural people to maintain and rebuild such connections against the hegemonies imposed on them, and thus ensure their survival as rural people.

If those who describe contemporary and past societies do not pay attention to those events that challenge the hegemonic views of procedural landscapes or relegate them to the status of anomalies, they are actively promoting the agenda of those who impose them. The assumption that the values of the most powerful group in a society are those that will be imposed on, and be held by, everybody else and in all circumstances is absurd in the abstract, and yet we so often fall into its trap. As an illustration in contrast to such ideas, Martha Harroun Foster (2006:223) showed how Métis identities persevered as private identities, "supported by kinship networks and maintained by elders" against the political pressures to give them up. The Métis, she found, "were able to absorb labels and rigid ethnic definitions as layers that did not disrupt their private sense of self." Similarly, Gagnon (2004:37) maintained that "while political elites can attempt to construct peoples' views about ethnicity from above, such attempts have their effect mostly in perceptions about such relations *outside of* their own lived experiences. The impact on their perceptions of their own communities is minimal." The impact of essentialized hegemonic narratives of ethnic identity, contemporary and historical, on real communities can be debated and depends on the strength of the community to withstand such narratives. Their uncritical acceptance by academia, however, always supports the agendas of elites who construct such identity narratives to protect or gain resources for themselves (see Braun 2013).

In order to notice nonevents in narratives, we need "to listen to one another and keep our ears open" (DeMallie 1993:534). In order to truly understand the history of community interactions and to ensure a healthy future for these local communities—on the plains and elsewhere—we need to break the structures of procedural, hegemonic landscapes and, instead, return to an investigation of reciprocal kinship relations as structuring communities. Listening is not only an act of attention, but also a deeply political act. The investigation of history is at the same time the creation of history. To paraphrase Augé (1982:102), "If [ethnohistory] is to have any urgency, it must lie in denouncing all those pseudoculturalist attempts at recuperation, which, in the name of a bastardised and idealist definition of culture, would employ specialists simply to gather vestiges of the work of artisans and of folkloric customs" and to string a straight series of events from the contemporary into the historic. In *Teaching to Transgress,* bell hooks (1994:27) writes about Martin Luther King's notion of community and his urging that we need a "revolution of values" to truly liberate society and (re)build kinship communities. In that vein, then, I would suggest that in order to *see* real communities, to write the history of community relations on the plains and elsewhere, we liberate ourselves from hegemonic procedural landscapes, build true bridges between disciplines and people, break the conventional structures, and follow Ray DeMallie's teaching in a similar revolution that is based on the practice of listening in humility. Ethnohistory, as DeMallie has pointed out, should be in a perfect position to write the history of communities in *their own* landscapes. After all, who should have better ears to hear their voices than ethnohistorians?

NOTES

1. There are, of course, exceptions, for example Christina Gish Hill's (2013) study of Northern Cheyenne kinship as the foundation for sovereignty different from the concept of the state. I propose, though, that contemporary tribal sovereignty in the United States is much more reminiscent of the state, and that it attempts to create a landscape that is procedurally similar to the one constructed by the state, although different in content, agenda, and practice. Kinship communities, in the way I use the term here, might best be seen in a similar relationship to contemporary state and tribal procedural landscapes as Kurkiala (2002) described oral tradition as standing in relation to both academic and indigenous nationalist historical narratives.

2. Burnett's (2010) study provides a fascinating complementary reading to Regular's (2009). They both deal with roughly the same landscape, at roughly the same time, yet from very different perspectives. While Regular approaches the historic landscape through a study of economic interactions, Burnett provides a view of personal interactions in the realm of the exchange of medical knowledge. Together, these books provide a picture of personal, cultural, social, and political (non)cooperation in an interesting (non)dialogue with each other.

3. One of the distinct ironies of the procedural landscape on the plains is the argumentation in *U.S. v. Mission Golf Course and City of Mission* in 1982. The central point of the case was the definition of community. The government argued that "a community was not necessarily limited to an area circumscribed by legal boundaries," while the city argued that Indian and non-Indian communities were "socially and culturally distinct" (Biolsi 2001:87). The government, in other words, argued for a definition of community that is not tied to procedural landscape, while the city argued that communities had to be determined according to procedural landscapes. The case shows that even the state sometimes—when it fits its interests—acknowledges the constructed nature of procedural landscapes.

4. Alpha Blondy, "Les Imbeciles," from the Album *Yitzhak Rabin* (1998). My favored translation is "the globalization of the one-way economy." Procedural dependencies, or perhaps better the expansion of procedural landscapes through dependency, also, of course, create new relationships of similarities across ethnic and national lines: the "imagined" kinship of new, global "imagined communities." Global networks, for example of "indigenous peoples" (Niezen 2003, 2004) are a good example. The fact that, as Anderson (2000:vi) points out, Siberian reindeer herders—and others, everywhere (Braun 2008; Christen 2008; Strang 1997)—are "as firmly rooted in the dilemmas produced by industrial development . . . as are the lives of any factory-worker in Yekaterinburg or Manchester" shows how procedural landscapes have been globalized. It also shows the potential of resistance provided by the realization of similarities and the activation of kinship communities across ethnic boundaries.

Epilogue

RAYMOND FOGELSON

It is a pleasure to be grandfathered into this excellent assemblage of essays honoring Professor Raymond J. DeMallie, a practitioner extraordinaire of the fine art of ethnohistory.

First, I sadly note that the term "Festschrift" seems to be in disrepute. Publishers may fear dismal sales for volumes put into that category, what they suspect to be collections of perfunctory, pedestrian papers that my former University of Washington colleague Melville Jacobs used to file under the category "Travel Money," referring to slight meeting presentations never destined to see the light of published day. All one had to do was smear on a dash of hagiography praising the honoree and, as the logic goes, one had a ready Festschrift article. However, as I scan my library shelves, I find that Festschriften done right are an underappreciated academic genre. Among more memorable contributions, I can recall Malinowski's piece on Melanesian material culture for the C. G. Seligmann Festschrift (Evans-Pritchard 1934); Julian Steward's essay on the economic basis of bands for the Kroeber volume (Lowie 1936); A. Irving Hallowell's now classic article on Ojibwa ontology, which first appeared in a volume in honor of Paul Radin (Diamond 1960); Meyer Fortes's significant study of time and social structure among the Ashanti, which was published in a Festschrift for Radcliffe Brown (1963[1949]); John Goggin and William Sturtevant's account of the Calusa, included in the volume honoring George Peter Murdock (Goodenough 1964); Lévi-Strauss's exploration of the sex of the stars, found in the Jakobson Festschrift (1967); and many others. Festschriften often liberate untapped sources of creative energy and passionate scholarship. Such, I feel, is the case with the contributions to the present volume.

These essays have gone through several drafts and make important theoretical points. Sebastian Felix Braun deserves special credit for organizing and editing these papers in such a fashion that they form a coherent whole. Together the authors of these essays advance the field of ethnohistory in significant new directions, while duly acknowledging the positive influence of Ray DeMallie.

Sebastian invited me to present an epilogue to this volume. I always imagined that an epilogue was produced by the union of two or more dialogues
by intercourse or, perhaps better, by stimulating generative discourse—what
New Millennium people might call sexting. But, after checking my dictionary, I find that epilogue means a closing section of a novel, play, or a speech
sometimes delivered as poetry by one of the actors after the drama's conclusion. Rather than systematically commenting on each chapter, my epilogue
is organized around three interrelated themes that emerge from my reading
of the interdigitated individual contributions.

RAYMOND J. DEMALLIE

The first of these themes revolves around the person of Ray DeMallie. While
all authors pay tribute to Ray's inspirational mentorship and his rigorous
and vigorous humanism, it is David Miller who offers a detailed overview of
Ray's career development and achievements. David diligently searched the
documentary record and conducted direct interviews with Ray; he also
makes use of his own cogent insights while a student at Indiana and his experiences as an active fieldworker in the northern plains. He presents valuable data on the early influences that led DeMallie to become a scholar of
Native North America. David senses that Ray was something of a "straight
arrow," if not an antiquarian, before he became an anthropologist. This coincides with my first impressions of Ray as an undergraduate when I arrived
at Chicago in 1965. He seemed energetic, archivally constricted, with a clear
agenda to study Lakota kinship objectively in a straightforward structural-
functional fashion.

I recently discovered a delightful autobiographical fragment about John
Andrew Rice, the genius behind the revolutionary education experiment,
Black Mountain College:

> While he was an infant he absorbed knowledge taking it in through
> his tissues, without thought or care. Then in boyhood, he became a
> collector of birds' eggs, stamps, tobacco tags, baseball averages, dates
> —anything that can be arranged in series. But if he is to become a man
> —some do—he grows tired of counting and collecting and a terrifying
> thing happens: he ceases to be a scientist; he begins to ask, "what does
> it mean?" and with the coming of this question there comes the first
> step into manhood. To know is not enough.
> [cited in Katherine C. Reynolds 1998:22]

Ray's intellectual journey seemed to reach a similar juncture. He was well
prepared for a sheltered career as a secluded ethnological scientist sifting

through endless documents and artifacts. The wonderful Margaret Blaker had already dusted off J. Owen Dorsey's desk should Ray seek permanent refuge at the Smithsonian. However, such was not to be.

At Chicago we readily accepted a slightly revised version of Ray's exceptional BA paper as the equivalent of a master's thesis, but we insisted that he do fieldwork for his PhD. Although he had previously made some brief excursions into the northern plains, Ray was a bit nervous about venturing into the field for an extended period. Some of his hesitation arose because of the recent condemnation of anthropologists by Vine Deloria, Jr. (1988). Among the Sioux, Ray's reticence and nonthreatening demeanor served him well, and he made a rapid and successful adjustment to fieldwork. I recall receiving a letter from him asking, "Where are the hostile Sioux? Everyone's so nice" (or words to that effect).

In his usual assiduous way, Ray collected a voluminous amount of valuable field data that supplemented and amplified his understanding of Lakota social structure from the literature. More importantly he began to view kinship relations from a Native perspective and to empathize with the Lakota's struggle to cope with the impinging modern world while attempting to preserve their traditions. Sometimes these conflicts bore bitter fruit. He was deeply depressed by the suicide of a Lakota youth whom he had befriended. Ray's objective, empirical approach to anthropology began to take a more subjective, humanistic turn as a result of his immersion in the field.

Miller also notes that the emergence of symbolic anthropology at the University of Chicago coincided with Ray's brief tenure as a graduate student. (I emphasize "brief," because Ray holds the modern record at Chicago for speed in completing his PhD, finishing in just over two years.) While not yet fully exfoliated, symbolic anthropology was already strongly represented in the department by David Schneider and Clifford Geertz, both of whom were influenced by the theoretical paradigm of Talcott Parsons. Schneider's approach, while considering culture to be "a system of symbols and meanings," seems in retrospect more closely akin to Ruth Benedict's notions of cultural configurations as abstracted summarizations of a society's values and ethos. Geertz attended more to Weberian and philosophical ideas about meaning, though couched in Native terms and bolstered by extensive field data. Later, Victor Turner and Terry Turner joined the faculty, followed soon thereafter by Nancy Munn; each offered their own versions of symbolic anthropology as ultimately derived from French sociology and British social anthropology. I remained faithful to implicit Boasian approaches to symbolism, as well as drawing inspiration from Freudian dreamwork (actually my published undergraduate paper involved an experimental study of sexual symbolism as aroused by music).

DeMallie was enthusiastic about Schneider's cultural analysis of kinship systems and hoped to combine it with Fred Eggan's more formal synthesis of historical and structural-functional analysis to gain a more comprehensive understanding of Sioux kinship. Unfortunately, Ray was rebuffed by Schneider who didn't regard him as a very promising student, one, he felt, who was too tied to Eggan's and Tax's teachings. Schneider's misjudgment was dramatically exposed years later when Ray gave a sparkling presentation on the cultural dimensions of Lakota kinship at the departmental Monday seminar; Schneider belatedly embraced him as a long-lost disciple, but it was too late.

Miller ably documents the development of Ray's close association with Vine Deloria, Jr. The 1970 American Anthropological Association meeting in San Diego was, indeed, a pivotal moment in their relationship. Ray was well prepared for the encounter by having already worked on language with Vine's father, Vine Deloria, Sr., and by having made the acquaintance of two important women relatives: Vine Jr.'s aunt Ella Deloria and his cousin, anthropologist Bea Medicine. Despite these personal connections and his recent fieldwork at Cheyenne River, Vine didn't see much practical value in Ray's proposed research. Nevertheless, this and subsequent encounters quickly became more cordial. Ray's work on Sioux economic development for Sam Stanley's project at the Smithsonian may have helped change Vine's estimation of Ray's relevance; Stanley was a close confidant of Vine's. Later, Ray's archival skills made him a valuable consultant for Vine's work on treaties and federal law. However, at base, I think it was their shared interests in issues of Native spirituality that really solidified the relationship. They remained close friends until Vine's death.

Miller's accurate and informative account, nevertheless, inevitably misses some influential unwritten and unspoken factors in the unfolding of DeMallie's career. It is important to note that Ray was an only child and his relations with his parents were very close. After receiving his doctorate, I was invited to join him and his parents for a celebratory dinner at Café Bohemia, a wild game restaurant. His parents took extreme pride in Ray's accomplishments and the evening took on special meaning. I not only sensed mutual affection, but also a lack of generational distance. Ray was clearly a coequal member of this small, closely knit family. Ray's father died a few short years after this memorable event, and his warm, supportive mother succumbed to cancer soon thereafter. Ray was painfully distraught over the sudden disintegration of his family. A long period of private mourning and loneliness was only partially mitigated by intense work and the solace of personal friendships.

The period after Ray received his PhD in December of 1971 was particularly decisive for his subsequent career. He continued his productive postdoctoral work at the Smithsonian. If he wanted to, he might have remained there indefinitely, since he was, so to speak, "to the manor [or castle] born." He would have enjoyed a secure and successful life as a Smithsonian scientist. But the Smithsonian, for all its glorious reputation, had become an increasingly stodgy, bureaucratic, and conservative research center. The abiding "natural history" approach eschewed experimentalism and cutting-edge theory. Instead, Ray accepted an assistant professorship at the University of Wyoming in 1972. Teaching and being on the other side of the academic firing lines were new challenges, since in those days, Chicago provided few opportunities for graduate students as teaching assistants.

Ray's initial teaching experience at Wyoming was positive, and he enjoyed the lifestyle of Laramie, but when the call came from Indiana University, he was ready to move on. Indiana seemed a perfect fit, with its rich tradition of Native American, linguistic, and folkloric studies, and as the original home of the fledgling subfield of ethnohistory, toward which Ray's attention was increasingly drawn. Among others at Indiana, Carl Voegelin proved a valued friend and mentor. Ray also developed close friendships with some of the younger faculty members, but he felt slightly alienated from many of his senior colleagues who provided the department with a strong Africanist orientation. During his first few years at Indiana, Ray spent much time away from campus pursuing research in Washington and at other archival sites and in the field. He once complained to me that he had trouble attracting graduate students. I responded by saying something to the effect that if he spent more time at home, they would come. The contributors to this volume and many others not included bear testimony to the accuracy of my prediction. Ray's close relationships with his students are based on mutual respect and loyalty. He treats students as colleagues and frequently accompanies them into the field, as well as coauthoring papers with them. As Paula Wagoner points out, the American Indian Studies Research Institute (AISRI) that he founded on campus became a beehive of activity and a literal community of scholars, Indiana graduate students, and visitors and others brought in for special expertise.

Ray and I engaged in an informal exchange system in which I sent to Bloomington some promising graduates of our college and MA program—Dennis Kristoferson, Kristen Alten, and Meredith Johnson come to mind. Chicago also sent some advanced graduate students for additional training. I am reminded here of the late Sharon Stephens, Tony Seeger, Jeff Anderson, and two contributors to this volume, Ray Bucko and David Dinwoodie. In return, I had the good fortune of working, however briefly, with Indiana students interested in the Southeast; these included Max White, Wyman Kirk, Matthew Bradley, and most especially another contributor, Jason Jackson. Without Jason's later crucial support, the Southeastern *Handbook of North American Indians* would never have been completed. But Ray and I also ran into discouraging delays, organizational obstacles, and editorial incompetence in completing our respective handbooks. The final, in some ways compromised products reflect the decline in the formerly high standards of the Smithsonian.

The vital presence of Douglas Parks at Indiana deserves special mention. Ray and Doug continue to be a dynamic research team with complementary, yet overlapping interests in ethnology and linguistics, in both the Northern and Southern Plains, and in Siouan- and Caddoan-speaking peoples. Both are prodigious library scholars and skilled fieldworkers who are committed to giving back to the communities they study. Their interests intersect in the elicitation, collection, transcription, translation, and interpretation of Native texts. While they maintain their individual scholarly identities, they are constructive critics of each other's work. Doug's arrival in Bloomington also seemed to encourage Ray's move toward a more humanistically oriented anthropology.

THE STATUS AND FUTURE OF ETHNOHISTORY

The second theme that runs through these contributions concerns the status and future trajectory of ethnohistory. Much material that inevitably fell between the cracks of David Miller's biographic account reflects problems endemic to the writing of ethnohistory. The written record is always selective and incomplete, if not subtly or blatantly biased. When one tries to supplement the documentation by employing ethnological data and anthropological techniques, the picture may come into clearer focus. Direct observation and experience, such as Miller's insights as a student of DeMallie, are valuable, as are his one-on-one interviews with Ray. However, even here it is evident that we are our own worst informants. Memories are fragile and subject to inevitable secondary revision. Facts fit the structure of stories rather than vice versa. These processes are wonderfully demonstrated in the chapters presented by Ray Bucko and Patrick Moore.

Father Bucko's account of William Bordeaux's book, *Conquering the Mighty Sioux,* not only records the present ambivalence of the Rosebud community about republishing it, but also documents Bordeaux's self-serving grandiosity and inherent biases in trying to provide an authentic view of Sioux history. Despite the book's shortcomings, however, Bordeaux collected valuable, if filtered, testimony from the elders. He deserves to be remembered as a clear voice in trying to promote Native well-being. Patrick Moore's eloquent rendering of elder Arthur John's memory of an encounter between a Gwich'in Anglican minister and a Kaska-speaking community at Ross River, doubtless contains significant lacunae and distortions. Yet, John's account comes across as an unadulterated version of a past event. I was particularly impressed with the directional, deitic complexity preserved in Moore's text. Because the account concerns the outlawing of the traditional stick gambling game, which has now been revived, the narrative continues to resonate with its audience.

At this point it seems appropriate to consider the joker in this deck, Paula Wagoner's "The Search for an Honest Man." Her essay echoes the self-proclaimed tricksterish qualities of an elusive man she identifies as Ivan Drift. Ivan, indeed, may have been a white drifter who hooked up with the influential Red Cloud family at Pine Ridge in the 1930s. However, in his self-promoting correspondence with commissioner of Indian Affairs John Collier, Drift identifies himself as Cree-Sioux. Is this, then, his unstable trickster character at play? Or was he an early version of a hippie wannabe? Drift was clearly knowledgeable about environmental planning, as well as informed about details of Lakota ceremonialism and tribal politics; he even displays some proficiency in the language.

Drift produced an enigmatic illustrated volume *America Needs Indians!* (1937) under the pseudonym Iktomi Hcala. Among other things, the book provides a scathing critique of Collier's Indian New Deal (or as Drift calls it, "nude eel"). I have a personal interest in this book, since my father bought (for $1) a rare copy for me at a flea market and inscribed it, "Ray this book looks screwball to me." Drift's sharp insights on Indian policy, expressed in playful typographic variations and intricate satirical drawings, make for a spiderweb-like journey into the trickster's twisted mind. This spiderman trickster not only deceives others, but ultimately deceives himself. Supposedly he drifted off and became a sort of hermit, living in a cave, and like the prototypical Diogenes searching unsuccessfully for "the last honest man." Paula's chapter rightfully raises as many questions as it answers. R.I.P. Ivan Drift.

The status of ethnohistory, like the trickster, remains perpetually problematic. Perhaps, some useful perspective can be gained by briefly reviewing the history and ethnohistory of ethnohistory. For many decades ethnohistory existed as an unmarked category. It was embodied to some degree by such renowned scholars as Adolph Bandelier, James Mooney, H. H. Bancroft, Herbert Spinden, H. E. Bolton, John R. Swanton, and Joseph Jablow, among many others. The nominal subfield finally arose with the founding of the journal *Ethnohistory*, at Indiana University in Bloomington, under the leadership of Erminnie Wheeler-Voegelin. It is interesting that from the beginning the term "ethnohistory" was unhyphenated, unlike most other so-called ethno-sciences. The assumed closeness of the relationship between ethnography or ethnology and history, however, was deceptive. The primary focus of this original group of ethnohistorians was on Indian land claims cases. Consequently the emphasis was on written documentary evidence or treaties. These data were only slightly tempered by anthropological and linguistic interpretations concerning maximal and minimal social units, Indian occupancy of the land, and utilization of resources. Oral testimony took a back seat to the written record. Ethnohistory, thus, was defined primarily as an applied enterprise, and reports were factually oriented and intentionally atheoretical. This approach, apart from playing to the court system in which it was used, also avoided discussions between the disciplines.

As an academic field, ethnohistory might be viewed as a bastard offspring of history and anthropology. Despite the absence of a hyphen, ethnohistory fell far short of achieving a legitimate union between history and anthropology. Rather, it resembled the Iroquois two-row wampum belt in which European and Native ways represented two separate streams flowing in opposite directions. The collaborative endeavor resulted in accounts of Native history that conformed to Western historiographic frameworks. Native voices were, at best, muffled, and anthropological data were only utilized sparingly. These tensions are reflected in the early work of Ray DeMallie. Historic materials concerning the Sioux, brought to life from the archives, were left to speak for themselves with only minor commentary and minimal interpretation; some linguistic nuances might be offered, and perhaps a few clarifying remarks about Native social structure and subsistence patterns might be appended. However, these early efforts were far removed from Native conceptions of the past or what I have called "ethno-ethnohistory." In Ray's collaborations with the formidable Mildred Wedel (1980), ethnohistory was viewed as a method of employing a cultural lens to sharpen understanding of the primary written historical record.

About this time a recognition of Native history written by Native historians began to emerge. A program to encourage the work of Native historians was instituted at the Newberry Library. Allen Slickpoo, a Nez Perce scholar, produced an interesting book on his tribe's history from a Native perspective (Slickpoo and Walker 1973). Slickpoo took issue with the glorification of Chief Joseph, whom he regarded as a minor figure, as compared to the neglect of the more significant, lesser-known warriors who died during the Nez Perce War. I recall Wilcomb Washburn praising Slickpoo's effort in a review of his book, but he believed that Slickpoo had failed to measure up to the standards of historical scholarship. Indeed, whose rules did we have to follow? Nevertheless, the emergence of recognized Native historians stimulated greater appreciation of oral testimony and raised the question, taken up by many, of who owns the past.

Several articles signal DeMallie's gradual move toward a more Native-oriented ethnohistory: his 1977 essay on Siouan concepts of power (with Robert Lavenda); the important paper on Siouan notions of time (1976a); his brilliant analysis of the Ghost Dance (1982); and of course, his magisterial presidential address to the American Society for Ethnohistory, "'These Have No Ears': Narrative and the Historical Method" (1993). Here DeMallie indicates and demonstrates the possibilities of a closer listening to and appreciation of Native texts. Braun, in the final section of the Introduction to this volume, "An Ethnohistory of Listening," clearly articulates DeMallie's contributions to a more sensitive understanding of the relations between spirituality and social structure as mediated through language, kinship, and community. Braun also rightly stresses Ray's moral commitment to mutual engagement with and humble participation in Native communities; to treat Native interlocutors as coequals; and to master, perhaps, the most difficult task of all—to learn to listen.

Sarah Quick has learned to listen well not only to Métis fiddling, but also to the pulse of heritage making and maintenance. Scholars seem overly eager to pronounce the death of Native institutions and practices. Revivals are dismissed as inauthentic or denounced as reinvented traditions. What goes unappreciated is the fact that practices can either go underground or their memories can linger latently in the cultural mind-set for long periods and suddenly spring back to life—albeit in often modified form—when circumstances permit. This is frequently the case with supposed language death, with long lapses in the performance of ceremonies, or in regard to aspects of material and expressive culture. Where we perceive discontinuity, the Natives see continuity. Quick's musical ear is sensitive to these issues in modern Métis fiddling.

Again, Braun in his astute contribution "Against Procedural Landscapes" succinctly sets forth the fundamental problematic for ethnohistory when he writes, "a history without ethnology and an ethnology without history can be read as essentializations: one of culture, the other of change." History he sees as a connected series of events, whereas culture is involved with the meaning of continuous nonevents. History is concerned with diachrony; culture, or ethnicity, with synchrony. This inherent disconnect between dynamics and statics harkens back in social science to the work of Herbert Spencer. The problem posed for ethnohistory, however, is how to bridge this existential chasm. I suggest that one way of resolving this dilemma is through the idea of interpolation.

Interpolation has multiple meanings, including the insertion into a text of spurious or new matter; or, in mathematics, to find intermediate points in a sequence. However, my use of the term derives from a much simpler etymology of "between the poles." Interpolation is, implicitly, used in the fine bit of ethnohistoric detective work provided by Jason Jackson in this volume. Jason tries to track down the meaning of an ambiguous eighteenth-century reference by James Adair to "a great solemn feast of love" among "the Mississippian Floridians." Jason's method utilizes a careful analysis of comparative historical and ethnographic data to reach a plausible, but qualified conclusion that this calendrical ritual was a widespread Southeastern spring observance that was connected with ideas of planting, fertility, and rebirth following the winter doldrums.

TRANSFORMATION

This brings me to the final theme that I find running through many of these contributions, and that is the idea of transformation and the possibilities of a transformative ethnohistory. Transformation, in essence, refers to a change from one form to another. One problem here is accommodating both gradual change, in which the differentiation is only recognized in retrospect, and rapid or abrupt change, in which the alteration is dramatically apparent in the consciousness of the members of the society. It is one thing to acknowledge that a transformation has taken place; it is another matter to ascertain what motivated the change. The vague, undefined term "transformation" slides slickly off the tongue in far too much social science discourse.

I think the notion of transformation often reveals a close affinity to the idea of transcendence. Transcendence can be conceived as the elevated product of a synthesis of two (or more) different phenomena. Without getting entangled in Hegelianism, I will quote my friend, the artist, novelist, poet, and anecdotalist Donald Weismann (1984:viii):

> Let us say that we are riding in a twin-engine aircraft and that we are seated midway between two engines. With a little effort we can hear first the left engine and then the right one. Rarely can both such engines sound *exactly* alike. Almost always one is pitched higher than the other. One engine is producing sound vibrations of a certain frequency per second while the other is producing vibrations of a greater or lesser frequency. These vibrations affect our hearing differently, making one engine sound higher in pitch than the other. And besides being able to hear the particular sound of each of the engines, we can, if we listen closely, hear a *third* sound. This third sound is the result of the other two sounds as they beat against each other. It's what is called the *beat-note*: a note or pitch whose frequency equals the *difference* in the frequencies of the two sounds. It is exactly and inexorably related to the two sounds, but it is neither of these—like the son is neither his mother nor his father, nor is he both.

Analogously, this example expresses what happens when history and culture ideally lose their separateness and merge into a transformative or transcendental ethnohistory.

In her highly original contribution, "Swing Time: Narrative, Collective Improvisation, and the Ethnohistorical Method," Kellie Hogue proves to be intuitively in tune with the process that Weismann describes. Here, Kellie invokes the jazz idiom to demonstrate how transformation operates in ethnohistory. In effect, James Mooney transforms into James Moody; and the mind boogies! The variations of the storyteller become analogous to the virtuosity of the tenor sax player. And just as stories are collective endeavors in which each rendition takes on its own embellishments, so do the collective improvisations of a jazz combo produce new sounds that are more than the sum of the melodic lines of the individual musician. To "swing" is more than repetitive rhythmic pulsation. It is a complex interplay involving downbeats and upbeats, overtone and undertones, different registers (which Kellie likens to "having any number of metaphorical planes in the air, all at different altitudes—some occupying higher ranges, some lower"), and the often spontaneous combination of melodic lines in polyphony, creating new harmonics. Knowledgeable jazz aficionados can do a verbal riff on these and other techniques, but it is only a consummate jazz musician, like Wynton Marsalis, who can both feel and articulate what jazz is all about. I once asked a prominent jazz trumpeter about "swing" and "swinging," and he said it simply meant "getting the notes in the right place."

Kellie then recenters her discussion on DeMallie's approach to narrative. DeMallie sees the ethnohistorical method as a little like the actions of Lévi-Strauss's *bricoleur* in bringing together diverse sets of seemingly noncompatible sources into a common frame of analysis to reveal a previously unperceived structure. The newly juxtaposed materials hopefully "speak for themselves and . . . tell their own story." This strategy resembles the "object epistemology" favored by Frank Hamilton Cushing as a technique of museum display in which the material objects are allowed to speak for themselves (Conn 1998).

At the core of DeMallie's method are Native narratives or "stories." However, as Braun cautions, stories are generally composed of episodic events and not the noneventual matrix into which culture is normally embedded. This is especially true when Native narratives become textualized. Our Aristotelian bias forces stories into a mold characterized by a discernible beginning, middle, and end. In ethnographic reality the lines of Native narrative tend to curl in and out, around and about. Past, present, and future become indeterminate; thus, for instance, history becomes prophecy, and prophecy becomes history. Some missing portions of the narrative are assumed to be known by the audience and are successfully interpolated, while other portions demand formulaic repetition. By holding interpretations and reinterpretations to a minimum, DeMallie hopes to get closer to the Native *mentalité*. Indeed, stories can become animate, and some even "have ears."

I end my rambling epilogue here. Maybe some of what I have said will stimulate continuing dialogue among the authors of these worthy contributions. Furthermore, I hope my remarks will encourage rejoinders and correction from the person who inspired this volume, the honored and honorable Raymond J. DeMallie.

Afterword

Thinking Ethnohistorically

RAYMOND J. DEMALLIE

Recent debate over the legitimacy of ethnohistory as a specialization distinct from good history or good anthropology has led some scholars to declare the end of ethnohistory.[1] After all, historians have integrated culture and society into their studies and anthropologists have become more aware of the value of examining the past, both for its own sake and for understanding the present. Conceptualizing ethnohistory within disciplinary boundaries rather than between them has hindered its development. Yet ethnohistory persists and continues to attract young scholars. It has established a niche in academia as exemplified both by the American Society for Ethnohistory and its vibrant annual meetings and by the success of the journal *Ethnohistory*.

As a college student majoring in anthropology at the University of Chicago in the mid-1960s, I found it natural to combine my interest in American Indian history with the social anthropology that I had come there to study. The general disinterest in history within the field of social anthropology seemed to me to offer an opportunity for innovation. I wanted to bring history to social structure by combining American historical anthropology with British social anthropology, integrating the two approaches by using the documentary methods of history. In this I had strong support and advice from my teachers, notably Fred Eggan, Sol Tax, Raymond D. Fogelson, George W. Stocking, James W. VanStone, and Bernard Cohen. Their classes and countless hours of conversation profoundly shaped my thinking.

Few of my classmates shared that enthusiasm for history or for American Indians. Most were focused on fieldwork overseas and seemed to have little patience for historical study. None of them, as far as I knew, shared another of my great interests—the study of museum collections, both objects and manuscripts. I spent three summers on National Science Foundation Research Participation grants for undergraduates at the Smithsonian Institution (and later a summer as a graduate student and a year as a National Endowment for the Humanities postdoctoral fellow). There I came to appreciate the invaluable collections amassed over the course of more than a century by anthropologists who had engaged in the same scholarly pursuits that occupy us today.

At the Smithsonian, John C. Ewers and William C. Sturtevant, each in his own way, imparted their ethnological perspectives and emphasized the importance of taking a historical approach to the study of culture. Margaret C. Blaker, head of the Bureau of American Ethnology Archives, taught me how to understand manuscript collections and to work with them effectively. Mildred Mott Wedel introduced me to the historical French sources on North America and to the importance of a critical approach to evaluating those sources. Waldo R. Wedel gave me an appreciation for the value of archaeology to ethnohistorical study. Together, the Wedels educated me in the potential synergy among archeological, cultural, and historical approaches. Equally important to my education, Paul Voorhis introduced me hands-on to the methods of field linguistics.

In October 1967 Bill Sturtevant visited Chicago and took me along on my first visit to the Newberry Library. Bill had arranged to drive with James VanStone (North American curator at the Field Museum of Natural History) to Lexington, Kentucky, for the annual meeting of the American Society for Ethnohistory and they invited me to join them. Margaret Blaker also attended the meeting, where she assiduously introduced me to many scholars whose work I had read. I had the opportunity to hear Ella C. Deloria, the Dakota linguist and student of Sioux culture, present a paper on Yankton place names, listened intently to papers on Alaskan research—including VanStone's progress report on his ethnohistorical study of the Nushagak River Eskimo—and even enjoyed an arcane bibliographical survey presented as the presidential address by Ernest S. Dodge (Peabody Museum at Salem) of American sources for Pacific ethnohistory. It may not have been my cultural area, but it was the kind of work I enjoyed. By the time I returned to Chicago I knew that "ethnohistorian" would be a part of my professional identity.

Subsequently, I developed the habit of thinking ethnohistorically by bringing together diverse material: documents, some written in the distant past that were gleaned from archives, others written more recently, such as the field notes of anthropologists who preceded me, and even my own field notes, which, as Sturtevant (1966:18–19) insisted, should be treated like any other historical documents: books; newspapers; drawings, paintings, photographs; sound recordings; artifacts; and linguistic data. My preoccupation has been looking for connections among them, how one thing explains or contextualizes another, always with the goal of understanding the past.

By thinking ethnohistorically it is possible to see in the record of the past the evidence of social structures, of cultural symbols, of linguistic patterns. Since I work with the Sioux, who became literate in their own language in the nineteenth century, I am fortunate to have access to a plentitude of material written in the Native language by Sioux individuals. These documents are rarely self-explanatory and require interpretation on the basis of other evidence. For me, a source that I have found to be of tremendous ethnohistorical value is the vast record compiled by government stenographers of councils and meetings with Indian tribes, from early nineteenth-century treaty councils down through mid-twentieth-century congressional hearings. Interpreters tended to have limited vocabularies; the English translations they provided, and that were preserved in writing, often directly reflect Native concepts that are invaluable for cultural understanding—though they, too, require comparison with other sources for analysis.

The results of such study are less conducive to constructing narratives embracing long time periods than to explicating specific patterns or events. In my own work I prefer to think in terms of "ethnohistorical perspective" rather than "ethnohistory." My goal has been to publish the most important of these sources in critical editions so that they can be used in the future for large-scale synthesis. But there are many such sources, and, happily, new ones keep appearing. It seems to me now that what I conceptualized for the Sioux is comparable, on a small scale, to the type of comparative historical reconstruction of North American cultures envisioned by Franz Boas. It cannot be accomplished in a single lifetime. There, in short, lies the importance of teaching, in the hope that a few scholars in the coming generations will continue the work.

Thinking ethnohistorically implies a willingness to amass diverse materials that may be relevant for many different projects, keeping on the lookout for new material, and being alert to possible connections among them. It leads to many ideas, problems, or partially developed projects that one returns to again and again when new material becomes available, or when new meanings are seen in material that one has studied repeatedly over the course of years. By way of illustration—though at the cost of revealing my embarrassingly slow progress on a small problem—I decided to discuss my interest in the name "Oglala," the designation of one of the seven tribes that by the middle of the nineteenth century comprised the Lakota or Teton Sioux. It is useful as an example since it involves ethnographic data, a variety of historical documents, and the need for understanding the Native language to resolve even a simple problem.

• • •

In fall 1968 as a first-year graduate student I had the good fortune (thanks to Jim VanStone) to obtain an internship in the Anthropology Department at the Field Museum. Donald Collier, son of Commissioner John Collier, the architect of the Indian Reorganization Act, chaired the department. His specialty was Latin America, but as a graduate student in the 1930s he had carried out ethnographic fieldwork on the Plains. When I mentioned to him my interest in the Sioux, he told me about his work with the Oglalas at Pine Ridge. Working with Fred Eggan (who was my advisor at the University of Chicago), Collier had sought to define the variety of "camping groups," that is, social structures, that characterized the Plains tribes. What surprised him about the Oglalas, he said, was that the name was not applied to all the constituent groups living on Pine Ridge until after the reservation was established in 1879. The bands, essentially independent camping groups, were each named; one was called "Oglala," and only in the reservation context was the name generalized to them all. He based this conclusion on his interviews with elders and on his study of the published annual reports of the commissioner of Indian Affairs that predated the establishment of Pine Ridge, in which he found an abundance of evidence of the various band names as well as the use of the term "Oglala." He suggested that I read his neatly typed 1939 field notes and allowed me to make a photocopy.

I was intrigued and challenged, as Collier clearly intended me to be, to make sense of what had suddenly become the mystery of the Oglalas. First I turned to the standard history of the Oglalas by George Hyde. He traced first mention of the name to 1700, when the French explorer Pierre-Charles Le Sueur met a group of Sioux on the Blue Earth River in Minnesota that he designated "Ojalespoitans or Village Divided into Many Small Bands" (Hyde 1957:8). However, the next citation of the name does not occur until nearly a century later, in 1795, in the journals of Jean-Baptiste Truteau, a fur trader from St. Louis who visited tribes on the upper Missouri River; he writes the name as *Occononas* (Douglas R. Parks in DeMallie 2001:757). After Truteau, there are frequent references to the Oglalas in the historical record.

The writings of traders Rufus Sage (Hafen and Hafen 1956) and David Adams (Hanson 1994), and of the traveler Francis Parkman (Wade 1958), document a momentous event in Oglala history. Competition among the fur companies and independent traders was fierce, and illegal liquor was used to entice Indians to trade their buffalo robes. Parkman identified two chiefs, Bull Bear and Smoke, as bitter rivals. In November 1841, during a drunken brawl, the jealousy between their two factions ended in the deaths of Bull Bear, the leading chief, and seven others. This split the Oglalas into two groups, the followers of Bull Bear, who moved south, and those of Smoke, who moved north. By the time Pine Ridge Agency was established in 1879, Little Wound, a son of Bull Bear, had emerged as principal chief of the southern group, while Red Cloud, a nephew of Smoke, had become recognized as the principal chief of the northern group.

John Robinson, an Episcopal missionary to the Sioux, recorded the Lakota names with translations of the seven Oglala bands at Pine Ridge in 1879; the next year J. Owen Dorsey of the Smithsonian Institution's Bureau of Ethnology confirmed the list with an Oglala who was visiting Washington, D.C. (Dorsey 1897:220):[2]

(1) *Phayábya,* Pushed Aside

(2) *Thaphíšeleca,* Spleen (of an animal)

(3) *Kiyúksa,* Breaks His Own (marriage custom)[3]—Little Wound's band

(4) *Wažáže* (meaning unknown)

(5) *Itešíca,* Bad Face, or *Oglálaȟca,* Real Oglala—Red Cloud's band

(6) *Oyúȟpe,* Thrown Down or Unloaded

(7) *Wágluȟe,* Followers or Loafers

Hyde (1957:313–14), notes that the first three of these seven bands represent the followers of Bull Bear and the last three represent the followers of Smoke; he states that they were known as the Bear People and the Smoke People (1957:40). The fourth group, the *Wažáže,* was a Brule band that had been associated with the Oglalas at least since armed warfare between the Lakotas and the U.S. Army began in 1854. The majority of the band remained with the northern Oglalas until 1871 when they came with Red Cloud's Oglalas to the agency named after him on the North Platte River in Wyoming, just west of the Nebraska line. In 1873, when the agency was moved seventy-five miles east to the White River, the *Wažáže* moved there with the Oglalas (Hyde 1957:189, 201). In 1877, however, the *Wažáže* band was transferred to Spotted Tail Agency by government order (Hyde 1961:248). In 1879 and 1880, when Robinson and Dorsey recorded Lakota band names, *Wažáže* was listed with the Oglalas, and not with the Brules, but in 1884 William J. Cleveland (also an Episcopal missionary) recorded the reverse—the *Wažáže* band was included with the Brules and not the Oglalas (Dorsey 1897:218–21). It would seem that this shift back to the *Wažáže's* former tribal identity may have been a gradual one. It is also relevant to keep in mind that the areas administered by the two agencies were contiguous.

A.1 Oglala Bands at Pine Ridge, 1879

"Bear People," Southern Oglalas	"Smoke People," Northern Oglalas	Originally Brule, but associated with the Oglalas
Phayábya 'pushed aside' (?)	*Itešíca* or *Oglálaȟca* 'bad face' or 'real Oglala'	*Wažáže*
Thaphíšeleca 'spleen'	*Oyúȟpe* 'unload'	
Khiyúksa 'break in half' (?)	*Wágluȟe* 'loafers'	

In light of this historical background I studied Collier's field notes. One of the old men he interviewed, Kills Above, age seventy-three, was a member of

Red Cloud's Bad Face band, and thus represents Smoke's people. He stated: "The Bad faces were called ogalala before settling on the Reservation. I don't know how they got that name. Before the reservation, the Bad faces were the only ones called ogalala. I don't know what ogalala means." Another of his consultants, Lone Bull, age eighty-six, was from the *Khiyáksa* band, representing Bull Bear's people. (All of Collier's consultants used the form *Khiyáksa* rather than *Khiyúksa*. Both forms are still used today at Pine Ridge, with no agreement as to whether one is correct.) Lone Bull also asserted that the term "Oglala" came into general use only after settling on the reservation, but he added an origin story for the name:

> *The name ogalala*
> There were two brothers-in-law, one in the Badger Eater (xókayùta [ȟokáyuta]) camp and the other in Red Cloud's camp.[4] They were arguing [about] who was the bravest. The Badger Eater was able to count more coups. So the Red Cloud got mad and threw dust in the other's face, and he did the same. That's how the name started. *Ogalala* means to pick something up and throw it. That happened in Red Cloud's camp three years before Sitting Bull made a treaty with the govt. That was when the Agency was at Ft. Robinson, before we settled on the Pine Ridge reservation.[5] At first the name applied only to Red Cloud's camp, but after we were on the reservation it came to mean all the Pine Ridge Indians. I guess this was because Red Cloud was considered the biggest chief on the reservation, and was recognized as the head chief by the govt.

Walks Out, age seventy-seven, a Minneconjou married to an Oglala woman, told Collier the same origin story but attributed it to a different band:

> *Origin of the name ogalala*
> This happened at the time the agency was moved to Fort Robinson from the Sod Agency (ca. 1874?). It was among the oyoxpe [oyúȟpe]. Two men got in an argument over the Ring and Stick game, and one threw dirt in the other's face. The word *ogalala* came from *itókala* (to throw something).[6] At first it was a nickname just for the oyoxpe, but when the different camps were up in the northwest (Wyoming, and Tongue R., Mont.), they all got to be called that. These were as follows:
> kiaksa
> Loafers (wágluxe)
> Bad faces (itecitca)

oyoxpe
waaZi [*wažáže*]

Walks Out's list of the bands that formed the Oglalas omits the *Phayábya* and *Thaphíšeleca* bands, both of which were in the Bull Bear faction that lived farther south.

The information Collier recorded from Alex Adams, a member of the Bad Face band and a nephew of Chief Red Cloud, is especially important for understanding Oglala history. At age ninety-two, Adams was the oldest of his consultants, but Collier found working with him to be frustrating. He complained that Adams's "memory was poor, and it was extremely difficult to keep him on the subject of discussion. Every half hour or so he would fall asleep." Nonetheless, he was the only consultant to give Collier an account of the events that led to the separation between the followers of Bull Bear and Smoke.

Adams stated that the name of the parent group of those later known as the *Khiyáksa* and Bad Faces was *Guhía,* and that the separation occurred when his mother was about six years old, which Collier estimated to have been between 1810 and 1830. During a drunken brawl, one or more members of the Bull Bear faction killed Lone Man (Red Cloud's father), White Hawk, and Little Shield. Later, in revenge, Red Cloud shot and killed Bull Bear (whom Adams calls "Little Wound the Older"), Short Bull, and Standing Bull (brother of Little Wound the Older). Collier recorded: "Red Cloud's camp later got the name itecita [*itéšica*] (bad face) in the following manner. Smoke got drunk. He went up to his relatives and said, 'You nephews, all your faces are bad.' From that time on they were called bad Faces. That happened about the time that Maj. Twiss became agent [1855]."

It seems remarkable that Collier was able to record information about the feud between the Smoke and Bull Bear factions that occurred nearly a century earlier. The dating was off—Bull Bear was killed in 1841—but Adams's memories fit well with historical accounts.

Collier's field notes continue Adams's account:

The name ogalala
      After old Red Cloud killed those men he fled. He was gone three years, staying among the minikoZu [*mnikhówožu*, 'Plants by Water' (Minneconjou)]. Then he returned. There were some men, including young Smoke, Old Red Cloud's nephew, drinking.[7] They got in an argument, and Smoke threw dirt in their faces. This happened about 60 years ago (sic!), about two years before Major Twiss came [1855].[8] Red Cloud's band had the name Bad Faces before they got the name ogalala. It was only the bad faces who were called that—it happened among them.

The Kiaksa made friends again at the time of the big annuity issue [the 1851 treaty]. . . . The chiefs shook hands and exchanged horses. The kiaksa got to be called ogalala also, later when they went to visit the bad faces.

Young Man Afraid of his Horse's camp (payabya) used to visit the Bad Faces. After awhile they got to be called ogalala too.

The oyoxpe (unload) had few horses, and they loaded their horses and dogs with very big packs. The oyoxpe were poor.

cikcítsila [*šikšícala*] (bad [ones])—the name of a group that used to camp with the Bad Faces; but I don't think we used to call them ogalala.[9]

The minikoZu [*mnikʻówožu*] were not called ogalala. They stayed up north with the itaziptco [*itázipcho* 'No Bows'].

In short, there is no consensus among Collier's consultants concerning the origin of the name Oglala or the groups to which the name was applied. Kills Above, a member of Red Cloud's band, believed that Oglala was an old band name later replaced by Bad Face. Lone Bull, a *Khiyáksa* from the opposite faction, traced the origin of Oglala directly to Red Cloud's action in throwing dust on an adversary and believed that the name Oglala was generalized to all the bands at Pine Ridge because of the government's support for Red Cloud as head chief. Adams, also a member of Red Cloud's band, stated that the older name Bad Face was replaced by Oglala but that the original name of the band was *Guhía*. Walks Out, not himself an Oglala, said the Bad Face band was previously known as *Oyúhpe*. Among these accounts, the main commonality is the idea that use of the term "Oglala" was extended more widely over time, even, as Walks Out said, being applied to the *Wažáže* when they were with the Oglala groups in the north fighting against the U.S. Army.

Collier worked at Pine Ridge from February 18 through March 11, 1939. He was discouraged that he had been unable to find consultants who were able to give extensive genealogies and remember the composition of camps from their childhood. However, he underestimated the value of the material he recorded. The consultant with whom he spent the most time was Lone Bull. He told Collier that when he was eight years old (around 1861) his family lived in the camp of Pawnee Killer, chief of the *Khiyáksa* band. The band actually was a conglomeration of three distinct groups, the *Khiyáksa, Škokpá,* and *Guhía;* collectively they were called *Khiyáksa,* but each of the three maintained a separate identity. During that winter they camped south of the North Platte River on White Man's Creek. The *Khiyáksa* had their own camp and the other two groups camped together about a half mile away. In the spring, when they moved to hunt buffalo, they formed a single camp circle, the *Guhía* on the northeast, the *Škokpá* on the west, and the *Khiyáksa* on the south.

The names of these two additional groups presented me with another puzzle. Collier was unable to obtain any translation for the name *Guhía*. In 1931, according to Hyde (1957:317), He Dog, a member of Red Cloud's band, identified the name of the band of Red Cloud's father as "Kuhee or Kuhinyan (Stand-offish)." This seems clearly to be Collier's *Guhía*, although the English name does not seem to be a translation of the Lakota. Some years later, as I discuss below, I found this name listed as an Oglala band by Joseph N. Nicollet, writing in 1839. He recorded the name as "Ku-Inyan, he gives the rock" (DeMallie 1976b:261). Thus the name seems to have been *Kʼu-íŋyaŋ* 'Gives-rock', but whether this is the actual origin of the name or a folk etymology of a name whose original meaning was lost cannot be known.[10] The second name, *Škokpá*, is also mentioned by Hyde (1957:313) in the form "Shkopa (bent)" as an alternate name for the Spleen (*Thaphíšeleca*) band. These are two closely related words: *škópa* 'crooked, concave', like a creek bed; and *škokpá* 'concave, hollow', like a shell. It is not clear whether one of these forms is correct or whether both were used. Collier's interpreter translated the name as "no flesh," suggesting bellies concave from starvation. Shortly before Collier's fieldwork Ella Deloria (ca. 1937) recorded a text in Lakota from an anonymous Oglala woman who mentioned the name "Skokpaya" as an example of a recent band name that had replaced an older one. Deloria translated it as "In the dip, hollow."[11]

Overall, Collier's consultants confirm Hyde's (1957:9) observation that there was a surprising lack of unanimity among Lakotas concerning the meaning of group names; most names had several contradictory, seemingly trivial, explanations. Since most originated as nicknames it seems reasonable to conclude that the stories of their origins and significance changed from generation to generation.

Concerning the name Oglala, at Pine Ridge in 1915 Paul Bear Robe and Wood Leg told Eugene Buechel, S.J. (1915–43) that the original name for the Oglalas was *Chahóta Ištá Oglála* 'They Threw Ashes into Their Own Eyes'. In the 1930s Deloria's anonymous Oglala woman narrator related a tradition that she had learned from her grandfather that explained the name Oglala. In the distant past a group of brothers quarreled with one another over possession of a metal arrowhead, metal being a rare commodity. One threw ashes from a cold fireplace into the eyes of the others to incapacitate them. The group was named after this shameful incident. The narrator commented, "It is only after it was shortened into the single word *Oglála* that people made up all sorts of stories to explain it" (Deloria ca. 1937).

In fact, this tradition was attested almost a century earlier by Nicollet, who heard the story during his visit to Fort Pierre, a trading post on the

Missouri River, in 1839. He wrote: "The Oglalas, or the people who throw ashes in their own eyes . . . tradition says it was ashes that two young people threw in each other's eyes during a quarrel" (DeMallie 1976b:259). The persistence of this story over such a long period suggests that it may actually represent the origin of the name.

To understand the history of Lakota ethnonyms it is essential to begin with an examination of social organization. The basis for group identity was the *thiyóšpaye,* a word that literally translates as 'bunch of lodges' (*thí* 'dwelling place' + *ošpáye* 'bunch, herd'). A *thiyóšpaye* was a group of related nuclear families *(thiwáhe),* each living in its own tipi. Minimally, the *thiyóšpaye* was an extended family, but larger ones comprised a network of related families. *Thiyóšpaye* were named, usually with nicknames, and each had a recognized chief, who, with the advice of other respected men, oversaw the affairs of the camp. A camp was called *wichóthi,* literally, 'place where they live', though the term *waníthipi* 'they live in winter' was used for the winter camp. Two or three *thiyóšpaye* might habitually camp together during the summer, then split up during the winter to make better use of scarce resources—game and forage for horses (see DeMallie 1971, 2009).

Lone Bull's account, as recorded by Collier, provides a valuable illustration of Lakota social organization. During his childhood the three *thiyóšpaye—Khiyáksa, Škokpá,* and *Guhía—*camped together in the summer and were known collectively as *Khiyáksa.* Pawnee Killer was the leading chief (*wakíchuŋza* 'decider') and so they were commonly referred to as Pawnee Killer's camp. But, according to Lone Bull, each of the *thiyóšpaye* had four chiefs, one of whom was recognized as the leader of the *thiyóšpaye.* Although there are contradictions in the material as recorded by Collier, it seems that Pawnee Killer's *thiyóšpaye* was the Škokpá, but that as he aged his duties fell to Yellow Bear, his nephew. The leader of the *Khiyáksa thiyóšpaye* was Little Wound, Pawnee Killer's son-in-law. The *Guhía thiyóšpaye* was led by Whistler, who was unrelated to Pawnee Killer; they were a small and very poor group, owning few horses, and probably affiliated with the others for protection. The *Khiyáksa* and *Škokpá* were united through marriages over several generations and doubtless the *Guhía* were intermarried with them as well.

Corroboration of Lone Bull's account is found in the 1931 Pine Ridge field notes of anthropologist H. Scudder Mekeel. In an interview with Charles Turning Hawk Mekeel learned that the *Khiyáksa* comprised four "bands": *Khiyáksa, Thašnáheca, Škokpá,* and Owl Feather Headdress (the last two said to have originated among the Brules). In addition, Turning Hawk noted that He Dog's *Thašnáheca* camp also included the "Kunhinyan." Combining the information from Collier, Hyde, and Mekeel provides a picture of the social organization of the southern Oglalas as it existed in the mid- to late-nineteenth century:

A.2 Southern Oglala (*Khiyáksa*) Bands

Retranscription and translation	Collier (1939)	Hyde (1957)	Mekeel (1931)
Khiyáksa 'bite in two' (?)	Kiaksa	Kiyuksa	Kiyaksa
Thaphíšeleca 'spleen'	Tapícletca	Tapishlecha	
Kʼuíŋyaŋ 'gives rock' (?)	Guhía	Kuhee or Kuhinyan	Kuhinyan
Škokpá 'concave'	Ckokpa	Shkopa (alternate name for Tapishlecha)	Sokpaiya
Hiŋháŋśuŋ wapʼáha 'Owl Feather Headdress'			Owl Feather Headdress
Thašnáheca 'ground squirrel'			Tashńáitca

Understanding that *thiyóšpaye,* although they were named, independent social groups, frequently camped together and were at those times identified by the name of the dominant *thyóšpaye,* allows us to make sense of seemingly contradictory data. For example, Hyde's conclusion that *Škokpá* and *Thaphíšeleca* are alternate names for the same band can be explained by the fact the *Škokpá* was a smaller *thiyóšpaye* associated with the larger *Thaphíšleca thiyóšpaye.* Similarly, when Black Moccasin told Mekeel (1931:38) that the "Ku hin yan" were "mostly of Khiyaksa, had name first," we can understand it as an expression of the fact that the smaller *Kʼuíŋyaŋ thiyóšpaye* had previously been associated with the *Khiyáksa.*

Historical records and the testimony of many Lakotas from the late nineteenth century to the mid-twentieth make it clear that *thiyóšpaye* were always in flux during the prereservation period. Successful chiefs attracted followers, their *thiyóšpaye* grew in size, and when they died or became incapacitated their sons frequently succeeded them, breaking the *thiyóšpaye* into two or three separate camping groups, one of which sometimes, but not always, retaining the original *thiyóšpaye* name. When the seven *thiyóšpaye* that formed Pine Ridge settled there in 1879 it is apparent that each one was a composite of two or more subgroups, with recognized chiefs. The Indian agent at Pine Ridge sought to weaken the power of the leading chiefs and encouraged the minor chiefs to establish their own camps. In 1884, according to Episcopal missionary William J. Cleveland, the original seven *thiyóšpaye* at Pine Ridge had increased to twenty-one (Dorsey 1897:220–21). The process of fission continued with the division of the reservation into administrative districts and, in 1910, the allotment of land to individuals. In 1915 Buechel (1915–43) compiled a list of twenty-four *thiyóšpaye,* each represented by a separate community on Pine Ridge, and listed an additional five said to be extinct. Mekeel, based on his field work at Pine Ridge, identified forty-one communities derived from *thiyóšpaye* (Macgregor 1946:77, n.1).

Uncertainty surrounds an important issue for the study of Lakota society—the question of recruitment to the *thiyóšpaye.* My dissertation advisor, Fred Eggan, on the basis of his own studies and on those of Collier, characterized Lakota social structure as based on "a bilateral extended family centered on a group of siblings" (Eggan 1955:513). This structure, in Eggan's words, was " 'horizontal' or generational in character." The extended family groups were "amorphous but flexible." He wrote: "The bilateral or composite band organization, centered around a chief and his close relatives, may change its composition according to various circumstances—economic or political" (1955:518). This fits well with ethnographic and historical data but leaves open the question of recruitment. When Mekeel queried *Makʿúla* (Breast), who in 1931 was eighty-one years old, he replied: "If a Minneconjou marries an Oglala woman and lives with her people, the children became Oglala, and it is optional with the man which tribe he calls himself" (Mekeel 1931:51). Royal Hassrick, who did fieldwork in the early 1940s at Pine Ridge, suggested that children belonged to the families (meaning *thiyóšpaye*) of both their father and mother, but that in fact boys tended to identify with the father's family and girls with the mother's. Residence was another factor influencing the choice. In the end, Hassrick concludes, "there were no rigid rules for family membership" (1964:98). Nor was there any strict rule for residence after marriage. Whether the couple lived in the camp of the husband's or wife's family or chose to live elsewhere depended on circumstances, including the type of marriage, the couple's ages, social status, and personal preference. A *thiwáhe* (nuclear family) was counted as belonging to the camp (*wichóthi*) in which they lived, though the members might identify with other *thiyóšpaye.* In other words, it is necessary to distinguish between a camp as a residential unit of greater or lesser duration and a *thiyóšpaye* as a culturally recognized group of related families. Most camps comprised one or more *thiyóšpaye* (like Pawnee Killer's camp as recalled by Lone Bull for Collier) plus any number of temporary residents from other *thiyóšpaye.* Individuals could and did change their *thiyóšpaye* identity, particularly after long residence with another group.

In 1974, when visiting the American Museum of Natural History in New York to look for Clark Wissler's and Mekeel's field notes, I came across a collection of manuscripts by the geographer Joseph N. Nicollet, famous for his 1842 map of the upper Mississippi region. Among his papers was a list of

Sioux tribes and bands that he recorded at Fort Pierre in 1839 (DeMallie 1975, 1976b). In it, Nicollet gave the names of three Oglala bands: "Onkp'hatinas [*Húŋkpathila*], the lodges at the end of the circle," chief Yellowish Eagle; "Ku-Inyan [*Kʼuíŋyaŋ*], he gives the rock," chief Mad Dog; and "Oyúrpe [*Oyúȟpe*], those who put down (the burden that they carry)," chief White Earrings (1976:261). According to Hyde (1957:313) the *Húŋkpathila* band was that of Man Afraid of Horse, but after his position as head chief of the Oglalas was usurped by Red Cloud, the band was renamed *Phayábya* 'Pushed Aside', and is one of the seven bands that settled on the reservation in 1879. The *Guhía*, according to Lone Bull, were absorbed by the *Khiyáksa/Khiyúksa*, and the *Oyúȟpe* continued as a major band into the reservation period.

Complicating the picture, however, is Nicollet's listing of Brule bands. Of the four he lists, three are names later associated with the Oglalas: "Wajaji. Name which the Sioux give to the Osage, and which this band took" (Nicollet comments, "this Sioux band had marriages with Ponca-Osage families"), chief Black Horn; "Minishanan, the little band of Red Water," chief *Le Borgne*; "Kiuksa, those who divide, who separate," chief Two Elks (DeMallie 1976:361). The *Wažáže*, as Hyde (1957:312) noted, maintained an identity distinct from the Oglalas until settling on the reservation. The other two bands, *Mnišála* 'Little Red Water', and *Khiyúksa* 'Those Who Divide', were visited in 1849 by Francis Parkman, who identified them as Oglala (Wade 1947). At that time Red Water was an elderly chief whose son, Big Crow, was Parkman's host. *Le Borgne* (the one-eyed) was the brother of Bull Bear, who had been killed in 1841. The *Khiyúksa* were Bull Bear's band; the name Two Elk as chief does not reoccur in later lists. Significantly, an Oglala named Eagle Feather told Parkman "that since Bull Bear's death, there had been nothing but divisions and separations among them—they were a body without a head" (Wade 1947:457).

The Brules and Oglalas were the southernmost of the Lakota tribes, so it is not surprising that *thiyóšpaye* from one might over time join the other, reflecting marriage alliances and the influence of prominent chiefs. Individual genealogies reveal a high degree of intermarriage among all the Lakota tribes and with the Cheyennes, and in a large number of cases the husband moved to the wife's *thiyóšpaye* and became identified with it.

The issue of band names remained an intriguing puzzle for me.[12] When planning the *Plains* volume of the *Handbook of North American Indians*, I decided to construct a concordance of band names for all the Sioux tribes. Pulling the names together in one chart made me look at them in a new light (DeMallie 2001:736–48). A number of band names reappear in various tribes, for example, *Šikšíca* 'Bad Ones' (Upper Yanktonai, Hunkpapa, Minneconjou, Oglala), *Chaŋkhúte* 'Shoot at Wood' (Sisseton, Yankton), and *Wakháŋ* 'Holy' (Oglala, Hunkpapa). The band name *Khiyúksa/Khiyáksa* appears among the Mdewakanton and Upper Yanktonai as well as among the Oglalas and Brules but, without evidence, I see no justification for assuming that the commonality of names necessarily represents actual migrations of social groups from one tribe to another.[13] In fact, if Nicollet's translation "Those Who Divide" is correct, *Khiyúksa* may simply be a name given to a camp that secedes from another, a regular occurrence reflecting the usual process by which new *thiyóšpaye* were formed.

In some cases, of course, a shared name may represent historical connection. For example, given their proximity, it seems likely that the Oglala and Brule *Khiyúksa/Khiyáksa* may have originated as a single *thiyóšpaye*, part going to Pine Ridge and part to Rosebud. Genealogical study based on census records may shed light on the issue.

An interesting feature of the study of Sioux band names is that nineteenth-century observers started from the perspective of tribal camp circles, enumerating the bands in their relative positions (see Dorsey 1897). That is, they visualized social structure from the perspective of the summer camp during the time of the Sun Dance and communal buffalo hunts, when the tribe camped in a great circle with each band occupying its specific position in relation to the others. However, based on the field notes of twentieth-century anthropologists like Collier and Mekeel, none of the consultants whose words they recorded thought in terms of the structure of the camp circle. Their field notes amply exemplify the fact that when asked about social divisions Lakotas began by talking about their own *thiyóšpaye*, moved on to other *thiyóšpaye* to which they were related, named others with which they were familiar in their own tribe, then, moving farther out, named other Lakota tribes. Individuals identified first with their *thiyóšpaye* and identified others of their own tribe in terms of their *thiyóšpaye* affiliation. However, when speaking of Lakotas from other tribes, they identified them by the tribal, not band name (*Mnikhówožu*, for example). These two factors taken together may explain why Collier's consultants were so indecisive about the tribal name Oglala; it was not the way in which they were used to thinking about themselves.

Historical sources from Truteau in 1795 onward confirm that Oglala tribal identity was not a product of the reservation system. Nonetheless, tribal boundaries began to solidify when the Lakotas moved to their agencies on the Great Sioux Reservation in the 1870s and they became fixed after 1889 when half of the reservation was opened for settlement and the Lakotas were isolated from one another on five separate reservations. Reservation boundaries became de facto tribal boundaries. Historically, individuals, families, and even *thiyóšpaye* had moved freely from one Lakota tribe to another. Under the supervision of the Office of Indian Affairs, however, transferring from one reservation to another was a complicated bureaucratic matter requiring formal permission from the Indian agents.

A significant but largely overlooked government document provides insightful evidence of the social processes at work during the early reservation period (Commission Report 1892). In 1889, when the Sioux signed the agreement with the United States to surrender half of their reservation lands, the newly created Pine Ridge and Rosebud Reservations were contiguous, the boundary between them set at the mouth of Pass Creek on the White River. Before the agreement was passed into law, an Oglala delegation visiting Washington persuaded the commissioner of Indian Affairs that the boundary should be moved sixteen miles east, to the mouth of Black Pipe Creek, thereby enlarging Pine Ridge and reducing Rosebud. This was done, and Black Pipe Creek became the legal boundary between the two reservations. It soon became apparent that most of the Lakota living between those two creeks were Brules, enrolled at Rosebud. The situation presented a crisis for the Office of Indian Affairs. Short of congressional action to relocate the boundary back to Pass Creek (which would have required the signatures of at least three-fourths of adult males at Pine Ridge), the Brules living on Pine Ridge either would have to leave their homes and move east of the Rosebud line or be transferred to the Pine Ridge rolls.

During summer 1891 a government commission visited Pine Ridge and Rosebud to resolve the situation. They found that the Pine Ridge Lakotas were unwilling to cede the land between the two creeks to Rosebud but the vast majority were supportive of accepting the Brules living there as members of Pine Ridge. Most of the Brules living in that area were from the *Wažáže* band, which, as I noted earlier, had been transferred in 1877 from Red Cloud Agency (later Pine Ridge) to Spotted Tail Agency (later Rosebud). In 1881, Spotted Tail, the leading Brule chief, who was a member of the *Wažáže* band, was murdered. Big White Horse, a Brule, told the commissioners: "The man who was at the head of us over there [at Rosebud] was killed and we were made orphans, and as we used to be under Red Cloud before we were transferred we thought about him and came back here" (Commission Report 1892:33).

But the commissioners learned that the Brules were not the only "orphans" seeking to be enrolled at Pine Ridge. There were also Lakotas who were enrolled at Standing Rock who had fled to Pine Ridge after the killing of Sitting Bull in 1890 as well as survivors of Big Foot's ill-fated band of Ghost Dancers from Cheyenne River, most of whom were killed at Wounded Knee in 1890. The commissioners were firm in explaining to the Lakotas that each individual could belong to only one reservation; those who chose to move to Pine Ridge would forfeit all rights in their previous reservation.

Young Man Afraid of His Horses, one of the Oglala chiefs, told the commissioners, "we would like to have those people who want to stay here remain." Just as the white men are all one, he said, so "Indians are all one" (Commission Report 1892:42). Torn Belly, a headman of the Badger Eaters (*Ȟokáyuta*) band, declared:

> I am an Ogalalla. I belong to this agency, and to those people who
> want to remain here I shall give part of my name. My name is Ogalalla.
> That is what I am, and we shall call them Ogalallas, and have them
> belong to this agency hereafter. They have asked permission of the
> Ogalallas, and they have secured it. I do not give them that name for
> nothing. They came here wishing to remain, and we have given them a
> large number of horses. We want them to hereafter be called Ogalallas.
> [1892:48]

For the Lakotas, bestowing a name required validation by the gift of horses,
so Torn Belly's speech affirms the legitimacy of the name "Oglala" as applied
to these newcomers. Although he does not specify it, the gift of horses was
likely made to the followers of Sitting Bull and Big Foot, not to the Brules.
Torn Belly's speech may be taken to represent the evolution of tribal identity.
Even as early as 1891, Oglala identity was being extended to all Lakotas enrolled at Pine Ridge.

Concluding that "Oglala" as an ethnonym long antedated the reservation
period leaves open the question of how old the name might be. As I mentioned above, in his history of the Oglalas, Hyde (1957:8) followed earlier
writers in tracing the name back to the late seventeenth century. The source
of this information is Le Sueur, the previously mentioned French explorer
and trader who visited the Sioux in Minnesota from the 1680s to 1701 (Wedel
1974; DeMallie 2001:720–24, 2006). In 1695 he escorted a Sioux chief to Mon-
treal to meet with the governor, and to ask that traders be sent to his people.
The chief presented the governor with twenty-two arrows, representing the
number of what the French called "*nations*" (apparently villages) of his
people. In 1697, while Le Sueur was in France, he worked the cartographer
Jean-Baptiste Louis Franquelin to draft a map of the upper Mississippi region and to locate on it twenty-three Sioux villages. The French at that time
distinguished between the Sioux of the East and the Sioux of West, using the
Mississippi River as the dividing line. On the map (reproduced in Wedel
1974:167; DeMallie 2001:722), eleven villages are shown east of the river and
twelve west. Le Sueur also provided a list of twenty-four names in Dakota
with translations that was written on the upper left corner of the map, and
three additional names, without translation, appear to have been added
later.[14] In his 1700 journal Le Sueur provides a list of twenty village names, of
which seven are Sioux of the East and thirteen are Sioux of the West. Among
those named as western groups are four given on the Franquelin map as
Sioux of the East, a possible indication of westward movement of some of the
eastern Sioux.

In his journal Le Sueur estimated the population of the seven villages of
Sioux of the East at about three hundred lodges, an average of nearly forty-
three lodges per village. If that average held for the thirteen villages of the

Sioux of the West their population would amount to 559 lodges. Yet Le Sueur wrote of the Sioux of the West, "I have seen only one part of more than a thousand lodges. They make no use at all of canoes. They do not cultivate the ground and do not gather wild rice at all. They remain in the prairies which are between the upper Mississippi and the River of the Missouris and live only by hunting." On the Franquelin map, written in large letters on either side of the Mississippi, are the legends "Sioux de l'Est" and "Pays et Nation des Sioux de l'Ouest" ("Sioux of the East" and "Country and Nation of the Sioux of the West"). These are the groups with which Le Sueur was familiar. In equally large letters around Big Stone Lake ("Lac des Tintons") at the head of the Minnesota River is the legend "Pays et Nation des Tintons" ("Country and Nation of the Tetons"). Le Sueur spent seven months, from fall 1700 until spring 1701, at a fort he and his men constructed on the Blue Earth River in Minnesota. He did not visit the Tetons in their territory nor did he record any visits by them to his fort (Delisle 1702). On this basis I believe it is safe to conclude that Le Sueur's list of "nations" of the Sioux of the East and Sioux of the West, although extensive, represents only the Dakotas (eastern Sioux) and the Yanktons-Yanktonais, and does not include any of the Teton bands.

Some of the names given by Le Sueur are easily identified with nineteenth-century ethnonyms (see list in DeMallie 2001:723–24). However, Hyde's (1957:8) identification of the "Ojalespoitans or Village Divided into Many Small Bands" as the Oglala must be rejected. Hyde assumed that the "Ojale" represent "Oglala," and since the name Oglála was said to mean "scattered," the idea of a village divided into small bands fit the general meaning. Hyde's source for the name was the compilation of French documents published by Pierre Margry (1876–86, 6:87). However, Le Sueur's name list as published there reproduces many changes from the original manuscript (Delisle 1702; see Wedel 1974). The manuscript reads "Oüiatespouitons—village dispersed in several small bands." In the Dakota dialect this may represent *oyáte* 'people' + *sbu(ya)* 'fine(ly), small' + *thuŋ* 'village,' perhaps signifying "Village of people in small groups," but it must be understood that reconstructing the exact linguistic form and its meaning is necessarily conjectural. In any case, there is no reason to associate this name with the Oglalas or, as far as I know, with any other nineteenth-century ethnonym.

If the ancestors of the Oglalas are represented among the names recorded by Le Sueur they were a part of the "Tinton" or "Nation of the Prairies." This designation, from *thiŋtá* 'prairie' + *thuŋ* 'village', became in the Lakota dialect *Thíthuŋwaŋ* 'Teton', the name by which all the Lakotas are known. (The same name also appears on Le Sueur's list as a village of the Sioux of the West; "Prairie Village" was still a prominent Mdewakantonwan band in the nineteenth century.) Hyde conjectured that the Oglalas moved westward from Minnesota to the prairies east of the Missouri, then crossed west after the way was cleared when the many villages of earthlodge-dwelling Arikaras along the river were decimated by smallpox epidemics between 1772 and 1780 (Hyde 1957:17). Historically, this is undoubtedly true, but when the Oglala name originated remains a mystery.

This brief investigation into the name "Oglala" and the issues of naming and social organization into which it has led offers a good example of the range of challenges ethnohistorical study can present. The data lend themselves to historical, anthropological, and linguistic analyses, but none of these should be confused with the perspectives of native oral traditions, which are concerned with the interpretation of the past for explicating the present. Whether the name *Oglála* originated from the throwing of dust or ashes; whether the incident occurred among the Badger Eaters, *Oyúȟpe,* or Bad Faces; why and when it happened—all these are details that vary among the tellers.

A more aberrant version of the story than those recorded by Collier and presented above is the account given to Mekeel by Black Moccasin (1931:38):

> The original Oglala came from the Hunkpapa. They scattered dust in the faces of the Hunkpapa and so got the name. After this they separated from the Hunkpapa—The name of the Oglala before they were called this was Sage Brush (Pe ji hota [*phežíȟota*]). Then their name was Oyukpe and then finally they got the name Oglala.

A clue to understanding this transformation of the origin story may be found in Collier's interview with Eagle Elk, who claimed that Red Cloud was a Hunkpapa who married an Oglala woman. At first this seemed to me inexplicable; Eagle Elk was an *Oyúȟpe,* and so from a different band than Red Cloud; perhaps Eagle Elk wanted to distance Red Cloud from the other Oglalas. Subsequently, however, Alex Adams (a nephew of Red Cloud) told Collier that after killing Bull Bear, Red Cloud fled to the Minneconjous and stayed with them for three years. Throughout Collier's interviews his Oglala consultants tended to lump together the Hunkpapas and Minneconjous (both northern Lakota tribes whose chiefs resisted white incursion), so the two stories are compatible. Exile for a period of years was the usual punishment for murderers, so Adams's story makes good cultural sense. By incorporating the northern Lakotas into the Oglala origin story, Eagle Elk's tradition solidifies the connection between Red Cloud and the origin of the name Oglala.

The important fact is that these stories explain why the people are called "Scatters Their Own." The oral traditions recorded by Collier date the origin of the name to the 1850s or 1870s, but written sources first mention the name in 1795. The purpose of the oral traditions was to keep the name relevant to the present by assigning its origin to a remembered past. Recognizing that the epistemology underlying oral traditions is of a radically different nature from that characterizing western scholarship is important for ethnohistory.

In a similar vein it is essential to differentiate between folk etymologies and linguistic etymologies. Folk etymologies have cultural significance and may reveal a good deal about social realities, while linguistic etymologies have the potential to reveal the history of the term. Among the Oglala bands, *Khiyáksa/Khiyúksa* provides an instructive example: *khi-* 'through the middle'; *yaksa* 'to bite off'/*yuksa* 'to break off by hand': 'to bite through the middle'/'to break in half'. Both forms make linguistic sense and both forms are attested by different oral traditions. Wood Leg told Buechel (1915–43) that the name means "Bite in two in the middle: These people broke loose from their band in consequence of a dispute." Hyde (1957:313) reports two traditions concerning the name. One is that it refers to a test of a woman's virginity in which she made her vow while biting a leather snake. One woman, "on being rejected as not a virgin became so infuriated that she bit the leather snake in two." A second is that the name reflects the band splitting off after the death of Bull Bear. Additionally, Hyde mentions Riggs's (1897:157) interpretation of the name as referring "to the breaking of the tribal marriage customs" by marrying into their own group; in this case the Lakota form would presumably be *Kiyúksa* 'breaks his own' (*ki* 'his own' rather than *khi* 'through the middle'). In short, this *thiyóšpaye* name has multiple interpretations. Neither folk etymologies nor linguistic etymologies are sufficient to determine its original form or meaning.

The uncertainties surrounding ethnonyms such as *Oglála* and *Khiyáksa* provide a valuable warning of the necessity for caution and careful evaluation in using historical sources ethnohistorically. Wrenching words out of context—Le Sueur's Sioux village names, for example—and weaving conjectural historical narratives based on assumed continuities through time and across geographical space is detrimental to scholarship, misleading to readers, and fosters a false sense of certainty. Ethnohistorical analysis proceeds slowly and is necessarily built on demonstrable connections, not speculation.

• • •

After nearly forty years of lecture classes, seminars, reading classes, oral exams, defenses, professional conferences, endless late-night discussions with students, one remembers the frustrations, failures, and embarrassments—misspeaking, lapses of memory, misjudging the audience, inarticulate responses to questions, not being at one's sharpest—more readily than the successes. Those dark memories are compounded by the nature of the anthropology I have professed. My first anthropology teacher, Sol Tax, insisted that anthropology was not just a profession but a vocation; it is all-encompassing and provides the context in which an anthropologist experiences life. It is impossible to teach a vocation. I have never felt that there was a privileged body of information that I wanted to pass on to students. Rather, what I could offer is what I received from my own professors—inspiration. One can teach methods, present theories and perspectives, lead students through the history of the discipline, but in the end what counts is offering one's own work as it develops over time as an example of what anthropology is or can be. Each of us, as anthropologists, develops a highly personalized vision of the discipline, and that diversity weaves the fabric of anthropology.

I came to anthropology with a love of history and a deep interest in American Indians, particularly the Sioux. As a student I read the classic ethnographies and studied anthropological theories, but at the same time immersed myself in documents, including correspondence and reports from the Office of Indian Affairs and the War Department in the National Archives; the unpublished manuscripts of J. Owen Dorsey and other anthropologists in the Bureau of American Ethnology Archives; Lewis Henry Morgan's papers at the University of Rochester; and the manuscripts of George A. Dorsey and the ethnographic collections (documents of another kind) at the Field Museum. I came to appreciate the writings of nineteenth- and early twentieth-century anthropologists, not as outdated antiquarian curiosities but as ongoing conversations to which I could contribute. I consoled myself that if I was interested enough in something to pick up where an anthropologist one or more generations before me left off, then in the future there would be others like me who would continue the conversation.

Now, looking back over my shoulder, across the years (and back through the pages of this book), it is gratifying to realize that I am not traveling alone. The conversation will continue.

NOTES

1. See, for example, Meyer and Klein, "Native American Studies and the End of Ethnohistory" (1998). Krech (1991:365) argues for abandoning the term "ethnohistory" in favor of "anthropological history and historical anthropology."

2. The English translations of Lakota band names are subjects of much debate and uncertainty; I have modernized the Lakota transcriptions. The list that appears in Dorsey (1897) is the source used by Hyde.

3. The translation originated with Riggs, who provided it for a *Mdewákhaŋthuŋwaŋ* band that bore the same name. The transcription system used by Riggs and Dorsey does not differentiate between aspirated and unaspirated consonants. In this case, the difference is crucial to the meaning. The prefix *ki-* (unaspirated) means 'his own', as reflected in the translation 'breaks his own'. However, the prefix *khi-* (aspirated) means 'through the middle', in which case the name would be 'break through the middle'. Oglalas today pronounce the name with the aspirated prefix.

4. During the reservation period the Badger Eaters became an independent band under Chief No Water (Buechel 1915–43).

5. Sitting Bull never signed a treaty with the government, but the reference must be to the 1868 treaty. Camp (later Fort) Robinson was established in 1874 near Red Cloud Agency, which had moved to that location near present Crawford, Nebraska, the previous year. The move to Pine Ridge occurred in 1879.

6. From *ité* 'face' + *okála* 'to scatter in or on'.

7. This seems to reflect confusion in translation. According to Hyde (1957:67) Red Cloud was Smoke's nephew.

8. The bracketed date is Collier's. In fact, Bull Bear was killed in 1841 so this event must have happened about 1843, more than a decade before Thomas Twiss arrived as Indian agent and nearly a century before this interview. Adams seems to be attributing to Smoke both the names Bad Face and Oglala.

9. This name appears in Buechel's 1915 list of Oglala bands (Buechel 1915–43).

10. The expected form would be *iŋyaŋ kʾú* 'he gives rock'; the fact that the name is ungrammatical suggests that the translation is a folk etymology.

11. Deloria was uncertain about the name; she did not mark stress on it nor mark the initial consonant as *š* rather than *s*.

12. Kingsley Bray has done extensive work on the history of Oglala bands (Bray 1982, 1985a, 1985b).

13. Bray (1982, 1985a, 1985b) assumes that when a name is found among the Oglalas that matches the name of a band documented at an earlier date elsewhere, it reflects an actual migration of social groups. This can only be inference, however, unless there is historical or linguistic evidence to back it up.

14. Additions to the map were made in 1702 by the cartographers Claude and Guilliame Delisle from Le Sueur's dictation (Wedel 1974:158).

ACKNOWLEDGMENTS

I would like to thank Patrick Warren, Douglas R. Parks, and Kingsley Bray for critical readings of drafts of this paper.

References

Abler, Thomas S.

    1982   Ethnohistory: A Choice between Being Anthropology or Being Nothing. *Central Issues in Anthropology* 4 (1): 45–61.

Abu-Lughod, Lila

    1990   The Romance of Resistance: Tracing Transformations of Power through Bedouin Women. *American Ethnologist* 17 (1): 41–55.

Adair, James

    1775   *History of the American Indians.* London: Edward and Charles Dilly.

    1930 [1775]   *Adair's History of the American Indians,* edited by Samuel Cole Williams. Johnson City, Tenn.: Watauga Press.

    2005 [1775]   *The History of the American Indians,* edited by Kathryn E. Holland Braund. Tuscaloosa: University of Alabama Press.

Agha, Asif

    2007   *Language and Social Relations.* Cambridge: Cambridge University Press.

Ahlers, Jocelyn

    2006   Framing Discourse: Creating Community through Native Language Use. *Journal of Linguistic Anthropology* 16 (1): 58–75.

Allen, George

    2000   Contexts without Absolutes. In *Being and Dialectic: Metaphysics as a Cultural Presence,* edited by William Desmond and Joseph Grange, pp. 101–23. Albany: SUNY Press.

Andersen, Chris

    2011   Moya 'Tipimsook ("The People Who Aren't Their Own Bosses"): Racialization and the Misrecognition of "Métis" in Upper Great Lakes Ethnohistory. *Ethnohistory* 58 (1): 37–63.

Anderson, Benedict

    1991   *Imagined Communities: Reflections on the Origin and Spread of Nationalism.* London: Verso.

Anderson, David G.

    2000   *Identity and Ecology in Arctic Siberia: The Number One Reindeer Brigade.* Oxford: Oxford University Press.

Augé, Marc

1982   *The Anthropological Circle: Symbol, Function, History.* Cambridge: Cambridge University Press and Paris: Editions de la Maison des Sciences de l'Homme.

1995   *Non-Places: Introduction to an Anthropology of Supermodernity.* London: Verso.

1999   *An Anthropology for Contemporaneous Worlds.* Stanford: Stanford University Press.

Baerreis, David A.

1955   A Footnote to Dwight L. Smith's Shawnee Captivity Ethnography. *Ethnohistory* 2 (2): 183.

Bakhtin, Mikhail

1981   *The Dialogic Imagination: Four Essays by M.M. Bakhtin,* edited by Michael Holquist. Austin: University of Texas Press.

1984   *Problems of Dostoevsky's Poetics.* Minneapolis: University of Minnesota Press.

Bashkow, Ira

2004   A Neo-Boasian Conception of Cultural Boundaries. *American Anthropologist* 106 (3): 443–58.

Basso, Keith

1988   "Speaking with Names": Language and Landscape among the Western Apache. *Current Anthropology* 3 (2): 99–130.

1996   *Wisdom Sits in Places: Landscape and Language among the Western Apache.* Albuquerque: University of New Mexico Press.

Bateman, Rebecca

1996   Talking with the Plow: Agricultural Policy and Indian Farming in the Canadian and U.S. Prairies. *Canadian Journal of Native Studies* 16 (2): 211–28.

Bateson, Gregory, and Mary Catherine Bateson

1987   *Angels Fear: Towards an Epistemology of the Sacred.* New York: Bantam.

Bauman, Richard

2012   Performance. In *A Companion to Folklore,* edited by Regina F. Bendix and Galit Hasan-Rokem, pp. 94–118. Malden, Mass.: Wiley-Blackwell.

Begg, Alexander

1871   *Dot It Down: A Story of Life in the Northwest.* Toronto: Hunter, Rose.

Bell, Amelia Rector

1990   Separate People: Speaking of Creek Men and Women. *American Anthropologist* 92 (2): 332–45.

Benedict, Ruth Fulton

1922   The Vision in Plains Culture. *American Anthropologist* 24 (1): 1–23.

Berkhofer, Robert F., Jr.

1969   *A Behavioral Approach to Historical Analysis.* New York: The Free Press.

1973   Clio and the Culture Concept: Some Impressions of the Changing Relationship in American Historiography. In *The Idea of Culture in the Social Sciences,* edited by Louis Schneider and Charles Bonjean, pp. 77–100. Cambridge: Cambridge University Press.

1995   *Beyond the Great Story: History as Text and Discourse.* Cambridge, Mass.: Harvard University Press.

Berlin, Isaiah

1960   History and Theory: The Concept of Scientific History. *History and Theory* 1 (1): 1–31.

Bettelyoun, Susan Bordeaux, and Josephine Waggoner

1998   *With My Own Eyes: A Lakota Woman Tells Her People's History,* edited by Emily Levine. Lincoln: University of Nebraska Press.

Biolsi, Thomas

1997   The Anthropological Construction of "Indians": Haviland Scudder Meekel and the Search for the Primitive in Lakota Country. In *Indians and Anthropologists: Vine Deloria Jr. and the Critique of Anthropology,* edited by Thomas Biolsi and Larry Zimmerman, pp. 133–59. Tucson: University of Arizona Press.

2001   *Deadliest Enemies: Law and the Making of Race Relations on and off Rosebud Reservation.* Berkeley: University of California Press

Black-Rogers, Mary

1986   Varieties of 'Starving': Semantics and Survival in the Subarctic Fur Trade, 1750–1850. *Ethnohistory* 33 (4): 353–83.

Blondin, George

1990   *When the World Was New: Stories of the Sahtú Dene.* Yellowknife, NWT: Outcrop.

Boas, Franz

1912   *Tsimshian Texts.* Publications of the American Ethnological Society 3: 65–285. Leiden: E.J. Brill.

1936   History and Science in Anthropology: A Reply. *American Anthropologist* 38: 137–41.

1982 [1940]   *Race, Language, and Culture.* Chicago: University of Chicago Press.

Boas, Franz, and Ella C. Deloria

1941   *Dakota Grammar.* Memoirs of the National Academy of Sciences 23 (2). Washington, D.C.: U.S. Government Printing Office.

Bordeaux, Dorine

1958a   Indian Difficulties. *Argus Leader,* January 12, 1958, p. 6A.

1958b   Indians Need Help. *Argus Leader,* October 17, 1958, p. 4.

Bordeaux, William J.

  1926   The Early Day Squaw Man. *The Sunshine State* 7 (1): 26.

  1927   Sioux Indian Orator: Chief Hollow Horn Bear. *The Sunshine State* 8 (4): 30–31.

  1929   *Conquering the Mighty Sioux.* Sioux Falls, S. Dak.

  1934a   Chief Spotted Tail. *The Dakotah Traveler* 1 (4): 11, 27.

  1934b   Indian Progress. *The Dakotah Traveler* 1 (5): 20–21.

  1934c   Indian Ceremonies. *The Dakotah Traveler* 1 (6): 10–11.

  1935a   Sioux—Hunters and Trailers. *The Dakotah Traveler* 1 (7): 18–19.

  1935b   The Dead. *The Dakotah Traveler* 1 (8).

  1948   *Custer's Conqueror.* Smith and Company.

  1958   Indians in Want. *Argus Leader,* March 10, 1958, p. 4.

  1974   *Sitting Bull, Tanka-Iyotaka.* Grand Rapids, Mich.: Custer Ephemera Society.

Brady, Cyrus Townsend

  1971   *Indian Fights and Fighters.* Lincoln: University of Nebraska Press.

Braroe, Niels Winther

  1975   *Indian and White: Self-Image and Interaction in a Canadian Plains Community.* Stanford: Stanford University Press.

Braudel, Fernand

  1958   *On History.* Chicago: University of Chicago Press.

Braun, Sebastian Felix

  1997   Interethnische Beziehungen der Traditionellen Gesellschaften Alaskas und Nordwestkanadas. Lic. phil. I thesis, Universität Basel.

  1998   Ceremonies of Contact: Warfare and Exchange in Traditional North America. *Bulletin de la Société Suisse des Américanistes* 62: 29–33.

  2008   *Buffalo Inc.: American Indians and Economic Development.* Norman: University of Oklahoma Press.

  2013   Imagining Unimagined Communities: The Politics of Indigenous Nationalism. In *Tribal Worlds: Critical Studies in American Indian Nation Building,* edited by Brian Hosmer and Larry Nesper, pp. 141–60. Albany: SUNY Press.

Braund, Kathryn E. Holland

  1990   Guardians of Tradition and Handmaidens to Change: Women's Roles in Creek Economic and Social Life During the Eighteenth Century. *American Indian Quarterly* 14 (3): 239–58.

Bray, Kingsley M.

  1982   *Making the Oglala Hoop: Oglala Sioux Political History (1804–1825), Part I, 1804–1825.* London: English Westerners Society, American Indian Studies Series 2.

  1985a   *Making the Oglala Hoop: Oglala Sioux Political History (1804–1825), Part II.i, 1825–1841.* London: English Westerners Society, American Indian Studies Series 4.

1985b *Making the Oglala Hoop: Oglala Sioux Political History (1804–1825), Part II.ii, 1841–1850*. London: English Westerners Society, American Indian Studies Series 4.

2006 *Crazy Horse: A Lakota Life*. Norman: University of Oklahoma Press.

Briggs, Charles

1996 The Politics of Discursive Authority in Research on the "Invention of Tradition." *Cultural Anthropology* 11 (4): 435–69.

Briggs, Charles and Richard Bauman

1999 "The Foundation of All Future Researches": Franz Boas, George Hunt, Native American Texts, and the Construction of Modernity. *American Quarterly* 51 (3): 479–528.

Brown, Jennifer S. H., and Elizabeth Vibert

2003 Introduction. In *Reading Beyond Words: Contexts for Native History*. 2nd edition, edited by Jennifer S. H. Brown and Elizabeth Vibert, pp. xi–xxxii. Peterborough, ON: Broadview Press.

Brown, Joseph Epes

1953 *The Sacred Pipe: Black Elk's Account of the Seven Sacred Rites of the Oglala Sioux*. New York: Penguin Books.

Brown, Kate

2001 Gridded Lives: Why Kazakhstan and Montana Are Nearly the Same Place. *The American Historical Review*, 106 (1): 17–48.

Brumann, Christoph

2009 Outside the Glass Case: The Social Life of Urban Heritage in Kyoto. *American Ethnologist* 36 (2): 276–99.

Bruner, Edward

2005 *Cultures on Tour: Ethnographies of Travel*. Chicago: University of Chicago Press.

Buckley, Thomas

1989 The Articulation of Gender Symmetry in Yuchi Culture. *Semiotica* 74: 289–311.

Buechel, Eugene

1915–43 *Lakota Ethnological Notes*. Holy Rosary Mission-Red Cloud Indian School Records, Series 7-1, Raynor Memorial Libraries, Marquette University, Milwaukee, Wis.

1939 *A Grammar of Lakota: The Language of the Teton Sioux Indians*. Saint Francis, S. Dak.: Rosebud Education Society, St. Francis Mission.

1970 *Lakota-English Dictionary*, edited by Paul Manhart. Pine Ridge, S. Dak: Red Cloud Indian School.

⁂ Bunten, Alexis Celeste

2008 Sharing Culture or Selling Out? Developing the Commodified Persona in the Heritage Industry. *American Ethnologist* 35 (3): 380–95.

Bunzl, Matti
    2004   Boas, Foucault, and the "Native Anthropologist": Notes toward a Neo-Boasian Anthropology. *American Anthropologist* 106 (3): 435–42.
Burch, Ernest S., Jr.
    2005   *Alliance and Conflict: The World System of the Iñupiaq Eskimo.* Lincoln: University of Nebraska Press.
Burke, Peter
    1990   Historians, Anthropologists, and Symbols. In *Culture through Time: Anthropological Approaches,* edited by Emiko Ohnuki-Tierney, pp. 268–83. Stanford: Stanford University Press.
✳ Burnett, Kristin
    2010   *Taking Medicine: Women's Healing Work and Colonial Contact in Southern Alberta, 1880–1930.* Vancouver: UBC Press.
Cahill, Cathleen
    2011   *Federal Fathers and Mothers: A Social History of the United States Indian Service, 1869–1933.* Chapel Hill: University of North Carolina Press.
Campisi, Jack, and William A. Starna
    2004   Another View on "Ethnogenesis of the New Houma Indians." *Ethnohistory* 51 (4): 779–91.
Capron, Louis
    1953   *The Medicine Bundles of the Florida Seminole and the Green Corn Dance.* Bureau of American Ethnology Anthropological Paper No. 35. Washington, D.C.: Government Printing Office.
    1956   Notes on the Hunting Dance of the Cow Creek Seminole. *The Florida Anthropologist* 9 (3–4): 67–78.
Carpenter, Jock
    1977   *Fifty Dollar Bride: Marie Rose Smith, a Chronicle of Métis Life in the 19th Century.* Sidney, BC: Gray's Pub.
Cash, Joseph H., and Herbert T. Hoover (editors)
    1971   *To Be an Indian: An Oral History.* New York: Holt, Rinehart and Winston.
Castile, George
    2004   Federal Indian Policy and Anthropology. In *A Companion to the Anthropology of American Indians,* edited by Thomas Biolsi, pp. 268–83. Oxford: Blackwell Publishing.
Christen, Kimberly.
    2008   *Aboriginal Business: Alliances in a Remote Australian Town.* Santa Fe: SAR Press.
Clark, Robert A. (editor)
    1988   *The Killing of Chief Crazy Horse: Three Eyewitness Views.* Lincoln: University of Nebraska Press.
Clifford, James
    1983   On Ethnographic Authority. *Representations* 1 (2): 118–46.

1988   *The Predicament of Culture: Twentieth-Century Ethnography, Literature, and Art.* Cambridge, Mass.: Harvard University Press.

2004   Looking Several Ways: Anthropology and Native Heritage in Alaska. *Current Anthropology* 45 (1): 5–30.

Collier, Donald

1939   Ogalala Field Notes Pine Ridge Feb.-March, 1939. Fred Eggan Collection, Box 72, Folder 5, Special Collections Research Center, University of Chicago Library.

Collins, James

1998   Our Ideologies and Theirs. In *Language Ideologies: Practice and Theory,* edited by Bambi Schieffelin, Kathryn Woolard, and Paul Kroskrity, pp. 256–70. Oxford: Oxford University Press.

Commission Report

1892   *Letter from the Secretary of the Interior in Relation to the Affairs of the Indians at the Pine Ridge and Rosebud Reservations in South Dakota.* Senate Ex. Doc. 58, 52nd Congress, 1st Session (Serial 2900).

Conn, Steven

1998   *Museums and American Intellectual Life, 1876–1926.* Chicago: University of Chicago Press.

2004   *History's Shadow: Native Americans and Historical Consciousness in the Nineteenth Century.* Chicago: University of Chicago Press.

Cruikshank, Julie

1990a   *Life Lived Like a Story.* Lincoln: University of Nebraska Press.

1990b   Getting the Words Right: Perspectives on Naming and Places in Athabaskan Oral History. *Arctic Anthropology* 27 (1): 52–65.

1997   Negotiating with Narrative: Establishing Cultural Identity at the Yukon International Storytelling Festival. *American Anthropologist* 99 (1): 56–69.

1998   *The Social Life of Stories: Narrative and Knowledge in the Yukon Territory.* Vancouver: UBC Press.

2005   *Do Glaciers Listen? Local Knowledge, Colonial Encounters, and Social Imagination.* Vancouver: UBC Press.

Culin, Stewart

1907   Games of the North American Indians. Pp. 3–809 in *24th Annual Report of the Bureau of American Ethnology for the Years 1902–1903.* Washington, DC.

D'Arcus, B.

2003   Contested Boundaries: Native Sovereignty and State Power at Wounded Knee, 1973. *Political Geography* 22: 415–37.

Daniels, Robert E.

1970   Cultural Identities among the Oglala Sioux. In *The Modern Sioux: Social Systems and Reservation Culture,* edited by Ethel Nurge, pp. 198–245. Lincoln: University of Nebraska Press.

Darnell, Regna

    1992   The Boasian Text Tradition and the History of Anthropology. *Culture* 12 (1): 39–48.

    2001   *Invisible Genealogies: A History of Americanist Anthropology.* Lincoln: University of Nebraska Press.

Davis, Dave D.

    2001   A Case of Identity: Ethnogenesis of the New Houma Indians. *Ethnohistory* 48 (3): 473–94.

De Groot, Jerome

    2009   *Consuming History: Historians and Heritage in Contemporary Popular Culture.* Abingdon: Routledge.

Delisla, Claude

    [1702]   "Mémoires de Mr le Sueur," 1699–1702. Aix-en-Provence, Archives Nationales, Archives de la Marine, 2JJ 56/9.

Deloria, Ella

    ca. 1937   *Og.lála Name Story.* American Philosophical Society Library, ms. no. 497.3 B63c (X8a.21), part 10.

    1998 [1944]   *Speaking of Indians.* Lincoln: University of Nebraska Press.

    ✗ 2006 [1932]   *Dakota Texts.* Lincoln: University of Nebraska Press.

    2009   *Waterlily. New Edition.* Lincoln: University of Nebraska Press.

Deloria, Philip J.

    2004   *Indians in Unexpected Places.* Lawrence: University Press of Kansas.

Deloria, Vine, Jr.

    1988 [1969]   *Custer Died for Your Sins: An Indian Manifesto.* Norman: University of Oklahoma Press.

    1999   *Singing for a Spirit: A Portrait of the Dakota Sioux.* Santa Fe: Clear Light Publishers.

Deloria, Vine, Jr., and Raymond J. DeMallie (editors)

    1999   *Documents of American Indian Diplomacy: Treaties, Agreements and Conventions, 1775–1979.* 2 Vols. Norman: University of Oklahoma Press.

DeMallie, Raymond J.

    1968   Kinship Systems of the Dakota Indians. Honors thesis, University of Chicago.

    1970a   Kinship in Teton Dakota Culture. MA thesis, University of Chicago.

    1970b   A Partial Bibliography of Archival Manuscript Material relating to the Dakota Indians. In *The Modern Sioux: Social Systems and Reservation Culture,* edited by Ethel Nurge, pp. 316–23. Lincoln: University of Nebraska Press.

    1971   Teton Dakota Kinship and Social Organization. PhD dissertation, University of Chicago.

    1972   Using Historical Data: A Dakota Example. Paper given to the symposium session "Historical Documents and North American Indians." 71st American Anthropological Association meeting in Toronto, November 30, 1972.

1975   Joseph N. Nicollet's Account of the Sioux and Assiniboine in 1839. *South Dakota History* 5 (4): 343–59.

1976a   Teton Dakota Time Concepts: Methodological Foundations for the Writing of   Ethnohistory. *Folklore Forum* (Special Issue: Trends and New Vistas in Contemporary   Native American Folklore Study), Bibliographic and Special Series, 15 (9): 7–17.

1976b   Nicollet's Notes on the Dakota. In *Joseph N. Nicollet on the Plains and Prairies*, translated and edited by Edmund C. Bray and Martha Coleman Bray, pp. 250–81. St. Paul: Minnesota Historical Society Press.

1977a   Treaties Are Made between Nations. In *The Great Sioux Nation*, edited by Roxanne Dunbar Ortiz, pp. 110–15. New York: The American Indian Treaty Council Information Center and Berkeley: Moon Books.

1977b   American Indian Treaty Making: Motives and Meanings. *American Indian Journal* 3 (1): 2–10.

1978a   George Bushotter: The First Lakota Ethnographer. In *American Indian Intellectuals* (1976 American Ethnological Society Proceedings), edited by Margot Liberty, pp. 91–102. St. Paul: West Publishing Co.

1978b   Pine Ridge Economy: Cultural and Historical Perspectives. In *American Indian Economic Development*, edited by Sam Stanley, pp. 237–312. The Hague: Mouton.

1979   Change in American Indian Kinship Systems: The Dakota. *Currents in Anthropology: Essays in Honor of Sol Tax*, edited by Robert Henshaw, pp. 221–41. The Hague: Mouton.

1980   Touching the Pen: Plains Indian Treaty Councils in Ethnohistorical Perspective. In *Ethnicity on the Great Plains*, edited by Frederick C. Luebke, pp. 38–53. Lincoln: University of Nebraska Press.

1981   Fort Laramie Treaty of 1851. *Montana the Magazine of Western History* 31 (3): 42–50.

1982   The Lakota Ghost Dance: An Ethnohistorical Account. *Pacific Historical Review* 51: 385–405.

1984   *The Sixth Grandfather: Black Elk's Teachings Given to John G. Neihardt.* Lincoln: University of Nebraska Press.

1987   Lakota Belief and Ritual in the Nineteenth Century. In *Sioux Indian Religion: Tradition and Innovation*, edited by Raymond J. DeMallie and Douglas R. Parks, pp. 25–44. Norman: University of Oklahoma Press.

1988a   Introduction to the Reprint Edition. In *Among the Sioux of Dakota: Eighteen Months' Experience as an Indian Agent 1869–70*, edited by DeWitt Clinton Poole, pp. xi–lii. St. Paul: Minnesota Historical Society Press.

1988b   Lakota Traditionalism: History and Symbol. In *Native North American Interaction Patterns*, edited by Regna Darnell and Michael K. Foster, pp. 2–21. Hull: Mercury Paper No. 112. (Canadian Ethnology Service), Canadian Museum of Civilization, National Museums of Canada.

* 1993 "These Have No Ears": Narrative and the Ethnohistorical Method. *Ethnohistory* 40 (4): 515–38.

⟡ 1994 Kinship and Biology in Sioux Culture. In *North American Indian Anthropology: Essays on Society and Culture,* edited by Raymond J. DeMallie and Alfonso Ortiz, pp. 125–46. Norman: University of Oklahoma Press.

⟡ 1998 Kinship: The Foundation of Native American Society. In *Studying Native America: Problems and Prospects,* edited by Russell Thornton, pp. 306–56. Madison: University of Wisconsin Press.

1999 "George Sword Wrote These": Lakota Culture as Lakota Text. In *Theorizing the Americanist Tradition,* edited by Lisa Philips Valentine and Regna Darnell, pp. 245–58. Toronto: University of Toronto Press.

2001a Teton. In *Plains,* edited by Raymond J. DeMallie, pp. 794–820. *Handbook of North American Indians,* Vol. 13, William C. Sturtevant, general editor. Washington, D.C.: Smithsonian Institution.

2001b Procrustes and the Sioux: David M. Schneider and the Study of Sioux Kinship. In *The Cultural Analysis of Kinship: The Legacy of David M. Schneider,* edited by Richard Feinberg and Martin Oppenheimer, pp. 46–59. Urbana: University of Illinois Press.

2001c Sioux until 1850. In *Plains,* edited by Raymond J. DeMallie, pp. 983–95. *Handbook of North American Indians,* Vol. 13, William C. Sturtevant, general editor. Washington, D.C.: Smithsonian Institution.

2001d Yankton and Yanktonai. In *Plains,* edited by Raymond J. DeMallie, pp. 1011–25. *Handbook of North American Indians,* Vol. 13, William C. Sturtevant, general editor. Washington, D.C.: Smithsonian Institution.

2006a Introduction to the Bison Books Edition. In *Dakota Texts,* by Ella Deloria, pp. v–xix. Lincoln: University of Nebraska Press.

2006b Vine Deloria Jr. (1933–2005). *American Anthropologist* 108 (4): 932–35.

2006c The Sioux at the Time of European Contact: An Ethnohistorical Problem. In *New Perspectives on Native North America: Cultures, Histories, and Representations,* edited by Sergei A. Kan and Pauline Turner Strong, pp. 239–60. Lincoln: University of Nebraska Press.

2009 Community in Native America: Continuity and Change among the Sioux. *Journal de la Société des Américanistes* 95 (1): 185–205.

DeMallie, Raymond J. (volume editor)

2001 *Handbook of North American Indians, Volume 13: Plains.* William C. Sturtevant, general editor. Washington: Smithsonian Institution.

DeMallie, Raymond J., and John C. Ewers

2001 History of Ethnological and Ethnohistorical Research. In *Plains,* edited by Raymond J. DeMallie, pp. 23–43. *Handbook of North American Indians,* Vol. 13, William C. Sturtevant, general editor. Washington, D.C.: Smithsonian Institution.

DeMallie, Raymond J., and Robert H. Lavenda

1977   *Wakan*: Plains Siouan Concepts of Power. In *The Anthropology of Power: Ethnographic Studies from Asia, Oceania, and the New World*, edited by Raymond D. Fogelson and Richard N. Adams, pp. 153–65. New York: Academic Press.

DeMallie, Raymond J., and David Reed Miller

2001   Assiniboine. In *Plains*, edited by Raymond J. DeMallie, pp. 572–595. *Handbook of North American Indians*, Vol. 13, William C. Sturtevant, general editor. Washington, D.C.: Smithsonian Institution.

DeMallie, Raymond J. and Douglas Parks

2001   Tribal Traditions and Records. In *Plains*, edited by Raymond J. DeMallie, pp. 1062–73. *Handbook of North American Indians*, Vol. 13, William C. Sturtevant, general editor. Washington, D.C.: Smithsonian Institution.

Dempsey, Hugh

1979   Introduction. In *My Tribe the Crees*, edited by Joseph F. Dion and Huge Dempsey, pp. v–viii. Calgary: Glenbow-Alberta Institute.

DeWall, Robb

1983   *Crazy Horse and Korczak*. Crazy Horse, S. Dak.: Korczak's Heritage, Inc.

Dinwoodie, David W.

1998   Authorizing Voices: Going Public in an Indigenous Language. *Cultural Anthropology* 13 (2): 193–223.

1999   Textuality and the "Voices" of Informants: The Case of Edward Sapir's 1929 Navajo Field School. *Anthropological Linguistics* 41 (2): 165–92.

2002   *Reserve Memories: The Power of the Past in a Chilcotin Community*. Lincoln: University of Nebraska Press.

2010   Ethnic Community in Early Tsilhqut'in Contact History. *Ethnohistory* 57 (4): 651–78.

Dorsey, J. Owen

1897   Siouan Sociology. Pp. 205–44 in *15th Annual Report of the Bureau of American Ethnology for the Years 1893–1894*. Washington, D.C.

Duncan, Starkey

1992   Face-to-Face Interaction. In *Folklore, Cultural Performances, and Popular Entertainments: A Communications-Centered Handbook*, edited by Richard Bauman, pp. 21–28. Oxford: Oxford University Press.

Dussel, Enrique

1998   Beyond Eurocentrism: The World System and the Limits of Modernity. In *The Cultures of Globalization*, edited by Fredric Jameson and Masao Miyoshi, pp. 3–31. Durham: Duke University Press.

Eagleton, Terry

2000   *The Idea of Culture*. Oxford: Blackwell.

Eastman, Charles Alexander

    1894   The Sioux Mythology. *Popular Science Monthly* 46 (November): 88–91.

    1906a   Rain-in-the-Face: The Story of a Sioux Warrior. *Outlook* 84 (October 27): 507–12.

    1906b   The War Maiden of the Sioux. *The Ladies Home Journal* 23: 14.

    1915   *The Indian Today: The Past and Future of the First American.* Garden City, N.Y.: Doubleday.

    1976 [1904]   *Red Hunters and the Animal People.* New York: AMS Press.

    1980 [1911]   *The Soul of the Indian: An Interpretation.* Lincoln: University of Nebraska Press.

    1991a [1902]   *Indian Boyhood.* Lincoln: University of Nebraska Press.

    1991b [1918]   *Indian Heroes and Great Chieftains.* Lincoln: University of Nebraska Press.

Eastman, Charles Alexander, and Elaine Goodale Eastman

    1990 [1909]   *Wigwam Evenings: Sioux Folk Tales Retold.* Lincoln: University of Nebraska Press.

Eggan, Fred

    1952   The Ethnological Cultures and Their Archeological Background. In *The Archeology of Eastern United States,* edited by James B. Griffin, pp. 34–45. Chicago: University of Chicago Press.

    1954   Social Anthropology and the Method of Controlled Comparison. *American Anthropologist* 56 (1): 743–63.

    1966   *The American Indian: Perspectives for the Study of Social Change.* Chicago: Aldine.

Eggan, Fred (editor)

    1955 [1937]   *Social Anthropology of North American Tribes, Enlarged Edition.* Chicago: University of Chicago Press.

Ellis, Richard N.

    1975   Introduction. In *My People the Sioux,* by Luther Standing Bear. Lincoln: University of Nebraska Press.

    1978   Introduction. In *Land of the Spotted Eagle,* by Luther Standing Bear. Lincoln: University of Nebraska Press.

Ens, Gerhard J.

    1996   *Homeland to Hinterland: The Changing Worlds of the Red River Metis in the Nineteenth Century.* Toronto: University of Toronto Press.

Fenske, Michaela

    2007   Micro, Macro, Agency: Historical Ethnography as Cultural Anthropology Practice. *Journal of Folklore Research* 44 (1): 67–99.

Fenton, William N.

    1952   The Training of Historical Ethnologists in America. *American Anthropologist* 54 (3): 328–39.

1987   *The False Faces of the Iroquois.* Norman: University of Oklahoma Press.

1991 [1953]   *The Iroquois Eagle Dance: An Offshoot of the Calumet Dance.* Syracuse: Syracuse University Press.

Fisher, Dexter

1985   Introduction. In *American Indian Stories*, by Zitkala-Sa. Lincoln: University of Nebraska Press.

Fisher, Robin

1977   *Contact and Conflict: Indian-European Relations in British Columbia, 1774–1890.* Vancouver: UBC Press.

Fletcher, Matthew L. M.

2007–2008   Retiring the "Deadliest Enemies" Model of Tribal-State Relations. *Tulsa Law Review* 43: 73–87.

Fletcher, Matthew L. M., and Peter S. Vicaire

2012   Indian Wars: Old and New. *The Journal of Gender, Race & Justice* 15 (2): 201–30.

Fogelson, Raymond D.

1962   The Cherokee Ballgame: A Study in Southeastern Ethnology. PhD dissertation, University of Pennsylvania. University Microfilms, Ann Arbor.

1971   The Cherokee Ballgame Cycle: An Ethnographer's View. *Ethnomusicology* 15 (3): 327–38.

1974   On the Varieties of Indian History: Sequoyah and Traveller Bird. *Journal of Ethnic Studies* 2: 105–12.

1989   The Ethnohistory of Events and Nonevents. *Ethnohistory* 36 (2): 133–47.

2001   Schneider Confronts Componential Analyses. In *The Cultural Analysis of Kinship: The Legacy of David M. Schneider,* edited by Richard Feinberg and Martin Oppenheimer, pp. 33–45. Urbana: University of Illinois Press.

Fogelson, Raymond D. (volume editor)

2004   *Handbook of North American Indians. Vol. 14: Southeast.* William C. Sturtevant, general editor. Washington, D.C.: Smithsonian Institution.

Fogelson, Raymond D., and Amelia B. Walker

1980   Self and Other in Cherokee Booger Masks. *Journal of Cherokee Studies* 5: 88–101.

Fortes, Meyer

1963 [1949]   Time and Social Structure: An Ashanti Case. In *Social Structure: Studies Presented to A.R. Radcliffe-Brown*, edited by Meyer Fortes, pp. 54–84. New York: Russell and Russell.

Foster, Martha Harroun

2006   *We Know Who We Are: Métis Identity in a Montana Community.* Norman: University of Oklahoma Press.

Fowler, Loretta

    1987   *Shared Symbols, Contested Meanings: Gros Ventre Culture and History, 1778–1984*. Ithaca: Cornell University Press.

Fox Family

    2008   *Fox Family Fiddle: Métis Tunes from Montana*. Sweetgrass Music, B001D080CG.

Fox, Richard

    1991   For a Nearly New Culture History. In *Recapturing Anthropology: Working in the Present*, edited by Richard G. Fox, pp. 93–114. Santa Fe: School of American Research Press.

Gagnon, V. P., Jr.

    2004   *The Myth of Ethnic War: Serbia and Croatia in the 1990s*. Ithaca: Cornell University Press.

Galloway, Patricia, and Jason Baird Jackson

    2004   Natchez and Related Groups. In *Southeast*, edited by Raymond D. Fogelson, pp. 598–615. *Handbook of North American Indians*, Vol. 14, William C. Sturtevant, general editor. Washington, D.C.: Smithsonian Institution.

Gardner, Beeth

    1992   *Edmonton's Musical Life: 1892–1930*. Fort Edmonton Park, AB.

Gardner, Susan

    2009   Introduction. In *Waterlily, New Edition*, by Ella Deloria, pp. v–xxviii. Lincoln: University of Nebraska Press.

Geertz, Clifford

    1973   *The Interpretation of Cultures*. New York: Basic Books.

    1983   *Local Knowledge: Further Essays in Interpretive Anthropology*. New York: Basic Books.

Gennette, Gerard

    1979   *Narrative Discourse: An Essay in Method*. Ithaca: Cornell University Press.

Georges, Robert

    1972   Recreations and Games. In *Folklore and Folklife: An Introduction*, edited by Richard M. Dorson, pp. 173–90. Chicago: University of Chicago Press.

Gibson, James R.

    1992   *Otter Skins, Boston Ships, and China Goods: The Maritime Fur Trade of the Northwest Coast, 1785–1841*. Seattle: University of Washington Press.

Gillespie, Susan D.

    1991   Ballgames and Boundaries. In *The Mesoamerican Ballgame*, edited by Vernon L. Scarborough and David R. Wilcox, pp. 317–45. Tucson: The University of Arizona Press.

Glassie, Henry H.

    1968   *Pattern in the Material Folk Culture of the Eastern United States*. Philadelphia: University of Pennsylvania Press.

Glenn, James R.
  1996 *Guide to the National Anthropological Archives, Smithsonian Institution, Revised and Enlarged.* Washington, D.C.: National Anthropological Archives.

Goffman, Erving
  1961 Role Distance. In *Encounters: Two Studies in the Sociology of Interaction,* pp. 85–99. Indianapolis: The Bobbs-Merrill Company, Inc.
  1983 *Forms of Talk.* Philadelphia: University of Pennsylvania Press.

Goggin, John M., and William C. Sturtevant
  1964 The Calusa: A Stratified, Non-Agricultural Society (with Notes on Sibling Marriage). In *Explorations in Cultural Anthropology,* edited by Ward H. Goodenough, pp. 179–219. New York: McGraw Hill.

Goldenweiser, Alexander
  1937 *Anthropology: An Introduction to Primitive Culture.* New York: F. S. Crofts and Company.

Goodard, Pliny
  1904 *Hupa Texts.* University of California Publications in Archaeology and Ethnology 1(2). Berkeley: University of California Press.

Goode, Judith
  1992 Food. In *Folklore, Cultural Performances, and Popular Entertainments: A Communications-Centered Handbook,* edited by Richard Bauman, pp. 233–45. Oxford: Oxford University Press.

Goodyear, Frank H.
  2003 *Red Cloud: Photographs of a Lakota Chief.* Lincoln: University of Nebraska Press.

Graeber, David
  2001 *Towards and Anthropological Theory of Value: The False Coin of Our Own Dreams.* New York: Palgrave.

Grinnell, George Bird
  1956 *The Fighting Cheyennes.* Norman: University of Oklahoma Press.

Grumet, Robert S. (editor)
  2001 *Voices from the Delaware Big House Ceremony.* Norman: University of Oklahoma Press.

Gumperz, John
  1972 [1968] Speech Community. In *Language and Social Context,* edited by Pier Paolo Giglioli, pp. 219–31. Hammondsworth: Penguin Books.

Hafen, P. Jane (editor)
  2001 *Dreams and Thunder: Stories, Poems, and the Sun Dance Opera, by Zitkala-Sa.* Lincoln: University of Nebraska Press.

Hafen, LeRoy R., and Ann W. Hafen (editors)
  1956 *Rufus B. Sage: His Letters and Papers 1836–1847 with an Annotated Reprint of His "Scenes in the Rocky Mountains and in Oregon, California, New Mexico, Texas, and the Grand Prairies."* The Far West and the Rockies Series, Vols. 4–5. Glendale, Calif.: Arthur   H. Clark.

Hallowell, A. Irving

1926   Bear Ceremonialism in the Northern Hemisphere. *American Anthropologist* 28 (1): 1–175.

1960   Ojibwa Ontology, Behavior, and World View. In *Culture in History: Essays in Honor of Paul Radin,* edited by Stanley Diamond, pp. 19–52. New York: Columbia University Press.

Handler, Richard, and Jocelyn Linnekin

1984   Tradition, Genuine or Spurious. *Journal of American Folklore* 97: 273–90.

Hanks, William F.

2005   Explorations in the Deictic Field. *Current Anthropology* 46 (2): 191–220.

2010   *Converting Words: Maya in the Age of the Cross.* Berkeley: University of California Press.

Hanson, Charles E., Jr.

1966   James Bordeaux. *The Museum of the Fur Trade Quarterly* 2 (1): 2–13.

1969   The Battle of Crow Butte. *Museum of the Fur Trade Quarterly* 5 (3): 2–4.

1972   Reconstruction of the Bordeaux Trading Post. *Nebraska History* (Summer): 137–65.

1991   James Bordeaux, Chapter Two. *The Museum of the Fur Trade Quarterly* 27 (4): 2–9.

Hanson, Charles E., Jr. (editor)

1994   *The David Adams Journals.* Chadron, Nebr.: Museum of the Fur Trade.

Hardorff, Richard G.

2001   *The Death of Crazy Horse: A Tragic Episode in Lakota History.* Lincoln: University of Nebraska Press.

Harkin, Michael

1997   *The Heiltsuks: Dialogues of Culture and History on the Northwest Coast.* Lincoln: University of Nebraska Press.

Harper's New Monthly Magazine

1859   The People of the Red River and the Red River Trail. *Harper's New Monthly Magazine,* January 18 (104): 169–76; June 19 (109): 37–55.

Harries-Jones, Peter

1995   *A Recursive Vision: Ecological Understanding and Gregory Bateson.* Toronto: University of Toronto Press.

Hassrick, Royal

1964   *The Sioux: Life and Customs of a Warrior Society.* Norman: University of Oklahoma Press.

Havard, Gilles

2008   "So amusingly Frenchified": Mimetism in the French-Amerindian Encounter (XVIIth–XVIIIth c.). *Le Journal* (Center for French Colonial Studies) 24 (1): 1–7.

Healy, W. J.

1923   *Women of Red River; Being a Book Written from the Recollections of Women Surviving from the Red River Era.* Winnipeg, MB: Russell, Lang & Co.

Helm, June and Nancy Lurie

1966   *The Dogrib Hand Game.* Anthropological Series 71, National Museum of Canada Bulletin 205. Ottawa.

Herskovits, Melville J.

1948   *Man and His Works: The Science of Cultural Anthropology.* New York: Alfred A. Knopf.

Heth, Charlotte

1975   The Stomp Dance Music of the Oklahoma Cherokee: A Study of Contemporary Practice with Special Reference to the Illinois District Council. PhD dissertation, University of California. University Microfilms, Ann Arbor.

Hill, Christina Gish

2013   Kinship as an Assertion of Native Nationhood. In *Tribal Worlds: Critical Studies in American Indian Nation Building,* edited by Brian Hosmer and Larry Nesper, pp. 65–109. Albany: SUNY Press.

Hill, Jane

1985   The Grammar of Consciousness and the Consciousness of Grammar. *American Ethnologist* 12 (4): 725–37.

Hobsbawm, Eric, and Terence Ranger (editors)

1983   *The Invention of Tradition.* New York: Cambridge University Press.

Holmes, Clara L. K.

1930   The Great West Festival at Calgary. *Canadian Geographical Journal* 1 (3): 268–75.

hooks, bell

1994   *Teaching to Transgress: Education as the Practice of Freedom.* New York: Routledge.

Howard, James H.

1981   *Shawnee! The Ceremonialism of a Native Indian Tribe and Its Cultural Background.* Athens: Ohio University Press.

Howard, James H. (in collaboration with Willie Lena)

1984   *Oklahoma Seminoles: Medicine, Magic, and Religion.* Norman: University of Oklahoma Press.

Howey, Meghan C. L., and John M. O'Shea

2006   Bear's Journey and the Study of Ritual in Archaeology. *American Antiquity* 71 (2): 251–82.

Hudson, Charles

1977   James Adair as Anthropologist. *Ethnohistory* 24 (4): 311–28.

Hudson's Bay Company

1837–40   Fort Chilcotin Post Journal. MS B.37/a/. Hudson's Bay Company Archives, Archives of Manitoba.

Hyde, George E.

1957 [1937]　*Red Cloud's Folk: A History of the Oglala Sioux Indians, Revised Edition.* Norman: University of Oklahoma Press.

1961　*Spotted Tail's Folk: A History of the Brulé Sioux.* Norman: University of Oklahoma Press.

Hymes, Dell

1981　*"In vain I tried to tell you": Essays in Native American Ethnopoetics.* Philadelphia: University of Pennsylvania Press.

Iktomi Hcala

1937　*America Needs Indians! (Unexpurgated Version).* Denver: Bradford-Robinson.

Indian Chiefs of Alberta

1970　*Citizens Plus.* Edmonton: Indian Association of Alberta.

Indian House Records

1970　*Songs of the Muskogee Creek, Part 1.* [IH 3001] Indian House Records, Taos, N.M.

Ingold, Tim

2000　*The Perception of the Environment. Essays in Livelihood, Dwelling and Skill.* New York: Routledge.

Iverson, Peter

1994　*When Indians Became Cowboys. Native Peoples and Cattle Ranching in the American West.* Norman: University of Oklahoma Press.

Jackson, Jason Baird

1997　Making Faces: Eastern Cherokee Booger Masks. *Gilcrease Journal* 5 (2): 50–61.

2000　Customary Uses of Ironweed (*Vernonia fasciculta*) by the Yuchi in Eastern Oklahoma, USA. *Economic Botany* 54 (3): 401–403.

2002a　Gender Reciprocity and Ritual Speech among the Yuchi. In *Southern Indians and Anthropologists: Culture, Politics, and Identity,* edited by Lisa J. Lefler and Frederic W. Gleach, pp. 89–106. Athens: University of Georgia Press.

2002b　*Spirit Medicine: Native American Uses of Common Everlasting* (Pseudognaphalium obtusifolium) *in Eastern North America.* Occasional Papers of the Sam Noble Oklahoma Museum of Natural History No. 13. Norman: Sam Noble Oklahoma Museum of Natural History.

2002c　A Yuchi War Dance in 1736. *European Review of Native American Studies* 16 (1): 27–32.

2003a　The Opposite of Powwow: Ignoring and Incorporating the Intertribal War Dance in the Oklahoma Stomp Dance Community. *Plains Anthropologist* 48 (187): 237–53.

2003b　*Yuchi Ceremonial Life: Performance, Meaning and Tradition in a Contemporary American Indian Community.* Lincoln: University of Nebraska Press.

2004   Recontextualizing Revitalization: Cosmology and Cultural Stability in the Adoption of Peyotism among the Yuchi. In *Reassessing Revitalization: Perspectives from North America and the Pacific Islands,* edited by Michael Harkin, pp. 183–205. Lincoln: University of Nebraska Press.

2007   The Paradoxical Power of Endangerment. *World Literature Today* 81 (5): 37–41.

Jackson, Jason Baird, and Mary S. Linn

2000   Calling in the Members: Linguistic Form and Cultural Context in a Yuchi Ritual Speech Genre. *Anthropological Linguistics* 42 (1): 61–80.

Jackson, Jason Baird, and Victoria Lindsay Levine

2002   Singing for Garfish: Music and Community Life in Eastern Oklahoma. *Ethnomusicology* 46 (2): 284–306.

Jackson, Michael

1998   *Minima Ethnographica: Intersubjectivity and the Anthropological Project.* Chicago: University of Chicago Press.

2007   *Excursions.* Durham: Duke University Press.

Jacobs, Melville

1959   *Content and Style of an Oral Literature: Clackamas Chinook Myths.* Chicago: University of Chicago Press.

Jacoby, Sally, and Elinore Ochs

1995   Co-Construction: An Introduction. *Research on Language and Social Interaction* 28 (3): 171–83.

Jahner, Elaine A.

1983   Introduction. In *Lakota Myth*, by James R. Walker, edited by Elaine A. Jahner, pp. 1–40. Lincoln: University of Nebraska Press.

1992   Transitional Narratives and Cultural Continuity. *boundary 2* 19 (3): 148–79.

Jameson, Fredric

1998   *The Cultural Turn: Selected Writings on the Postmodern, 1983–1998.* London: Verso.

Jolivétte, Andrew J.

2007   *Louisiana Creoles: Cultural Recovery and Mixed-Race Native American Identity.* Lanham: Lexington Books.

Jonaitis, Aldona

1995   Introduction: The Development of Franz Boas's Theories on Primitive Art. In *A Wealth of Thought: Franz Boas on Native American Art*, edited by Aldona Joanitis, pp. 3–36. Seattle: University of Washington Press.

Joynt, Carey B., and Nicholas Rescher

1961   The Problem of Uniqueness in History. *History and Theory* 1 (2): 150–62.

Kaeppler, Adrienne L.

1992   Dance. In *Folklore, Cultural Performances, and Popular Entertainments: A Communications-Centered Handbook,* edited by Richard Bauman, pp. 196–203. Oxford: Oxford University Press.

Kane, Paul

1971   *Paul Kane's Frontier; Including Wanderings of an Artist among the Indians of North America,* edited by J. Russell Harper. Austin: Published for the Amon Carter Museum, Fort Worth, and the National Gallery of Canada by the University of Texas Press.

Kavanaugh, Thomas W.

1991   Whose Village? Photographs of William S. Soule. *Visual Anthropology* 4: 1–24.

Keane, Webb

1999   Voice. *Journal of Linguistic Anthropology* 9 (1–2): 271–73.

Keenan, Jerry

1972   The Wagon Box Fight. *Journal of the West* 11: 51–74.

Kemp, Randall Harold

1909   *A Half-Breed Dance, and Other Far Western Stories: Mining Camp, Indian and Hudson's Bay Tales based on the Experiences of the Author.* Spokane: Inland Printing Co.

Kennedy, Michael

1961   *The Assiniboines: From the Accounts of the Old Ones Told to First Boy (James Larpenteur Long).* Norman: University of Oklahoma Press.

Khalid, Adeeb

2007   The Soviet Union as an Imperial Formation. A View from Central Asia. In *Imperial Formations,* edited by Ann Laura Stoler, Carole McGranaham, and Peter C. Perdue, pp. 113–39. Santa Fe: School for Advanced Research Press.

Kirshenblatt-Gimblett, Barbara

1995   Theorizing Heritage. *Ethnomusicology* 39 (3): 367–80.

1998   *Destination Culture: Tourism, Museums, and Heritage.* Berkeley: University of California Press.

Kniffen, Fred B.

1965   Folk Housing: Key to Diffusion. *Annals of the Association of American Geographers* 55 (4): 549–77.

Krech, Shepard, III

1991   The State of Ethnohistory. *Annual Review of Anthropology* 20: 345–75.

Kroeber, A. L.

1935   History and Science in Anthropology. *American Anthropologist* 37: 539–69.

1939 *Cultural and Natural Areas of Native North America.* University of California Publications in American Archaeology and Ethnology 38. Berkeley: University of California Press.

1963 [1948] *Anthropology: Culture Patterns and Processes.* New York: Harcourt, Brace, and World.

1991 Introduction. In *American Indian Life,* edited by Elsie Clews Parson, pp. 5–16. Lincoln: University of Nebraska Press.

Kulchyski, Peter

2005 *Like the Sound of a Drum: Aboriginal Cultural Politics in Denendeh and Nunavut.* Winnipeg: University of Manitoba Press.

Kunitz, Stephen J.

1971 The Social Philosophy of John Collier. *Ethnohistory* 18 (Summer): 213–29.

Kurkiala, Mikael

1997 *"Building the Nation Back Up." The Politics of Identity on the Pine Ridge Indian Reservation.* Acta Universitatis Upsaliensis, Uppsala Studies in Cultural Anthropology 22. Uppsala: University of Uppsala Press.

2002 Objectifying the Past: Lakota Responses to Western Historiography. *Critique of Anthropology* 4 (22): 445–60.

Lafond Historical Society

1981 *Dreams Become Realities: A History of Lafond and Surrounding Area.* Lafond, AB: Lafond Historical Committee.

LaGrand, James B.

2002 *Indian Metropolis: Native Americans in Chicago, 1945–75.* Urbana: University of Illinois Press.

Leach, Edmund

1976 *Culture and Communication: The Logic by Which Symbols Are Connected.* Cambridge: Cambridge University Press.

Leer, Jeff

1989 Directional Systems in Athabaskan and Na-Dene. In *Athapaskan Linguistics, Current Perspectives on a Language Family,* edited by Keren Rice and Eung Do Cook, pp. 575–622. New York: Mouton.

Lesser, Alexander

1933 *The Pawnee Ghost Dance Handgame: A Study of Culture Change.* New York: Columbia University Press.

Lévi-Strauss, Claude

1960 Four Winnebago Myths: A Structural Sketch. In *Culture in History: Essays in Honor of Paul Radin,* edited by Stanley Diamond, pp. 351–62. New York: Columbia University Press.

1963 *Structural Anthropology.* New York: Basic Books.

1966 *The Savage Mind.* Chicago: University of Chicago Press.

1967 Le Sexe des Astres. In *To Honor Roman Jakobson: Essays on the Occasion of His Seventieth Birthday*, pp. 1163–70. The Hague: Mouton.

1969 *The Elementary Structures of Kinship.* Boston: Beacon Press.

1970 *The Raw and the Cooked.* New York: Harper and Row.

1992 *Tristes Tropiques.* New York: Penguin Books.

1997 *Look, Listen, Read.* New York: Harper Collins.

Levine, Emily

1998 Introduction. In *With My Own Eyes: A Lakota Woman Tells Her People's History,* by Susan Bordeaux Bettelyoun and Josephine Waggoner, edited by Emily Levine, pp. xv–xl. Lincoln: University of Nebraska Press.

Levine, Victoria Lindsay

1990 Choctaw Indian Musical Cultures in the Twentieth Century. PhD dissertation, University of Illinois at Urbana-Champaign. University Microfilms, Ann Arbor.

1991 Arzelie Langley and a Lost Pantribal Tradition. In *Ethnomusicology and Modern Music History,* edited by Stephen Blum, Philip V. Bohlman, and Daniel M. Newman, pp. 190–206. Chicago: University of Chicago Press.

2004a Choctaw at Ardmore, Oklahoma. In *Southeast,* edited by Raymond D. Fogelson, pp. 531–33. *Handbook of North American Indians,* Vol. 14, William C. Sturtevant, general editor. Washington, D.C.: Smithsonian Institution.

2004b Music. In *Southeast,* edited by Raymond D. Fogelson, pp. 720–33. *Handbook of North American Indians,* Vol. 14, William C. Sturtevant, general editor. Washington, D.C.: Smithsonian Institution.

Linnekin, Jocelyn

1983 Defining Tradition: Variations on the Hawaiian Identity. *American Ethnologist* 10: 241–52.

Linton, Ralph

1936 Status and Role. In *The Study of Man,* pp. 113–31. New York: Appleton-Century-Crofts, Inc.

Livingston, Tamara

1999 Musical Revivals: Toward a General Theory. *Ethnomusicology* 43 (1): 66–85.

Looby, Christopher

1996 *Voicing America: Language, Literary Form, and the Origins of the United States.* Chicago: University of Chicago Press.

Lowenthal, David

1996 *Possessed by the Past: The Heritage Crusade and the Spoils of History.* New York: The Free Press.

1998 Fabricating Heritage. *History & Memory* 10 (1): 6–22.

Lowie, Robert

1912   *Chipewyan Tales.* New York: American Museum of Natural History.

1940   *An Introduction to Cultural Anthropology.* 2nd edition. New York: Farrar and Rinehart.

1983 [1935]   *The Crow Indians.* Lincoln: University of Nebraska Press.

Macbeth, R. G.

1897   *The Selkirk Settlers in Real Life.* Toronto: W. Briggs.

MacGregor, Gordon

1946   *Warriors without Weapons: A Study of the Society and Personality Development of the Pine Ridge Sioux.* Chicago: University of Chicago Press.

Mackie, James

1993   History of the Society. In *Pioneer Families of Southern Alberta.* Calgary: Southern Alberta Pioneers and their Descendants.

2010   About Us. Southern Alberta Pioneers Association. http://www.pioneersalberta.org/about_us.html (accessed September 3, 2010).

Malinowski, Bronislaw

1934   Stone Implements in Eastern New Guinea. In *Essays Presented to C.G. Seligmann,* edited by E. E. Evans-Pritchard, Raymond Firth, Bronislaw Malinowski, and Isaac Schapera, pp. 189–96. London: Kegan Paul, Trench, Trubner and Co.

Manning, Frank E.

1992   Spectacle. In *Folklore, Cultural Performances, and Popular Entertainments: A Communications-Centered Handbook,* edited by Richard Bauman, pp. 291–99. Oxford: Oxford University Press.

Marble, Maton

1860   Red River and Beyond. *Harper's New Monthly Magazine,* August 21 (123): 289–311; October 21 (125): 581–606.

Margry, Pierre (editor)

1876–86   *Découvertes et établissements des Français dans l'ouest et dans le sud de l'Amérique septentionale, 1614–1754.* Mémoires et documents originaux. 6 Vols. Paris: D. Jouaust.

Marsalis, Wynton

1995   *Marsalis on Music.* New York: W.W. Norton & Company, Inc.

2008   *Moving to Higher Ground: How Jazz Can Change Your Life.* New York: Random House.

Marshall, Joe

1992   The Lakota (Western Sioux) in 1868. In *The Historical Significance of the Fort Phil Kearny Sites,* edited by Patty Myers and Mary Ellen McWilliams, pp. 41–44. Story, Wyo.: Fort Phil Kearny/Bozeman Trail Days Association.

Mauss, Marcel

    1990 [1950]   *The Gift: The Form and Reason for Exchange in Archaic Societies.* New York: Norton.

McCrady, David

    2006   *Living with Strangers: The Nineteenth-Century Sioux and the Canadian-American Borderlands.* Lincoln: University of Nebraska Press.

McCreight, Major Israel, and Flying Hawk

    1947   *Firewater and Forked Tongues; a Sioux Chief Interprets U.S. History.* Pasadena, Calif.: Trail's End Pub. Co. Inc.

McDermott, John Dishon, Jr.

    1965   James Bordeaux. In *Mountain Men and the Fur Trade of the Far West,* edited by LeRoy R. Hafen, pp. 65–80. Glendale, Calif.: A. H. Clark.

McKinley, Robert

    2001   The Philosophy of Kinship: A Reply to Schneider's *Critique of the Study of Kinship.* In *The Cultural Analysis of Kinship: The Legacy of David M. Schneider,* edited by Richard Feinberg and Martin Oppenheimer, pp. 131–67. Urbana: University of Illinois Press.

Meadowcraft, Enid La Monte

    1954   *The Story of Crazy Horse.* New York: Grosset & Dunlap.

Meandering Michael

    2009   Michael's Meanderings: 22nd Annual Yukon Stick Gambling Championships. http://www.michaelsmeanderings.com/2009/08 /22nd -annual-yukon-stick-gambling.html (accessed December 15, 2012).

Mekeel, Haviland Scudder

    1930–31   Field Notes Summer of 1930–31, White Clay District, Pine Ridge Reservation, South Dakota. Department of Anthropology, American Museum of Natural History, New York.

Mercatante, Frank

    1974   Introduction. In *Sitting Bull: Tanka-Iyotaka*, by William Bordeaux, p. 1. Grand Rapids, Michigan: Custer Ephemera Society.

Meyer, Melissa L., and Kerwin Lee Klein

    1998   Native American Studies and the End of Ethnohistory. In *Studying Native America: Problems and Prospects*, edited by Russell Thornton, pp. 182–216. Madison: University of Wisconsin Press.

Mignolo, Walter and Arturo Escobar (editors)

    2007   Globalization and the De-Colonial Option. *Cultural Studies* 21: 2–3.

Miller, Jay

    1997   Old Religion among the Delawares: The Gamwing (Big House Rite). *Ethnohistory* 44 (1): 113–34.

Mommsen, Wolfgang J.

1978   Social Conditioning and Social Relevance of Historical Judgments. *History and Theory* 17 (4): 19–35.

Moore, Patrick

2002   Point of View in Kaska Historical Narratives. PhD dissertation, Indiana University.

Moore, Patrick, and Daniel Tlen

2007   Indigenous Linguistics and Land Claims: The Semiotic Projection of Athabaskan Directionals in Elijah Smith's Radio Work. *Journal of Linguistic Anthropology* 17 (2): 266–86.

Morice, A. G.

1978 [1906]   *The History of the Northern Interior of British Columbia.* Smithers, BC: Interior Stationary Limited.

Morgan, Mindy J.

2005   Constructions and Contestations of the Authoritative Voice: Native American Communities and the Federal Writers' Project, 1935–41. *American Indian Quarterly* 29 (1–2): 56–83.

Munro, Pamela, and Catherine Willmond

1994   *Chickasaw: An Analytic Dictionary.* Norman: University of Oklahoma Press.

Nahachewsky, Andriy

2001   Once Again: On the Concept of "Second Existence Folk Dance." *Yearbook for Traditional Music* 33: 17–28.

Neihardt, John G.

1932   *Black Elk Speaks: Being the Life Story of a Holy Man of the Ogalala Sioux.* New York: William Morrow [see *Black Elk Speaks: Being the Life Story of a Holy Man of the Oglala Sioux: The Premier Edition,* as told through John G. Neihardt (Flaming Rainbow), annotated by Raymond J. DeMallie, with illustrations by Standing Bear. Albany: State University of New York Press, 2008].

Nelson, Grace

1958   Time, Arthritis Slow Fingers of Artist. *Argus Leader,* May 11, 1958, p. C5.

Nerdball3

2008   21st Annual Yukon Stick Gambling Competition. YouTube. http://www.youtube.com/watch?playnext=1&index=2&feature=PlayList&v=VeXAkC7xhPk&list=PL075F02DABB3447F2 (accessed December 18, 2012).

Niezen, Ronald

2003   *The Origins of Indigenism: Human Rights and the Politics of Identity.* Berkeley: University of California Press.

2004   *A World beyond Difference: Cultural Identity in the Age of Globalization.* Malden, Mass.: Blackwell.

Noble, David W.

1971   *The Progressive Mind, 1890–1917.* Chicago: Rand McNally.

Norris, Frank

2002   *Alaska Subsistence: A National Park Service Management History.* Alaska Support Office, National Park Service, U.S. Department of the Interior. http://www.cr.nps.gov/history/online_books/norris1/ (accessed August 8, 2011).

Northern Alberta Pioneers and Descendants Association

n.d.   About Us. http://www.northernalbertapioneers.com/about-us.asp (accessed September 3, 2010).

Noyes, Dorothy

2003a   *Fire in the Plaça: Catalan Festival Politics after Franco.* Philadelphia: University of Pennsylvania Press.

2003b   Group. In *Eight Words for the Study of Expressive Culture,* edited by Burt Feintuch, pp. 7–41. Urbana: University of Illinois Press.

2012   The Social Base of Folklore. In *A Companion to Folklore,* edited by Regina F. Bendix and Galit Hasan-Rokem, pp. 13–39. Malden, Mass.: Wiley-Blackwell.

Noyes, Dorothy, and Regina Bendix

1998   In Modern Dress: Costuming the European Social Body, 17th–20th Centuries. *Journal of American Folklore* 111 (440): 107–14.

Ohnuki-Tierney, Emiko

1990   Introduction: The Historicization of Anthropology. In *Culture through Time: Anthropological Approaches,* edited by Emiko Ohnuki-Tierney, pp. 1–25. Stanford: Stanford University Press.

Olson, James C.

1965   *Red Cloud and the Sioux Problem.* Lincoln: University of Nebraska Press.

Olwig, Karen F.

1999   The Burden of Heritage: Claiming a Place for a West Indian Culture. *American Ethnologist* 26 (2): 370–88.

Ortiz, Roxanne Dunbar (editor)

1977   *The Great Sioux Nation. Sitting in Judgment on America: An Oral History of the Sioux Nation and Its Struggle for Sovereignty.* New York: The American Indian Treaty Council Information Center and Berkeley: Moon Books.

Parks, Douglas R.

1988   The Importance of Language Study for the Writing of Plains Indian History. In *New Directions in American Indian History,* edited by Colin Calloway, pp. 153–97. Norman: University of Oklahoma Press.

1999   George A. Dorsey, James R. Murie, and the Textual Documentation of Skiri Pawnee. In *Theorizing the Americanist Tradition,* edited by

Lisa Philips Valentine and Regna Darnell, pp. 227–44. Toronto: University of Toronto Press.

Parks, Douglas R., and Raymond J. DeMallie

1992a   Plains Indian Native Literatures. *boundary 2*, 19 (3): 105–47.

⯈ 1992b   Sioux, Assiniboine, and Stoney Dialects: A Classification. *Anthropological Linguistics* 34 (1–4): 233–55.

Parsons, Elsie Clews (editor)

1991 [1922]   *American Indian Life.* Lincoln: University of Nebraska Press.

Passmore, John

1987   Narratives and Events. *History and Theory* 26 (4): 68–74.

Peacock, James

2005   Geertz's Concept of Culture in Historical Context: How He Saved the Day and Maybe the Century. In *Clifford Geertz by His Colleagues,* edited by Richard A. Shweder and Byron Good, pp. 52–62. Chicago: University of Chicago Press.

Pirsig, Robert M.

1992   *Lila: An Inquiry into Morals.* New York: Bantam Books.

Plumwood, Val

2000   Deep Ecology, Deep Pockets, and Deep Problems: A Feminist Ecosocialist Analysis. In *Beneath the Surface: Critical Essays in the Philosophy of Deep Ecology,* edited by Eric Katz, Andrew Light and David Rothernberg, pp. 59–84. Cambridge, Mass.: MIT Press.

Quick, Sarah

2009   Performing Heritage: Métis Music, Dance and Identity in a Multicultural State. PhD dissertation, Indiana University.

2012   "Frontstage" and "Backstage" in Heritage Performance: What Ethnography Reveals. *Canadian Theatre Review* 151 (Summer): 24–29.

Radin, Paul

1911   The Ritual and Significance of the Winnebago Medicine Dance. *Journal of American Folklore* 24 (92):149–208.

1963 [1923]   *The Autobiography of a Winnebago Indian. Life, Ways, Acculturation, and the Peyote Cult.* New York: Dover.

1987 [1966]   *The Method and Theory of Ethnology: An Essay in Criticism.* South Hadley, Mass.: Bergin and Garvey Publishers.

Rappaport, Roy A.

1992   Ritual. In *Folklore, Cultural Performances, and Popular Entertainments: A Communications-Centered Handbook,* edited by Richard Bauman, pp. 249–260. Oxford: Oxford University Press.

1999   *Ritual and Religion in the Making of Humanity.* Cambridge: Cambridge University Press.

Ray, Arthur J.

2005 [1974]   *Indians in the Fur Trade.* Toronto: University of Toronto Press.

Reed, Ann

> 2011 [2009]   Interview with Merry Ketterling. On Disk 1 of three companion DVDs to Sebastian F. Braun, Gregory Gagnon and Birgit Hans, *Native American Studies: An Interdisciplinary Introduction.* Dubuque: Kendall/Hunt.

Regular, W. Keith

> 2009   *Neighbours and Networks: The Blood Tribe in the Southern Alberta Economy, 1884–1939.* Calgary: University of Calgary Press.

Restall, Matthew

> 2003a   *Seven Myths of the Spanish Conquest.* Oxford: Oxford University Press.

> 2003b   History of the New Philology and the New Philology in History. *Latin American Research Review,* 38 (1): 113–34.

Reynolds, Katherine Caddock

> 1998   *Visions and Vanities: John Andrew Rice of Black M*ountain College. Baton Rouge: Louisiana State University Press.

Ricker, Eli Seavey

> 2005   *The Indian Interviews of Eli S. Ricker, 1903–1919,* edited by Richard E Jensen. Lincoln: University of Nebraska Press.

Ricoeur, Paul

> 1981   The Narrative Function. In *Hermeneutics and the Social Sciences,* edited by Paul Ricoeur, pp. 274–305. Cambridge: Cambridge University Press.

Ridington, Robin

> 1968   The Medicine Fight: An Instrument of Political Process among the Beaver Indians. *American Anthropologist* 70 (6): 1152–60.

Riggs, Stephen Return

> 1893   Dakota Grammar, Texts, and Ethnography. In *Contributions to North American Ethnology,* Vol. 9. U.S. Geographical and Geological Survey of the Rocky Mountains Region, Department of the Interior. Washington, D.C.: Government Printing Office.

Riney, Scott

> 1999   *The Rapid City Indian School, 1898–1933.* Norman: University of Oklahoma Press.

Robinson, H. M.

> 1879   *The Great Fur Land, or, Sketches of Life in the Hudson's Bay Territory.* New York: G.P. Putnam's Sons.

Roginsky, Dina

> 2007   Folklore, Folklorism, and Synchronization: Preserved-Created Folklore in Israel. *Journal of Folklore Research* 44 (1): 41–66.

Rosaldo, Renato

> 1980   *Ilongot Headhunting, 1883–1974: A Study in Society and History.* Stanford: Stanford University Press.

Royce, Anya Peterson

2002 [1977]   *The Anthropology of Dance.* Hampshire, UK: Dance Books, Ltd.

Ruoff, A. LaVonne Brown

1991   Introduction. In *Old Indian Days,* by Charles Eastman, pp. ix–xxiv. Lincoln: University of Nebraska Press.

Sahlins, Marshall

1981   *Historical Metaphors and Mythical Realities: Structure in the Early History of the Sandwich Islands Kingdom.* Ann Arbor: University of Michigan Press.

2000   *Culture in Practice: Selected Essays.* New York: Zone Books.

Sandoz, Mari

1942   *Crazy Horse: The Strange Man of the Oglalas.* New York: Alfred E. Knopf.

Sapir, Edward

1916   *Time Perspective in Aboriginal American Culture: A Study in Method.* Canada Department of Mines, Geological Survey Memoir 90. Anthropological Series 13. Ottawa: Government Printing Bureau.

Sapir, Edward, and Harry Hoijer

1942   *Navajo Texts.* Iowa City: Linguistic Society of America

Scherer, Joanna Cohen (editor)

1990   Picturing Cultures: Historical Photographs in Anthropological Inquiry. *Visual Anthropology* 3 (2–3).

Schneider, David M.

1984   *A Critique of the Study of Kinship.* Ann Arbor: University of Michigan Press.

Schneider, Manfred

1987   Liturgien der Erinnerung, Techniken des Vergessens. *Merkur* 41 (8): 676–86.

Schouls, Tim

2003   *Shifting Boundaries: Aboriginal Identity, Pluralist Theory, and the Politics of Self-Government.* Vancouver: UBC Press.

Sharfstein, Daniel J.

2003   The Secret History of Race in the United States. *The Yale Law Journal* 112: 1473–1509.

Sharp, Henry S.

2001   *Loon: Memory, Meaning, and Reality in a Northern Dene Community.* Lincoln: University of Nebraska Press.

Sheldon, Addison E.

1941   A Memorial to the Sioux Nation. *Nebraska History: Sioux Memorial Issue* 22 (1): 39–44.

Sherzer, Joel, and Anthony C. Woodbury (editors)

1987   *Native American Discourse: Poetics and Rhetoric.* Cambridge: Cambridge University Press.

Shoemaker, Nancy

2004   *A Strange Likeness: Becoming Red and White in Eighteenth-Century North America.* Oxford: Oxford University Press.

Silverstein, Michael

1993   Metapragmatic Discourse and Metapragmatic Function. In *Reflexive Language: Reported Speech and Metapragmatics,* edited by John A. Lucy, pp. 33–58. Cambridge: Cambridge University Press.

1997   Encountering Language and Languages of Encounter in North American Ethnohistory. *Journal of Linguistic Anthropology* 6 (2): 126–44.

1998   Contemporary Transformations of Local Linguistic Communities. *Annual Review of Anthropology* 27: 401–26.

1999   NIMBY Goes Linguistic: Conflicted "Voicings" from the Culture of Local Language Communities. Paper presented to the Department of English/Discourse Studies, Texas A&M University.

Simmons, William S.

1988   Culture Theory in Contemporary Ethnohistory. *Ethnohistory* 35: 1–14.

Singer, Beverly

2001   *Wiping the Warpaint Off the Lens: Native American Film and Video.* Minneapolis: University of Minnesota Press.

Slickpoo, Allen P., and Deward E. Walker, Jr.

1973   *Noon Nee-me-poo (We the Nez Perces): Culture and History of the Nez Perces.* Lepwai, Idaho: Nez Perce Tribe of Idaho.

Sneve, Virginia Driving Hawk

1995   *Completing the Circle.* Lincoln: University of Nebraska Press.

Speck, Frank G.

1945   *The Celestial Bear Comes Down to Earth: The Bear Sacrifice Ceremony of the Munsee-Mahican in Canada as Related by Nekatcit.* Reading, Pa.: Reading Public Museum and Art Gallery.

1950   *Concerning Iconology and the Masking Complex in Eastern North America.* Philadelphia: University Museum, University of Pennsylvania.

Speck, Frank G., and Leonard Broom (in collaboration with Will West Long)

1951   *Cherokee Dance and Drama.* Berkeley: University of California Press.

Spence, Mark David

1999   *Dispossessing the Wilderness: Indian Removal and the Making of National Parks.* Oxford: Oxford University Press.

Sprague, Donovin Arleigh

2005   *Rosebud Sioux: Images of America.* Chicago: Arcadia Publishing.

Standing Bear, Luther

1975 [1928]   *My People the Sioux.* Lincoln: University of Nebraska Press.

Stauffer, Helen Winter (editor)

1992 *Letters of Mari Sandoz.* Lincoln: University of Nebraska Press.

Steward, Julian H.

1936 The Economic and Social Basis of Primitive Bands. In *Essays in Anthropology Presented to A.L. Kroeber,* edited by Robert H. Lowie, pp. 331–50. Berkeley: University of California Press.

Stocking, George W., Jr.

n.d. About the Department: History. http://anthropology.uchicago.edu /about/history.shtml (accessed September 10, 2009).

1992 *The Ethnographer's Magic and Other Essays in the History of Anthropology.* Madison: University of Wisconsin Press.

Stoeltje, Beverly J.

1992 Festival. In *Folklore, Cultural Performances, and Popular Entertainments: A Communications-Centered Handbook,* edited by Richard Bauman, pp. 261–71. Oxford: Oxford University Press.

Stoler, Ann Laura

2009 *Along the Archival Grain: Epistemic Anxieties and Colonial Common Sense.* Princeton: Princeton University Press.

Strang, Veronica

1997 *Uncommon Ground. Cultural Landscapes and Environmental Values.* Oxford: Berg.

Sturtevant, William C.

1955 The Mikasuki Seminole: Medical Beliefs and Practices. PhD dissertation, Yale University. University Microfilms, Ann Arbor.

1966 Anthropology, History, and Ethnohistory. *Ethnohistory* 13 (1–2): 1–51.

1968 Lafitau's Hoes. *American Antiquity* 33 (1): 93–95.

Swanton, John R.

1908 Social Conditions, Beliefs and Linguistic Relationship of the Tlingit Indians. Pp. 391–485 in *26th Annual Report of the Bureau of Ethnology for the Years 1904–1905.* Washington, D.C.

1928a Religious Beliefs and Medical Practices of the Creek Indians. *Annual Report of the Bureau of American Ethnology* 42: 473–672.

1928b Social and Religious Beliefs and Usages of the Chickasaw Indians. *Annual Report of the Bureau of American Ethnology* 44: 173–273.

1931 *Source Material for the Social and Ceremonial Life of the Choctaw Indians.* Bureau of American Ethnology Bulletin No. 103. Washington, D.C.: Government Printing Office.

Tanner, Helen Hornbeck

2007 In the Arena. An Expert Witness View of the Indian Claims Commission. In *Beyond Red Power: American Indian Politics and Activism since 1900,* edited by Daniel M. Cobb and Loretta Fowler, pp. 178–200. Santa Fe: SAR Press.

Taylor, Mark C.

1986   Introduction: System . . . Structure . . . Difference . . . Other. In *Deconstruction in Context: Literature and Philosophy,* edited by Mark C. Taylor, pp. 1–34. Chicago: University of Chicago Press.

Tedlock, Dennis

1983   *The Spoken Word and the Work of Interpretation.* Philadelphia: University of Pennsylvania Press.

1999   *Finding the Center: The Art of the Zuni Storyteller.* Lincoln: University of Nebraska Press.

Thiong'o, Ngũgĩ

1986   *Decolonizing the Mind: The Politics of Language in African Literature.* New Hampshire: Heinemann.

Thompson, Niobe

2008   *Settlers on the Edge: Identity and Modernization on Russia's Arctic Frontier.* Vancouver: UBC Press.

Thornton, Thomas F.

2008   *Being and Place among the Tlingit.* Seattle: University of Washington Press.

Todorov, Tzvetan

1992   *The Conquest of America: The Question of the Other.* New York: Harper Collins.

Tonkin, Elizabeth

1992   Mask. In *Folklore, Cultural Performances, and Popular Entertainments: A Communications-Centered Handbook,* edited by Richard Bauman, pp. 225–32. Oxford: Oxford University Press.

Trigger, Bruce G.

1986   Ethnohistory: The Unfinished Edifice. *Ethnohistory* 33 (3): 253–67.

Trouillot, Michel-Rolph

1995   *Silencing the Past: Power and the Production of History.* Boston: Beacon Press.

Troutman, John

2007   The Citizenship of Dance. Politics of Music among the Lakota, 1900–1924. In *Beyond Red Power: American Indian Politics and Activism since 1900,* edited by Daniel M. Cobb and Loretta Fowler, pp. 91–108. Santa Fe: School for Advanced Research Press.

Turino, Thomas

2008   *Music as Social Life: The Politics of Participation.* Chicago: University of Chicago Press.

Turkel, William J.

2007   *The Archive of Place: Unearthing the Pasts of the Chilcotin Plateau.* Vancouver: UBC Press.

Urban, Greg and Jason Baird Jackson

    2004   Social Organization. In *Southeast,* edited by Raymond D. Fogelson, pp. 697–706. *Handbook of North American Indians,* Vol. 14, William C. Sturtevant, general editor. Washington, D.C.: Smithsonian Institution.

Veyne, Paul

    1988   *Did the Greeks Believe in Their Myths? An Essay on the Constitutive Imagination.* Chicago: The University of Chicago Press.

Voegelin, Erminie W.

    1954   An Ethnohistorian's Viewpoint. *Ethnohistory* 1 (2): 166–71.

Wade, Mason (editor)

    1947   *The Journals of Francis Parkman.* 2 vols. New York: Harper and Brothers.

Wagoner, Paula L.

    2002   *"They treated us just like Indians." The Worlds of Bennett County, South Dakota.* Lincoln: University of Nebraska Press.

Walker, James R.

    1980   *Lakota Belief and Ritual,* edited by Raymond J. DeMallie and Elaine A. Jahner. Lincoln: University of Nebraska Press.

    1982   *Lakota Society,* edited by Raymond J. DeMallie. Lincoln: University of Nebraska Press.

    1983   *Lakota Myth,* edited by Elaine A. Jahner. Lincoln: University of Nebraska Press [see DeMallie's introduction to the 1989 reprint edition].

Wallis, Wilson D.

    1930   *Culture and Progress.* New York: Whittlesey House.

Waselkov, Gregory A.

    2004   Exchange and Interaction since A.D. 1500. In *Southeast,* edited by Raymond D. Fogelson, pp. 686–96. *Handbook of North American Indians,* Vol. 14, William C. Sturtevant, general editor. Washington, D.C.: Smithsonian Institution.

Washburn, Wilcomb E.

    1961   Ethnohistory: History "in the Round." *Ethnohistory* 8 (1): 31–48.

Webster, Anthony

    2009   *Explorations in Navajo Poetry and Poetics.* Albuquerque: University of New Mexico Press.

Wedel, Mildred Mott

    1974   Le Sueur and the Dakota Sioux. In *Aspects of Great Lakes Anthropology: Papers in Honor of Lloyd A. Wilford*, edited by Elden Johnson, pp. 157–71. St. Paul: Minnesota Historical Society.

    1976   Ethnohistory: Its Payoffs and Pitfalls for Iowa Archeologists. *Journal of the Iowa Archeological Society* (25): 49–77.

Wedel, Mildred Mott, and Raymond J. DeMallie

1980   The Ethnohistorical Approach in Plains Area Studies. In *Anthropology on the Great Plains,* edited by W. Raymond Wood and Margot Liberty, pp. 110–28. Lincoln: University of Nebraska Press.

Wedel, Waldo R.

1938   The Direct Historical Approach in Pawnee Archeology. *Smithsonian Miscellaneous Collections* 97 (7): 1–21.

Weismann, Donald L.

1984   *Duncan Phyfe and Drum with Notes for the Bugle Corps.* Bryn Mawr, Pa.: Dorrance and Company.

White, Richard

1983   *Roots of Dependency: Subsistence, Environment, and Social Change among the Choctaws, Pawnees, and Navajos.* Lincoln: University of Nebraska Press.

2001 [1991]   *The Middle Ground: Indians, Empire, and Republics in the Great Lakes Region, 1650–1815.* Cambridge: Cambridge University Press.

Whiteley, Peter M.

2004   Why Anthropology Needs More History. *Journal of Anthropological Research* 60 (4): 487–514.

Wilson, Everett Pitt

1941   The Story of Oglala and Brule Sioux in the Pine Ridge Country of Northwest Nebraska in the Middle Seventies. *Nebraska History: Sioux Memorial Issue* 22 (1): 15–33.

Wilson, Raymond

1983   *Ohiyesa: Charles Eastman, Santee Sioux.* Urbana: University of Illinois Press.

Wissler, Clark

1971 [1938]   *Red Man Reservations.* New York: Collier Books.

Wolf, Eric R.

1982   *Europe and the People without History.* Berkeley: University of California Press.

Yeager, Anson

1948   Crazy Horse's Story Is Chronicled Here. *Argus Leader,* May 2, 1948, p. 28.

Yoder, Don

1976   Folklife Studies in American Scholarship. In *American Folklife,* edited by Don Yoder, pp. 3–18. Austin: University of Texas Press.

Yukon Native Brotherhood

1973   *Together Today for Our Children Tomorrow: A Statement of Grievances and an Approach to Settlement by the Yukon Indian People.* Whitehorse: Yukon Native Brotherhood.

yukonfawn

2008   21st Annual Yukon Stick Gambling Competition. YouTube. http://www.youtube.com/watch?v=VeXAkC7xhPk (accessed December 16, 2012).

2009   22nd Annual Yukon Stick Gambling Competition. YouTube. http://www.youtube.com/watch?v=52YlcRmNjWE (accessed December 16, 2012).

Zelinsky, Wilbur

1958   The New England Connecting Barn. *Geographical Review* 48 (4): 540–53.

Zitkala-Sa

1985a   *American Indian Stories.* Lincoln: University of Nebraska Press.

1985b   *Old Indian Legends.* Lincoln: University of Nebraska Press.

Contributors

Sebastian Felix Braun studied ethnology, history, and philosophy at Universität Basel, Switzerland, before taking his PhD in anthropology from Indiana University. He is associate professor and chair of the Department of American Indian Studies at the University of North Dakota. Braun is the author of *Buffalo Inc. American Indians and Economic Development* (University of Oklahoma Press, 2008), and, among other things, has written for the International Work Group for Indigenous Affairs' (IWGIA) *The Indigenous World* since 2004. His current interests are with the impacts of oil extraction on rural and Native communities in North Dakota and the West.

Raymond Bucko earned his PhD in anthropology from the University of Chicago. He is professor of anthropology and Native American studies in the Department of Sociology, Anthropology, and Social Work at Creighton University, and currently Visiting Research Scholar at Fordham University. He co-founded the Lakota Immersion Mentorship Program and was the director of Native American studies at Creighton. Bucko is a member of the Red Cloud Pastoral Ministry and of the Red Cloud Heritage Center commission. Apart from many articles, he is the author of *The Lakota Ritual of the Sweat Lodge. History and Contemporary Practice* (University of Nebraska Press, 1998).

Raymond J. DeMallie is Chancellor's Professor in the anthropology department at Indiana University, where he is also the co-director of the American Indian Studies Research Institute, and curator of North American ethnology at the Mathers Museum. Among many other publications, he is the author and editor of numerous books, including the Plains volumes of the *Handbook of North American Indians* (Smithsonian 2001), *The Sixth Grandfather* (Nebraska 1984), with Douglas Parks of *Sioux Indian Religion* (Oklahoma 1987), with Alfonso Ortiz of *North American Indian Anthropology* (Oklahoma 1994), with Vine Deloria, Jr. of *Documents of American Indian Diplomacy* (Oklahoma 1999), and as an annotator of *Black Elk Speaks* (SUNY 2008).

David W. Dinwoodie received a PhD in anthropology from the University of Chicago. He is associate professor of anthropology at the University of

New Mexico. His interests include the political, cultural dynamics of the greater Pacific Northwest, the history and politics of culture in Canada, historical anthropology, and language and communication. Dinwoodie's publications include articles in Anthropological Linguistics, Cultural Anthropology, Ethnohistory, and Histories of Anthropology Annual, and he is the author of *Reserve Memories: The Power of the Past in a Chilcotin Community* (Nebraska 2002).

Raymond Fogelson is professor of anthropology, of human development, and of social sciences at the University of Chicago. He is the editor of the Southeast volume of the *Handbook of North American Indians* (Smithsonian 2004), as well as author and editor of numerous articles and books on ethnohistory, Cherokee history and culture, and related interests. Among them are (with Richard Adams) *The Anthropology of Power* (Academic Press 1977), and *The Cherokees: A Critical Bibliography* (Indiana 1978). He has contributed to many edited volumes and journals from *Ethnohistory* to *Anthropological Linguistics*.

Kellie J. Hogue is a research associate with the American Indian Studies Research Institute (AISRI) at Indiana University, Bloomington. She received her PhD in anthropology and American studies from Indiana University. Her dissertation explored ideas of kinship, identity, and pilgrimage within the contemporary context of the modern movement to canonize Kateri Tekakwitha, a 17th century Native woman. Hogue has published in the *Journal de la Société des Américanistes*. She is currently working on a study of representations of Native females in the Jesuit Relations. Her interests include kinship, identity, race/ethnicity, religion, and ethnohistorical method and theory.

Jason Baird Jackson is director of the Mathers Museum of World Cultures at Indiana University, where he is also an associate professor of folklore. His interests span folklore studies, museum work, linguistic anthropology, ethnohistory, and cultural anthropology. He holds a PhD from Indiana and has collaborated in research with Woodland Indian communities in Oklahoma since 1993. Jackson is the author of *Yuchi Ceremonial Life: Performance, Meaning, and Tradition in a Contemporary Native American Community* (University of Nebraska Press, 2003) and the editor of *Yuchi Indian Histories Before the Removal Era* (University of Nebraska Press, 2012) as well as the journal Museum Anthropology Review.

David Reed Miller earned an MA in history from the University of North Dakota and a PhD in anthropology from Indiana University. He was dean of instruction at Fort Peck Community College and a postdoctoral fellow at the Smithsonian before joining the First Nations University as head of the department of Indian studies. His most recent work (with Dennis Smith, Joseph McGeshick, James Shanley, and Caleb Shields), *The History of the Assiniboine and Sioux Tribes of the Fort Peck Indian Reservation, Montana, 1800-2000* (FPCC 2008) showcases his long-established mastery of great plains Native histories and cultures, especially Assiniboine and Sioux, as well as his commitment to deep ethnohistorical, collaborative work with Native communities.

Patrick Moore is an associate professor of anthropology at the University of British Columbia. His work has focused on the languages and oral traditions of Northern Athabaskans in Alberta, British Columbia, and the Yukon where he lived from 1976 until 2001. He has participated in collaborative digital language and culture documentation and archiving projects with the Kaska, Tagish/Tlingit, and Beaver First Nations (www.virtualmuseum.ca /Exhibitions/Danewajich). He is the author (with Angela Wheelock) of *Wolverine Myths and Visions. Dene Traditions from Northern Alberta* (University of Nebraska Press 1990).

Mindy Morgan is associate professor of anthropology and an affiliated faculty member of the American Indian studies program at Michigan State University. She received her Ph.D. in anthropology from Indiana University. Her book, *"The Bearer of This Letter": Language Ideologies, Literacy Practices, and the Fort Belknap Indian Community* was published by University of Nebraska Press in 2009. Ethnohistorical research conducted in the course of this project led her to investigate tribal members' participation in the Federal Writers' Program in the late 1930s and early 1940s throughout Montana. She is currently working on a new project stemming from this research regarding the periodical, *Indians At Work,* published by the Office of Indian Affairs between 1933 and 1945.

Sarah Quick is assistant professor of anthropology and sociology at Cottey College. She earned a PhD in anthropology from Indiana University, and an MA in anthropology from University of Missouri. Her research focuses on Métis culture and history, performance studies, dance, ethnomusicology, and heritage. She has published in the Canadian journals *Ethnologies* and *Canadian Theatre Review* and is currently preparing a manuscript based on her doctoral research for the series *Folklore Studies in a Multicultural World.* She also researches the slow food movement and heritage ideals through food and is active in the Rock Hill Educational Community Garden.

Paula L. Wagoner received her PhD in anthropology from Indiana University. She taught at Oglala Lakota College and is currently associate professor of anthropology at Juniata College. She is the author of *They Treated Us Just Like Indians* (University of Nebraska Press, 2002). Her research has focused on Great Plains Native cultures and histories, cultural pluralism, relationships between communities, treaties, and the cultural attachment to place. More recently, she has done research on chemical weapons in the United States and the way communities surrounding facilities perceive their storage, disposal, and existence.

Index

CPSIA information can be obtained at www.ICGtesting.com
Printed in the USA
LVOW08s0948120813

347449LV00004B/7/P